DOUBLE LIVES: STORIES OF BIGAMY IN ENGLAND AND WALES, 1604–2024

This book explores the fascinating backstories and unexpected sequels of bigamous marriages from the 17th century to the present day.

A woman remarries after hearing that her husband has drowned, only for him to turn up alive and well. Is she now a criminal? A deserted husband, unable to afford a divorce, finds happiness in a new union. How many do the same? A conman advertises for a wife and then disappears with her lifesavings; he has already done the same to many other women. How is he brought to justice?

These are just a few of the hundreds of bigamous remarriages put under the microscope in Double Lives. As a companion volume to *Double Trouble: Bigamy and the Law in England and Wales, 1604–2024*, this book goes behind the law reports to reconstruct the stories of those involved. Drawing on archival sources, pamphlets, newspapers, census data, parish registers, divorce petitions and family histories, it shows the different forms that bigamy might take – accidental, consensual, deceptive or exploitative – and how bigamists' stories in turn helped to shape the law.

Double Lives shows how bigamy should not be dismissed as a comical or victimless crime. Every case has its own complex mix of desire and deception, and, all too often, heartbreak for someone.

Double Lives

Stories of Bigamy in England and Wales, 1604–2024

Rebecca Probert

•HART•

OXFORD • LONDON • NEW YORK • NEW DELHI • SYDNEY

HART PUBLISHING

Bloomsbury Publishing Plc

Kemp House, Chawley Park, Cumnor Hill, Oxford, OX2 9PH, UK

1385 Broadway, New York, NY 10018, USA

Bloomsbury Publishing Ireland Limited, 29 Earlsfort Terrace, Dublin 2, D02 AY28, Ireland

HART PUBLISHING, the Hart/Stag logo, BLOOMSBURY and the Diana logo are trademarks of Bloomsbury Publishing Plc

First published in Great Britain 2026

A catalogue record for this book is available from the British Library.

A catalogue record for this book is available from the Library of Congress.

Library of Congress Control Number: 2026934359

ISBN: HB: 978-1-50997-948-6
ePDF: 978-1-50997-949-3
ePub: 978-1-50997-947-9

Typeset by Compuscript Ltd, Shannon

For product safety related questions contact productsafety@bloomsbury.com

To find out more about our authors and books visit www.hartpublishing.co.uk. Here you will find extracts, author information, details of forthcoming events and the option to sign up for our newsletters.

Peter Robert Calver
Founder of Lost Cousins
1 October 1950–19 January 2026

ACKNOWLEDGEMENTS

This book has taken shape over many years, and I am hugely grateful to all those who have provided advice, assistance and encouragement along the way.

First, I want to acknowledge the huge contribution of the many research assistants who have worked on different sources with me. Their roles are described more fully in *Double Trouble*, but David Brookman, Emma Hinxman, Nell Stephenson, Rachel Pimm-Smith, Mary Hinxman and Elizabeth Farrand will all no doubt recognise some of the names in this book from their research, and I hope that they will enjoy seeing what else I have uncovered.

I would also like to acknowledge the institutional support provided to me by both the University of Warwick, where this project started, and the University of Exeter, where the bulk of the research and writing was done. Both provided schemes for undergraduates to get involved in academic research, the Undergraduate Research Support Scheme at Warwick and the Access to Internships scheme at Exeter. The library team provided support in sourcing books. The University of Exeter was also hugely generous in providing me with a research assistant during my first two years and additional funding to spend time at the National Archives.

At the National Archives, the super-helpful staff supplied documents, interpreted confusing reference numbers that I was trying to follow up, and alerted me to useful sources. I am particularly grateful to Dr Charlotte Smith for telling me about the National Archives' index to ASSI 45, as well as for reading and commenting on my sources section in chapter 1, and to both her and Amanda Bevan for many fascinating conversations during breaks from the reading rooms. I am also grateful to Kate Faulkner and David Wills for giving me access to the Maitland Legal History Room in Cambridge, to Renae Satterley and Harpeet Dhillon for allowing me to consult the manuscript notes of Sir Soulden Lawrence in Middle Temple Library, to the Cheshire Archives and Local Studies team for providing scans of one seventeenth-century case, to the Parliamentary Archives for providing a scan of the original 1604 Act, to the staff at Bristol Library for helping to track down an elusive pamphlet, and to the helpful staff at the British Library, Lambeth Palace Library, London Guildhall Library and the London Archives for their assistance over the course of many visits.

Over the years I have presented papers on different aspects of bigamy to colleagues at both Warwick and Exeter, including the latter's Bracton Centre for Legal History Research and the Centre for Early Modern Studies, as well as to the Selden Society, the Cambridge Centre for English Legal History, the Social Science History Association, the Society of Legal Scholars, the British Legal History Conference, the Law & History Network, the Northern Legal History Group and the Institute for Historical Research. I am very grateful to everyone who attended any of these talks and for their insightful questions and helpful feedback. Together with my fabulous 'bigamy buddy', Mélanie Méthot, I co-organised an entire conference on bigamy at Macquarie University and spent a happy month entirely devoted to discussing the topic in what became dubbed as the 'bigamy house' in Parramatta with her and her fantastic team of research assistants, Parmida Beedle, Katie Stobbe and Hannah Boiler.

I have also given talks on the topic of bigamy to the Society of Genealogists, the Society of Australian Genealogists, the Institute for Heraldic and Genealogist Studies, the Association of Genealogists and Researchers in Archives, *Who Do You Think You Are? Live* at the NEC, and to dozens of family history groups, U3As and other societies. I have chatted to Hollywood actress Kim Cattrall and Australian chef Maggie Beer about their bigamous ancestors on *Who Do You Think You Are?* as well as to many others who have traced a bigamist in their family tree. I am very grateful to Peter Calver for advertising my call for information about suspected bigamists who were never prosecuted via the Lost Cousins' newsletter and to all those family historians who responded. Some completed the online survey, others preferred to remain anonymous, but among those who provided information and were happy for their involvement to be acknowledged were Cindy Alder, Rian Anderson, David Andrews, Rosie Ansell, Jenny Armour, Val Bachelor, Elaine Banks, Sandra Bates, Richard Bawden, Paul Billington, Brian Binns, Marina Black, Alan Bloor, Wilson Bolsover, Ann Bond, Elaine Bonneau, David Bovington, Jill Bradbury, Elizabeth Briggs, Colin Broughton, Shirley Brown, Simon Bull, Steve Bumstead, Adam Bunting, Mike Burnham, Irene Caldwell, Sally Canham, Gill Chesney-Green, Christopher Clegg, Ian Cole, Chris Coleman, Elizabeth Conway, Dorothy Cooper, Jan Costin, Lorna P. Cowan, Alan Craxford, Carlè Crozier, Ian Day, Shelagh Delphyne, Linda Dennis, John Durham, Denis Edwards, Christine Ensor, Ian Evans, Wayne Farmer, Barbara Fisher, Gordon Foulkes-Jones, Lucinda Ganderton, Jo-Anne Gannon, Shelagh Garside, Lorna Gibson, Carole Giffen, Heather Goff, Carolyn Greenwood, Rebecca Gurney, Kevin Haley, Linda Hall, Kay Halley, Barbara Handley, Heather Hayes, Sue Heys, Norman Holloway, Eric Hopley, Susan Hora, Paul Howes, Sarah Hughes, Yvonne Hughes, Peter Humphrey, Clare Humphreys, Linda Hutton, Janet James, Pat Jones, Richard Jones, Gillian Kendrigan, Geoff King, Frances Lake, Stephen Larkin, David Leach, Bridget Lewis, Ailsa Logan, Maggie Luscombe, Donna Maycock, Rob McBride, Jane Milbourne, Normandie Miller, Eileen Milton, Neil Mitchell, Liz Mitchell, Yvonne Mitchell, Pat Mundell, Rose Murrell, Shirley Oakland, Sid Norman, Josie Norris, Katerina Papatheodoropoulos, Liz Parmenter, Brenda Paternoster, Alexander Paterson, Jennie Parfitt, Sandra Parker, Jenny Pedley, Alex Pinhorn, Ann Piper, Bill Piper, Hannah Plowman, Jan Polkinghorne, Tim Powys-Lybbe, Mary Hartley Price, Leigh Prideaux, Rosemary Probert, John Pruce, Maureen Rawson, Pat Ribbans, Ann-Maree Richardson, Barbara Roberts, Jean Ross, Katy Russell-Duff, Peter Scott, Susan Sherman, Barbara Smith, Maggie Smith, Dianne Shenton, Sue Shore, Jean Spelman, Neil Spurgeon, Gill Taylor, Karen Taylor, Rose Taylor, Marie Teasdale, Elaine Thomas, Jeanette Thornell, Brian Thompson, Jim Tidmarsh, Mervyn Tims, Joyce Trousdale, Jennifer Tucker, Jerry Turner, Ali Walker, Rob Walsh, Colin Ward, Amanda West, David Wharton, Bill Whykes, Jane Williams, Liz Williams, Helen Wright and John Young. Other family historians who have since provided me with additional information about bigamy include Abigail Axton, Karen de Bruyne, Jennifer Crawford,

Sarah Dal, Melissa Ellis, Jeremy Geere, Alex Halliday, Sheila Harris, Shirley Oakland, Sue Shore, Susan Stanforth, Julia Stoker, Andy Turner, Jan Wain, Roger Woodhouse, and many more. All the information they provided has informed my broader conclusions, but I have not shared the details: their stories are for them to tell. I am also grateful to Alec Farquharson, a descendant of Richard Archibald Farquharson, who features in chapter 11, for getting in touch with additional details about his 2 x great-grandfather's life.

I am hugely grateful to Chris Barton and Peter Calver for reading and commenting on draft chapters, and to Stephanie Dropuljic for advice on the law of evidence. I have also benefited from conversations and exchanges with Paul Cavill, Ian Dodd, Rachel Gimson, Maebh Harding, Daniel Hill, Martin Ingram, Ruth Lamont, Carol McKinven, Joanna Miles, Zainab Naqvi, Alan Norrie, Gail Savage, Gwen Seabourne, Findlay Stark and Cassie Watson.

The team at Hart Publishing have been brilliant through the process. I would like to thank Sinead Molony for her enthusiasm for the double book idea when I first mooted it, to Verity Stuart for her patience with me as I asked for extra time to complete it, and to David Stott for his careful copy-editing. The illustrations for the covers were designed by my very talented friend Oda Sonju.

It would take far too long to list all the friends and family members who have listened to my stories about bigamy over the years, but there are two who are no longer with us that I would like to mention. Through Rachael Brookman, my brilliantly clever and much-missed friend, her dad became one of my research assistants, something none of us would have imagined when I first went round to their house for tea as a shy eleven-year-old. And Russell Joslin, a journalist with BBC Coventry and Warwickshire, was responsible for alerting me to the case at Warwick Crown Court that ignited my interest in bigamy – and so was indirectly responsible for the whole project.

But the person to whom I am most grateful is my husband, Liam D'Arcy-Brown, who has been my main research assistant, reader and cheerleader over the course of the project. He has been both my first reader and my last, as well as perusing countless drafts in-between. With such a wonderful husband, I have no reason ever to think of committing bigamy.

CONTENTS

1

Introduction

I. At the Scene

Back in 2008, I went to my local Crown Court to see a bigamist being sentenced. When I arrived and made my way to the cramped public gallery, there were several women already seated there, all visibly upset. I suddenly had the horrible thought that these might well be the bigamist's wives.[1] And the only spare place was on the far side of them. Feeling somewhat abashed at being there out of mere curiosity, I hesitated. But it was too late to back out: the judge had spotted me hovering and instructed me in no uncertain terms to sit down immediately. I had no choice but to squeeze past them, hoping that I looked as apologetic as I felt.

It reminded me to think of the people behind the trial. Bigamy is often seen as a somewhat old-fashioned crime, the stuff of Victorian melodrama and Golden Age murder mysteries. It is often portrayed as a comical crime, the basis of farces such as Ray Cooney's 1983 play *Run for Your Wife* – which has spawned West End productions, am-dram stagings, adaptations around the globe in different languages and cultures, and a widely panned film. The poster for an Indian stage version went so far as to describe it as the 'world's longest running and funniest comedy ever written'. But *Run for Your Wife* is, we should remember, a play about a man who is leading a double life, deceiving two women, neither of whom is aware of the other's existence. And deception, as the case studies in this book will show, is a key part of the crime of bigamy.

Unlike *Run for Your Wife*, across the 10,000 or so cases from the past 420 years that I have analysed, only a *very* small number of individuals were carrying on a 'double life' in the sense of maintaining two households simultaneously. But every form of bigamy by its very nature involves an element of duplicity. Any bigamist, even one in a stable second marriage who has been honest with their second spouse, will have had to tell some lies – at the very least to the authorities involved in conducting the second marriage, and probably to others.

In any case, only a small minority of bigamy cases involved stable second unions in which the bigamist had been honest with their new spouse. Most second

[1] From the newspaper report of the case, I subsequently discovered that only his legal wife was at court that day ('Bigamist gets 3 years', *Coventry Telegraph*, 6 December 2008), although all three of the women he had married had been present a few weeks earlier when he was found guilty (F Yeoman, 'Wives cheer as bigamist is found guilty', *The Times*, 14 November 2008).

spouses simply had no idea that they were entering into a marriage that was bigamous and void. They thought that their marriage was legal, and were often shocked and distressed to discover it was not. So the 'double lives' of my title is not merely a reference to the obvious fact of an individual having (at least) two spouses. It is also intended to evoke the impact on those spouses of discovering that they are married to a bigamist – the potential for relationships and homes to be fractured or torn apart, lives turned upside down, the revelation demanding a re-evaluation of what has gone before, with every comment or action assuming a new significance.

There were, inevitably, degrees of deception. There were the straightforward cases where the bigamist had simply claimed (or let it be assumed) that they were single, or that their first spouse had died, or (in later periods) that they were divorced. There were the slightly more complex situations where the bigamist had compounded their deception by using an alias, fabricating evidence, or asking family and friends to lie for them. There were also trials where the question of what the second spouse had known was hotly contested, or where it appeared that both the bigamist and the second spouse had been labouring under the same misunderstanding about the validity of their marriage – making these cases of mutual self-deception.

There were also some bigamists for whom one has to have sympathy. Many simply wished to move on from a first spouse who had proved violent, or unfaithful, or who had deserted them (and sometimes all three) but were unable to obtain a divorce. At the other end of the scale, however, there were those who deliberately set out to deceive and exploit a sequence of women, moving on from one relationship to another in a matter of months, weeks, or even days. The victims in such cases were rarely wealthy individuals but rather women who had saved up a small amount of money over years of hard work, only to lose it all.[2]

As all this indicates, bigamy is – or at least has been – a hugely varied offence. The incidence of different types of bigamy has fluctuated over time, depending on factors such as the availability of divorce and the acceptability of cohabitation. Even so, in any given period one will find people committing bigamy for a whole range of reasons. Looking at their lives in detail – including what happened to them and their various spouses after their bigamy was discovered – allows for a more nuanced assessment of the significance of bigamy than just focusing on the trial.

So my aim in this book is to tell the tale of bigamy from the early seventeenth century to the twenty-first, through the stories of those who were accused of committing the offence. Using case studies obviously involves going beyond conventional legal sources and approaches. As the legal historian Brian Simpson long ago pointed out, there was traditionally a most peculiar convention within law of 'suppressing curiosity about cases', of studying precedent without knowing or caring about the people involved.[3] Simpson himself did much to encourage a different approach, and modern scholarship provides many brilliant examples of how being curious about the parties

[2] See chapter 12 (John Woodgate Kinsella) and *Double Trouble*, ch 5.

[3] AWB Simpson, *Leading Cases in the Common Law* (Oxford, Oxford University Press, 1995) 10. cf the approach adopted by social historians, with the case study approach adopted by L Stone, *Uncertain Unions and Broken Lives: Intimate and Revealing Accounts of Marriage and Divorce in England* (Oxford, Oxford University Press, 1995) being a particular inspiration for the current work.

provides new insights.[4] Sometimes understanding the story behind the case helps to explain an otherwise baffling legal decision.[5] On other occasions, knowing more about the parties raises questions about whether a different result might have been reached if all the facts had been presented to the court. And sometimes the disparity between the details as they originally emerged and those that formed the basis of the court's decision are so striking as to raise the suspicion of some deliberate 'massaging' of the facts to achieve a particular result. There is rarely just one 'story' behind a case.

This is an appropriate point to say a little more about the sources that I have used in researching these case studies, and how they have shaped my selection.

II. The Sources Underpinning the Stories

The sources that are available vary considerably over time. For much of the period, the official documentation that has been preserved is somewhat scanty. Only a few records of bigamy trials have survived from the seventeenth century. More are available for the eighteenth century, but the picture remains patchy, with some areas having better records than others. Even when records exist, the information is limited: all that survives from the assizes of that time is the indictment (usually very formulaic), the verdict, and the sentence – helpful in building up the bigger picture, but not particularly illuminating about the individuals involved. More information is available for cases that were tried at the Old Bailey (from 1834, the Central Criminal Court), but its published *Proceedings* were never a full transcript of the trial and do not generally include the judge's direction to the jury.

From the early nineteenth century onward, such sources can be supplemented by an increasing number of national and local newspapers. The latter were particularly important as they regularly carried detailed reports of their county assizes – not just the high-profile cases, but a summary of all the cases that had been tried.[6] Local newspapers also reported the proceedings in the magistrates' courts – sometimes providing a much more detailed insight into the case than the subsequent trial report, particularly where the accused pleaded guilty.

The nineteenth century also saw the publication of an increasing number of formal law reports – initially as a matter of private initiative and then, from 1865, on an official

[4] See eg R Auchmuty, 'Whatever happened to Miss Bebb? *Bebb v The Law Society* and women's legal history' (2010) 31 *Legal Studies* 199; RW Ireland, 'Sanctity, superstition and the death of Sarah Jacob' in A Musson and C Stebbings (eds), *Making Legal History: Approaches and Methodologies* (Cambridge, Cambridge University Press, 2012); D Watkins, 'Recovering the lost human stories of law: Finding Mrs Burns' (2013) 7 *Law and Humanities* 68; E Rackley and R Auchmuty (eds), *Women's Legal Landmarks: Celebrating the History of Women and Law in the UK and Ireland* (Oxford, Hart, 2019); J Aston, 'Petitions to the Court for Divorce and Matrimonial Causes: A New Methodological Approach to the History of Divorce, 1857-1923' (2022) 43 *Journal of Legal History* 161; R Auchmuty, E Rackley and M Takayanagi (eds), *Women's Legal Landmarks in the Interwar Years: Not For Want of Trying* (Oxford, Hart, 2024).

[5] See eg the case of Eliza Dent in chapter 9.

[6] Although not inevitably: a detailed report on the trials at the Glamorganshire assizes at Swansea ends with 'The case was still proceeding when our Reporter was despatched by the train at 7 o'clock': *The Silurian*, 5 March 1853.

basis. As we shall see, what got reported was key to shaping how the law evolved.[7] But law reports, even the official ones, are not without their flaws. Some get the most basic details wrong – as I discovered when trying to trace the individuals involved in a particular case.[8] Even when they accurately reported the case as stated to the court, this did not necessarily reflect the reality of what had happened. There is more than one example in my case studies of the story being altered as the case proceeded through its different stages.[9]

The scope for finding out what happened behind the scenes – both before and after the trial – also changes over time. For the seventeenth century, there is the difficulty of corroborating the most basic of personal details, even the dates of the alleged marriages.[10] As we move into the eighteenth century, the greater availability of marriage registers makes it viable to build up a picture of what happened before the trial, but finding out what happened afterwards remains a challenge. By the time we get to the mid-nineteenth century, the combination of civil registration and decennial censuses makes it easier to ascertain the details of the marriages and trace the subsequent lives of those involved.[11] That said, even with the benefit of modern databases, finding out what happened to bigamists and their spouses can be surprisingly difficult. Sometimes their name is too common to be sure that the person traced is the right one, especially if they had moved to a different area and were no longer living with either of their spouses. In other cases, however, their name is so uncommon that the lack of any later records hints that they may have assumed an alias; indeed, on occasion, a change of name and subsequent remarriage was only revealed when the individual was arrested and tried for a second time.[12]

As we edge closer to the present day, the question is not so much what information is available as what it is appropriate to access. The shift to emotive, story-led journalism has meant that precise details of the two (or more) marriages are now less likely to be reported than in the nineteenth century. Genealogical databases are, for obvious reasons, less likely to include marriage registers from recent marriages. There is also the intrusiveness of investigating the lives of people who are still living. When searching the 1939 register to discover what happened to various bigamists after their trial, I found blacked-out entries that remain officially closed – a reminder that these households included people who are still alive. In my twentieth-century case studies I have accordingly been mindful as to what material is in the public domain.

So far I have been talking only about cases that came to trial. But for a full understanding of bigamy – both legally and socially – it is also important to look at those who, for whatever reason, were never prosecuted. Here again the sources are very

[7] On the growing sophistication of the criminal law in this period, see P Handler, 'Legal development in Victorian criminal trials' in M Dyson and D Ibbetson (eds), *Law and Legal Process: Substantive Law and Procedure in English Legal History* (Cambridge, Cambridge University Press, 2013).

[8] *R v Henry Allen* (1872) LR 1 CCR 367 (chapter 3).

[9] See in particular the case of Martha Ann Tolson (chapter 7).

[10] As illustrated in the case study of Mary Carleton (chapter 2).

[11] The first census to record specific individuals was taken in 1841. Each subsequent census, all the way up to 1921, included additional details that help to verify the identity of those named.

[12] See eg the case of Gloucester Gale (chapter 12).

varied. Indeed, some of the unprosecuted cases are far more richly documented than those that came to trial, with the individuals involved writing at great length as to why they felt that they were justified in remarrying, or contesting the allegations that had been made against them. Some of these cases demonstrate the challenges of bringing a prosecution, for example where the evidence of one or other of the marriages was lacking. Others involve individuals who probably should not be labelled 'bigamists' at all, since they would have had a good defence to any potential charge. Their stories nonetheless help to illustrate the scope of the offence, providing a useful reminder that individuals would only be tried if a prosecutor was able to establish a *prima facie* case against them.

So there is, inevitably, far more to say about some bigamists than others. Some were well-known individuals whose lives were richly documented, with hundreds if not thousands of pages of material and commentary. Others were just briefly in the spotlight at the time of their arrest and trial and then vanished from public view. In choosing my case studies, I have tried to maintain a balance between the high-profile and the humdrum, to ensure that the full range of experiences is represented, and to make it clear which are exceptional and which can be seen as illustrative of broader trends. But understanding the significance of any given case obviously requires a knowledge of the legal framework, to which we now turn.

III. Setting the Stories in Context: The Changing Legal Framework

Double Lives is a companion piece to *Double Trouble*, which explains the evolution of the crime of bigamy from 1604 to the present day. Each has been written so that they can be read either together or independently. Within *Double Lives*, necessary details of the changing legal framework are woven through the case studies by way of explanation, so readers who want to get straight to the stories can skip over the following three subsections without fear of missing out on crucial information. But for ease of reference, and for those who prefer to have a sense of the bigger picture before diving into specific cases, a brief overview of the legal background is provided here.

(i) The Bigamy Act 1604

We start in 1604, when Parliament made it a felony, punishable by death, to 'marry' one person while legally married to another, unless one of the specified exceptions applied.[13]

There is quite a lot to unpack here. Since an individual could only commit bigamy if they were validly married in the first place, it makes sense to start with what was

[13] Bigamy Act 1604. Previously, bigamy had been dealt with by the church courts, whose powers of punishment were limited to penance and excommunication: M Ingram, *Church Courts, Sex and Marriage in England, 1570-1640* (Cambridge, Cambridge University Press, 1987).

required for a valid marriage at this time. In terms of the formalities of getting married, the only recognised ceremony was one conducted by an ordained Anglican clergyman.[14] The age of consent to marry was set at a level that seems shockingly low to modern eyes: 12 for girls and 14 for boys.[15] Couples could not validly marry if they were within the 'prohibited degrees' (that is to say, too closely related to each other by blood or marriage),[16] or of the same sex,[17] and, obviously, neither could be already married to anyone else.

So one potential answer to a charge of bigamy was that the first marriage was void.[18] Another was that one of the specific exceptions in the Bigamy Act applied. There was an exception for those who had remarried after their spouse had been absent for seven years, 'not knowing the other to be living within that time'.[19] This exception, it should be noted, did not require the remarrying spouse to have received a false report of the other spouse's death, or even to have a genuine, if mistaken, belief that they had died; all that was needed was the absence of knowledge of the other spouse being alive. A second exception involved those whose spouse had been absent 'beyond the seas' for seven years – in which case the mere fact of their absence was sufficient, regardless of whether or not the other spouse knew they were alive. There were also exceptions for those who had married under the age of consent, those whose first marriage had been annulled by the church courts,[20] and those who had been 'divorced'.[21]

Here some further explanation is necessary. In 1604, divorce in the modern sense of a decree ending a valid marriage was not an option.[22] The only formal remedy available to the unhappily married was what was called a divorce *a mensa et thoro* – essentially

[14] The canon law of the Church of England also contained various directions as to how and where this ceremony should be conducted, but a marriage could still be valid even if it did not comply with these. Marriage law was put on a statutory basis by the Clandestine Marriages Act 1753. The Marriage Act 1836 then gave couples two new options: getting married in a registered place of worship or in a register office.

[15] This did not change until the Age of Marriage Act 1929, which raised the minimum age of marriage to 16.

[16] The law here is particularly complex, both in terms of who was prohibited from marrying and the consequences of doing so. For present purposes the list of prohibited relationships set out in the Church of England's Table of Kindred and Affinity in 1563 can be taken as definitive. This stated that an individual was prohibited from marrying their parent/child, sibling, grandparent/grandchild, uncle/aunt, or nephew/niece, along with the spouse of any of these relations (eg a step-parent) or any of these relations of a spouse (eg a parent-in-law). Marriages to in-laws were treated as voidable, rather than void, which in essence meant that they were valid up until they were annulled. This remained the case until the Marriage Act 1835, which made any future such marriages simply void. Marriages to the closest blood relations were almost certainly void, even if the 1835 Act described them as voidable. Over the course of the twentieth century, the restrictions on marrying in-laws were gradually lifted, as discussed in the case of James Chadwick in chapter 3 (which also deals with the controversy over whether marriage to a deceased wife's sister was within the prohibited degrees).

[17] See further the case of Katharine Jones in chapter 3. Same-sex marriage was finally made possible by the Marriage (Same Sex Couples) Act 2013.

[18] Or, to add a further layer of complexity, that the second marriage was void for some reason other than it being bigamous: see the case of Henry Allen in chapter 3.

[19] Bigamy Act 1604, s 2, and see further chapter 6.

[20] An annulment could be granted if the marriage was void on any of the grounds set out above. It could also be granted if one spouse was incapable of consummating the marriage or if their consent to it had been vitiated by duress.

[21] Bigamy Act 1604, s 3, and see further chapter 5.

[22] The practice of granting divorces by means of a private Act of Parliament only began in the 1670s. In 1857 a new civil court was established with the power to grant divorces.

an order permitting the parties to live apart, to separate 'from bed and board'. Such 'divorces' were granted by the church courts to authorise a separation from an adulterous or violent spouse, but did not permit either to remarry. It was this kind of 'divorce' to which the 1604 Act was alluding.[23]

So if there had been a divorce *a mensa et thoro*, or if any of the other exceptions in the Bigamy Act applied, an individual was not guilty of the crime of bigamy. But even if they had no defence, and were convicted, it was unlikely that they would be sentenced to death. Many men successfully pleaded 'benefit of clergy' – which by this time was essentially a test of literacy, to see if they could read a passage from the Bible. However, this did not mean that they escaped punishment altogether: they were still branded – burnt 'in the hand', or on the thumb.[24] Women, by contrast, were not entitled to plead benefit of clergy – so juries were warned that they had to be very certain before convicting alleged female bigamists.[25]

(ii) Defences: Interpretation and Key Changes

The 1604 Act remained in force all the way through until 1828, when it was repealed and replaced by the Offences Against the Person Act. This kept the core of the offence but abolished various defences. The absence of a spouse overseas for seven years was no longer sufficient; only those who had no knowledge of their spouse being alive in the seven years preceding their remarriage still had a defence. The defence for those divorced a *mensa et thoro* was also abolished. In its place was a new exception for those 'divorced from the bond of the first marriage' – a reference to the possibility of being divorced by private Act of Parliament. The geographical scope of the offence was also expanded: it was now an offence that could be committed anywhere in the world by any British subject.[26]

The 1828 Act was itself replaced in 1861, but this new Offences Against the Person Act made no changes to the scope of the offence.[27] There were, however, important changes in how the various exceptions were interpreted and applied in the courts. From 1865, once a separation of seven years had been established, the onus was on the prosecution to show that the remarrying spouse had known their first spouse to be alive during that time.[28] From 1872, the invalidity of the second marriage for some reason other than its being bigamous did not necessarily shield the remarrying spouse from conviction.[29] And from 1889, a genuine and reasonably held belief in the death of the first spouse was confirmed to be a defence.[30]

[23] See the cases of Penelope Rich and Margaret Porter in chapter 5.
[24] *Double Trouble*, ch 2.
[25] As we shall see in the case of Mary Carleton in chapter 2.
[26] *Double Trouble*, ch 6.
[27] *Double Trouble*, ch 8.
[28] *R v John Curgerwen* (1865) LR 1 CCR 1 (chapter 6).
[29] *R v Henry Allen* (1872) LR 1 CCR 367 (chapter 3).
[30] *R v Tolson* (1889) 23 QBD 168 (chapter 7).

(iii) Punishment: Implementation and Key Changes

From the early 1700s, branding became the de facto punishment for bigamy, with women having been given the right to plead benefit of clergy on the same terms as men,[31] and the reading test being abolished altogether.[32] From mid-century, branding was increasingly likely to be accompanied by a period of imprisonment, and from 1779 imprisonment or whipping could be ordered instead of branding. From this point, the most common sentence handed down at the Old Bailey was a year in prison and a small fine, but at the provincial assizes the full range of punishments were used.[33]

In 1795, legislation was passed allowing bigamists to be transported to Australia for seven years.[34] At the same time, an alternative was provided: imprisonment in England and Wales for up to two years. The necessity of determining whether any given case was bad enough to justify a sentence of transportation meant that understandings of the offence became more nuanced. It became standard to refer to bigamy as the most variable of offences – as the Old Bailey's Common Serjeant put it in a case from 1798, one that more than any other 'afforded room either for mitigation or aggravation, according to the circumstances'.[35] And in assessing the degree of mitigation or aggravation, it was the harm done to the second spouse that was key. The deception, seduction, financial exploitation, and abandonment of the second spouse were all factors that could, whether individually or in combination, result in a higher sentence. Where such factors were combined and repeated, a sentence of transportation was almost always ordered. Between 1805 and 1836, just over a quarter of all those convicted of bigamy were sentenced to transportation.[36]

From the 1830s, the use of transportation declined, being ordered in only the most serious cases.[37] In the 1850s, the end of transportation required alternative arrangements to be made. Legislation in 1853 accordingly changed the maximum penalty to four years' penal servitude.[38] Four years later this was extended to seven,[39] and this was retained by the Offences Against the Person Act 1861.[40] Only a very few bigamists were ever sentenced to penal servitude, however: around 6 per cent of those convicted between 1857 and 1913. After the First World War such sentences became even rarer, and by the 1930s most convicted bigamists were either being bound over or given a prison sentence of a month or less. And after the Second World War only a shrinking percentage of known bigamists was being prosecuted at all.[41] Up until 1945, around

[31] See the case of Mary Stokes (chapter 12).
[32] *Double Trouble*, ch 3.
[33] *Double Trouble*, ch 4.
[34] *Double Trouble*, ch 5.
[35] *True Briton*, 25 October 1798.
[36] This figure is calculated from data obtained from the *Criminal Registers*. This source, and the dataset constructed from it, is discussed further in *Double Trouble*, ch 1. In total, 181 individuals were sentenced to transportation of the 714 convicted between 1805 and 1836.
[37] *Double Trouble*, ch 6.
[38] Penal Servitude Act 1853, s 4.
[39] Penal Servitude Act 1857, s 2; *Double Trouble*, ch 8.
[40] Offences Against the Person Act 1861, s 57.
[41] *Double Trouble*, ch 10.

85 per cent of cases known to the police had resulted in a prosecution. After that date it fell dramatically. By 1950, only around half of all known cases were coming to trial, by 1963 it was one-third, and by the late 1970s just one-tenth.

This brings us on to a further question: how did cases of bigamy come before the courts in the first place?

IV. A Very Brief History of Prosecuting Bigamy

This overview explains how accusations of bigamy came to trial, how cases were tried, and what happened thereafter, first outlining the key elements of the process in 1604 (and for quite some time after), and the key changes over the centuries.[42] I also explain some of the key differences between bigamy and other crimes in terms of detection and motivations for prosecution.

(i) Key Elements

In 1604 there was no police force in the modern sense, and no public prosecutor. The parish constable might play a role in taking the accused into custody, but prosecutions for bigamy (and indeed most other crimes) were primarily brought by private individuals.[43] The first step was for the accused to be brought before the local Justice of the Peace. Having heard from the accused and their accusers, this magistrate would decide whether to commit the former for trial at the assizes.[44]

The assizes dealt with the most serious forms of crime.[45] The judges who presided over them were not local men, but members of the legal elite, judges who for most of the year were based in Westminster, in the three common law courts of King's Bench, Common Pleas, or Exchequer. There they primarily dealt with civil cases, along with the occasional point of criminal law referred for their consideration. But twice a year, in spring and summer, they travelled round the country in pairs, each within a defined 'circuit', during which time they spent a few days in designated towns and cities to hear both criminal cases and civil suits.[46] Within London, the assize court for the City of London and Middlesex was the Old Bailey, where sessions were held on a more regular basis (eight per year from 1669).[47] The common law judges sat here too, but there were

[42] An expanded version of this section, with additional references, appears in *Double Trouble*, ch 1.

[43] P Cox, R Shoemaker and H Shore, *Victims and Criminal Justice: A History* (Oxford, Oxford University Press, 2023) ch 4.

[44] Bail could be granted but depended on whether the accused could find sufficient surety that they would attend their trial, generally by third parties providing financial guarantees on their behalf.

[45] There were occasional examples of bigamy cases being tried at the 'quarter' sessions, which, as their name suggests, were held four times each year. These were presided over by Justices of the Peace and generally dealt with less serious offences: JH Baker, 'Criminal Courts and Procedure at Common Law 1550-1800' in JS Cockburn (ed), *Crime in England 1550-1800* (London, Methuen, 1977).

[46] JS Cockburn, *A History of the English Assizes, 1558-1714* (Cambridge, Cambridge University Press, 1972) 23.

[47] ibid 31.

also two dedicated judges, the Recorder and the Common Serjeant, both legal officers within the City of London.

The formal indictment against the accused was generally drawn up by the clerk of assize and then sent to the Grand Jury. Consisting of between 13 and 23 'respectable men',[48] its role was to consider the prosecution evidence and decide whether the trial should proceed. They could take the view that the accusation was groundless, in which case they would write upon the bill either 'ignoramus' ('we do not know') or, later, 'not a true bill' or 'not found'.[49] In this case the accused would then be discharged.

If the Grand Jury was satisfied that there was a case to answer, then the bill would be endorsed as a 'true bill'. The defendant would be 'arraigned', which meant that the charge would be read to them, and they were asked if they pleaded guilty or not guilty. In the event of a guilty plea, the only remaining question related to the sentence. But at least in the seventeenth century, most of those accused of bigamy pleaded not guilty. Their trial would then proceed before the petit (or petty) jury, consisting of 12 men – typically craftsmen, shopkeepers, and tenant farmers.

The prosecutor was responsible for presenting the evidence against the accused (who would therefore be discharged if the prosecutor failed to appear). Seventeenth-century trials were almost entirely conducted without lawyers: only on rare occasions did counsel appear for the prosecution, and those accused of bigamy (or any other felony) were not permitted to have counsel to speak in their defence. The one exception was if there was a genuine point of law to be debated.[50] This was a narrower exception than it might sound, given the rudimentary state of the criminal law in this period. Moreover, once the legal arguments were concluded, counsel had no further role to play in the trial. In the absence of counsel, it was up to the judge (and, to a lesser extent, the jury) to ask questions of the prosecutor and any witnesses.[51] The defendant could also cross-examine the prosecution witnesses, make a speech challenging any of the evidence they had given, and call their own witnesses.

Once all the evidence had been heard, the judge summed up as necessary. In cases where the applicable law was clear, the jury then gave their verdict, guilty or not guilty. Where the applicable law was in doubt, the judge had the power to reserve a question for the consideration of the twelve common law judges at Westminster. In such cases the jury could give either a 'special verdict' (essentially limited to findings of fact, leaving open the question of whether those facts gave rise to criminal liability) or, increasingly, a 'general verdict'.[52] The twelve judges would hear arguments from counsel on the disputed point of law and give their opinion, and if they thought that the conviction was wrong, a pardon could be granted. In the absence of any process of appeals against

[48] ibid 67.

[49] Sir JH Baker, *An Introduction to English Legal History*, 5th edn (Oxford, Oxford University Press, 2019) 546; R Ireland, *Land of White Gloves? A history of crime and punishment in Wales* (London, Routledge, 2015) 34.

[50] As in the case of Mary Porter (chapter 5).

[51] As in the case of Mary Carleton (chapter 1).

[52] JH Langbein, *The Origins of Adversary Criminal Trial* (Oxford, Oxford University Press, 2003, ppbk 2005) 329.

conviction or sentence, seeking a pardon was also the only route for those convicted of bigamy to challenge the outcome of the trial.[53]

(ii) Key Changes

From the early eighteenth century, defence counsel began to appear in at least some bigamy trials at the Old Bailey.[54] Even then, their role remained limited: they could examine (and cross-examine) witnesses, but they were not permitted to address the jury on the defendant's behalf.[55] From 1836, however, they were also able to make opening and closing statements, and directly challenge the evidence against the accused.[56] There were, of course, still many defendants who were unable to afford the fees of counsel. Only in the twentieth century were efforts made to ensure that those accused of a crime had legal representation, provided free to those without the means to pay.

From the mid-eighteenth century, those who decided to prosecute had increasing support from the state to do so, being entitled to be reimbursed for their expenses in bringing the prosecution. The shift from private to public prosecutions began in the nineteenth century, with the establishment of professional police forces. There was also the new Director of Public Prosecutions, a post created in 1879, who advised on whether a prosecution should be brought and, on occasion, also initiated prosecutions. By the mid-twentieth century, police prosecutions had become the norm. With the creation of the Crown Prosecution Service in 1985, state responsibility for the prosecution of criminal offences was entrenched, and private prosecutions became very rare.[57]

The role of the magistrate underwent change in the nineteenth century as processes became formalised. Nineteenth-century magistrates heard cases in public buildings (rather than, as previously, in their own homes) and, from 1839, in dedicated police courts. The process of preliminary examination was reformed in 1848 with the accused being given the opportunity to respond to the prosecution evidence.[58] Magistrates also took on responsibility for trying a whole range of less serious offences – including, in the late twentieth century, bigamy cases.[59]

The system of assizes lasted until the 1970s, although it underwent various changes over the centuries. The petty jury remained a central part of the process of trial, although the Grand Jury was abolished in 1933.[60] The old system of assizes (and

[53] For an example, see the case of William Martin Lolley (chapter 5).

[54] See *Double Trouble*, ch 3.

[55] The impact of these restrictions can be seen in the case of Lucy Ahier (chapter 6).

[56] As a result of the Trials for Felony Act 1836, s 1 (usually referred to as the Prisoner's Counsel Act 1836). For examples of counsel making full use of their new powers, with some impassioned rhetoric, see the cases of Sarah Horsfield (chapter 6) and Eliza Dent (chapter 9).

[57] Cox, Shoemaker and Shore (n 43) 130.

[58] Indictable Offences Act 1848, s 18.

[59] Criminal Law Act 1977; discussed in *Double Trouble*, ch 11.

[60] Administration of Justice (Miscellaneous Provisions) Act 1933, s 1. Certain exceptions remained, but none that are relevant to prosecutions for bigamy.

quarter sessions) was finally swept away and replaced with the modern system of Crown Courts in 1972.

As regards the possibility of appeals, the process of referring legal points to the twelve judges was put on a formal basis in 1848 with the establishment of the Court for Crown Cases Reserved (CCCR). Again, it remained for the trial judge to decide which cases to refer, and the role of the CCCR remained limited to ruling on points of law. Only from 1908, with the establishment of the Court of Criminal Appeal, did it become possible for those convicted of a crime to appeal against their conviction or sentence.[61]

Across the centuries, women accounted for only a minority of those facing trial for bigamy. Until the twentieth century, however, they would have been tried in an all-male environment. Only in the wake of the Sex Disqualification (Removal) Act 1919 did it become possible for women even to sit on juries, let alone to qualify as solicitors or barristers or sit as judges.[62]

(iii) Key Differences between Bigamy and Other Offences

The absence of a police force for much of the period may have been less significant for bigamy than for other crimes, largely because the process of detection was very different in this context. After all, there was no doubt as to *who* had committed the offence. But it might be some time before anyone realised that a crime had been committed. That said, there were multiple different ways in which bigamy came to light. The discovery that the marriage was bigamous often happened within the family circle, whether by the discovery or receipt of an incriminating letter,[63] a chance comment, or the first spouse turning up.[64] Family and friends who were aware of the first marriage might inform the second spouse.[65] Outside the family circle, a bigamous marriage might be discovered when parish officials were tracking down an errant husband to enforce his financial obligations to his wife (or supposed wife), or where the bigamist had been charged with another offence.[66]

There was a similarly wide range of reasons – personal, legal and financial – that could motivate an individual to bring a prosecution. There were aggrieved first spouses, second spouses who were angry at being deceived, violent second husbands who resented their bigamist wife's attempts to invoke the law's protection against them, and relatives who were embroiled in some wider quarrel with the bigamist or who prosecuted out of spite.[67] There were prosecutions by second spouses who simply wanted to be free,[68]

[61] See *Double Lives*, ch 8 on the conditions that had to be satisfied.

[62] For brilliant insights into the various feminist campaigns and legislative landmarks that finally led to women being able to do all of these things, see Rackley and Auchmuty (n 4) and Auchmuty, Rackley and Takayanagi (n 4).

[63] As apparently happened in the case of Mary Carleton (chapter 2).

[64] See the case of Richard Leaver (chapter 2).

[65] See the case of Peter Thomson (chapter 7).

[66] See the case of Alexander Borromeo (chapter 12).

[67] See the case of Eliza Corbett (chapter 10).

[68] See the cases of Eliza Lumley (chapter 4), Philip Blake (chapter 13), and the examples discussed in the case study of Emily Scully (chapter 9).

or by members of their family who wanted to free them.[69] First husbands prosecuted to establish they were no longer responsible for a bigamist wife, and second husbands prosecuted to prove that they never had been. First wives, conversely, prosecuted to establish their husband's financial obligations, while second wives, particularly before the married women's property legislation of the 1870s and 1880s, did so to reclaim their assets from bigamist husbands. Family members also prosecuted to ensure that the bigamist did not inherit assets that would otherwise have gone to the family.[70] But the person bringing the prosecution did not have to have such a close personal link with the bigamist: in one case it was the jilted fiancée of the second husband who instigated proceedings,[71] while in another the prosecution seems to have been an attempt to get the bigamist out of the way so that he would not be able to give evidence in a trial for treason.[72] There were also plenty of prosecutions brought by the parish[73] and, on occasion, by private organisations.[74]

V. The Approach

I begin by showing the parameters of the crime of bigamy. To be convicted of bigamy, the accused had to have been validly married, and that marriage still had to be subsisting at the time of the second marriage. Chapter 2 looks at cases where the evidence of one of the marriages was contested, and chapter 3 explores the disputes that arose over their legal status, either because of some formal defect in the ceremony or because of some more fundamental objection to the validity of the marriage. Chapter 4 examines two cases where questions were raised as to the fate of the first spouse and where the burden of proof lay in such cases. There was then the question of whether any of the statutory exceptions applied, raising questions about the meaning of the reference to 'divorce' in the 1604 Act (chapter 5) and how the seven-year exceptions should be interpreted (chapter 6). Over time, courts also held that certain mistaken beliefs would constitute a defence (chapter 7). But there were plenty of others who had mistakenly believed that they were entitled to remarry because they had misunderstood the law – which was not a defence (chapter 8).

I then explore different types of bigamy. There were cases where the first marriage never really got off the ground or had broken down long before the bigamous marriage (chapter 9). In other cases the parties to the first marriage had agreed to separate, or both had committed bigamy (chapter 10). There were then more complex cases involving affairs, overlapping relationships, and simultaneous relationships, which undermine any neat sequential account of bigamy as involving an unhappy first marriage being replaced by a stable second one (chapter 11). And there were the fraudsters, fortune-hunters, and 'super-bigamists', some of whose stories could justify an entire book in

[69] See the case of Eliza Dent (chapter 9).
[70] See the cases of Thomas Gordon and Dorothy Josephine Wagstaff (chapter 13).
[71] See the case of Sarah Horsfield (chapter 6).
[72] See the case of John Taylor (chapter 9).
[73] See the cases of Ambrose Rowe (chapter 3) and Benjamin Griffiths (chapter 9).
[74] See the cases of Alexander Borromeo and Gloucester Gale (chapter 12).

themselves (chapter 12). In chapter 13 I look at what happened after the trial, focusing on those cases where there was a subsequent legal dispute of some kind, and in chapter 14 I showcase various examples of those who were never prosecuted.

So, some cases were chosen because of their legal significance, whether because they established a new approach or illustrate a particular point. Others were selected to illustrate the variability of the offence, from the entirely inadvertent, through the more-or-less excusable, to the nastiest and most calculated of crimes. And some I just had to include simply because they are great stories.

2

Married or not? Denying the Ceremony

From 1604 until the early nineteenth century, the most common reason for someone to be acquitted of bigamy was the absence of evidence of one or other of the weddings.[1] Bigamy was a serious offence, and the onus was on the prosecutor to provide evidence of both ceremonies. In the absence of any centralised system of registration – only in place from 1837 – finding the church where the weddings had taken place could be something of a challenge. Moreover, before the Clandestine Marriages Act 1753 there was always the possibility that the marriage had not taken place in a church at all, in which case documentary evidence might be open to challenge or entirely absent.

Understandably, then, when faced with an accusation of bigamy, some individuals simply denied that one or other of the ceremonies ever happened. The seven case studies chosen for this chapter all illustrate different variations on that theme. Sometimes, of course, the accused may well have been telling the truth. That is certainly a possibility in the case of Mary Carleton, who was tried and acquitted at the Old Bailey in 1663. The supposed facts of her first marriage, recycled in various biographies, rest on the claims of her second husband and his family, and a single witness whose evidence was problematic in various respects. Richard Boyle similarly relied on the absence of any record of his alleged marriage to Loveday Billing, although in his case there were at least witnesses who could confirm that he had told them of it. By contrast, the second marriage of Richard Leaver, tried in 1737, was recorded, but only in the private registers kept by the Reverend Gainham, one of the disreputable Fleet parsons who conducted weddings without regard to the canonical requirements.

After 25 March 1754, all marriages were to be recorded in the parish register.[2] However, registration was not necessary for the marriage to be valid, and although tampering with the registers was a criminal offence, failing to register a marriage was not.[3] Even so, most clergy were assiduous in ensuring that marriages were registered, and parish registers were much better kept after the 1753 Act than before. Those accused of bigamy therefore had to come up with a reason why their name was in the marriage register.[4] The plausibility of such reasons varied wildly. In the case of Thomas Burgess, it was acknowledged that he had signed the register, but his second wife

[1] *Double Trouble*, chs 2–5.
[2] Clandestine Marriages Act 1753, ss 14–15.
[3] ibid s 16; see also R Probert, 'Offences in weddings law' in R Sandberg and R Riedel (eds), *Religion and the Criminal Law* (forthcoming).
[4] On this, see also the case of James Hugh Edwards, discussed in chapter 3.

claimed that this had happened before any ceremony had taken place. 'John Brown, the converted clown', not only denied his first marriage but assembled witnesses to prove that he was in a different part of the country at the time. Even more astonishing is the case of Frederick George Wharton, prosecuted at the Central Criminal Court in 1940, and his convoluted story about how someone else had assumed his identity and married a young Austrian countess to enable her to acquire British citizenship.

'I was Never Yet Married to Any but John Carleton': Mary Carleton, 1663

The Carleton bigamy trial of 1663 is both the best and the worst documented on record. On the one hand, there is Mary Carleton's own account of her arrest, committal, indictment and trial, providing a step-by-step guide to the process.[5] There is also a very full transcript of the proceedings at the Old Bailey, giving an unparalleled insight into the exchanges between the judge, jury and witnesses, as well as Mary's spirited defence.[6] There are then the pamphlets written by John Carleton after Mary's acquittal, which alleged that she had had not one but three husbands before him.[7] And there was a general pile-on from other contemporaries, with pamphlets being published both before and after the trial, their often lurid titles making their allegiances clear.[8] Mary's story was noted by the diarist Samuel Pepys, inspired some rather awful poetry, and even made it onto the London stage.[9] What we don't have is any evidence of whether Mary did in fact commit bigamy. No record exists of her alleged first marriage. We don't even know who she really was. Was she, as she herself claimed, Maria Van Wolway, a German gentlewoman from Cologne, of good birth and education?[10] Or was she, as one pamphlet alleged, the daughter of a poor fiddler from Canterbury?[11]

[5] M Carleton, *The case of Madam Mary Carleton, lately stiled the German Princess, truely stated with an historical relation of her birth, education, and fortunes; in an appeal to his illustrious Highness Prince Rupert* (London, 1663). Mary's authorship of this pamphlet has been questioned, but that does not detract from its utility as a contemporary guide to the process of a criminal trial. As one of Mary's biographers notes, the title 'Princess' was a label used by others rather than one claimed by Mary herself: MJ Kietzman, *The Self-Fashioning of an Early Modern Englishwoman* (Aldershot, Ashgate, 2004) 43.

[6] *The Arraignment, Trial, and Examination of Mary Moders* (London, 1663).

[7] J Carleton, *The Replication; or Certain Vindicatory Depositions* (London, 1663) and *The Ultimum Vale of John Carleton, of the Middle Temple* (London, 1663).

[8] See eg *The Lawyers Clark trappanned by the crafty Whore of Canterbury* (London, 1663).

[9] R Latham and W Matthews (eds), *The Diary of Samuel Pepys, Vol 4: 1663* (London, Harper Collins, 1971) 163, 177; see also *The Diary of Samuel Pepys, Vol 5: 1664* (London, Harper Collins, 1971) 124 for Pepys' visit to the theatre to see *The German Princesse* on stage, played by Mary herself; FB Gent, *Vercingetorixa; or the German Princess Reduc'd to an English Habit* (London, 1663).

[10] Carleton (n 5) 6. Kietzman (n 5) discounts this possibility, suggesting that Mary herself admitted it to be untrue. However, while Mary certainly admits to overstating her status, she does not abandon her insistence on her identity. There is a contemporary pamphlet that referred to Mary giving her answers in 'broken English' and noting how her 'grace and gallant deportment' had led spectators to argue that she could not be 'of any low birth and parentage': *The great tryall and arraignment of the late distressed lady otherwise called the late Germain princess* (London, 1663) 4, although there is of course the possibility that Mary herself was the author (see eg K Lilley, '"These Novels of My Life": Mary Carleton's Crimes' (2010) 25 *Australian Feminist Studies* 265, 271).

[11] *The Lawyers Clark* (n 8).

My aim here is not to try to unravel Mary's entire life history, but simply to assess whether her acquittal was justified. Most accounts of Mary's life present the details of her alleged previous marriages as established facts and assume that she was acquitted in 1663 simply because the prosecution 'bungled' their case.[12] Many have also repeated John Carleton's claim that Mary had been tried for bigamy previously.[13] Literary scholar Ernest Bernbaum confidently asserted that Mary 'ran away from her first husband, a shoemaker, in 1658, married a second in Dover, and escaped punishment for bigamy only through the failure of her first husband to appear against her', describing these as 'well attested fact'.[14] But repetition is not the same as attestation, and when we dig a little deeper into these supposedly solid facts, the foundation for them disappears, and they begin to seem distinctly implausible.

The only facts that were not in dispute between John and Mary related to how they had met, and their brief courtship.[15] Mary had arrived in London towards the end of March 1663, travelling on a river barge from Gravesend. The owner of the Exchange Tavern where she was staying introduced her to his wife's brother, John Carleton. He wooed her on the understanding that she had a substantial dowry, and they were married at St Bartholomew's church in April 1663. This marriage at least was recorded in the parish register. Afterwards they lived together.[16]

But in May 1663 John's father received a letter alleging that his new daughter-in-law was not who she claimed to be. At this point the parties' stories begin to diverge, so it is better to set out who said what rather than try to compile a single narrative from their contradictory accounts. Both John's and Mary's versions agree that there was a letter, but they disagree as to who sent it, why, and what it said. According to Mary, the letter, while purporting to be an anonymous tip-off, in fact came from 'a servant and admirer' of her sister-in-law – the implication being that the Carletons had arranged for it to be sent.[17] It began, she later asserted, as follows:

> SIR, *I* Am unknown to you, but hearing that your Son Mr. *John Carleton* hath married a Woman of a pretended great Fortune, and high Birth, I thought fit to give you timely notice of what I know, and have heard concerning her, that she is an absolute Cheat, hath married several Men in our County of *Kent*, and then run away from them, with what they had. If it be the same Woman I mean, she speaks several Languages fluently, and hath very high Breasts, *&c.*[18]

[12] J Todd and E Spearing (eds), *Counterfeit Ladies: The Life and Death of Mal Cutpurse; The Case of Mary Carleton* (London, William Pickering, 1994) xxviii; K Lilley, 'Mary Carleton's false additions: the case of the "German Princess"' (2010) 16 *Humanities Research* 79, 79–80.

[13] J Hudson, *Crime and Consequence in Early Modern Literature and Law* (Edinburgh, Edinburgh University Press, 2022) 168, describing Mary as a 'female adventurer, thief and polygamist' and stating that she 'twice cheated justice with acquittals on bigamy charges'.

[14] E Bernbaum, *The Mary Carleton Narratives, 1663-1673: A Missing Chapter in the History of the English Novel* (Cambridge, Massachusetts, Harvard University Press, 1914) 1, 2. See also K Lucenko, '"Meerly my own free Agent": Liberty and Civility in The Case of Madam Mary Carleton' (2019) 14 *Early Modern Women: An Interdisciplinary Journal* 50, 50–51 ('We know that she fled her first husband, a shoemaker, and married a second man, a surgeon, and was arrested and tried for bigamy').

[15] M Matchinske (ed), *The Carleton Bigamy Trial* (New York/Toronto, Iter Press, 2023) 4.

[16] John, it appears, had no reason to believe that Mary was anything other than a virgin at the time of their wedding, although he later alleged that he was willing to prove (privately) 'what an artificial made [sic] she was, whose seeming purity of a true Maiden Bride, was sophisticated and made strict by the power of Druggs & help of Art': Carleton, *Ultimum Vale* (n 7) 24.

[17] Carleton (n 5) 69.

[18] Carleton (n 5) 70.

By contrast, in his later pamphlet titled *The Ultimum Vale of John Carleton*, John presented the letter sent to his father as a response to various inquiries that had been made in Dover. 'By what I can discover', his version runs, Mary was 'a Gentlewoman that is the greatest Cheat in the World'.

> She hath now two Husbands living in this Town, the one a Shoemaker named Thomas Steadman, the other a Chirurgion [surgeon] named Thomas Day. She was borne in Canterbury, her maiden name is Mary Modders, her Father was a Musician belonging to Christ-church Canterbury. She was lately in Dover-Castle a Prisoner, taken out of a ship bound for the Barbadoes, where she cheated the M[aste]r of £50. If it be she, I am sorry for your friends misfortune.[19]

John also claimed that Mary was recognised by a gentlewoman as 'the same person that formerly lay at her house, behind the Feathers Tavern in St Paul's churchyard'.[20]

Mary was arrested and, as she indignantly noted, 'haled and pulled by Beadles, and such like rude and boisterous Fellows, before a Tribunal, like a lewd Criminal'.[21] The 'tribunal' in question was the magistrate Sir Edmund Berry Godfrey. This was the first formal stage of criminal proceedings. Magistrates were required to 'take the examination of such Prisoner, and information of those that bring him, of the fact and circumstance … as much thereof as shall be material to prove the felony'.[22] As legal historian John Langbein has observed, this meant that the pre-trial procedure was very much slanted towards the prosecution, with magistrates being directed to assemble 'not the whole case, but only the prosecution case'.[23]

In this case Godfrey does not appear to have delved too deeply into the case for the prosecution either. Mary's father-in-law explained the case against her, and Godfrey asked Mary whether it was true. Her pert response was that if she had two husbands, he was one of them. This did her no favours, and she was committed for trial.[24] Mary was accordingly confined in the Gatehouse prison, adjacent to Westminster Abbey, before being transferred to Newgate for the start of the next Old Bailey sessions.[25]

On the evening of 3 June, Mary was brought up from Newgate to be arraigned. The indictment against her was read. As this provides a good illustration of the standard form for an indictment for bigamy in the seventeenth and eighteenth centuries, I shall reproduce it in full, apart from modernising the dates.

> That she the said Mary Moders, late of London, Spinster, otherwise Mary Stedman, the Wife of Thomas Stedman, late of the City of Canterbury, in the County of Kent, Shoemaker [on 12 May 1654] did take to Husband the aforesaid Thomas Stedman, and him the said Thomas Stedman then and there had to Husband. And that she the said Mary Moders, alias Stedman, [on 21 April 1663], at London, in the Parish of Great Bartholomew's, in the Ward

[19] Carleton, *Ultimum Vale* (n 7) 27. It should be noted that the spelling of surnames varies between sources: unless quoting directly, I will refer to Steadman and Moders.

[20] ibid 28. This may well have been true, but the woman in question did not specifically identify Mary as being from Canterbury, her complaint instead being that Mary had stolen from her.

[21] Carleton (n 5) 73.

[22] Criminal Law Act 1555, s 1.

[23] JH Langbein, *The Origins of Adversary Criminal Trial* (Oxford, Oxford University Press, 2005) 43.

[24] Carleton (n 5) 74.

[25] ibid 76.

> of Farringdon without, feloniously did take to Husband one John Carleton, and to him was married, the said Thomas Stedman her former Husband then being alive, and in full Life, against the Form of the Statute in that case provided, and against the Peace of our said Sovereign Lord the King, his Crown and Dignity, &c.[26]

To this she pleaded 'not guilty'.

The trial began the following morning, before Judge Howel. The first witness for the prosecution was James Knot, who said that he had been present at Mary's first wedding to Thomas Steadman nine years earlier. In response to a question from the judge, he confirmed that Mary and Thomas had lived together for four years after the wedding and had two children together, both of whom had since died.[27]

That Knot was being questioned by the judge – and also, as the trial went on, by members of the jury – was nothing out of the ordinary. Seventeenth-century trials were, as Langbein has noted, a 'lawyer-free altercation'.[28] Only on rare occasions did counsel appear for the prosecution, and those accused of a felony were not permitted to have counsel to speak in their defence. As a result, both the judge and members of the jury took a far more active role in the proceedings.[29]

But the questions they asked did suggest that they had some doubts about Knot's evidence. Members of the jury asked whether he was sure of her identity ('Friend, did you give this very Woman?') and tested his story that he had given her away.[30] And the judge returned to the question of when and where the wedding had taken place:

> *Court.* You are sure they were married in the Church, and this is the Woman?
>
> *Knot.* Yes, I am sure of it.
>
> *Court.* How long ago?
>
> *Knot.* About nine Years ago.[31]

The reason why this was so important was that if the ceremony *had* taken place as alleged in May 1654, then it would not have been a valid marriage by the laws then in force. On 24 August 1653, Cromwell's Barebones Parliament had passed new legislation requiring all marriages to take place before a local Justice of the Peace.[32] This had explicitly provided that, from 29 September 1653, no other form of marriage 'shall be held or accompted a Marriage according to the Laws of England'.[33]

[26] *Arraignment* (n 6) 1–2; Carleton (n 5) 75–76. The significance of the date when the first marriage was supposed to have taken place is explored further below.

[27] *Arraignment* (n 6) 5; Carleton (n 5) 81. The fact that the transcript of the trial that Mary included in her pamphlet is identical to that in the *Arraignment* is worth noting as a point in favour of Mary's credibility. For an example of a pamphlet that purports to include a transcript of the trial but which in fact selectively removed inconvenient evidence, see the case study of James Stamp Sutton Cooke in chapter 3.

[28] Langbein (n 23) 25.

[29] JS Cockburn, *A History of the English Assizes, 1558-1714* (Cambridge, Cambridge University Press, 1972) 122; N Lacey, *In Search of Criminal Responsibility: Ideas, Interests and Institutions* (Oxford, Oxford University Press, 2016) 114.

[30] *Arraignment* (n 6) 5; Carleton (n 5) 81.

[31] *Arraignment* (n 6) 5; Carleton (n 5) 82.

[32] For the background to the legislation, see C Durston, '"Unhallowed Wedlocks": The Regulation of Marriage During the English Revolution' (1988) 31 *Historical Journal* 45.

[33] *An Act touching Marriages and the registering thereof; and also touching Births and Burials*: CH Firth and RS Rait (eds), *Acts and Ordinances of the Interregnum, 1642-1660: Vol 2* (London, HMSO, 1911) 716.

It is possible that Knot realised that he had made a mistake. Upon being questioned further, he said that Thomas and Mary were 'married according to the Order of the Land, a little before the Act came forth touching marriages by Justices of the Peace'.[34] At the very least, then, by Knot's own testimony, the date stated in the indictment could not have been when the wedding took place, given that the Act was passed and came into effect some eight months earlier.

But there was no other evidence that the alleged ceremony had taken place at all. The minister whom Knot claimed had conducted it had since died. The sexton, whom John Carleton's father had apparently visited very recently, was not to be found. Thomas Steadman, the alleged first husband, was not in court. It was explained that he had 'declared his willingness to come up to give evidence against her, but wanted money for his journey'.[35] While witnesses at the time were not reimbursed for their expenses in attending court, it would not have cost the Carletons much to pay for Thomas to travel from Canterbury – which lies only 60 miles from London, on the well-established route from Dover.

Of course, if Thomas was Mary's first husband, he would not have been able to give evidence against her even if he had been there, since spouses were barred from giving evidence against each other.[36] Even so, his presence in court would at least have established that he had not been invented by the Carletons and their witnesses. The judge gave short shrift to the claim by Mr Carleton senior (as he will be called to distinguish him from his son) that he had seen Thomas Steadman in Dover and that Thomas had acknowledged himself to be Mary's husband, demanding 'Where is this Man her Husband? Hearsays must condemn no Man'.[37] Pressed as to what he actually knew, Mr Carleton senior insisted that he knew Thomas was alive but had to admit that he had no direct knowledge of his being married to Mary.[38]

Incidentally, John Witte Jr provides a gripping backstory about Thomas Steadman and his father having tried to bully Mary into a marriage and having her arrested on trumped-up charges of theft. This, however, appears to be an entire invention, or rather a garbled version of Mary's relationship with the Carletons, Witte being under the mistaken impression that the 1663 prosecution was brought by Thomas Steadman's father, and that both Thomas and his father were in court.[39]

[34] *Arraignment* (n 6) 6; Carleton (n 5) 83.

[35] Evidence given by William Clark: *Arraignment* (n 6) 6; Carleton (n 5) 83. John subsequently told a different story, claiming that Thomas was a soldier and unable to get leave: *Ultimum Vale* (n 7) and see further below.

[36] *Mary Griggs's Case* (1659) Raym T 1; 83 ER 1; *Double Trouble*, ch 2. The bar remained in place until 1915.

[37] *Arraignment* (n 6) 6; Carleton (n 5) 84. As this indicates, there was already a concern that hearsay evidence was problematic, but hearsay statements were not specifically excluded: on the evolution of the law of evidence, see TP Gallanis, 'The Rise of Modern Evidence Law' (1999) 84 *Iowa Law Review* 499.

[38] It is entirely possible that there was a Thomas Steadman who had married a Mary in Canterbury. Kietzman (n 5) 97 found a record of a child being baptised in Canterbury who was the son of Thomas and Mary Steadman, but then Steadman was not that unusual a surname there, and Mary was probably the most common female name at the time.

[39] J Witte Jr, *The Western Case for Monogamy Over Polygamy* (Cambridge, Cambridge University Press, 2015) 311–12.

Crucially, there was no entry of the marriage in the register of St Mildred's church, where it was alleged to have taken place.[40] Mr Carleton senior sought to explain this away by claiming that the parish clerk (the former sexton) had told him that his predecessor had neglected to register it, marriages 'being then very numerous' ahead of the 1653 Act coming into force. That at least was plausible, supposing that the ceremony had taken place in late August or early September 1653, and not in May of 1654 as per the indictment. Couples were not enthusiastic about getting married before a Justice of the Peace, and there appears to have been something of a rush nationwide to marry ahead of the new law coming into force.[41] But Mr Carleton senior could not resist attempting to blacken his unwanted daughter-in-law's character still further by implying that she was somehow responsible for the lack of registration: 'If she intended this Trade, she likewise knew how to make the Clerk mistake Registring the Marriage.' Yet that hardly fitted with James Knot's claim that Mary and Thomas had then lived together for four years. The idea that a woman would deliberately take steps to conceal her legal marriage on the off chance that she might later marry bigamously was a little far-fetched.

It was also asserted in court that Mary had been tried for bigamy before. Another witness, William Clark, claimed that a person present at the Old Bailey that very day had been a juror at Canterbury in a trial that saw Mary accused of having two husbands.[42] But it was later admitted that the man in question was not in fact sure if Mary was the woman who had been tried.[43] Once again, we have a claim being made that the prosecution was unable to substantiate.

Mary herself addressed the court at length, attributing the prosecution to the 'malice' of her father-in-law, and denying that she was ever married to anyone except John Carleton. She claimed that various persons had been bribed to give evidence against her, and that 'my Innocence shall be my Counsellor'.[44] She concluded by pointing out that since she had been in prison, various supposed schoolmates from Canterbury had been to visit her and upon seeing her 'they all declared that they did not know me'.[45]

This prompted Judge Howel to ask whether there was anyone who could prove that Mary had lived in Canterbury: 'Have you none in that whole City, neither for Love of Justice nor Right, will come to say she lived there?'[46] But no such witness was forthcoming. At one point Mr Carleton senior claimed to have found a man named Davis who had been at Mary's father's house in Canterbury, but the man in question had mysteriously disappeared before he was able to give evidence.

[40] Cf Kietzman (n 5) 27, whose suggestion that 'John claimed to be able to discover Mary's truth by doing genealogical research in Canterbury parish churches (giving priority to the fixity of writing)' does not sufficiently reflect the absence of any written sources.

[41] D Rosman, *The Evolution of the English Churches, 1500-2000* (Cambridge, Cambridge University Press, 2003) 102.

[42] *Arraignment* (n 6) 6; Carleton (n 5) 83–84.

[43] *Arraignment* (n 6) 14; Carleton (n 5) 100. The trial, if it took place, must have been at the quarter sessions rather than the assizes, the latter being held in the county town of Maidstone: JS Cockburn (ed), *Calendar of Assize Records: Kent Indictments, 1649-1659* (London, HMSO, 1989).

[44] *Arraignment* (n 6) 13; Carleton (n 5) 96.

[45] ibid.

[46] *Arraignment* (n 6) 13; Carleton (n 5) 97.

Mary's witnesses then gave evidence to support her claim that the case against her had been fabricated. Elizabeth Collier recounted how a Mr Billing – yet another of Mary's supposed former husbands – had turned up at the Gatehouse prison and mistakenly identified her as his wife.[47] One Jane Finch said that she had been offered £5 to give evidence against Mary.[48] Most compelling of all was the evidence of Mr Bailey, the jailor of the Gatehouse, who said that at least 500 people had been to view Mary, of whom several were from Canterbury, 'but not one of them knew her'.[49]

When Judge Howel came to sum up, he was at pains to point out the gaps in the evidence.[50] The case, he noted, rested on the 'single testimony' of James Knot, whose recall of the details of the ceremony was somewhat hazy. If Mary had indeed been born in Canterbury, married there, lived with Thomas for four years and had two children, it would, as he pointed out, have been 'easy to have brought somebody to prove this'.[51] As for the allegation of the earlier trial, 'that there was a Trial, may be believed; but whether this be the Woman tried or acquitted, doth not appear'.[52] He also reminded the jury of the consequences of finding Mary guilty: 'a Woman hath no Clergy, she is to die by the Law, if guilty'.[53] With so many holes in the case presented by the prosecution, it is unsurprising that the jury returned a verdict of 'not guilty'.

Pepys recorded in his diary the following Sunday how he was glad that Mary had been cleared, praising her 'wit and spirit' and defending her against an acquaintance who 'enveighed mightily against the German princesse'.[54] The idea that Mary's eloquence saved herself from conviction and death has also proved popular with later commentators.[55] A recent collection of the pamphlets published about the trial are billed as relating to the 'sensational' case of Mary Carleton 'who may have saved herself from hanging by her eloquent self-defense'.[56] Yet it is worth bearing in mind that there were plenty of individuals who pleaded their innocence with equal fervour but who were nonetheless convicted. It seems far more likely that the jury, having heard and

[47] *Arraignment* (n 6) 13; Carleton (n 5) 97–98. Another contemporary pamphlet had Billing appearing in court and, after putting on his spectacles, identifying the woman standing next to Mary as the woman he had married – prompting Mary to note his mistake, adding 'he doth not know me here with his four eyes, how then is it possible that he should now know me with his two': *The great tryall* (n 10) 5.

[48] *Arraignment* (n 6) 13–14; Carleton (n 5) 98.

[49] *Arraignment* (n 6) 14; Carleton (n 5) 98–99.

[50] The very fact that he did so may indicate that this was a particularly difficult case. According to Cockburn, before the late eighteenth century it was 'unusual, indeed unnecessary, for a judge to sum up the evidence in routine criminal trials': JS Cockburn, *A History of the English Assizes, 1558-1714* (Cambridge, Cambridge University Press, 1972) 122.

[51] *Arraignment* (n 6) 15; Carleton (n 7) 100. Hudson (n 13) 178 suggests that Howel 'refused to engage with the question of Carleton's identity – potentially the weakest element of her argument', but it is clear that he did address the issue of *identification*, ie whether she was the same person who had supposedly already been tried. The question of her true identity was irrelevant.

[52] *Arraignment* (n 6) 15; Carleton (n 7) 100.

[53] ibid. His reference to a woman having 'no clergy' was an allusion to the anomalous privilege of 'benefit of clergy' that enabled literate men to escape the death penalty: see further *Double Trouble*, ch 2.

[54] *Diary* (n 9) 177.

[55] TB Hug, *Impostures in Early Modern England: Representations and Perceptions of Fraudulent Identities* (Manchester, Manchester University Press, 2010) 29, suggesting that Mary's 'power of invention and performance' saved her from the gallows.

[56] Matchinske (n 15).

weighed the evidence of various witnesses, simply took the view that the case against her had not been made out.

Despite Mary's acquittal, John Carleton continued to insist, in print, that she had committed bigamy in marrying him. He protested that there had been five or six witnesses ready to give evidence as to Mary's marriage to Thomas Day, along with the clergyman who had married her to one 'Mr Billing the Brickmaker'.[57] But he carefully refrained from giving any specific details as to when these marriages had taken place, claiming that it 'would be too tedious, to recite the full copy of her examination and tryal'.[58] It was not the only time during his rambling 48-page diatribe against Mary that he worried (with good reason) about being tedious. But the significance of the omission is obvious: the more specific an allegation, the easier it is to either prove or disprove.[59]

It is entirely possible that there was a Mary Steadman living in Canterbury who was suspected of having remarried while her first husband was still alive. Here, John did give some provenance for his claims: a letter about the woman in question from Francis Lovelace, the Recorder of Dover and Canterbury,[60] and an order from the quarter sessions that implied some doubt as to her marital status.[61] But again, there was nothing to prove that the woman in question was 'his' Mary.[62] Lovelace had not seen her, and declared himself to be too ill to come to London for the trial.

Other of John's allegations were patently ludicrous. He sought to explain the absence of Thomas Steadman from the Old Bailey on the basis that he was a soldier and could not leave Canterbury without the permission of the governor. That was plausible enough, although it was not the story that had been told at the trial. But John then alleged that Mary had written to the governor telling him that 'if they let Steadman come up, when she was dead she would haunt them'.[63] And this, he claimed, had meant that Thomas had been chained up in the castle to prevent him from leaving.[64]

[57] Carleton, *Ultimum Vale* (n 7) 35.

[58] ibid.

[59] Kietzman (n 5) 69 described John as undertaking 'genealogical research', and how he 'painstakingly records his "paper chase" – each piece of evidence found as well as each alleged piece that is missing'. In reality, far more was missing than was found or even sought. The idea of 'genealogical research' might imply that John had tracked down Mary's baptism (to prove her identity), or the baptisms and burials of the children that she was alleged to have had by Thomas Steadman or her supposed marriages to Day or Billing. There is no evidence that he even tried to do any of those things. The only parish register consulted is that of St Mildred's – which, as we have seen, turned out to have no record of the ceremony. But it seems highly unlikely that three clerks in three different churches would all be so careless as to neglect the registration of marriages.

[60] Lovelace at least was no invention: BD Henning (ed), *The History of Parliament: the House of Commons 1660-1690* (Woodbridge, Boydell and Brewer, 1983).

[61] This order, dating April 1660, required Mary to give sureties for her appearance at the next sessions and in the meantime 'to forbear to accompany with Tho. Day Chirurgion as his wife, unless (in the mean time) she brings a sufficient Certificate that Tho. Steadman is dead': Carleton, *Ultimum Vale* (n 7) 36.

[62] Or, indeed, that she had been tried for bigamy: John gave no details of the supposed trial, save to claim it had taken place in Dover (*Ultimum Vale* (n 7) 33), which contradicted the claim that had previously been made about her being tried at Canterbury (see text at n 42).

[63] Carleton, *Ultimum Vale* (n 7) 35.

[64] ibid. Kietzman (n 5) 97 also discovered a reference in the State Papers to a Thomas Steadman being arrested on 30 May 1663 and released on 6 June – his detention covering the exact period that Mary was being tried at the Old Bailey. This coincidence led her to speculate 'that perhaps a person of some influence and sympathy for the German Princess' plight had Steadman apprehended to prevent him from testifying against her'. Since this Thomas Steadman was described as being a husbandman of the parish of Woking, it seems

Overall, it seems entirely possible that the allegations of bigamy were concocted by the Carletons to rid themselves of a woman who had turned out not to be quite the catch they had assumed. At the very least, her acquittal was justified given the lack of credible evidence against her.

But whatever the truth about Mary's past, she faced a bleak future. Although her acquittal had saved her from a death sentence, it also left her in a very difficult position. Her marriage to John was effectively over, but because they had gone through a ceremony of marriage, and no earlier marriage had been proved, she could not risk marrying anyone else. Moreover, as her presumed husband, he was entitled to retain her jewels.[65] A few years later Mary was back at the Old Bailey, this time charged with theft, and was sentenced to transportation.[66] A further theft after her return led to her being sentenced to death.[67]

On 22 January 1673, she was taken to Tyburn to be hanged. Even then it was her marital history, rather than her more recent crimes, that continued to attract interest. A contemporary pamphlet reporting the event had one of the crowd asking Mary how many husbands she had had – with Mary replying 'Sir, I have been told myself I had fifty; but 'tis all false'.[68] The same author reported that Mary took a miniature portrait of John Carleton out of her pocket and asked that it be buried with her.[69]

Mary's execution led to a further flurry of publications.[70] The fact that she had been proved to be a thief made it easier for her detractors to believe that she had also been a bigamist.[71] But we should also consider the possibility that a young woman, deprived of her assets and tarnished by the allegations of the Carleton family, whether true or not, ended up sinking into poverty and stole in an attempt to survive. In her final speech, Mary asked for God's forgiveness for both herself and John, adding 'I beseech God lay nothing to his charge for my fault'.[72]

likely that this was a different person. There was at least one Thomas Steadman resident in Surrey at this time, who married at Cranleigh in 1658 – which was some 15 miles from Woking, as compared to the 80 miles separating Woking and Canterbury (FindMyPast, *Surrey Marriages 1653-1707*).

[65] Inevitably, there was a dispute between John and Mary as to whether these were worth anything. John contemptuously claimed that the 'Counterfeit Jewells, like the rest of her storys and her self, are scarce worth taking off from a Dunghill': Carleton, *Ultimum Vale* (n 7) 25.

[66] Hudson (n 13).

[67] *An Exact and True Relation of the Examination, Tryal and Condemnation of the German Princess, alias Mary Carleton, at Justice-Hall in the Old Baily, January 17, 1672* (London, 1672).

[68] Anon, *The Memoires of Mary Carleton, commonly stiled the German Princess being a narrative of her life and death interwoven with many strange and pleasant passages, from the time of her birth to her execution at Tyburn, being the 22th of January 1672/3: with her behaviour in prison, her last speech, burial & epitaph* (London, 1673) 108.

[69] ibid 113.

[70] *The Deportment and Carriage of the German Princess, Immediately before her Execution; And her last Speech at Tyburn* (London, 1673); *The Life and character of Mrs. Mary Moders, alias Mary Stedman, alias Mary Carleton, alias Mary -------, the famous German princess being an historical relation of her birth and fortunes, with the havock and spoil she committed upon the publick in the reign of King Charles the Second: together with her tragical fall at Tyburn, on the 22d of January 1678, added by way of appendix* (London, 1673).

[71] A biography of Mary compiled by Francis Kirkman simply asserted her marriage to Thomas Steadman as a matter of fact but was simply rehashing details from earlier publications: *The Counterfeit Lady Unveiled* (London, 1673) 20.

[72] *Memoires* (n 68) 117.

'No Proof of Marriage but by Circumstance': Richard Boyle, 1687

The case of Richard Boyle has interesting parallels with that of Mary Carleton. He too was tried for bigamy at the Old Bailey, around two-and-a-half decades after Mary's trial. And like Mary, he admitted his second marriage but denied his first. The terms in which he did so, though, were very different. Rather than denying that a ceremony had taken place at all, he simply insisted that 'there was no certificate appeared, or any person who married them, or saw them married, to give testimony against them';[73] in other words, that there was no good evidence with which to convict him. There were, however (and here again his case differed from Mary's), witnesses willing to say that Richard had told them he was indeed married to his alleged first wife.

According to the *Proceedings of the Old Bailey*,[74] Richard was accused of marrying the delightfully named Loveday Billing at Wanstead on 5 August 1685 and then one Susannah Moise at St James' Duke's Place on 29 January 1687. Witnesses for the prosecution gave evidence that Richard had courted Loveday but had met with resistance from her father. Richard had then apparently confessed to them that he had been married to Loveday privately, by 'an Irish minister'.[75] They also said that Richard had lived in lodgings with Loveday, publicly acknowledging her as his wife, that they had had a child together, and that he had referred to Loveday as his wife in formal legal documents. Some letters to Loveday's father were also produced in court, in which Richard had described himself as his 'dutiful son'. Even Richard's own witnesses said that he had offered Loveday money to 'disclaim the marriage'.[76]

The report in the *Proceedings* concluded by noting that Richard was 'upon the many probable circumstances and his own former confession of the first marriage etc found guilty of the felony'.[77] The court's willingness to accept witness testimony as to what Richard had said might seem to run counter to Judge Howel's insistence in Mary Carleton's case that 'hearsays must condemn no man'.[78] But, as later commentators

[73] *OBP*, 12 October 1687.

[74] First published in 1675, the *Proceedings* were intended for a popular audience, rather than as a legal record: T Hitchcock and WJ Turkel, 'The Old Bailey Proceedings, 1674-1913: Text Mining for Evidence of Court Behaviour' (2016) 34 *Law and History Review* 929, 937. There was no attempt to provide a full transcript of a case, just a brief summary. When we contrast the 30-line report of Richard's case with the transcript of Mary Carleton's, which runs to as many *pages*, it is frustrating to think how much we are missing. Even so, there is no better source available for the period.

[75] *OBP*, 12 October 1687. The fact that the wedding had taken place privately, rather than in a church, would not in itself have had any impact on its validity, as long as the person conducting it was an ordained Anglican clergyman. There does not appear to have been any discussion as to the religious affiliation of the officiating minister, but the Anglican Church was the Established Church in Ireland, even if it catered to only a minority of the largely Catholic population.

[76] ibid.

[77] It is possible that the references to the 'probable circumstances' and Richard's confession were the reporter's own summary, but it seems more likely that they reflect the judge's summing up of the evidence for the jury. While there are other contemporary reports where it seems likely that their compiler was adding his own commentary on the case (see eg *Double Trouble*, ch 2, for some of his mordant asides on the fate of those who were unable to read), we know from Mary Carleton's case that judges did sum up the evidence, at least in complex cases, and that this was not simply a later innovation.

[78] See above.

explained, hearsay evidence as to admissions made by the defendant *was* admissible.[79] The reference to the 'many probable circumstances' also illustrates the importance attached to evidence that the parties had lived together and been reputed to be husband and wife. Such evidence was insufficient to establish a marriage by itself, but could provide corroboration of identity, and of the likelihood of there having been a ceremony.[80]

Since Richard was clearly literate, he was not facing the death penalty. Instead, he was able to plead benefit of clergy, and was burnt in the hand.[81] But the fact that he had been convicted had consequences beyond his punishment, with implications for his now-void marriage to Susannah.[82] His next step was to petition for a new trial. In his letter, he noted that he had been indicted for bigamy by Loveday, 'a lewd woman', and found guilty although there was no proof of his marriage to her 'but by circumstance'.[83] His letter was referred to the Attorney General on 17 March 1688.[84]

Richard's personal petition reflected the absence of any other avenue of appeal. It was to be several centuries before those convicted of a crime had the right to appeal to a higher court against their conviction or sentence.[85] Given everything that was going on politically in 1688, it is unsurprising that his case was not seen as a priority. As was noted the following year, his petition was 'not proceeded with by reason of the late stop of the execution of the laws' – a terse allusion to the arrival in England of the Protestant William of Orange and his army, the subsequent flight of his Catholic father-in-law James II, and the dilemma as to who should succeed James on the throne.[86]

Eventually, in February 1689, William and his wife Mary were declared joint rulers, and normal business could resume. At Hampton Court, on 2 May 1689, the Attorney General was warranted to issue a writ of *certiorari* in Richard's favour, quashing his conviction. This noted that Richard had shown that he had been 'seduced' by Loveday, and had cohabited with her, but that he, 'being willing to live virtuously', had gone on to marry Susannah 'according to the law of the land'. The verdict against him had been given 'without proof or certificate of any marriage with the said Billing' and without Richard being able to call witnesses – 'they being absent, and he under confinement'.[87]

Yet it is worth noting that there was only Richard's word for any of this. Loveday had since died, and there was in any case no new investigation into the circumstances. Nor was any mention made of Richard's earlier admission that Loveday was his wife.

[79] Gallanis (n 37) 517–18.

[80] On the role played by evidence of cohabitation and reputation, see R Probert, 'The presumptions in favour of marriage' (2018) 77 *Cambridge Law Journal* 375.

[81] The *Proceedings* did not explicitly refer to him pleading benefit of clergy, but this can be inferred from the fact that he was branded rather than being sentenced to death.

[82] Proceedings in the church courts regarding the marriage were stopped upon evidence of his conviction being given: *Boyle v Boyle* (1687) 3 Mod 164; 87 ER 106.

[83] EK Timings (ed), *Calendar of State Papers Domestic: James II, 1687-9: Vol 3* (London, 1972) 167.

[84] TNA, *State Papers*, SP 44/71, 420.

[85] The right of appeal – as opposed to the possibility of a judge referring questions of law for resolution – was only conferred in 1907, with the creation of the Court of Criminal Appeal: see *Double Trouble*, ch 1.

[86] M Kishlansky, *A Monarchy Transformed: Britain 1603-1714* (London, Penguin, 1997) 277–85.

[87] WJ Hardy (ed), *Calendar of State Papers Domestic: William and Mary, 1689-90* (London, 1895) 86; TNA, *State Papers*, SP 44/338, 316.

Rather than the process being used to set aside a wrongful conviction, it may simply have replaced it with an unwarranted acquittal.

'Who are You!': Richard Leaver, 1737

During his trial at the Old Bailey in 1737, Richard Leaver refused to acknowledge Alice Allington as his wife, claiming to remember nothing about any wedding:

> I was fuddled over Night, and next Morning I found myself abed with a strange Woman, – and who are you! – how came you here says I! O, my Dear, says she, we were married last Night at the Fleet.[88]

It was a defence that has proved irresistibly quotable.[89] It was also a story that would have confirmed some people's worst fears about the Fleet prison and the various activities that took place within its environs. Only the previous year, Parliament had passed legislation banning the sale of gin, but a merry trade in distilling, distribution and drinking continued within the Rules of the Fleet, the area surrounding the prison where those imprisoned for debt could pay to reside.[90] Another problematic activity was the trade in clandestine marriages. Various clergymen operating out of the alehouses around the Fleet were willing to conduct wedding ceremonies without any of the preliminaries required by the canon law. The ready availability of both alcohol and marriage was known to have led to some hasty and ill-advised unions. One such case had just recently come to the attention of the civil courts: Mary Hill, described as being 'in mean circumstances and of bad character', was alleged to have inveigled a young gentleman into marriage by getting him drunk at an alehouse near the Fleet – for which the Court of Chancery had committed her to the prison for contempt, the gentleman in question being under their jurisdiction as a ward of court.[91]

As that case showed, being drunk at the time of the ceremony did not affect the validity of the marriage. Nor was it a defence to a subsequent charge of bigamy.[92] Indeed, our Richard Leaver's real defence was that the whole story of the ceremony had been made up. This was a defence that had worked for one Edmund Dangerfield the previous year – upon his explaining that the certificate had been obtained as part of a scam, the jury had acquitted him. As in Edmund's case, one of Richard's witnesses produced a certificate that he had obtained from the Fleet the previous Tuesday, telling the court, 'this is a Certificate of my being married to one I never saw in my Life; they'll give Certificates to any Body'.[93]

[88] *OBP*, 20 April 1737.

[89] By me, as well as others: see *Double Trouble*, ch 2; B McConnell, 'For bad or worse' (1992) 142 *New Law Journal* 1250; DM Turner, 'Popular Marriage and the Law: Tales of Bigamy at the Eighteenth-Century Old Bailey' (2005) 30 *London Journal* 6.

[90] J Warner, *Craze: Gin and Debauchery in an Age of Reason* (London, Profile Books Ltd, 2003) 46.

[91] *Hill v Turner* (1737) 1 Atkyns 515; 26 ER 326 – reporting the sequel, where Lord Hardwicke ordered that Mary be restrained from suing in the ecclesiastical court for alimony or restitution of conjugal rights.

[92] For other examples of men being convicted of bigamy despite claiming to have no recollection of the ceremony, see *OBP*, 3 March 1720 (Thomas Cox); *OBP*, 4 July 1730 (John Ward); *OBP*, 26 May 1736 (Robert Wilson).

[93] *OBP*, 20 April 1737.

Richard was probably banking on the poor reputation (and poor eyesight) of the Reverend Gainham, who Alice was claiming had married them. The previous year, one jury, frustrated at the acquittal of an alleged bigamist whom Gainham had no recollection of marrying, had asked the court if something could be done to suppress his 'iniquitous' trade in marriages.[94] Indeed, Gainham's inability to remember the individuals he had married was notorious. Called as a witness in Edmund Dangerfield's case, he had simply read from his register book. When pressed as to whether he had any recollection of Edmund, he claimed to have married 2,000 persons in the intervening three years.

So Richard's story of waking up in an alcohol-induced stupor and being conned by the woman sharing his bed into believing that he had married her, with a fake certificate to give credibility to the story, was, on the face of it, all too plausible. But given the other facts in the case, it seems unlikely that it was true. Richard, after all, was no teenager beguiled by a designing older woman. His first marriage, to Catherine Avery, had taken place at Halstock in Dorset some 13 years earlier. He had left Catherine behind when he came up to London. The *Proceedings* give no hint as to when he first met Alice, but she claimed Richard was perfectly sober at the time of the ceremony, adding tartly that 'he had no Money to make himself drunk'.[95] Any drinking that had been done, she added, had happened afterwards: one woman had paid for 'half a Pint of Gin', and upon the couple arriving home 'there were 5 or 6 People to wish us Joy, and they were all forced to club for a little more Gin to make us drink'. After all that, it would be unsurprising if Richard's recollection of events was hazy.

But the strongest evidence against Richard's story is that he had lived quite openly with Alice after the ceremony, and the pair had had two children together. The parish registers of St John the Evangelist, in London's Smith Square, confirm this part of Alice's evidence: there was a Catherine Liver baptised there in December 1734, some 11 months after the alleged ceremony in the Fleet, followed by a John Leaver in February 1736. Both were recorded as the children of Richard 'and Alice his wife'.[96] It might even have proved to be a happy and long-lasting marriage, had it not been for the unexpected arrival of Catherine, Richard's first wife, in the summer of 1736. Upon realising that her marriage to Richard was bigamous, Alice left him.

'When We Got there We Changed Our Minds': Thomas Burgess, 1838

In 1838, a 35-year-old blacksmith named Thomas Burgess was prosecuted for bigamy at the Cheshire assizes. Evidence of both weddings was provided by way of copies from the marriage registers. Less than a year had separated the two ceremonies,

[94] *OBP*, 13 October 1736 (John Smart).
[95] *OBP*, 20 April 1737.
[96] Ancestry, *Westminster Church of England Parish Registers*, SJSS/PR/1/1. Catherine had been born on 10 December and was baptised on 30 December, so there is nothing to suggest that Richard and Alice were having sex before their wedding.

but it was stated that his first wife, Mary, had left him after just seven weeks on account of his ill treatment of her.[97] And Sarah Podmore, his second, was there in court, ready to give evidence. It seemed as if it was going to be a straightforward case. But when the Attorney General started to question Sarah, he got something of a shock:

> Q. You know the prisoner?
>
> A. Yes!
>
> Q. You were married to him in the Manchester Old Church in May, 1838?
>
> A. No! Sir!

At this point the Attorney General suggested that Sarah's words 'should be taken down', and warned her that she would be prosecuted for perjury if she did not tell the truth. Nonetheless, she maintained that she was not married to Thomas. But when asked by the judge whether she was ever 'at church with the prisoner', she was forced to admit that she had at least been in the building:

> Oh! yes! at the old church in Manchester where we intended to be married, but when we got there we changed our minds. We went into the vestry, when the clerk produced the marriage lines, which the prisoner paid for, and I received them; when at the communion table he turned round, took his hat, and we both went out again.

She went on to explain that she had been, and still was, Thomas' housekeeper and had told other people that they were married 'for my own credit's sake'. But she insisted that 'I never swore we were married; and *we are not married*'.[98]

It might seem like a highly implausible story, concocted by a supportive second wife to try to ensure that her 'husband' would escape conviction. But the location of the alleged non-wedding did make it plausible. The Collegiate Church of St Mary, St Denys and St George was the parish church for the whole of Manchester – the largest city in England and Wales outside London, with a population of around 300,000 at this time.[99] Couples living in Manchester did not have to be married at the parish church – there were at least some other churches in the city that were authorised for weddings.[100] But they were required to pay the marriage fee of 3s 6d to the parish church's officials whether they married there or not.[101] As a result, the Collegiate Church was host to an astonishing number of weddings – some 2,615 in 1838 alone.

With legal restrictions on when weddings could take place (only between 8 am and 12 noon), and practical limitations on when working-class couples were available to marry, weddings were often conducted in batches. Local author Isabella Banks, writing a few decades after Thomas and Sarah's alleged non-wedding, provided a vivid

[97] 'Assize Intelligence', *Chester Chronicle*, 6 April 1838.

[98] ibid.

[99] The 1841 census recorded a population of 311,000: J Ellis, 'Regional and County Centres, 1700-1840' in P Clark (ed), *The Cambridge urban history of Britain: volume II, 1540–1840* (Cambridge, Cambridge University Press, 2000) 679.

[100] See eg CH Timperley, *Annals of Manchester* (Manchester, Bancks & Co, 1839) 67, recording a wedding at St John's, some 35 years after it was founded.

[101] The original charter had given the church's chaplains the right to these fees to supplement their meagre salary: ibid 24.

description of one such occasion in her novel *The Manchester Man*. Her characters, after enjoying some refreshment in one of the nearby hostelries, arrived just as the chaplain was pronouncing a benediction over the first instalment of 'some twenty couples closely packed around the altar'. There followed a 'jostle and scramble for "first kisses"', before these couples were 'hustled away to sign the church books, with their attendant witnesses'.[102] The next batch were then packed into place, the chaplain started again from the top, with the general part of the service being read before each couple in turn were approached for their vows. There was some consternation when one bride realised that her husband-to-be was still in the pub, but the chaplain dealt with this absence by peremptorily telling the man kneeling next to her, one Tom, to act as proxy. Poor Tom 'looked aghast at the prospect of marrying the wrong woman … or, what was worse, of being saddled with two wives', but the chaplain proceeded relentlessly.[103] Happily, the errant bridegroom was fetched from the pub in time to say his own vows, and all was concluded satisfactorily.

Even if some of Mrs Banks' descriptions may have been embroidered or imagined,[104] the batch weddings were true enough, and they were still taking place in the 1830s. According to the register book, Thomas and Sarah were the fourteenth of 16 couples waiting to be married that morning – 'all stood in a ring', as Sarah later noted in court.[105] It appears that they had stayed for at least some of the ceremony but, according to Sarah, had slipped away without the knowledge of the clergyman or the clerk before the crucial words 'I take thee' had been spoken.[106]

It seems that the Collegiate Church, when dealing with dozens of weddings on a single day, had adopted the decidedly irregular practice of getting couples to sign the register before the ceremony had taken place. As the parish clerk admitted under cross-examination, it was not unknown for couples to leave without getting married, but he thought that there were no more than two cases each year. He also insisted that he personally only signed the register *after* the ceremony, and that if the couple left before the ceremony 'we always write "not married"'. But although he had signed the register as a witness – as he had for several of the other couples getting married on 9 May 1836 – he had no personal recollection of Thomas and Sarah going through the ceremony. The judge gave him a good ticking off, warning him that he was 'making a false entry' by signing the register in these circumstances.[107]

In summing up the case for the jury, the judge implied that Sarah's evidence did have to be viewed with some scepticism, given that she had been living with Thomas up until the time of his arrest 'and was in a great degree under his influence'. Nonetheless, the fact that the certificates were signed before the ceremony took place could not be overlooked. The jury almost immediately returned a verdict of not guilty.[108]

[102] GL Banks, *The Manchester Man* (Manchester, Printwise Publications, 1991, first published 1876) 176.
[103] ibid 178.
[104] Joshua Brookes was certainly 'supposed to have baptized, married, and buried more persons than any other clergyman in the kingdom' during his 31-year tenure (Timperley (n 100) 78). However, Mrs Banks was born in 1821, the year that he died, so could never have witnessed his marrying style.
[105] Ancestry, *Anglican Parish Registers*; 'Assize Intelligence', *Chester Chronicle*, 6 April 1838.
[106] 'Assize Intelligence', *Chester Chronicle*, 6 April 1838.
[107] ibid.
[108] 'Chester Assizes', *Morning Herald*, 5 April 1838.

The *Manchester Courier*, commenting on the case a week later, was certainly sceptical as to whether Sarah had been telling the truth. As it explained, the practice at the church was for the vicar to be given a list of all the couples marrying, in the order in which they were to be placed at the altar, and then to address each separately by name when joining them in marriage, so he would know if anyone had left without marrying.[109] Had Charles explained this at the time, the verdict of the jury might well have been different.

So it is at least possible that Thomas and Sarah were bigamously married, rather than not being married at all. But whatever their precise marital status, their union endured. The 1851 census found them living in Cheshire with three daughters, with another appearing in the 1861 census, and they remained together until Thomas' death in 1864.[110]

Manchester Collegiate Church, and its batch weddings, was to go on to play a significant role in the history of bigamy. Of those tried at the Lancashire assizes in the 1840s and 1850s, 22 per cent of the second weddings had taken place there. Perhaps even more surprisingly, 28 per cent of these had also had their *first* wedding there.[111] Clearly, they were hoping that the huge number of weddings would enable them to escape detection, or at least conviction. If so, they were to be disappointed. Most of those standing trial had been detected and prosecuted within a year of their bigamous wedding.[112] And although there were occasional cases where those who had married at the Collegiate Church were acquitted, these acquittals were all based on the statutory exceptions. It may be that the parish clerks had heeded the judge's warning and tightened up their procedures for registering weddings. But certainly no one else escaped conviction as a result of their second wife claiming that they had changed their mind.

'One Story was Good Till the Other was Told ...': The Converted Clown, 1881

In July 1880, it was reported that a clown-turned-preacher had spent his Sunday addressing a (largely uninterested) crowd at Dudley. Open-air preachers were no

[109] 'Registration of Marriages at the Collegiate Church', *Manchester Courier* 14 April 1838.

[110] TNA, 1851 census, HO107/2161, folio 217, p 12; 1861 census, RG9/2579, folio 4, p 1. That this was the correct couple was confirmed by Thomas' occupation of blacksmith, which matched that recorded at the time of his trial, and by matching the place of birth recorded for Sarah in the census with a baptism for a Sarah Royle in 1809 (Ancestry, *Cheshire, England, Select Bishop's Transcripts, 1576-1933*), and a subsequent marriage of a Sarah Royle to James Padmore in 1831 (which had taken place, inevitably, at the Collegiate Church: Ancestry, *Anglican Parish Registers*).

[111] These calculations are based on 222 cases tried at the Lancashire assizes between 1840 and 1859 for which it was possible to ascertain the location of the second marriage from the newspaper report of the trial, either because it was reported or because the details given allowed it to be traced via Ancestry. Of these, 49 individuals had married at the Collegiate Church (or, as it became in 1847, Manchester Cathedral), and of them, 14 had had their first marriage there.

[112] Perhaps the most striking example was that of Robert Mellow, who had married his first wife in Manchester Collegiate Church in 1837 and his second there in January 1845, but was arrested within two or three hours and brought before the borough court the following day (*Morning Post*, 21 January 1845). Of those tried in the 1840s, the median gap between their second wedding at Manchester Collegiate Church and the trial was 346 days (n = 25).

novelty, but this one, in addition to discoursing on the Book of Revelations, had caught the attention of a journalist by his cryptic allusions 'to a martyrdom he was suffering'. The people of nearby Tipton had, the preacher claimed, accused him of being someone else and 'all sorts of dreadful things'.[113] He had concluded his peroration by paraphrasing Shakespeare's Iago:

> He who steals my purse steals trash,
> But he who steals my good name
> Steals that which not enriches him
> And not ennobles me.

The incident at Tipton to which he was referring had taken place a few months earlier. Then passing under the soubriquet of 'John Brown, the converted clown', he had made his appearance at the Prince's End Primitive Methodist chapel, where he was instantly identified by several members of the congregation as being a man named Henry John Llewellyn. Among them was his wife Mary Ann, whom he had deserted some 13 years earlier. Her identification of him had led to the trustees of the chapel turning him out of the pulpit – not just on account of his desertion of Mary Ann, but because he was accompanied by a different woman whom he had claimed was his wife.[114] Placards were put up denouncing him as an imposter.[115] His response – as his choice of quotation hinted – was to threaten to sue them for libel.

But the months passed without his taking any steps to make good on this threat. In January 1881, he was finally brought before the Chester City Police Court and charged with bigamy.[116] Evidence was given of a marriage of a Henry John Llewellyn to Mary Ann Davies at the parish church of Quinton in Worcestershire in 1865 and of a James Brown having married Mary Macaloone at a Presbyterian chapel in Chester in 1868. This was sufficient for him to be detained while witnesses were sought, despite him continuing to protest his innocence. At the next hearing, one witness came forward to say that he had accompanied Henry to Quinton church and seen him married to Mary Ann. Another, with whom Henry had been lodging at the time, also recalled Henry going to church to be married, returning with Mary Ann, introducing her as his wife, and that the pair had lived there 'as man and wife' for a few months. This witness had also been one of those present at the chapel in Tipton who had identified 'John Brown' as Henry.[117] But the prisoner still denied being Henry, or knowing either of the witnesses. Another week was allowed for the defence case to be prepared, but the next hearing only brought more detailed evidence for the prosecution, with no witnesses appearing for the defence. After some deliberation, the magistrates finally decided that the prisoner should be committed to stand trial.[118]

The fact that it had taken three hearings for the magistrates even to get to this stage provides an insight into the way that pre-trial proceedings had developed by

[113] *County Advertiser & Herald for Staffordshire and Worcestershire*, 17 July 1880.
[114] 'An "Evangelist" Charged with Bigamy', *Manchester Courier*, 31 January 1881.
[115] 'A "Converted Clown" Charged with Bigamy', *Cheshire Chronicle*, 12 February 1881.
[116] 'Charge of Bigamy Against an Evangelist', *Cheshire Observer*, 29 January 1881.
[117] 'The Charge of Bigamy Against an Evangelist', *Cheshire Observer*, 5 February 1881.
[118] 'The Charge of Bigamy Against A "Converted Clown"', *Cheshire Observer*, 12 February 1881.

the 1880s. It was no longer a matter of the magistrate simply reviewing the evidence for the prosecution. Legislation passed in 1867 had allowed magistrates to hear from witnesses for the defence, and for such witnesses to be bound over to attend the trial.[119] But a failure to bring forward witnesses before the magistrates did not preclude them giving evidence at a subsequent trial – as we will shortly see.

At the Chester assizes in May 1881, the evidence given on behalf of the prosecution was unusually detailed.[120] Between them, the various witnesses supplied not only the details of the prisoner's two marriages but his entire employment history, to try to establish his identity as Henry John Llewellyn. His sister spoke of their early upbringing in Coventry, of their father's death in 1849 when Henry was just five years old, of his time in the workhouse before being taken to Dudley by their uncle, and of his being employed by a baker. This job gave him his teenage nickname, and a shoemaker named Hall explained how he had taken 'Hot Rolls' on as an apprentice in around 1857 or 1858, confirming that he had served the full seven years. A boot and shoe manufacturer gave evidence that he had employed Henry for two years after he had finished his apprenticeship – around 1864 or 1865 – and that the marriage to Mary Ann Davies had taken place during that time. It all appeared pretty seamless, all the way through to Henry's desertion of Mary Ann in around 1867. And all the witnesses were confident that the prisoner was the man in question. Three of them even reported having had conversations with him the previous year in which reference was made to his earlier life. One had discussed mutual acquaintances, while another had introduced him to others as Llewellyn. The third was the prisoner's sister, who said that he had initially claimed not to know her but had acknowledged the relationship when bidding her farewell.

The only witness for the prosecution who did not agree with this version of events was the second wife, who was clearly reluctant to give evidence against a man who had been a 'good husband' to her. She asserted not only that he had never worked as a shoemaker while he was with her, but that he 'did not know how to put a patch on a boot'. That attempt to shake the evidence as to his identity was easily countered: as counsel for the prosecution pointed out, the prisoner had described himself as a shoemaker in the marriage register.[121] But then counsel for the defence, a Mr Higgins, stepped forward. He began by warning that he would be producing evidence which was in direct conflict with what the jury had already heard: as he declared, 'one story was good till the other was told'. In support of the prisoner's claim that he was not who the prosecution said he was, two witnesses came forward with a completely different

[119] Criminal Law Amendment Act 1867, s 3.

[120] Unless otherwise indicated, the account of the trial is taken from the report that appeared under the headline 'Henry John, The Evangelist, And His Wives', *Chester Chronicle*, 7 May 1881. A substantially similar, but slightly shorter, account appeared in the *Cheshire Observer*, 7 May 1881, which noted that the case had already been fully reported when the prisoner was committed by the city magistrates. Some other newspapers were quicker to report the trial, which had clearly caught the public imagination, but may have been relying on second-hand information rather than having reporters at the trial (see eg 'Bigamy by the Converted Clown', *Echo*, 2 May 1881, which noted that it had received its information as to Henry's conviction by telegram).

[121] The *Cheshire Observer*, 7 May 1881, reported the same words, but in a different order, with Mary's line about her husband not knowing how to patch a boot being a riposte to counsel for the prosecution saying that the marriage register recorded him as a shoemaker.

backstory. In this version of events, the prisoner was 'Jim Brown': sometime clown, briefly a purveyor of teetotal drinks, and occasional shoe-repairer. One of these two witnesses, who said he had acted in various shows with the prisoner, stated that they were both performing in Bradford in 1865. The other, a shoemaker, claimed that it was he who had taught the prisoner how to repair shoes when the latter came to him as a 'stripling lad' in 1862, and that the prisoner 'did not appear to know anything about shoe-making then'. After going off to perform as a clown, the prisoner had come back to him in June 1865 and remained with him for four months. In other words, according to this version of events, the prisoner had been in Bradford during the crucial time in August 1865 when he was alleged to have married Mary Ann Davies. More fundamentally, he could not be the Henry John Llewellyn who had begun his apprenticeship as a shoemaker in Staffordshire in the late 1850s. Never had the ability to patch a boot assumed so much significance in determining whether an individual was guilty of bigamy.[122]

The hearing occupied most of the day.[123] As the judge observed in summing up the case for the jury, while the evidence given by the witnesses for the prosecution 'certainly seemed conclusive', the evidence put forward by the defence was 'very startling'. There was simply no way that both versions could be true, and the jury would need to give the case their 'most careful attention'. And if they were in any doubt as to whether the prisoner was in fact Henry John Llewellyn, they should give him 'the benefit of that doubt', and acquit him.[124]

After a deliberation of around a quarter of an hour, the jury returned with a verdict of 'guilty'. At the close of the assizes, the judge announced that Henry – as we can now call him – would be sentenced to four months' imprisonment with hard labour, a punishment that balanced his positive behaviour towards his second wife with his desertion of his first, and the relatively short gap between the two marriages.[125]

A 'converted clown' was always going to have an interesting backstory. But Henry's stint as a clown and subsequent conversion to Methodism was probably the least bizarre aspect of his story. By this time, it was rare enough for those accused of bigamy to seek to deny it: by 1881, most were simply pleading guilty. The few who maintained their innocence were mostly those who had been separated from their first spouse for a long time before marrying their second. There was still the occasional case where the evidence of one or other of the marriages was not forthcoming. But claims as to mistaken identity were, for obvious reasons, pretty rare in the context of bigamy. Cases where the two competing life stories were both so detailed and internally consistent but at the same time mutually incompatible were rarer still.

The story told by the prosecution does at least tally with the evidence that can be traced from other surviving sources. The 1861 census has a 17-year-old John Llewellyn from Coventry living in Rowley Regis in Staffordshire as an apprentice cordwainer with

[122] 'Henry John, The Evangelist, And His Wives', *Chester Chronicle*, 7 May 1881.
[123] 'An "Evangelistic" Bigamist – An Extraordinary Career', *Liverpool Daily Post*, 2 May 1881.
[124] 'Henry John, The Evangelist, And His Wives', *Chester Chronicle*, 7 May 1881.
[125] This was the same sentence as that handed down to the other bigamist convicted at the same assize, who had deceived his wife and left her on a couple of occasions: 'The Bigamists', *Cheshire Observer*, 7 May 1881; TNA, *Calendar of Prisoners*, HO 140/53.

Laban Hall and his wife.[126] And Mary Ann Davies appears in the 1871 census with the surname Llewellyn and a daughter whose age tallies with Henry's abandonment of her.[127]

I have not been able to ascertain what happened to Henry after he was released from prison, partly because it is difficult to know what name one should search for, or which occupation he might be following. There is no evidence that he resumed his old identity of Henry Llewellyn, and James Browns were too common to be sure of any match. He may even have assumed yet another name.

'I am a Ghost-wife Married to Some Spectre who has Disappeared into Thin Air': The Countess and the Clerk, 1940

In January 1940, Frederick George Wharton, a 34-year-old clerk from Wembley, was accused of bigamy. His first marriage was not in dispute: he had married Emily Wheway in Manchester in 1927.[128] And a ceremony had certainly taken place at the Marylebone register office in 1937 between an Austrian woman named Edeltrud Neuwirth and a man going by the name of Frederick Wharton. But Frederick denied that this was him.[129]

This later marriage had come under scrutiny because Scotland Yard were investigating Edeltrud, who was also known as the Countess von Costenza.[130] She had been questioned by them in November 1939, a couple of months after the outbreak of the Second World War. As she admitted, her marriage to Frederick had been purely one of convenience.[131] She had come to England in 1936 in the hope of pursuing her career as a film actress and had wanted to obtain British nationality to avoid having to return to the Nazi's German Reich. The following year, she said, she had encountered Frederick in a café near to Marble Arch, thought that he looked 'a clean, typical Englishman', and struck up a conversation with him.[132] Upon learning that he was in

[126] TNA, 1861 census, RG9/2039, folio 31, p 21.

[127] TNA, 1871 census, RG10/3020, folio 98, p 11. Just to add to the confusion, Mary Ann was recorded as Hannah, but this seems simply to have been the name by which she was known within the family (see her entry in the 1841 census, TNA, HO107/1196, Book 12, folio 44, p 31). The presence of her father, Lot Davies – matching the name on her marriage certificate – and daughter Leah, with whom she was living in 1881 under the name Mary Ann (1881 census, RG11/2885, folio 114, p 35), provides confirmation of the match.

[128] Ancestry, *Manchester, Non-Conformist Marriages*, GB127.M275/2169/1.

[129] 'Young Austrian Countess: Englishman Denies He "Married" Her', *Yorkshire Post and Leeds Intelligencer*, 3 January 1940.

[130] According to the statement that she made when interviewed at New Scotland Yard, she was the daughter of the Count von Costenza, with Neuwirth being the surname of her stepfather: TNA, HO 405/50232/1, 'Statement of Edeltrud Claudette von Costenza', Central Office, New Scotland Yard, 14 November 1939. Given the different names by which she was known, it is convenient to refer to her simply as the countess, although counsel for the prosecution somewhat snarkily noted that the use of titles was more 'free and easy' in Austria than in England: 'Countess Tells of One-Day Wedding', *Birmingham Daily Gazette*, 3 January 1940.

[131] TNA, HO 405/50232/1, 'Statement of Edeltrud Claudette von Costenza', Central Office, New Scotland Yard, 14 November 1939.

[132] TNA, HO 405/50232/1, 'The Truth about my Marriage – by Countess Manna von Costenza'.

financial difficulties, she offered him £25 to marry her, along with the funds necessary to redeem his suit from the pawnshop. The ceremony took place a few days later. Afterwards, they had gone back to the house of one of the witnesses for tea, she had given Frederick the money, and he had then left. They met up again a few days later to go to the passport office to get a British passport for her. Their next meeting was in 1939, after the police had been to see her. She had arranged for him to be at her flat when the police were there, but he had refused to answer any questions and referred them to his solicitors.[133]

When the countess appeared before the magistrates to give evidence against Frederick, the case attracted huge press coverage.[134] Although bigamy cases were far from uncommon in 1940, few had could rival this one in terms of the ingredients likely to capture the public imagination. Newspapers made much of the fact that the countess was an extremely attractive 22-year-old redhead, splashing pictures of her – in a succession of very stylish hats – across their pages.[135] And if that wasn't enough, there was the added drama and suspense generated by the fact that Frederick had a very different story to tell.

Frederick's version of events was that he had been approached by a man in Hyde Park in 1937 and offered a position as secretary to a society set up to assist foreign residents in London.[136] He had worked for them for a few weeks, during which time he had handed over his birth certificate in preparation for obtaining a passport for himself. After three weeks, he was told that he was no longer needed, but the countess had helped him find a new job.[137] The next contact between them, he claimed, had been in October 1939, after the outbreak of war, when she had told Frederick to expect a call from the police and asked him to say that he was her husband.[138]

A handwriting expert gave evidence that the signature on the marriage register was similar to that on other documents written by Frederick, and he was committed for trial.[139] At the Central Criminal Court, he doggedly stuck to his story that someone had used the details from his birth certificate to pretend to be him and had forged his signature on the marriage register.[140] He also denied having written a letter to the countess in Paris, despite it bearing his address, claiming that this too was a forgery.[141] Such denials

[133] TNA, HO 405/50232/1, 'Statement'.

[134] See eg 'Countess of 22 "Wed To Be British"', *Daily Herald*, 3 January 1940: 'Countess says "I asked man in café to wed me"', *Daily Express*, 3 January 1940; 'Countess Tells of £25 "Marriage" to Briton', *Daily News*, 3 January 1940; 'Woman: "I Paid to Wed"', *Daily Mirror*, 3 January 1940. 'Countess Says She Wed Clerk to Escape Concentration Camp', *Birmingham Daily Gazette*, 10 January 1940; '"I Fled From My People" – Countess', *Daily Mirror*, 10 January 1940; 'Countess Says "I am not a spy"', *Daily News*, 10 January 1940.

[135] 'Countess Tells of "Wedding" to Become British', *Daily Express*, 3 January 1940; '"I am Victim of Marriage": Countess' Story', *Daily Herald*, 10 January 1940; 'Countess tells of her "friendship" wedding', *Daily Express*, 7 February 1940; 'Countess says: "Am I British or not?"', 9 February 1940.

[136] 'Queer Sequels to Meeting Alien in Hyde Park', *Daily Record*, 8 February 1940.

[137] This aspect of his story tallied with her subsequent statement: 'The Truth about my Marriage – by Countess Manna von Costenza', TNA, HO 405/50232/1.

[138] 'Countess says "I asked man in café to wed me"', *Daily Express*, 3 January 1940.

[139] 'The Clerk and the Countess: Handwriting Question In Bigamy Charge', *Wolverhampton Express and Star*, 23 January 1940; 'To Be Tried on Bigamy Charge', *Daily News*, 24 January 1940.

[140] 'Clerk Says Name Was Forged', *Manchester Evening News*, 8 February 1940.

[141] 'Denies He Wed Countess', *Daily Gazette for Middlesbrough*, 8 February 1940.

were met with polite incredulity by counsel for the prosecution, describing Frederick's testimony as a 'tall story'.[142]

But the person who had witnessed the ceremony at the Marylebone register office was unsure if Frederick was the man who had married the countess.[143] This was the portrait painter Alexander Christie, who had painted the countess back in 1937 and who one might imagine would have a good memory for faces. The countess herself was an occasionally evasive witness, refusing to answer some of the questions that were put to her until warned by the Recorder that the consequences of not doing so would be 'very unpleasant' for her.[144] After retiring for an hour, the jury came back with a verdict of 'not guilty'.[145]

Emily Wharton, Frederick's wife, certainly had no doubt as to his innocence. She had been present throughout the proceedings and burst into tears upon hearing the jury's verdict.[146] Outside the court she embraced him and declared that she had never believed the evidence against him. As she told the press, 'he would never do a thing like that'.[147]

And yet, of the two stories, Frederick's seemed far less plausible. The countess had also given various details that indicated that she knew quite a lot about him – more than might be expected if Frederick's story of their fleeting acquaintance was true. She knew his home address in Wembley.[148] She also claimed that he had promised to introduce her to the actor Robert Donat, with whom he said he had been at school.[149] It seems unlikely that this was a name plucked at random: Donat, who received an Oscar for his performance in *Goodnight, Mr Chips* a few weeks after Frederick's trial, was an exact contemporary of his, and both had attended school in Manchester.

Whatever the truth of the case, Frederick's acquittal left the countess in a very difficult position, with her marital status – and, crucially, her nationality – unclear. As the countess noted, in the eyes of the public she was 'a ghost-wife married to some spectre who has disappeared into thin air'.[150] She was still adamant that Frederick was the man she had married, and wrote plaintively that she had thought he was her friend as well as her husband. She also denied that she had come to Britain as a Nazi spy. But a few days after his trial, she was taken by the police to Holloway prison, where she was detained under the Defence Regulations.[151] She was to remain there for much of the war.[152]

142 'Case "Stranger than Fiction"', *Daily Herald*, 9 February 1940.

143 'Countess Warned in Friendship Marriage Case', *Evening Despatch*, 7 February 1940.

144 'Judge Warns Countess', *Evening News*, 7 February 1940.

145 'Bigamy With Countess Charge Fails: Man's Name in Register Was Forgery', *News Chronicle*, 9 February 1940.

146 'Mrs Wharton In Tears As Jury Free Husband', *Daily Record*, 9 February 1940.

147 'Bigamy With Countess Charge Fails: Man's Name in Register Was Forgery', *News Chronicle*, 9 February 1940.

148 The address she gave to New Scotland Yard was where Frederick and his wife were living in 1939: TNA, HO405/50232/1, 'Statement'; TNA, *1939 Register*, RG 101/948C.

149 'Countess Warned in Friendship Marriage Case: Story of Promised Introduction to Robert Donat', *Evening Despatch*, 7 February 1940.

150 TNA, HO405/50232/1, 'The Truth about my Marriage – by Countess Manna von Costenza'.

151 'Refugee Countess Now in Women's Prison', *Sunday Express*, 18 February 1940; 'Austrian Countess Interned', *Daily News*, 19 February 1940; 'Countess Goes to Prison', *Daily Mirror*, 19 February 1940.

152 TNA, HO405/50232/2.

In each of the cases we have looked at in this chapter, there have been contradictory stories to be sifted, sometimes with crucial evidence lacking. In Frederick and Edeltrud's, there is the added frustration that certain information is not yet accessible. Within the two bulging files in the National Archives detailing her pleas for release, certain names, details, and quite a few entire pages, have been redacted. There may yet be another twist in the story of the countess and the clerk.

3

Married or not? Questions about Validity

Ever since 1604, every conviction for bigamy has rested on two key elements: a valid first marriage, and a subsequent ceremony.[1] What changed over the years is whether or not it mattered that the second marriage would have been void regardless of it being bigamous. Three of the case studies in this chapter explore the evolving law on this point. At least in the seventeenth and eighteenth centuries, it seems clear that a person was not guilty of bigamy if their second 'marriage' was void for some other reason, as was evident in the acquittal of Katherine Jones in 1719. By the early nineteenth century, judges had come to realise that this allowed more devious individuals to escape conviction by (for example) having the banns called in a different name, and began to take a different line, as James Hugh Edwards discovered to his cost in 1814. Even so, it was not until the late nineteenth century that it was finally established, in the case of Henry Allen, that an individual whose second marriage would have been void regardless of its bigamous nature was still guilty of bigamy. And even today a person is not guilty of bigamy if their second marriage is in a form not recognised by the law.[2]

The criminal courts that heard bigamy cases did not, it should be noted, have the power to decide whether a marriage was valid. Until 1857, this was a matter for the church courts, and after that it was for the Divorce Court to determine. If the church courts had already decided on the validity of a marriage, then this was conclusive, and binding upon the criminal courts.[3] If the issue of validity had not yet been tested, then although a conviction (or acquittal) in a criminal court might be based on certain assumptions about the validity of the first or second marriage, it was not conclusive on those points, and a church court might subsequently take a different view, as in the

[1] My focus in this chapter is solely on what was required for a valid marriage within England and Wales. There were, of course, a number of cases where the question of whether an individual was guilty of bigamy depended on the validity of a marriage entered into outside England and Wales. The complexity of Irish marriage law underpinned some of the most high-profile bigamy cases of the nineteenth century, and I have written about these elsewhere ('*R v Millis* reconsidered: binding contracts and bigamous marriages' (2008) 28 *Legal Studies* 337; see also R Probert, M Harding and B Dempsey, 'A Uniform Law of Marriage? The 1868 Royal Commission Reconsidered' (2018) 30 *Child and Family Law Quarterly* 217, discussing the Yelverton litigation). Scottish marriages also featured in bigamy trials, particularly in areas adjacent to the border. For reasons of space, I have not included such cases in the current volume, but the case study of Eliza Dent, discussed in chapter 9, illustrates how the courts assessed what other jurisdictions required for a valid marriage.

[2] This has become especially relevant in recent years, with the rise in religious-only marriages (on which see further *Double Trouble*, chs 10–11).

[3] The Bigamy Act 1604, s 3, explicitly exempted those who had obtained an annulment. For a rare illustration of an acquittal on this basis, see the case study of John Troop Juert in chapter 5.

case of James Stamp Sutton Cooke in 1812. For non-lawyers, this can sometimes appear chaotic, inconsistent, or simply baffling. But it must be remembered that each court can only decide the question in front of it, and that different courts have different rules as to evidence and standards of proof. In bigamy trials, the question for the jury to decide was simply whether they were satisfied, on the evidence before them, that this person was already married when they went through a subsequent ceremony. Any doubts were to be resolved in favour of the accused, and the 1797 case of Ambrose Rowe provides a good example of the emerging idea that the case against the accused had to be proved 'beyond all reasonable doubt'.

In that particular case, the doubts related to whether Ambrose's first wife was already married when he married her. This was the most common challenge to the validity of the first marriage in bigamy trials, largely because it was one of the few scenarios where a marriage was automatically void without any need for the church courts to grant a formal annulment and without the possibility of subsequent ratification.[4] In 1835, Parliament also passed legislation stating that any future marriages within the prohibited degrees would be void. Exactly which marriages were within the prohibited degrees fell to be decided in a bigamy case, that of James Chadwick in 1846.

A marriage might also be void if it was not in the required form. Before 25 March 1754, the only precondition for recognition was for the marriage to be conducted by an ordained Anglican clergyman. Under the Clandestine Marriages Act 1753, however, a marriage was void if it was not celebrated in an Anglican church, after banns had been called or a licence had been granted.[5] Even if a licence had been granted, the marriage would still be void if either of the parties was under 21 and did not have parental consent. It was this latter provision that generated the most case law (and controversy), as the case study of James Stamp Sutton Cooke illustrates. On 1 November 1823,[6] the law changed again. From that date a marriage was only void if the parties had 'knowingly and wilfully' married other than in a church, or without banns or licence, and different solutions were adopted to deal with those minors who married without parental consent.[7] When new options for getting married were made available in 1837, the same rules about validity were carried over, with a few adaptations to reflect the different context. As the case study of Joseph Cooke shows, there were different views as to what was required for a valid marriage – a further illustration of the disjunction between law and religion that persists to this day.

[4] Same-sex marriages were void but rare (see further the case study of Katherine Jones below). Marriages where the bride was under 12 or the groom under 14 were void but could be ratified upon the underage party reaching that age. Such underage marriages were in any case expressly exempted by the 1604 Act (see further *Double Trouble*, ch 2). Marriages where one spouse was incapable of giving consent were also void, but similarly capable of ratification. For examples of individuals who claimed to have been forced into their first marriage and thought that they were entitled to enter into a second, see chapter 8.

[5] Clandestine Marriages Act 1753, s 8.

[6] The 1753 Act was actually repealed the previous year, and did not apply to marriages celebrated between 1 September 1822 and 25 March 1823. The new rules substituted by the Marriage Act 1822 in turn posed problems, and the 1753 Act was restored for marriages between 26 March and 31 October 1823. For an example of an individual who was caught out by these changes, see chapter 8.

[7] In essence, a lack of parental consent no longer rendered an underage marriage void, even if the parties had knowingly and wilfully married without it. However, those who obtained a licence by making a false statement would forfeit any property that would otherwise accrue to them by virtue of the marriage: on which see further R Probert, 'Parental responsibility and children's partnership choices', in R Probert, J Herring and S Gilmore (eds), *Responsible Parents and Parental Responsibility* (Oxford, Hart Publishing, 2009).

'The Woman was More Predominant in Her than the Man': Katharine Jones, 1719

At the Old Bailey in 1719, Katharine Jones stood accused of bigamy.[8] She had married John Nowland in April 1713, in a clandestine ceremony conducted by a clergyman in a house in Blue Ball Alley in the Mint, a district in Southwark that had special status as a 'liberty'.[9] Five years later, in April 1718, Katharine went through a second clandestine ceremony – in the same house as the first, but with one Constantine Boone.[10]

Katharine acknowledged both ceremonies, but argued that 'the last she was married to was no Man, and therefore could not be a Husband'.[11] One witness gave evidence that Constantine had been brought 'up as a Girl in Apparel and at School, and to handle the Needle' until the age of 12, 'when he turn'd Man and went to sea'. Others were called to prove that Constantine 'was a Monster, a Hermaphrodite, and had been shown as such at Southwark-Fair, Smithfield, and several other Places'. Constantine appeared in court and 'own'd her being a Hermaphrodite' and it was shown 'that the Woman was more predominant in her than the Man'. Katharine was accordingly acquitted.

The unusual facts of the case made it a favourite one for compilations of particularly noteworthy trials.[12] It is also a particularly useful one to bring out certain key points. English law did not (and still does not) have any special category for those born with both male and female characteristics. The classification of gender was strictly binary. An assessment therefore had to be made as to how any given individual should be classified if, as for Constantine, there was any doubt.[13] As a result, once it had been decided that Constantine was predominantly a woman, she *was* a woman as far as the law was concerned.[14] That meant that her marriage to Katharine was void. And a person could not be convicted of bigamy if their second marriage was void independently of its bigamous nature.

Katharine's was not the only bigamy case to raise the possibility of one of the spouses being what would today be described as intersex. This was implicit in the defence offered by John Davis at the Old Bailey in 1735, when he claimed that his first wife 'was no Woman' and called witnesses to prove this. The prosecution, however, produced evidence to contradict this, and John was duly convicted.[15]

The fact that a marriage between two persons of the same sex was simply void was so obvious for eighteenth-century legal writers that it did not even need to be stated. William Blackstone made no mention of it in his five-page discussion of void and

[8] *OBP*, 3 September 1719.

[9] On the celebration of clandestine marriages within this and other liberties, see R Probert, *Marriage Law and Practice in the Long Eighteenth Century: A Reassessment* (Cambridge, Cambridge University Press, 2009).

[10] *OBP*, 3 September 1719.

[11] ibid.

[12] *A compleat collection of remarkable tryals of the most notorious malefactors at the Sessions-House in the Old Bailey, from the year 1706, to the last sessions: Vol 4* (London, 1721) 311–12.

[13] M Sudai, 'Sex Ambiguity in Early Modern Common Law (1629–1787)' (2022) 47 *Law & Social Inquiry* 478.

[14] cf P Crawford and S Mendelson, 'Sexual Identities in Early Modern England: The Marriage of Two Women in 1680' (1995) 7 *Gender & History* 361, 366, who suggest that 'one of a double gender' could be a wife for a man and a husband for a woman 'and so guilty of bigamy'.

[15] *OBP*, 15 October 1735.

voidable marriages.[16] That said, the idea of a wedding ceremony involving two women, or two men, was not quite as unthinkable as Blackstone's silence might imply.[17] Back in the late seventeenth century, the London Consistory Court had annulled the marriage between Arabella Hunt and Amy Poulter – which was doubly invalid, on account of Amy being already married to a man.[18] Various cases of 'female husbands' came to light during the eighteenth century, the term being popularised by Henry Fielding in his account of Mary Hamilton.[19] Mary, in male garb and going by the name of James, had gone through a ceremony with a woman named Mary Price at St Cuthbert's church in Wells in July 1746. She was subsequently brought before the Somerset quarter sessions in December that year and, having been convicted, was sentenced to be publicly whipped. Nonetheless, such cases were exceedingly rare, and ones featuring multiple marriages were rarer still.[20] Although the newspaper coverage of the Hamilton trial alleged that Mary Price was Mary Hamilton's fourteenth wife,[21] this appears to have been an invention. Those who have investigated the original court records note that there is no mention in them of any other marriages, let alone another 13.[22] But those who made this claim were at least correct in noting that Mary Hamilton could not have been prosecuted for bigamy, 'because the law never contemplated a marriage among women'.[23]

By contrast, the immunity from prosecution for bigamy of those whose second marriage was void for some other reason did feature in quite a few trials. The late eighteenth century saw some unpopular acquittals, most notoriously that of Thomas Hornby Morland, whose second wife was underage when they married by licence and whose father had not consented to the match.[24] William Parker was similarly acquitted on the basis that his second wife Eleanor was already married at the time of their wedding.[25] This might have exposed Eleanor to prosecution, but she alleged in turn that her first husband had also had a first wife living when she married him. Clearly someone had committed bigamy at some point, but marrying someone who was already married was not (yet) a criminal offence.

By the start of the nineteenth century, judges were starting to disregard questions of validity where the claimed invalidity of the second marriage was due to the bigamist's own actions, for example in deliberately having the banns called in the wrong name.[26]

[16] W Blackstone, *Commentaries on the Laws of England: Vol 1* (Oxford, Clarendon Press, 1765) 422–27.

[17] On the broader history of female husbands, see J Mannion, *Female Husbands: A Trans History* (Cambridge, Cambridge University Press, 2020); C Derry, *Lesbianism and the Criminal Law: Three Centuries of Legal Regulation in England and Wales* (Cham, Palgrave Macmillan, 2020).

[18] Crawford and Mendelson (n 14).

[19] *The Female Husband* (London, 1746). The pamphlet is anonymous but has usually been attributed to Fielding.

[20] Caroline Derry, in a comprehensive investigation, identified the case of Ann Marlow, who had apparently married three women, although 'no details of those marriages … survive': Derry (n 17) 47.

[21] *Gloucester Journal*, 11 November 1746.

[22] Mannion (n 17); Derry (n 17) 44.

[23] A Knapp and W Baldwin, *Criminal Chronology; or, The New Newgate Calendar; Being Interesting Memoirs of Notorious Characters, Who Have Been Convicted of Outrages on The Laws of England, During The Seventeenth Century; and Brought Down to The Present Time: Vol 2* (London, 1809) 125.

[24] *Double Trouble*, ch 4.

[25] *OBP*, 9 December 1772.

[26] See the case of James Hugh Edwards, discussed below.

But it was only in 1872 that it was finally accepted that the invalidity of the second marriage on some more fundamental basis – for example, where the second spouse had a first spouse still living, or where the parties were within the prohibited degrees – did not preclude a conviction for bigamy.[27] And it was only towards the close of the twentieth century that an individual who was legally female was convicted of bigamy for 'marrying' a woman.[28]

'Did You Never Hear that Kitty Rowe had Another Husband?': Ambrose Rowe, 1797

On 20 October 1796, the wedding of Ambrose Rowe and Susannah Redwood took place by licence at St Mary's, Finchley.[29] Both parties made crosses next to their names in the marriage register – a hint that they did not belong to the class of society that usually married by licence. The wedding had in fact been instigated by the parish, the 'too great intimacy' between Ambrose and Susannah having resulted in her pregnancy.[30]

A few days after Susannah had given birth to their son, Ambrose was on trial for bigamy at the Old Bailey.[31] The prosecution had been brought by the parish officers of Islington, where Ambrose's first wife Kitty had recently claimed relief. The parish clerk of St Luke's, Old Street produced a copy of the entry in the register recording her marriage to Ambrose there in November 1793. He couldn't recollect Ambrose specifically, but another witness was able to confirm having attended the wedding, adding feelingly, 'I know it was in cold weather'.

But other witnesses then gave evidence that they had heard that Kitty had herself been married before, and that her husband was living in Ireland. No direct evidence of this marriage was produced, but there was the suspicious circumstance that Kitty had not wanted Ambrose to appear as her husband when they were travelling to Ireland. As the parish clerk noted, this had been 'a strong presumptive proof, to the magistrates, that she had a husband living, and that she wished to conceal her present marriage'. There was also the fact that Ambrose had raised the question of his marriage to Kitty at the time that the parish were 'arranging' his marriage to Susannah. This had resulted in advice being sought from Doctors' Commons; Ambrose 'told them the suspicion that his first wife was married, and they gave it as their opinion, at the Commons, that he might marry again, and he, being an ignorant man, was married'.[32]

With Ambrose unable to afford the fees of defence counsel, the judge stepped in to question the witnesses. Mr Justice Heath was clearly indignant at the criminal

[27] See the case of Henry Allen below.

[28] 'Woman posed as a man to marry the girl she loved', *Daily Mail*, 23 September 1977.

[29] Ancestry, *London Church of England Parish Registers*, DRO/032/A/01/013.

[30] *Oracle*, 14 January 1798.

[31] *OBP*, 11 January 1797. The baptism register of St John's Hampstead noted that Ambrose Rowe Jr was born on 9 January 1797: Ancestry, *London Church of England Parish Registers*, P81/JN1/099.

[32] *OBP*, 11 January 1797.

process being used 'merely to decide a settlement'.[33] He forced the beadle of Islington to admit that he had never actually enquired into whether Kitty's first husband was still alive: 'Did you never hear that Kitty Rowe had another husband? … And you never enquired to know whether he was alive or not?' He also expressed his strong disapproval of the parish's attempts to rid themselves of responsibility for a pauper.[34] Given the uncertainty as to whether Ambrose's marriage to Kitty was valid, the jury acquitted him.

Ambrose was one of only four people tried at the Old Bailey in the eighteenth century who were acquitted on account of the prior marriage of their first spouse. In the other three cases, which all occurred in the first half of the century, there appears to have been stronger evidence of the prior marriage. In the case of Mary Lewellin (alias Dennis, alias Freeman), it was proved that her supposed husband Dennis 'had a former wife living, at the time when the prisoner married him' and that Mary's marriage to him was therefore 'null in law'.[35] Martha Boucher had procured a copy of the register in which her first husband's prior marriage was recorded,[36] and in the case of George Horton it was 'fully proved' by the evidence of 'three captains of vessels, and one master of a vessel trading to Virginia' that his first wife's first husband was living on the York River in Virginia.[37] Conversely, defendants without such proof were convicted: Bridget Potter, for example, alleged that her first husband 'had another wife at Plymouth but could not prove it'.[38]

All this might give rise to the suspicion that the more circumstantial evidence of Kitty's first marriage was accepted in Ambrose's case simply because the judge and jury disapproved of the parish officials having brought the prosecution in the first place. But setting his case in the broader context of the evolution of the criminal law provides a different answer. The second half of the eighteenth century saw judges articulating the idea that the case against the accused had to be proved 'beyond all reasonable doubt'.[39] Ambrose's case is consistent with the application of that principle to cases where there were credible doubts as to the validity of the first marriage.

Clearly there still had to be *some* convincing evidence of the first spouse's prior marriage. It is unsurprising that the jury had convicted Thomas Parkinson two years earlier, given that his defence was solely that he had found a letter in his first wife's pocket 'from her husband she eloped from' and thought he 'had a right to marry again'.[40] But there does seem to have been a shift in practice, rather than simply a shift in language. When Sarah Baker was tried for bigamy in 1766, a witness claimed to have

[33] *OBP*, 11 January 1797.
[34] ibid, see also *Lloyd's*, 16 January 1797.
[35] *OBP*, 3 September 1707.
[36] *OBP*, 26 February 1739.
[37] *OBP*, 22 February 1749. No mention was made of whether the first wife's first *marriage* had been proved, but then the report in the *Proceedings* consisted of only a few lines.
[38] *OBP*, 10 January 1718.
[39] BJ Shapiro, *Beyond Reasonable Doubt and Probable Cause: Historical Perspectives on the Anglo-American Law of Evidence* (Berkeley and Los Angeles, University of California Press, 1991) 21; JM Beattie, 'Scales of Justice: Defense Counsel and the English Criminal Trial in the Eighteenth and Nineteenth Centuries' (1991) 9 *Law and History Review* 221, 249.
[40] *OBP*, 26 October 1791.

met an 'old woman' who had declared herself to be the prior wife of Sarah's supposed husband Nicholas Bedgood, adding 'she shewed her certificate to me, and I read it; and I really believe she was his lawful wife'.[41] With no more direct evidence of Nicholas' first marriage, Sarah was convicted. Half a century later, however, John Turner similarly had only indirect evidence that his first wife Maria was already married at the time he married her. As he told the court, he had been informed by Maria's cousin of her first husband being still alive, and had obtained a certificate from the War Office proving the existence of the man in question. In addition, Maria had apparently left John upon learning that he had been making inquiries about her prior marriage – in his words, 'knowing herself guilty'.[42] Such evidence would not, without proof of the actual ceremony, have been sufficient to convict Maria of bigamy in marrying John. But it was sufficient to acquit John of bigamy in marrying another woman.

This subtle shift in approaches to evidence was not reflected in contemporary legal treatises. The jurist Thomas Starkie, in his multi-volume work on evidence, simply noted that an accused person could, by way of defence, 'show that [their] first marriage was actually void',[43] without going into details about what was required. John Frederick Archbold was even less helpful, recycling an example from the eminent seventeenth-century judge Sir Matthew Hale in support of his statement that no indictment could be sustained if the first marriage was void, with no indication of who was responsible for proving what.[44] But the absence of discussion of this legal point was unsurprising: cases where the accused alleged that their first spouse was already married were rare, and none of them had made it into the law reports. It was not until *R v Wilson*, in 1862, that a judge was reported as having explicitly used the language of 'reasonable doubt' when referring to the question of whether the first spouse was already married.[45] But Ambrose's case suggests that the approach was established far earlier.

One final point needs to be made. The fact that some individuals were acquitted on the basis of their first spouse's prior marriage might give the impression that many bigamists were going unpunished. After all, if the first spouse was already married, then surely *they* had been guilty of bigamy when they remarried? But of course not every such remarriage was bigamous. In the case of John Turner, discussed above, it was noted that Maria had not heard of her first husband for seven or eight years; had she been prosecuted for bigamy, she too would have been acquitted. Similarly, we have no idea how long Kitty Rowe might have been separated from her first husband – and if he had been absent from her in Ireland for seven years or more before she married Ambrose, she would have had a good defence even if she had been aware that he was still alive.[46]

[41] *OBP*, 9 April 1766.

[42] *OBP*, 9 January 1811.

[43] T Starkie, *A practical treatise of the law of evidence: Vol 3* (London, J & WT Clarke, 1824) 1167.

[44] JF Archbold, *A summary of the law relative to pleading and evidence in criminal cases*, 3rd ed (London, Pheney, Sweet, 1828) 294.

[45] *R v Wilson* (1862) 3 F & F 119; 176 ER 53. Barbara Wilson has her own case study: see chapter 12

[46] The 1604 Act had exempted those whose spouse was 'beyond the seas' (s 2), which included Ireland.

'You will do Well to Consider if You are Prepared to Prove these Facts': James Stamp Sutton Cooke, 1812

James Stamp Sutton Cooke was born in London in April 1780 – 'in the rioting time', as his aunt confirmed at his trial for bigamy, the infamous Gordon riots having broken out in the city very soon after his birth.[47] She was being closely questioned about his age, because James was claiming he had been under 21 at the time of his first marriage. If so, given that this first marriage had taken place by licence, it would have been necessary for James' father to have given his consent. In the absence of such consent, the marriage would simply have been void,[48] making his second marriage valid and not bigamous.

James was not the first to try to run this defence. The late eighteenth century had seen a handful of individuals being acquitted on this basis.[49] But we know a little more about James' trial because of the detailed account that was published in 1823, some 11 years after it had taken place. The lengthy title of this 99-page pamphlet left the reader in no doubt as to its writer's agenda: *The Remarkable Trial of the Honourable James Stamp Sutton Cooke ... Wherein is Proved the Complete Innocence of this Much-Injured Gentleman*.[50] Though published anonymously, and referring throughout to James in the third person, it seems highly likely that it was written by James himself.

James' reason for publishing his *Remarkable Trial* a decade after the events had occurred was that he was again embroiled in legal proceedings. In the preface, written by one of his friends and addressed to the Lord Chief Justice, it was noted that publication was necessary in order 'that the malicious and false representations of a foul band of self-interested men should be distinctly confuted'.[51] He could hardly have given a clearer signal that the contents would be rather skewed towards presenting James in a positive light.[52] Besides, while the pamphlet was presented as if it was a transcript of the trial, there were some key differences from the version that had been published a decade earlier in the *Proceedings*. As we shall see, *The Remarkable Trial* omitted any evidence that was liable to put James in a bad light. It may also have embellished certain exchanges to put him in a more favourable light, as well as adding material that the court had deemed inadmissible.

James' case is clearly one where close attention needs to be paid to different sources. But as well as illustrating the dangers of taking any single source at face value, it also

[47] *OBP*, 8 April 1812.

[48] Clandestine Marriages Act 1753, s 11.

[49] See further *Double Trouble*, ch 4.

[50] *The Remarkable Trial of the Honourable James Stamp Sutton Cooke, accused of bigamy at the Old Bailey, on the 14th April 1812: wherein is proved the complete innocence of this much injured gentleman* (London, 1823) 23–24.

[51] ibid iv.

[52] Or at least that they were *intended* to show him in a good light. The footnotes in particular are unintentionally hilarious. The first hinted that both judge and jury in his trial were corrupt and asserted that 'the statute provides, that "they shall when found guilty be attainted, their meadows be ploughed up, their houses broken down, their woods grubbed up, and their lands, tenements, chattels, and goods forfeited to the King, and their vile bodies cast into prison, and be branded with the reproach and indignation of their fellow-countrymen, excluded from honorable society, and rendered perpetually infamous!!'. The over-use of exclamation marks was to be a recurring feature.

shows the importance of an understanding of the laws of evidence and legal procedure. Like many litigants-in-person before and since, James simply failed to appreciate how he needed to present his case.

The story of James' complex marital history begins in 1799, when he was stationed in Kent with his regiment. As an officer in the Royal South Gloucester militia, James would have cut a dashing figure. His romance with Jane Browning could have come straight out of the pages of *Pride and Prejudice.* According to James, Jane had been willing to come away with him within hours of their first meeting. Jane's brother John claimed that Jane had known James for a month, but did not deny that she had run away with him.[53] Like Lydia Bennett and George Wickham, the pair eloped to London together.[54]

On 12 September 1799, a licence was obtained from Doctors' Commons to authorise the marriage.[55] It stated that James had appeared before them in person and sworn on oath that he had attained the age of 21, and that Jane's father had given his consent. The latter at least was true: Mr Browning had come to London in the wake of Jane's elopement and had given his sanction to the marriage.[56] But James was still only 19, meaning that he too needed his father's consent.

The day after the licence had been obtained, the wedding of James and Jane took place at St James Westminster.[57] The couple lived together for the next two or three years. According to the evidence given at the Old Bailey by John Browning, James had made their father's house his home, and had been supported by him financially, to the tune of at least a hundred pounds and possibly more.[58] *The Remarkable Trial* strategically omitted those details, along with John's allegation that James had deserted Jane in Ramsgate in 1801, leaving her without any money and even pawning her clothes.

But John Browning was equally – and understandably – evasive about the reason for the breakdown of his sister's marriage.[59] It appears that Jane had begun a relationship with another man, an assistant surgeon attached to the 13th Regiment of Dragoons.[60] This prompted James to seek legal advice as to whether any redress was available to him. The barrister he consulted, John Ingram Lockhart, advised him that he would not be able to maintain any action for criminal conversation against the 'ungenerous invader' of his 'domestic peace', since his marriage to Jane was void on account of having been celebrated by licence when James was underage, without his father's consent.[61]

[53] *OBP*, 8 April 1812; *Remarkable Trial* (n 50) 14.

[54] *OBP*, 8 April 1812.

[55] Ancestry, *Marriage Bonds and Allegations.* A copy of this also appeared in the subsequent proceedings before the Court of Arches, Lambeth Palace Library, Arches, H 171/7.

[56] *OBP*, 8 April 1812.

[57] Ancestry, *Westminster Church of England Parish Registers*, STJ/PR/6/8.

[58] *OBP*, 8 April 1812.

[59] The pamphlet appended a footnote at this point in James' cross-examination of John, noting 'It was the woman's infidelity': *Remarkable Trial* (n 50) 13.

[60] The evidence for this was set out in detail in *The Remarkable Trial* (n 50) 28–30, including a letter that Jane had sent to her paramour, which, the author of the pamphlet darkly noted, the judge, 'for reasons best known to himself, would not at the trial suffer to be read'. Given that Jane's infidelity was irrelevant to the question of whether James had committed bigamy, it is hardly surprising that the judge refused to allow it to be read to the court.

[61] *Remarkable Trial* (n 50) 23–24.

Some years later, in September 1808, James met a young woman named Sophia Sanders.[62] Before the month was out, she had agreed to marry him. James even got her to sign a paper he had drafted, authorising him to have the banns called,[63] and checked again with Lockhart that he was free to marry.[64] The banns were called using a shortened form of his name – James Cooke – which, according to yet another footnote in *The Remarkable Trial*, was the name by which he was known at the time and was not done 'with any view to screen himself from the first inconsiderate marriage!'[65]

The wedding took place at St Luke's church on 10 October 1808. Their first child, John Sanders Cooke, was born the following year.[66] But by late 1811 this marriage too had run into difficulties, and the couple were living apart. James blamed others, later claiming that Sophia's affections had been 'estranged' from him 'by the unjust influence of a combination evidently formed for the unchristian-like purpose of finally ruining us'.[67] A letter from Sophia around this time suggests that she had not cut off all contact with him,[68] but the poem she enclosed was hardly affectionate:

> Oh! valiant Cooke, to Spain why don't you run,
> To fight the French, and leave your wife and son;
> And think'st thou not how happy we shall be;
> Should'st thou pop off – a dashing widow she:
> Then shall my days in one sweet tenor run,
> And end in bliss, as they in mirth begun.
> My parents still remain my joys to share,
> My mother's smiles, my father's tender care.
> Then pluck up courage, take your sword again,
> And may the first shot that's fir'd pass thro' thy brain;
> Then grant me Gods, when told of such your lot,
> I do not die with laughter on the spot.[69]

In March 1812, James was charged with bigamy and committed for trial at the Old Bailey.[70] He seems to have been somewhat dilatory in preparing his defence, and it was not until early April that he wrote to Lockhart asking him to give evidence.[71] Lockhart rather tetchily replied that he was occupied elsewhere, and that James should have asked earlier, but said that he would be able to attend if the trial was postponed.

[62] *OBP*, 8 April 1812; *Remarkable Trial* (n 50) 20.

[63] 'London, September 24, 1808. I, Sophia Saunders, give my free will and consent to James Cooke, Esq. to get published the banns of matrimony between him and myself, and to hold myself in readiness to marry him, within the rights of the church of England: witness my hand, Sophia Saunders.': *OBP*, 8 April 1812; *Remarkable Trial* (n 50) 20.

[64] *OBP*, 8 April 1812; *Remarkable Trial* (n 50) 24–25.

[65] *Remarkable Trial* (n 50) 20n.

[66] Another son was born to them but had died by the time of the trial.

[67] *Remarkable Trial* (n 50) 25.

[68] ibid 21.

[69] ibid. A truncated version of this also appeared in the *Proceedings*.

[70] TNA, *Newgate Prison Calendar*, HO77/19.

[71] *Remarkable Trial* (n 50) 31 includes Lockhart's reply, dated 9 April, saying that he had received James' letter 10 minutes earlier.

Having heard nothing further from James, he decided against setting off for London, explaining that his presence there would in any case be of little assistance:

> I recollect your consulting me on the subject of an action for criminal conversation, when, to the best of my recollection, a question arose as to the legality of your marriage, when the Statute Book was referred to, and I then said that a marriage celebrated (as yours) by licence, whilst underage, without your father's consent, was null and void to all intents and purposes whatsoever. And such are the words of the statute. I wish very much you would do yourself and friends the justice to consult some professional gentleman in town, who would, no doubt, inform you that the mere statement of the words of the statute, as mentioned by me in Bedford Row, cannot be of any real use to you on your trial; for there you have only to prove the facts – first, that you were under age; then, that the marriage was by licence; and lastly, that your father, mother, or other guardian, did not consent to it.

As he added:

> You will do well to consider if you are prepared to prove these facts, or if they can at any time be proved; and if you are not prepared to prove them, you must apply to the Court, and entreat them to put off your trial, until the next Session, by which time you must be sure to be prepared.[72]

James completely disregarded this very sensible legal advice. Instead, he decided to represent himself.

He made a bad impression from the start. Upon evidence of the first marriage being produced, James denied taking out the licence for his marriage to Jane, claiming that it was not his handwriting.[73] The judge, Newman Knowlys, was instantly sceptical, commenting that the affidavit could only have been sworn by one of the parties to the marriage. And Sophia – at least according to the *Proceedings* – subsequently confirmed that she believed the affidavit to be in his handwriting.[74] None of that made any difference to the validity of the first marriage, but it clearly damaged James' credibility, because it established that he had lied when procuring the licence. As Knowlys noted, when James had claimed to be of age, he had 'sworn falsely'.[75]

Throughout the prosecution's presentation of the case, James continued to jump in with questions and objections, with scant regard for procedure. He protested against Sophia being allowed to give evidence against him on the basis that she was 'in every sense of the word my lawful wife'.[76] But, as Knowlys seems to have tried to explain to him, it was well established that, once the fact of the first marriage had been proved, the second spouse could give evidence.[77]

[72] *Remarkable Trial* (n 50) 34.

[73] *OBP*, 8 April 1812. See also *Remarkable Trial* (n 50) 15–16.

[74] *OBP*, 8 April 1812. By contrast, *The Remarkable Trial* (n 50) 41 reported Sophia as saying 'the signature here, of James Stamp Sutton Cooke, I am positive was never written by him!!!!!'. It claimed that it was Jane's father who had procured the licence 'to cover the disgrace of her running away with that young officer!!!!!' (40).

[75] *OBP*, 8 April 1812. This was framed as a question to James' aunt Lucy, who simply replied 'He must'. Once again, *The Remarkable Trial* (n 50) 42 misrepresented what had been said. It reported Lucy as saying 'Whoever took such an oath swore falsely' – which conveyed the impression that it was not James who had taken the oath.

[76] *Remarkable Trial* (n 50) 17.

[77] *The Remarkable Trial* (n 50) reported Knowlys as having stated that 'the lawful wife can be a witness', but it seems highly unlikely that he would have phrased it in this way.

Some of the questions James posed were far from helpful to his case. Upon Sophia's poem being read out, he asked 'whether these lines were not written to me when I was in Clerkenwell prison, upon a charge of an assault brought against me by this lady's mother'.[78] Though it was not James' turn to ask questions, counsel for the prosecution had no objection to asking this one on his behalf: 'Miss Saunders, was he at that time confined for an assault committed upon your aged mother?' Sophia confirmed this had been the case. She also told the court that she and her surviving child had been living with her mother, and that James had never supported them – another detail not included in his *Remarkable Trial*.[79]

By the time James stood up to present his defence, it would be understandable if the judge was not feeling favourably inclined towards him. Even so, it seems unlikely that Knowlys was quite as rude and obstructive as *The Remarkable Trial* reported him as being.[80] And if James had been legally represented, the outcome would almost certainly have been different. His counsel would have quickly established that he was under 21 at the time of his first marriage and that there was nothing on the face of the register to show that his father had consented. He could then have made it clear that it was for the prosecution to show that consent *had* been given, rather than for the defence to prove that it had not. This had been the view of the twelve judges when two very similar cases had been referred to them around a decade earlier.[81]

But James clearly had no idea as to how to present his case. He wasted time showing off the legal research he had undertaken (not all of it accurate),[82] and trying to read out various letters (which Knowlys refused to allow, deeming them either irrelevant or inadmissible).[83] The only witness he called to prove that his father had not consented to his marriage to Jane was his younger cousin Sarah, whose only information on this point came from what she had heard Mr Cooke say.[84] And by this time such hearsay evidence was inadmissible, as Knowlys made clear.[85]

[78] *OBP*, 8 April 1812.

[79] ibid.

[80] The *Proceedings* certainly recorded Knowlys' objections to certain points of evidence, but nothing more, and the few newspapers that reported the case gave only the barest of details (see eg *Bell's Weekly Messenger*, 19 April 1812). Again, it needs to be borne in mind that *The Remarkable Trial* was published against the backdrop of pending legal proceedings, so James may have had a deeper agenda in wishing to present Knowlys as biased against him.

[81] *R v William James* (1802) Russ & Ry 17; 168 ER 660; *R v Charles Butler* (1803) Russ & Ry 61; 168 ER 683. While the 12 judges were only giving advice, rather than sitting as a formal appeal court, their views nonetheless carried significant weight.

[82] James does deserve some credit for at least citing the Clandestine Marriages Act 1753 correctly to establish that a marriage entered into by licence was void if one of the parties was underage and did not have the consent of their parent or guardian. He also reeled off a string of other references in support of this, although these were all references to the same settlement case in which Lord Mansfield had confirmed that there was no need for a decree of nullity to be obtained where the marriage was void. More bizarrely, he also claimed that it was written in the Bigamy Act 1604 that 'no person shall be found guilty of this offence, where they have married by licence, under age, without the consent of parents or guardians' – which was a pure invention on his part, since the Act contained no such provision.

[83] One was the letter written by Jane to her paramour, discussed above. The others were Lockhart's letters to James, which only established that he had been advised that his first marriage was void, not that it was void.

[84] *OBP*, 8 April 1812; *Remarkable Trial* (n 50) 37.

[85] On the exclusion of hearsay evidence, see TP Gallanis, 'The Rise of Modern Evidence Law' (1999) 84 *Iowa Law Review* 499, 517–18. According to *The Remarkable Trial*, several other family members were waiting to give evidence and Knowlys refused to hear any of them, but there is no hint of that in the *Proceedings*.

James then completed his defence where he should have started – by providing evidence that he was under the age of 21 at the time of his first marriage. That at least was clear, being confirmed by his aunt and his trustee, and by the baptism register of St James Clerkenwell. But by itself it was not enough.[86] The jury came back with a decision of guilty – upon which Knowlys sentenced James to seven years' transportation.[87]

In the weeks that followed, James and an apparently contrite Sophia seem to have been busy firing off letters to anyone who they thought might be able to help them.[88] The assassination of the Prime Minister, Spencer Perceval, in May 1812 caused some inevitable delay as political roles were reshuffled.[89] Knowlys was asked for his report on the case, and does not appear to have relented in his opinion of James. The upshot was that James and Sophia were advised that no steps would be taken until a decision had been obtained from the ecclesiastical court on the validity of James' first marriage.

On 12 December 1812, the case of *Cooke v Browning (falsely called Cooke)* came before the Court of Arches in London.[90] Depositions were taken from seven individuals: along with James' trustee and his cousin Sarah, who had given evidence at his trial, there was also his godfather, uncle, brother, sister, and an old acquaintance of the family.[91] Between them, they confirmed that James had been born in 1780 and that his father had not consented to his marriage to Jane. The judge, Sir John Nichol, duly declared James' first marriage to be void; or, as the front cover of *The Remarkable Trial* would later put it, 'By the same evidence that was tendered and denied to be good by the Old Bailey Court, it was decreed that his connexion with Jane Browning (falsely called Cooke) Was NO MARRIAGE!'[92] But the sentence confirming that James 'hath full liberty to contract and solemnize marriage with any other persons' was struck through with a thick black line – an acknowledgment that James had already remarried and was not at liberty to do so again.

It is easy to see why those unversed in the law might be baffled as to how two different courts, faced with substantially similar evidence, could come to opposite conclusions. But it needs to be borne in mind that the processes in the ecclesiastical court were entirely different from those at the Old Bailey. Rather than witnesses giving evidence on oath, and being cross-examined, they gave written answers to a series of questions.[93] There was no objection to them giving evidence about statements made by persons since deceased – in this case, evidence that James' late father had not

[86] According to *The Remarkable Trial*, Knowlys instructed the jury to regard the baptism register as a forgery, and his witnesses as having conspired together to present a false case to the court, which again seems highly unlikely: *Remarkable Trial* (n 50) 55.

[87] *OBP*, 8 April 1812.

[88] Sophia, according to *The Remarkable Trial* (n 50) 62, was 'conscious of having done Mr Cooke great injustice' and so was 'exhibiting some marks of contrition by endeavouring to restore him to liberty!!! !'.

[89] As noted by one of James' correspondents: *Remarkable Trial* (n 50) 61.

[90] Lambeth Palace Library, Arches, H 171/1-8.

[91] ibid, folio 8. Their depositions largely accord with those reprinted in the *The Remarkable Trial* (n 50), although minor edits were made to make the evidence seem even more convincing.

[92] *Remarkable Trial* (n 50).

[93] RB Outhwaite, *The Rise and Fall of the English Ecclesiastical Courts, 1500-1860* (Cambridge, Cambridge University Press, 2006) 10.

consented to his first marriage. This was also backed up by evidence of Mr Cooke's behaviour towards James after his first marriage.

The decision of the Court of Arches was duly forwarded to the Home Secretary, and on Christmas Eve 1812 the Prince Regent ordered that James be released from prison. *The Remarkable Trial* concluded by claiming that James had been restored 'blameless and unsullied to his former station in life' – at least 'in the estimation of the discerning and impartial part of the community'.[94]

For a while it looked as if James' story would have a happy-ever-after ending. He and Sophia, now confirmed as legally married, were reconciled. Several more children were born to them over the next decade or so: George Plantagenet, Margaret Plantagenet, Adelaide and Alfred. But in 1823 James became embroiled in his brother's attempt to claim the title of Lord Stafford. There followed accusations of trespass, a libel suit by James (only partially successful, and with a derisory single farthing in damages) and a conviction for conspiracy.[95] He died in the Marshalsea prison in 1828.

The Wrong Names: James Hugh Edwards, 1814

The marriage of James Hugh Edwards and Jemima Hart took place in November 1809.[96] The pair made their home with Jemima's married sister Frances in Walworth, by then already part of London's growing sprawl south of the Thames.[97] A son, George Frederick, was born the following September, and a daughter, Lavinia Jemima, early in 1812.[98] But at some point in 1813, James began to court a young woman named Susannah Timson, assuming the name of *Charles* Edwards. Susannah was just 19 at the time, and still living at home. As Susannah's father confirmed, James/Charles had represented himself to the family 'as a single man'. Upon receiving information that he was already married, Mr Timson had forbidden him to come to the house again.[99] It seems that his information had come from Jemima's brother William, who had learned of James' visits to Susannah. James promised William that he would 'leave off' visiting Susannah, and claimed that 'the acquaintance was all over'.[100]

That proved to be a lie. On Saturday 30 October, James told Jemima that he was going to the office – he was employed as a clerk in a firm of solicitors – and that he would return that same evening.[101] Evening came, but without him putting in an appearance. Instead, he sent a note saying that he had been required to go to Windsor and would not be back until the following Monday. He was in fact with Susannah. That morning, they had gone through a ceremony of marriage at St James' Piccadilly, with Susannah being

[94] *Remarkable Trial* (n 50) 99.
[95] *R v JSS Cooke* (1826) 5 B & C 201; 108 ER 201.
[96] Ancestry, *London Church of England Parish Registers*, P69/AND2/A/01/MS 6670/10.
[97] *OBP*, 26 October 1814.
[98] Their births were recorded in the register of an Independent chapel, the Walworth Locks Fields Chapel in York Street: TNA, *Registers of Births, Marriages and Deaths surrendered to the Non-parochial Registers Commissions of 1837 and 1857*, RG4/4202.
[99] *OBP*, 26 October 1814.
[100] ibid.
[101] ibid; *Public Ledger and Daily Advertiser*, 28 September 1814; *Star*, 4 November 1814.

married under the name of 'Anna' and James under the name of 'Charles' (the rather wonky 'C' in the marriage register indicating that he was not accustomed to signing his name in that way).[102]

He might have thought that he was being clever in getting Susannah to marry him in a false name. There was a growing body of case law holding marriages to be void where the banns had – as here – been called in a name by which the person in question had never been known.[103] Even a minor variation in the name might invalidate the marriage if it had been adopted for a fraudulent purpose.[104] It was also well established by 1813 that the invalidity of the second marriage was a bar to a successful prosecution for bigamy.[105]

On Monday, James returned to Jemima as promised and – according to her sister Frances – confessed that he had married Susannah. As Frances later told the court, 'we did not believe him; we thought he said what was really not true'.[106] At what point they decided that it *was* true is not clear. All we know is that in September 1814 James was arrested and charged with bigamy.[107]

At the Old Bailey, evidence of the two marriages was given by Jemima's brother William and by the clerk who had witnessed James and Susannah's wedding. The latter was not able to remember the occasion, noting that he had seen James before but 'cannot exactly say he was the person that was married'.[108] William, by contrast, was under no doubts as to James' guilt: when shown a note asking for the banns to be called for the second wedding, he confirmed the handwriting to be that of James. There was also the evidence of the landlord with whom Susannah had lodged after her wedding. James had, he reported, said that he was married to Susannah and would pay the rent of her room. The landlord, however, had been justifiably suspicious about the marriage, and forbade James to come to the house: as he told the court, while he was happy for Susannah to stay as long as she liked, 'I would not suffer him to cohabit with her there'.[109]

In response, James argued that although there was evidence of 'a person calling himself Charles Edwards' marrying Anna Timson, there was nothing to identify him as that person. He laid emphasis on the clerk's inability to remember him being married. He also challenged his brother-in-law's identification of his handwriting, arguing that men of a similar education were likely to write in a very similar way, and submitting, with apparent confidence, that the note arranging the calling of the banns 'was in pencil

[102] Ancestry, *Westminster Church of England Parish Registers*, STJ/PR/6/11.

[103] *Mather v Ney* (1807) 3 M & S 265n; 105 ER 610; *Wakefield v Mackay* (1807) 1 Hag Con 394; 161 ER 937n; *Wilson v Brockley* (1810) 1 Phill Ecc 132; 161 ER 937. For analysis of the case law on this topic, see R Probert, 'The Judicial Interpretation of Lord Hardwicke's Act of 1753' (2002) 23 *Journal of Legal History* 129.

[104] See also the slightly later case of *Wyatt v Henry* (1817) 2 Hag Con 215; 161 ER 720, in which the marriage was held to be void on account of Thomas Henry assuming the name of Charles Henry to conceal his identity and prior marriage.

[105] See *Double Trouble*, ch 2, and the case of Thomas Morland discussed in ch 4.

[106] *OBP*, 26 October 1814.

[107] 'Hatton Garden', *Public Ledger and Daily Advertiser*, 28 September 1814; *Morning Chronicle*, 1 October 1814; *The Times*, 1 October 1814.

[108] *OBP*, 26 October 1814.

[109] ibid. The context suggests that the term 'cohabit' was here used in its purely sexual meaning as James was only visiting the house, not proposing to move in.

writing, which … is not cognizable in a court of justice'.[110] He did not deny having told various people of his marriage to Susannah but claimed that this should not be taken into account against him. As he concluded, 'it is hard for a man to be convicted because the name of Edwards [is] in the book of marriages'.[111]

As his defence suggests, James had acquired a smattering of legal knowledge during the course of his employment as an attorney's clerk. He had clearly latched on to the fact that courts were becoming much stricter in terms of what was admissible as evidence.[112] But the rule that 'hearsay' was not admissible was subject to quite a number of exceptions, one of them being any admissions made by the accused himself.[113] His telling the landlord that he and Susannah were married might be seen as inconclusive, but his telling Frances was a direct and deliberate admission. Where he had acquired the idea that something written in pencil was inadmissible is harder to fathom. The jury had no hesitation in finding James guilty.

Before James' sentence could be pronounced, however, there was another legal issue that had to be decided. Susannah's father had told the court that she had never been known by the name of Anna – the name in which she had married, and the name that had been given in the indictment. The judge hearing the case, Newman Knowlys, accordingly raised the question of whether the indictment should instead have charged James with marrying Susannah 'by the name of Anna Timson'.[114] These doubts led him to reserve the case for the opinion of the twelve judges – the only avenue that then existed for any kind of review of the decisions made in criminal cases.[115]

This was not simply legal nitpicking. Considerable importance was attached to the indictment being correctly phrased. Only a few years earlier, a man named John William Bishop had escaped conviction for bigamy on account of his wife's name being misstated.[116] But the judges who met in the Exchequer Chamber on 12 November 1814 seem to have thought that they were being asked to decide a much broader question.[117] Their focus was more on the banns than on the indictment. As one of them recorded in his notes on the case, they 'expressly avoided considering the question how far the validity of a marriage was affected by a publication of banns in a wrong name'.[118] Their focus was purely on whether James was entitled to rely on the fact that the wrong name had been used to escape conviction for bigamy. And his actions, they thought, precluded him from doing so.[119] He had, after all, signed the note for the publication of the banns in the name of Anna Timson, and, subsequently, the register of their marriage, and so 'should not be permitted to defend himself on the ground that he did not marry Anna Timson, although such might not be her name'.[120]

[110] ibid.
[111] *OBP*, 26 October 1814.
[112] On which see Gallanis (n 85).
[113] ibid 518.
[114] *R v James Hugh Edwards, alias Charles Edwards* (1814) Russ & Ry 283; 168 ER 804.
[115] See further *Double Trouble*, ch 1.
[116] *OBP*, 15 April 1801. He was subsequently convicted of taking a false oath for the purpose of obtaining a licence for the second marriage: *OBP*, 1 July 1801.
[117] Middle Temple Library, Sir Soulden Lawrence MS, Crown Cases volume 6D, 459.
[118] ibid 459–60.
[119] ibid 460.
[120] *R v James Hugh Edwards, alias Charles Edwards* (1814) Russ & Ry 283; 168 ER 804.

James' conviction was accordingly upheld. The following January, he was informed of this decision.[121] He was sentenced to nine months in prison – a relatively light punishment, given that most bigamists convicted at the Old Bailey that decade were sentenced to transportation, but still hardly nominal.[122]

James' story provides a good example of how evidence sometimes needed to be pieced together from different sources to establish guilt. Having a witness to the wedding who could confirm the identity of the accused was good evidence, but not essential. Statements made to an outsider with a view to securing accommodation might be given little weight by themselves.[123] Similarly, statements by family members might well be regarded as partial. But collectively all these different pieces of evidence built up a convincing case.

As a legal precedent, *R v James Hugh Edwards* established that a bigamist could not escape conviction by having the banns for the second marriage called in the wrong names.[124] And it also eventually paved the way for courts to hold that the invalidity of the second marriage – independently of its bigamous nature – did not prevent a conviction.[125]

James' case also illustrates how complex the relationships involved could be. This was not a case of a marriage that had broken down and a husband seeking solace elsewhere. One of the damning details supplied by Frances was that James had slept with Jemima the very night before he married Susannah.[126] He had also continued to do afterwards: Jemima was pregnant at the time of his trial and gave birth to their third child two months after he was sentenced.[127] And from the birth of a *fourth* child in 1823, it appears that they were reunited after his trial.[128]

A New Mode of Marrying: Joseph Cooke, 1844

From July 1837, there were new options for getting married – and, with them, a whole new set of questions about what was required for a valid marriage. The Marriage Act 1836 had made it possible for couples to marry in a non-Anglican ceremony, in either a register office or a registered place of worship. In both cases, the ceremony had

[121] *OBP*, 11 January 1815.

[122] *London Chronicle*, 23 January 1815. The original of his trial in the *Proceedings* had stated that he was sentenced to transportation: *OBP*, 26 October 1814.

[123] As one treatise on evidence noted a few years later, assertions 'which have been made with a particular view during cohabitation, would indeed of themselves be entitled to very little credit': Starkie (n 43) 1186.

[124] See eg the case of John Palmer, indicted at the Durham assizes in 1827, whose bigamous marriage had been under the assumed name of John Leyster, his bride also assuming a different surname. John's counsel argued that those deficiencies meant that John could not be punished for bigamy (*Morning Chronicle*, 6 March 1827). The point was reserved, but at the following assizes John was sentenced to 10 months' imprisonment with hard labour – with the judge noting that the deliberate misstatement of the names 'was adding gross fraud to the offence of bigamy, and considerably added to the moral guilt' (*The Standard*, 15 August 1827). See also H Roscoe, *A digest of the law of evidence in criminal cases* (London, Saunders & Benning, 1835) 231.

[125] On which see *Double Trouble*, chs 6 and 8, and the case study of Henry Allen below.

[126] *OBP*, 26 October 1814.

[127] TNA, *Registers of Births, Marriages and Deaths surrendered to the Non-parochial Registers Commissions of 1837 and 1857*, RG4/4202.

[128] Ancestry, *London Church of England Parish Registers*, DL/T/013/011.

to be preceded by the giving of notice at a register office and take place in the presence of a registrar.[129]

In 1844, Joseph Cooke was indicted for bigamy at the Chester assizes. The prosecution had proved that he had gone through two ceremonies, with the first, to Sarah Parkinson, taking place at St Ignatius' Roman Catholic chapel in Preston in 1839. In his defence, Joseph argued that the chapel had not been registered for weddings as required by the 1836 Act.[130] There was a dispute as to whether the registrar had been present, and when in the process the register had been signed.[131] And Joseph also claimed that the priest who had conducted the ceremony had told him 'that the contract was not lawful until the wife's own priest had married them'.[132] Counsel for the prosecution tried to argue in return that a marriage by a Roman Catholic priest, in the presence of witnesses, was binding. But the judge, Mr Justice Maule, pointed out that the 1836 Act had made no mention of Catholic rites. In other words, the touchstone of legal validity was not whether the ceremony had been conducted by a Catholic priest, but whether the ceremony had taken place in accordance with the framework laid down by the 1836 Act. In the absence of evidence that the required formalities had been complied with, he directed the jury that Joseph was entitled to an acquittal.[133]

It then transpired that the chapel *had* been registered.[134] This emerged a few months later, when Joseph was brought before the Borough Court in Manchester charged with allowing Sarah and their two children to become chargeable to the parish. This time the registrar was present in court and able to confirm that the required paperwork had been duly completed, both for the chapel and for Joseph's specific marriage.

Joseph continued to protest that he was not liable for Sarah's support: 'She's not my wife, the judge said she was not, and I was acquitted.'[135] But as the magistrate pointed out to him, Maule had never said that Sarah was not his wife, having simply directed an acquittal on a point of law. Faced with the threat of being sent to prison for a month (with hard labour), Joseph changed his mind and agreed to pay seven shillings a week for the support of Sarah and their children.

Four years later he was back in court, still trying to argue that he was not liable for their support. There was renewed discussion as to what had taken place in 1839. But the clerk to the magistrates had the terms of the 1836 Act to hand, and pointed out that a marriage was only void if the parties 'knowingly and wilfully' married without notice to the registrar, and without the latter being present. With the onus being on Joseph to establish that both he *and* Sarah had deliberately failed to comply with the legal requirements, his challenge was dismissed.[136]

[129] On the requirements of the Marriage Act 1836, see further R Probert, *Tying the Knot: The Formation of Marriage, 1836-2020* (Cambridge, Cambridge University Press, 2021).

[130] 'Spring Assizes', *Morning Post*, 4 April 1844.

[131] This was not reported at the time but was alluded to in subsequent proceedings as having been part of his defence: 'An Awkward Situation', *Manchester Times*, 27 July 1844; 'A Man With Two Wives', *Daily News*, 20 January 1848.

[132] 'Bigamy', *Chester Chronicle*, 5 April 1844; 'Bigamy', *Chester Courant*, 9 April 1844.

[133] 'Cheshire Assizes', *Liverpool Mail*, 6 April 1844; 'Curious Case of Bigamy', *Liverpool Standard and General Commercial Advertiser*, 9 April 1844.

[134] It had in fact been among the first tranche of Catholic chapels to be registered, just after the 1836 Act came into force: *London Gazette*, 11 July 1837.

[135] 'An Awkward Situation', *Manchester Times*, 27 July 1844.

[136] 'A Man With Two Wives', *Daily News*, 20 January 1848.

Joseph's case is a reminder of how a court can only decide a case on the evidence before it – and of how an acquittal did not conclusively determine the question of which marriage was valid. It also hints at a potential misunderstanding of the new processes for getting married. Joseph kept bringing up the question of whether the registrar, Mr Walker, had been present at the ceremony. A witness confirmed that Walker had been in the vestry when the certificate was signed, but added that 'he could not swear that the gentleman was present at the marriage'. But as long as Joseph and Sarah had repeated the prescribed words to Walker in the vestry, this *was* the marriage under the terms of the 1836 Act.[137]

Marrying a Deceased Wife's Sister: James Chadwick, 1846

In September 1845, widower James Chadwick married Ann Fisher at Manchester Cathedral.[138] Ann was in fact the sister of James' late wife Hannah, whom he had married at the same Cathedral over two decades earlier. Such marriages were far from unusual, and James appears to have been a classic case of a widower seeking assistance in looking after his young family.[139] But marriages to a deceased wife's sister were listed in the Church of England's *Table of Kindred and Affinity* as being within the prohibited degrees, and in 1835 legislation had been passed specifying that any marriage within the prohibited degrees entered into after 31 August that year was void from the outset – rather than, as previously, merely voidable by a decree from a court.[140]

Having heard doubts raised about his second marriage's validity, James went to the Reverend Wilson, one of the Cathedral chaplains, for advice. From him he obtained a document stating that his marriage to Ann was void.[141] On 23 March 1846, James married Eliza Bostock at St John's church, about a mile from the Cathedral.[142] It is difficult to read anything into his choice of venue. On the one hand, it was not where his first two marriages had taken place. On the other, this marriage was preceded by the public calling of banns, and the Cathedral conducted so many marriages that it would have been a more natural choice for anyone wishing to avoid attention. Moreover, if James believed that his marriage to Ann was void, then he had nothing to hide.

In any case, Ann's friends quickly learned of the ceremony. Two weeks later, James was charged with bigamy and brought before the borough court.[143] His attorney having

[137] That this was standard practice is confirmed by later commentary: see eg JT Hammick, *The marriage law of England: a practical treatise on the legal incidents connected with the law of constitution of the matrimonial contract* (London, Shaw & Sons, 1887) 147–48, explaining that the practice of the parties was to 'leave the body of the church' after the Catholic rite had been performed and repeat the prescribed words to the registrar in the sacristy or vestry. On the disjunction between the religious and legal aspects of weddings, see R Probert, RC Akhtar and S Blake, *Belief in Marriage: The evidence for reforming weddings law* (Bristol, Bristol University Press, 2023).

[138] Ancestry, *Anglican Parish Registers* (marriage at St Mary, St Denys and St George, 14 September 1845).

[139] I have not been able to find him in the 1841 census, but the 1851 census lists him with five daughters aged between 18 and six: TNA, HO107/2227, folio 829, p 14.

[140] Marriage Act 1835.

[141] 'Curious Case of Bigamy', *Manchester Courier*, 8 April 1846; 'South Lancashire Assizes: Charge of Bigamy', *Manchester Times*, 18 December 1846.

[142] Ancestry, *Anglican Parish Registers*.

[143] 'Curious Case of Bigamy', *Manchester Courier*, 8 April 1846.

objected that his marriage to Ann was void, the court discharged him.[144] Despite this, a prosecution was subsequently instituted by a group of men who had themselves married the sisters of their deceased wives 'in order to have the question fairly raised before the judges'.[145] James accordingly found himself on trial at the South Lancashire assizes in December 1846.[146] Faced with competing arguments from counsel about the relationship between biblical injunctions, canonical prohibitions, and statute, Mr Justice Wightman understandably decided that the question was one that needed to be referred upwards.[147]

The answer was not quite as clear cut as the Church's *Table of Kindred and Affinity* made it appear. Back in 1540, Parliament had passed legislation railing against the church courts' willingness to issue dispensations to permit marriages between cousins as a blatant money-making exercise, intended to enhance their own position. It went on to say that the only prohibited marriages were those that fell within the 'Levitical degrees' – while at the same time making this subject to 'God's law'.[148]

Despite the references to God and the Book of Leviticus, the obvious implication of this was that it was Parliament, not the Church, that set the rules. The Church's only role was to interpret Parliament's words when called upon to determine the validity of any given marriage. This meant that the *Table of Kindred and Affinity* had no independent authority: it could be taken as an expression of the law, but it could not change what the law was. Over the decades, the common law courts issued prohibitions to prevent the church courts from annulling marriages regarded as falling outside the Levitical degrees.

The more difficult question was to decide which marriages were *within* the Levitical degrees. Here the fundamental problem was that the Book of Leviticus left quite a number of questions unanswered. The relevant chapter began with a general prohibition on sex between close relatives before going on to list various specific relationships that were prohibited. These included, as one would expect, close blood relations – mother, sister, granddaughter and aunt. It also listed the spouses of certain relations (father, son, brother) and the daughter or granddaughter of a sexual partner. No mention was made of a man's daughter or grandmother, but these were included within the prohibitions on the basis that they were just as close – within the same 'degree' of relationship – as others that were mentioned. And while a wife's sister was mentioned, the prohibition seemed to apply only while the wife was still alive: 'neither shalt thou take a wife to her sister, to vex her, to uncover her nakedness, beside the other in her lifetime'.[149] So a marriage to a

[144] 'Manchester Borough Court', *Manchester Times & Gazette*, 10 April 1846, noting dryly that 'there is no accounting for legislative wisdom'.

[145] 'Curious Case of Bigamy', *Morning Post*, 14 December 1846; 'South Lancashire Assizes: Charge of Bigamy', *Manchester Times*, 18 December 1846.

[146] TNA, PCOM 2/231.

[147] 'Curious Case of Bigamy', *Morning Post*, 14 December 1846; 'Marrying a Dead Wife's Sister', *The Tablet*, 19 December 1846 (noting that the arguments on both sides 'extended to an immense length'); 'Important Trial – Law of Marriage', *The Church and State Gazette*, 18 December 1846 (providing the most detailed account of the trial).

[148] Marriage Act 1540.

[149] *Authorized (King James) Version*, Leviticus 18:18. On polygamy within Judaism, see J Witte Jr, *The Western Case for Monogamy Over Polygamy* (Cambridge, Cambridge University Press, 2015).

deceased wife's sister was seemingly not within the Levitical degrees and so not prohibited by the 1540 Act unless prohibited by 'God's law'.

Before the Court of Queen's Bench, counsel for the Crown argued that the matter fell to be determined by reference to the 'scriptures', and that there was no prohibition on marrying the sister of a deceased wife.[150] Theologically, it was a strong argument. At the same time, it was a problematic argument to put to a secular court. Lord Denman somewhat wearily commented at the start of his judgment that he and his fellow judges 'have been occupied here by a discussion of five days, in which as many different interpretations have been put upon the texts under dispute'.[151] As he demanded:

> Are we to talk here of the opinions of the Scribes and the Pharisees? to sit as a Court of Error from the Karaites and Talmudists? to inquire into the doctrines of the Council of Eliberis? These are curious points, and may occupy men of leisure: but for us to decide upon them would be doing the very thing which the Legislature intended to prevent when it took upon itself to determine what were the prohibited degrees.[152]

Whatever the theological arguments, the judges were clearly far more comfortable in purporting to rest their decision on 'statute' (even if that statute led straight back to the scriptures) and on the consistent assumption since the late sixteenth century that marriage with a deceased wife's sister was prohibited. As a result, the Court finally confirmed what had been assumed from the start: that James Chadwick's second marriage was void and his third valid, and so by definition not bigamous.

There is not much more to be said about James. The 1851 census found him and Eliza living together in Manchester with a houseful of daughters.[153] Another daughter, Martha, was born in 1852.[154] But James then died, leaving Eliza to look after his children.[155]

But there is a lot more that could be said about marriages within the prohibited degrees.[156] Over the second half of the nineteenth century, there were occasional examples of individuals being acquitted of bigamy on the basis that their first marriage had been void for this reason.[157] Others did not even make it to trial: examples of individuals who had remarried after such a first marriage can be found in the newspaper reports of proceedings in the magistrates' courts, but such individuals were – quite rightly – discharged.[158] In such cases the prohibited marriage had generally involved in-laws, rather than blood relations, but there were occasional examples of close kin marrying.[159]

[150] *R v Chadwick* (1847) 11 QB 173, 206; 116 ER 441.

[151] ibid 232.

[152] ibid.

[153] TNA, 1851 census, HO107/2227, folio 829, p 14.

[154] Free BMD, RD Manchester, 1852 Q4 (mother's maiden name Bostock).

[155] TNA, 1861 census, RG9/2884, folio 33, p 20.

[156] The discussion above is just a very brief summary of the complex arguments made both at the assizes and before the Court of Queen's Bench. For a more detailed discussion of the evolving law on the prohibited degrees, see M Harding, 'The Curious Incident of the Marriage Act (no 2) 1537 and the Irish Statute Book' (2012) 32 *Legal Studies* 78.

[157] *OBP*, 20 November 1871 (Samuel Mills, acquitted as his first wife was his brother's widow).

[158] 'Marrying A Deceased Wife's Sister', *Birmingham Daily Post*, 8 December 1891 (James Totney, remarried while 'married' to wife of deceased sister, discharged).

[159] 'Singular Charge of Bigamy', *North-Eastern Daily Gazette*, 5 October 1891 (charge against Mary Ann Brice withdrawn when it was discovered that her first 'husband' was in fact her uncle).

Over the course of the twentieth century, however, the rules on who could marry whom were gradually relaxed, reducing the likelihood of an acquittal on this basis.[160]

In the meantime, however, questions had arisen as to whether an individual could be convicted of bigamy if it was their allegedly bigamous marriage that had been within the prohibited degrees.

'A Puzzle for the Judges': Henry Allen, 1872

Henry's first marriage, to Sarah Cummins, had taken place in 1853, in the parish church of Hurstbourne Tarrant, a village just outside Andover in Hampshire.[161] After Sarah's death in August 1867,[162] he did not wait long to remarry. In a little over three months, he had tied the knot with a 37-year-old widow, Ann Pearman Gutteridge, the wedding again taking place in the parish church.[163]

Four years later, on 2 December 1871, Henry went through a third ceremony of marriage – this time some distance away from the village, at an Independent chapel in Andover.[164] His latest bride was Hannah Crouch, a 27-year-old domestic servant who was pregnant with his child. She was also the niece of his late first wife, Sarah. This meant that their marriage was within the prohibited degrees and would have been void even if Henry had been free to marry. But Ann was still very much alive, and on 20 February Henry was arrested and charged with bigamy.[165]

Whether he was actually guilty of bigamy proved to be surprisingly difficult to answer. He was brought before the Hampshire assizes at Winchester in March 1872.[166] There his counsel relied on the fact that the marriage to Hannah was within the prohibited degrees, arguing that 'a man could not be found guilty of bigamy if it were a marriage with a person that was void in law'.[167] The judge, Baron Martin, wisely thought that this was a point that needed to be referred to the Court for Crown Cases Reserved.[168] Henry was accordingly advised to plead guilty and was released on bail pending the judges' decision.[169]

[160] The prohibitions were lifted one by one: deceased's wife's sister in 1907, deceased husband's brother in 1921, deceased's spouse's aunt/uncle or niece/nephew in 1931, divorced spouse's sibling, aunt/uncle, or niece/nephew in 1960. From 1986, marriage with a step-child was permitted if both were at least 21 and the step-parent had not been a *de facto* parent to the child, and marriage to the parent of a former spouse was also permitted, if both were 21 and their former spouses were dead (a harsh condition that was removed as the result of legal challenge in 2007).

[161] Ancestry, *Anglican Bishops Transcripts*, 79068/1/7. The 1861 census showed them living together in the village with their son: TNA, RG9/716, folio 36, p 6.

[162] Ancestry, *Church of England Burials, 1813-1921* (burial of Sarah Allen at Hurstbourne Tarrant on 25 August 1867).

[163] Nothing turned on this, but it points up the contrast between legal remarriages and bigamous ones.

[164] GRO, certified copy of certificate.

[165] TNA, *Calendar of Prisoners*, HO 140/18.

[166] TNA, ASSI 25/49/23.

[167] 'Hampshire Lent assizes', *Hampshire Independent*, 6 March 1872.

[168] TNA, ASSI 25/49/23 (noting that the case was being reserved for the 'Court of Criminal Appeal').

[169] 'Hampshire Lent assizes', *Hampshire Advertiser*, 6 March 1872.

The case came before the 'ordinary' court of five judges at the end of April,[170] but the point was deemed to be of sufficient difficulty and importance to require the presence of all 16 judges – a record for the court.[171] The following week, once the assembled judges had heard the various arguments, they retired to consider their judgment. Upon their return, the Lord Chief Justice, Lord Cockburn, announced that they still needed more time, and that judgment would be delivered the following term.[172]

One reason why the question was so difficult was that there were competing authorities to be considered. On the one hand there was the case of *R v Brawn*, heard at the Huntingdonshire assizes some three decades earlier, which had involved a married woman going through a ceremony with her deceased sister's husband. Lord Denman had firmly rejected the suggestion that the invalidity of the second marriage, on account of it being within the prohibited degrees, provided a defence, stating that it was 'the appearing to contract a second marriage, and the going through the ceremony, which constitutes the crime of bigamy'.[173] Were the law otherwise, he added, no one would ever be guilty of bigamy, since the second marriage was always by definition void. There was also *R v Penson*, in which Mr Baron Gurney had taken the view that the individuals involved could not escape punishment 'by contracting a *concertedly* invalid marriage'.[174]

That might seem clear enough. But these were the decisions of single judges on circuit. Being reported gave them wider currency, but no greater authority.[175] Judging from what was happening in practice at the assizes in the intervening years, the point was far from settled. Following *Brawn*, there certainly seems to have been an assumption that those whose second marriage was within the prohibited degrees were nevertheless guilty of bigamy. Amy Esaias, for example, was convicted at the Monmouthshire assizes in 1854, having acceded to her dying sister's request to marry the latter's husband despite being already married herself.[176] The following decade Joseph Pollard, whose second wife was his niece, was also convicted.[177] And various textbooks confidently asserted that it was 'no defence that the second marriage was void'.[178]

But at least one textbook just as confidently asserted the exact opposite: 'if either marriage be void … the party cannot be convicted'.[179] Only a few years earlier, in another case that had been referred to the CCCR, counsel for each side had taken opposing

[170] 'Criminal Appeal', *Hampshire Advertiser*, 1 May 1872.
[171] 'Bigamy Case – A Curious Point', *Hampshire Advertiser*, 8 May 1872.
[172] 'Court of Criminal Appeal', *London Evening Standard*, 6 May 1872; 'The Law Relating to Bigamy: Singular Case', *Sun & Central Press*, 7 May 1872; 'A Puzzle for the Judges', *Daily Telegraph*, 9 May 1872.
[173] *R v Brawn and Webb* (1843) 1 Car & K 144; 174 ER 751; *Morning Post*, 28 July 1843.
[174] *R v Penson* (1832) 5 Car & P 412, 413; 172 ER 1032, 1032.
[175] WHD Winder, 'The Rule of Precedent in the Criminal Courts' (1941) 5 *Journal of Criminal Law* 242.
[176] 'Bigamy', *Morning Post*, 3 April 1854.
[177] 'Extraordinary Charge of Bigamy', *Lloyd's*, 19 October 1862; *OBP*, 27 October 1862.
[178] JF Archbold, *The new system of criminal procedure* (London, Shaw & Sons, 1852) 614; RA Pritchard and W Tarn Pritchard, *A digest of the law and practice of the Court for Divorce and Matrimonial Causes* (London, W Maxwell, 1864) 203; J Jervis, *Archbold's Pleading and Evidence in Criminal Cases* (London, H Sweet, 1871).
[179] JF Archbold, *The justice of the peace and parish officer: Vol 4*, 6th edn (London, Shaw and Sons, 1859) 51 (who was presumably not cross-referencing between his own books).

views on the question.[180] And there were plenty of cases in which individuals had been acquitted of bigamy – or simply discharged without trial – upon it being shown that their second spouse had also been married to someone else at the time of the ceremony, on the basis that this marriage would have been void.[181] In other words, the approach in *Brawn* appears to have been applied only where the facts were more or less identical.

In the meantime, the Irish Court of Criminal Appeal had decided in *R v Fanning* that the invalidity of the second marriage *was* a defence to a charge of bigamy.[182] Although the context was different,[183] the reasoning was directly on point. There was also the decision of the Divorce Court in *Burt v Burt*, in which a wife had sought to divorce her husband on the ground of 'bigamy with adultery'.[184] In this case a woman had given evidence that she had married Burt in Australia, according to the form of the Kirk of Scotland. But in the absence of evidence as to whether this would be recognised as a valid marriage under Australian law, the court had held that the husband's bigamy had not been established, noting that '[t]here must be proof of such a ceremony as, but for the former marriage, would have constituted a valid marriage'.[185] In other words, by this reasoning the second ceremony *had* to have been capable of creating a valid marriage in and of itself.

Burt also hinted at a deeper question about what counted as a marriage for these purposes. It was one thing to decide that a person who went through a formal ceremony of marriage with one person while already married to another should not be able to escape conviction for bigamy simply because the new spouse was already married, or within the prohibited degrees, or because they had deliberately engineered that the second marriage would be void on account of some formal defect. But what if the second ceremony could never have amounted to a marriage under *any* circumstances?

Faced with these difficult questions, it is unsurprising that the judges took their time to come to their decision. But if there had been divisions among them, no hint of this appeared in the single judgment delivered by Cockburn on 23 May 1872.[186] Having reviewed the various authorities, he identified the 'mischief' that the legislation punishing bigamy was designed to address:

> The ground on which such a marriage is very properly made penal is, that it involves an outrage on public decency and morals, and creates a public scandal by the prostitution of a solemn ceremony, which the law allows to be applied only to a legitimate union, to a marriage

[180] *R v Clarke* (1867) 10 Cox CC 474. The allegation here was that the second marriage would have been void because it had taken place more than three months after the banns had been read; however, the CCCR had upheld Clarke's conviction on the basis that the parties had not 'wilfully' intermarried with knowledge that the banns had not been duly published (the wedding having taken place exactly three months after the third reading), making it unnecessary for them to decide what the result would have been if they had.

[181] See eg *OBP*, 14 December 1857 (Ann Alexander and John Wilkinson, discussed in chapter 10; 'Bigamy! – Wholesale Marrying', *Western Daily Press*, 5 August 1862 (William Hall, discharged without trial).

[182] (1866) 10 Cox CC 411. The judges had been split 7–4.

[183] The case had turned on a specific point of Irish law invalidating any marriage between a Protestant and a Catholic that had been conducted by a Catholic priest: Abductions Act 1745.

[184] *Burt v Burt* (1860) 2 Sw & Tr 88; 164 ER 925.

[185] ibid 88. The divorce was granted on the alternative ground of adultery and desertion.

[186] TNA, ASSI 29/49/23.

> at best but colourable and fictitious, and which may be made, and too often is made, the means of the most cruel and wicked deception. It is obvious that the outrage and scandal involved in such a proceeding will not be less, because the parties to the second marriage may be under some special incapacity to contract marriage.[187]

In other words, the harm to the second spouse was potentially the same regardless of whether the second marriage would have been void for some other reason.

From this he concluded that the court should not 'frustrate the operation of a very salutary statute' by adopting a narrow interpretation of its terms. If the terms of the 1861 Act *could* be construed to include a case like Henry's, they *should* be. The words 'shall marry another person' could, in his view, easily be interpreted as 'shall "go through the form and ceremony of marriage with another person"'.[188]

That said, the words 'form and ceremony' were key here. As Cockburn emphasised, the decision of the court did not mean 'that every fantastic form of marriage to which parties might think proper to resort' would expose the parties to prosecution for bigamy.[189] He explicitly left open the question of what the outcome would be if the ceremony had been performed 'by an unauthorized person, or in an unauthorized place'. As he noted, there would 'be time enough to deal with a case of this description when it arises'.[190]

All of this meant that the decision of the Court for Crown Cases Reserved had to be very precisely stated. It was not that the validity of the second marriage was irrelevant. Rather,

> where a person already bound by an existing marriage goes through a form of marriage known to and recognized by the law as capable of producing a valid marriage, for the purpose of a pretended and fictitious marriage, the case is not the less within the statute by reason of any special circumstances, which, independently of the bigamous character of the marriage, may constitute a legal disability in the particular parties, or make the form of marriage resorted to specially inapplicable to their individual case.[191]

The upshot was that Henry was guilty of bigamy even though the bigamous marriage would have been void on account of being within the prohibited degrees.

At the next Hampshire assizes, Henry surrendered to his bail, and was sentenced to a month's imprisonment with hard labour.[192] That it took 16 judges several weeks to resolve whether he had done anything for which he could be punished illustrates that the outcome was far from being a foregone conclusion. But his case did finally settle the law. In subsequent cases, individuals were found guilty of bigamy despite their second marriage being within the prohibited degrees.[193]

Henry's case also illustrates the growing sophistication of the criminal law. In addition to the careful consideration of competing precedents and the precise

[187] *R v Henry Allen* (1872) LR 1 CCR 367, 374–75.
[188] ibid 375.
[189] ibid 376.
[190] ibid. For discussion of how the courts dealt with such cases, see *Double Trouble*, chs 9–11.
[191] ibid.
[192] TNA, *Calendar of Prisoners*, HO 140/18.
[193] See eg *OBP*, 3 February 1890; 'Central Criminal Court', *Morning Post*, 5 February 1890 (Minnie Maria Langford, married her nephew, convicted of bigamy).

articulation of the court's decision, there was also its inclusion within a new 'official' series of law reports. Within such reports, it was the judgment that was given priority. As a resource for lawyers, the precise details of the case did not matter, except insofar as they identified the legal point at issue. The parties could just as well have been represented by letters, as in a mathematical formula.[194]

But putting the parties back into the picture does help to illuminate the impact of bigamy on those involved. The very day after Henry's conviction had been confirmed by the CCCR, Hannah applied to the local magistrates for a summons against Henry to support their daughter Blanche.[195] Hannah also took Blanche to her local church to have her baptised – with the register referring to her as 'Hannah Crouch, single woman'.[196] Whether Henry ever paid anything to support them is not recorded. By the end of the year, both Hannah and Blanche were dead. Hannah, it appears, had moved to London to find work: her death certificate recorded that she had been working as a scullery maid, and had died of typhoid fever, aged just 28.[197] Blanche had been left in the Andover workhouse, where she died the following month.[198]

At the time that Hannah was seeking support from Henry, it was noted in passing that he was back with Ann.[199] That, however, cannot be verified. The 1871 census, taken on the night of 2 April, shows Henry having moved to a different parish with his two children from his marriage to Sarah.[200] Subsequent censuses show him living with one or other of his now-married children, until his death in 1894.[201] It seems that the man who had acquired brief notoriety as a man who liked matrimony had spent most of his life effectively single.

[194] And to some extent they were. The official report misreported *all* the wives' names – Cunningham rather than Cummins, Pearson rather than Pearman, and Harriet rather than Hannah – necessitating multiple searches in order to track down their marriages. It also had Henry being tried at Manchester, rather than Winchester.

[195] 'County Bench, Friday, May 24th', *Reading Mercury*, 1 June 1872. Why she waited until then is unclear, given that there was no prospect of her marriage to Henry being valid, whatever the CCCR had decided.

[196] Ancestry, *Anglican Parish Registers*, 114M82/PR4 (baptism register of Penton Mewsey).

[197] GRO, Death certificate for Hannah Crouch, registered 14 October 1872.

[198] 'Deaths', *Hampshire Advertiser*, 30 November 1872; Burial register, Andover: Ancestry, *Anglican Bishops' Transcripts*, 21M65/F8/10/4.

[199] 'The Bigamy Case', *Hampshire Advertiser*, 29 May 1872.

[200] TNA, 1871 census, RG10/1242, folio 22, p 13.

[201] TNA, 1881 census, RG11/1262, folio 15, p 6; 1891 census, RG12/964, folio 13, p 4; *Civil Registration Death Index, 1837-1915*.

4

Alive or Dead? Presuming the Fate of the First Spouse

It was not enough for the prosecution to show that the accused had gone through two marriage ceremonies. They also had to prove that the first spouse was still alive when the second ceremony took place.[1] It was a simple enough point, and one that rarely led to legal disputes, largely because cases where such evidence was lacking would not get to trial in the first place. So the two case studies in this chapter are quite exceptional – both for this and for a whole host of other reasons.

In the case of Eliza Lumley, tried at the Central Criminal Court in 1868, there were witnesses who were willing to swear that they had seen her first husband after her second marriage. The question was whether they were to be believed and, if not, what approach the law should take to a case where the only firm evidence was that the husband had been alive fully five years before the second marriage.[2] The issue in the 1881 case of Henry Willshire was even more complex. The indictment assumed that the woman he had married in 1879 was his legal wife. But this was Henry's second trial for bigamy – the first having taken place in 1868 – and so questions were raised as to what had since become of Henry's very first wife, or, rather, who was responsible for *proving* what had become of her.

Both cases made it into the law reports, and into legal treatises and student textbooks. But even shorn of any legal significance, both Eliza and Henry would have merited their own case studies because of the sheer drama involved in their cases. Much of the drama in Eliza's case derives from the actions of her second husband, Major William Brownrigg Lumley, whose litigious nature is the mainspring of the whole narrative and provides some light relief. Henry's case, by contrast, is much darker, primarily on account of his appalling treatment of several of his wives.

[1] EH East, *A Treatise of the Pleas of the Crown: Vol 1* (London, 1803) 469 ('must … aver that the former consort was alive at the time of the second marriage').

[2] If the remarrying spouse had not seen the other spouse in the seven years prior to their remarriage, and had no reason to believe that they were alive, then the statutory exception applied: see further chapter 6.

What to Presume in the Absence of Evidence: Eliza Lumley, 1869

In the autumn of 1863, Major William Brownrigg Lumley and his wife Eliza were sojourning in Boulogne-sur-Mer. The town was a popular destination for English visitors – JM Turner had sketched it a few decades earlier, and Charles Dickens had passed more than one summer there in the 1850s. With little for the English residents to do except gossip, it was an environment in which rumours might quickly take hold. A Mrs Crow visited the Lumleys one day to tell them that one of William's relatives, Lady Lewis, was spreading a 'nasty rumour' about Eliza – claiming that she had been married before.[3]

Eliza dismissed Lady Lewis' scandalmongering 'with derision and thorough contempt'.[4] William was so convinced of her innocence that he resolved to bring proceedings for slander against Lady Lewis. Although these were later abandoned,[5] William's reaction gives a hint as to his litigious nature. Over the next decade or so, he was to be embroiled in proceedings in the criminal courts, the Court of Chancery, and the Court for Divorce and Matrimonial Causes.

The wedding of William and Eliza had taken place some 17 years earlier, in 1847.[6] At that time William had just returned from India, where he had been serving in the army. He had met Eliza at his aunt's house, and they were married within a few weeks. At the time of the ceremony, Eliza had described herself as a spinster and given her maiden name of Haines. During their marriage, the pair do not appear to have had a settled home, moving instead from one coastal resort to another.[7] But their union appears to have been a happy one, as in later letters William acknowledged the 'kindness and affection' he had received from Eliza over many years.

In January 1864, however, William left Eliza at the Hotel du Nord. He subsequently wrote to her from London, acknowledging that he had done wrong but adding that his 'sin and folly' had been such that his hands were 'completely tied'.[8] This was his coded admission that he had begun a relationship with another woman, Ellen Thompson. As he concluded:

> All I can add is that I pray to God that you may have strength granted to you to bear up against this most undeserved misery, and that I will most willingly and honourably do all that is in my power to remove or relieve its social consequences.[9]

[3] *OBP*, 11 January 1869.

[4] ibid.

[5] He was, as he later claimed, persuaded against pursuing the action by his solicitor 'in the strongest manner': 'The Extraordinary Charge of Bigamy Against a Lady', *London Evening Standard*, 4 November 1868.

[6] Ancestry, *London Church of England Parish Registers*, 10235997 (marriage at St John's, Hampstead, 9 July 1847). According to William, Eliza had gone to Hampstead for a fortnight to establish residence there in order for them to be married in that parish: 'The Extraordinary Charge of Bigamy Against a Lady', *London Evening Standard*, 4 November 1868.

[7] The 1861 census found them in a boarding house in Torquay: TNA, RG9/1412, folio 38, p 15. They had also lived at Shanklin on the Isle of Wight: TNA, *Divorce and Matrimonial Causes Files*, J77/104/1594.

[8] 'Extraordinary Charge of Bigamy Against a Lady', *Morning Post*, 29 October 1868.

[9] ibid.

His guilt about abandoning Eliza led him to make the generous settlement of £300 per year on her – in consideration, as the deed recited, of 'his natural love and affection for her'.[10]

A solicitor named Lawrence Desborough – who will recur more than once in our story – was appointed as one of the trustees of this settlement. Unfortunately, a disagreement between William and Lawrence over the resulting bill escalated to the point where there was an altercation in Lawrence's office. According to Lawrence, he had been standing by the door, asking William to leave his office, and had put his hand on William's shoulder. According to William, Lawrence had shaken his fist 'menacingly' in his face, and then 'completed the outrage by endeavouring to thrust me with such violence from the room that it amounted to the last indignity to which a gentleman can be exposed, viz., a blow'. The following day William sent Sir John Lewis (a relative and fellow officer) to Lawrence with a letter demanding either an apology or 'a meeting' – by which he meant a duel.[11]

Again, this challenge tells us quite a lot about William's character. Duelling may have been tacitly condoned in William's youth, but it had long fallen out of fashion as a means of settling disputes.[12] As one newspaper observed, 'in these days … a man is considered nothing less than a lunatic if on English soil he challenges another to fight a duel'.[13] Understandably, then, Lawrence calmly told Sir John that he did not intend to fight. He also made it clear that he had no intention of apologising, and gave him a very different account of William's visit to his office. This prompted a further furious letter from William:

> Sir John Lewis having delivered to me your reply to the honourable message I sent you yesterday through him, in which you decline to fight or apologise, and adopt, moreover, a tone of unexpected and barefaced denial, the only course that remains open to me now is to announce to you that I shall henceforth consider you as beneath the notice of all who are 'gentlemen to the manner born', and the only inconvenience you need further apprehend from me is a sound and wholesome flagellation whenever and wherever the chance of administering the same presents itself, my only hope and prayer being that the desired opportunity may occur in the vicinity of clear and running water, that I may be enabled to cleanse my hands as speedily as possible of that taint which must necessarily accrue from contact with a 'snob', a 'liar' and a 'coward'.

Lawrence prudently made no reply to this, but applied for a warrant for William's arrest.[14]

[10] TNA, C16/822/S57.

[11] 'Mansion House: A Challenge', *Morning Herald*, 27 December 1864; 'Challenge to Fight A Duel', *Globe*, 27 December 1864.

[12] Duels of honour had never been a legally accepted way of settling disputes in England and Wales – if one party was killed or injured, the other was in principle still criminally responsible. On the attitudes of juries, see DT Andrew, 'The code of honour and its critics: the opposition to duelling in England, 1700-1850' (1980) 5 *Social History* 409.

[13] 'Challenge to Fight a Duel', *Exeter and Plymouth Gazette*, 30 December 1864. The last known occasion on which a duel had been fought in England was in 1852, between two French exiles: M Mulholland, *The Murderer of Warren Street: The True Story of a Nineteenth-Century Revolutionary* (London, Hutchinson, 2018).

[14] 'Mansion House: A Challenge', *Morning Herald*, 27 December 1864; 'Challenge to Fight A Duel', *Globe*, 27 December 1864.

The result was that William was summoned to attend the Mansion House Police Court. There his attempts to justify his conduct generated considerable amusement – even the Lord Mayor could not help laughing.[15] Newspapers the length and breadth of the country reported on the case, some simply with the aim of amusing their readers, others intent on pointing out a moral lesson about changing ideas of acceptable conduct.[16] By the time of his appearance at the Central Criminal Court in mid-January, William had decided – or been advised – that any defence would be futile, and he pleaded guilty to unlawfully sending a letter containing a challenge to fight, and to sending a libellous and threatening letter.[17] Through his counsel, he also apologised to Lawrence. The Recorder noted that William had already incurred some punishment through 'making himself an object of public ridicule',[18] and ordered that he be released on his own recognizances.

In the meantime, Ellen Thompson had given birth to their son, who was given his father's name.[19] At a casual glance, there was nothing in the entry in the birth register to indicate that he was illegitimate. The only hint was that William, who had taken responsibility for registering the birth, was described as the occupier of the house where William Jr was born, rather than his father.[20]

We can skip over the next couple of years, to 1867. This is when William obtained proof of Eliza's former marriage.[21] His first response was to try to alter the deed which had settled £300 per year on Eliza. The trustees of that settlement – one of whom, we might recall, was Lawrence Desborough – were not amenable. William's next step, early in 1868, was to file a bill in Chancery to set aside the deed. And his third was to instigate a prosecution against Eliza for bigamy.

Eliza – described as 'a fashionably-dressed lady, with the remains of considerable personal attractions' – was brought before the magistrates at Marlborough Street in October 1868.[22] Evidence of her prior marriage having been provided, she was committed for trial at the Central Criminal Court – although not before William had himself been closely questioned as to his relationship with Ellen.[23] It will probably come as no surprise that William, when called upon to give evidence, 'entered the witness-box

[15] 'A Would-be Duellist', *Weekly Dispatch*, 1 January 1865.

[16] See eg 'Remarkable Challenge to Fight a Duel', *Bury and Norwich Post*, 3 January 1865, which jocularly noted that while William had sought to rely on the 'warlike weapons pertaining to his profession', Lawrence had availed himself 'of the strong arm of the law'. 'Duelling – The Law of "Honour"', *North Devon Journal*, 5 January 1865 more severely commented that 'men in this age and this country, whatever their rank or profession, and whatever their prejudices or instincts, should understand, or be taught by the severest lessons of justice, that duelling is illegal, criminal, and when resulting in death, felony and murder'.

[17] *OBP*, 11 January 1865; TNA, *Central Criminal Court: After Trial Calendars of Prisoners*, CRIM 9/11.

[18] 'Major Lumley and His Challenge', *Sun*, 10 January 1865; 'The Charge of Sending a Challenge', *Morning Advertiser*, 11 January 1865.

[19] GRO, birth of William Brownrigg Lumley, born 7 January 1865 at 23 Kildare Gardens – the address given by William at his trial.

[20] An illegitimate child was, in the eyes of the law, *filius nullius*, nobody's child, but under the Births and Deaths Registration Act 1836, s 19, the occupier of the house where the child was born was entitled to register the birth.

[21] He appears to have been in financial difficulties by this time (*OBP*, 11 January 1865), so may well have been looking for evidence to justify stopping Eliza's allowance.

[22] 'Extraordinary Charge of Bigamy', *Daily News*, 29 October 1868.

[23] 'Extraordinary Charge of Bigamy', *Weekly Dispatch*, 1 November 1868.

in a somewhat excited state'. He admitted that Ellen had assumed his name, but denied that they had gone through any form of marriage.[24]

Eliza's case finally came to trial in January 1869.[25] It was established by the prosecution that Eliza had been married, in January 1836, to a Frenchman named Alexander Victor.[26] The wedding had taken place on Jersey, where Eliza was then living with her father and two sisters. This prompted much questioning as to whether the ceremony would have been a good marriage by the law of Jersey and whether the copy of the register was admissible evidence.[27] The judge, Mr Justice Lush, retired to seek advice on this matter and, on his return, noted that the point would be reserved for consideration.

Various witnesses then spoke of their knowledge of Alexander and Eliza's married life together. Two gave evidence that Eliza had told them that Alexander had married her under an assumed name, that he was in fact a French convict, and that their marriage was not legal – after which Eliza had returned to Jersey. In his summing up for the jury, Eliza's defence counsel, Serjeant Ballantine, was to refer back to this, arguing that there were 'very good grounds' for believing that her first marriage was 'not a legal marriage' and that she might well have believed that she had a right to marry again.[28]

But with the only evidence being what Eliza had told people, there was no direct evidence to show that her first marriage was invalid. Even if she had believed that it was not binding on her, such a belief was, by itself, no defence.[29] And, crucially, Eliza had not been separated from Alexander for sufficiently long to satisfy the seven-year defence. They had certainly been living together in 1841,[30] and had run a school together for a brief time in Bristol. The governor of Bristol gaol gave evidence that Alexander had been admitted as a debtor in January 1842, and that Eliza had visited him there.

No one gave evidence of Eliza and Alexander being seen together after 1842, or of Eliza receiving any communication from him thereafter. But two witnesses swore that they had seen Alexander since then. A Mrs Oliver – described as an elderly lady wearing purple glasses – claimed to have seen him in Brighton in 1847, just four days before Eliza and William's wedding, fixing the date by reference to a book she had been given during that visit.[31] And Alexander's former employer, Dr John Stone, now aged 83, gave evidence that he had seen him in Bristol at some point in 1858 or 1859.

[24] 'The Extraordinary Charge of Bigamy Against a Lady', *London Evening Standard*, 4 November 1868.

[25] The Grand Jury had found a true bill against her in November, but the defence had requested a postponement: *Daily News*, 26 November 1868.

[26] Ancestry, *Jersey Parish Registers*, G/C/03/A3/4.

[27] At that time Jersey law did not require entries in the register to be signed by both parties.

[28] *Daily News*, 15 January 1869.

[29] At least at this point in time: for the evolution of the law, see chapter 7.

[30] The 1841 census recorded them as living together in Westbury Upon Trym in Gloucestershire: TNA, HO107/359, Book 6, Enumeration District 2, Folio 7, p 24.

[31] The description of her came from the proceedings before the magistrates, when it was also noted that 'much amusement' was generated by the tart way in which she responded to questions: 'The Extraordinary Charge of Bigamy Against a Lady', *London Evening Standard*, 4 November 1868. The evidence about the book came out at trial: *OBP*, 11 January 1869.

Both came in for close questioning from counsel for the defence, trying to shake their credibility as witnesses.[32]

If the evidence of Mrs Oliver and Dr Stone was to be believed, then Eliza was clearly guilty of bigamy. If not, then the last date that anyone could report having seen Alexander was in 1842. And it had long been established that to sustain an indictment for bigamy, it was necessary to prove that the first spouse was still alive at the time of the second marriage.[33] Despite this, Mr Justice Lush directed the jury that, in the absence of any circumstances leading to any reasonable inference that he had died, Eliza's first husband 'must be presumed to have been living at the date of the second marriage'.[34]

The complexity of this direction, with its inferences and presumptions, is probably why all the contemporary reports gave slightly differing accounts of what had to be decided: it seems no one had quite understood what Lush was saying.[35] Certainly the jury did not find it an easy case to decide. They retired to consider their verdict at a quarter to five. Two hours later, Lush sent for them to see if they had reached a decision, but they indicated that they were unable to agree.[36] According to *The Times*, one juror said they had been discussing the legality of the first marriage. Lush then informed them that this was a 'mere question of law', and that the point they needed to decide was whether they believed Alexander was alive in 1847.[37] After a few more minutes' discussion they returned a verdict of guilty – but added to the confusion by saying that this was on the basis of the evidence given by the gaoler as to Alexander being still alive in 1842 rather than that given by Mrs Oliver and Dr Stone.[38]

Lush then reserved the case for the consideration of the Court for Crown Cases Reserved.[39] After some delay, the case was finally heard towards the end of April.[40]

[32] *OBP*, 11 January 1869.

[33] T Starkie, *A practical treatise of the law of evidence: Vol 3* (London, J & WT Clarke, 1824) 1185.

[34] At least, this was how he put it at the subsequent hearing before the Court for Crown Cases Reserved (*R v Lumley* (1869) LR 1 CCR 196). Given that he was quite insistent that he had been wrong, he was clearly not trying to reframe what he had said to put himself in a good light.

[35] 'Central Criminal Court', *The Times*, 15 January 1869, gave the impression that the sole question for the jury was whether the evidence of Mrs Oliver and Dr Stone was to be believed. The *Proceedings* had Lush leaving the credibility of the evidence given by Mrs Oliver and Dr Stone to the jury but also directing them that there was 'some evidence' that Alexander was alive in 1847 (*OBP*, 11 January 1869). Other newspapers reported Lush as directing the jury that if they believed that Eliza was married to Alexander in 1836 and 'had no reasonable ground for believing that he was dead at the time she contracted the second marriage', they ought to find her guilty: 'The Charge of Bigamy Against a Lady', *Morning Post*, 15 January 1869; 'The Extraordinary Charge of Bigamy Against a Lady', *Daily News*, 15 January 1869.

[36] *Morning Post*, 15 January 1869; '*Daily News*, 15 January 1869; *The Times*, 15 January 1869.

[37] *The Times*, 15 January 1869.

[38] On this point all accounts agreed: *Morning Post*, 15 January 1869; *Daily News*, 15 January 1869; *The Times*, 15 January 1869; *OBP*, 11 January 1869.

[39] According to the account in the *Proceedings*, the points reserved related solely to the evidence of the first marriage (whether it had been sufficiently proved, whether the copy of the register had been properly admitted as evidence, and whether the evidence of an English barrister was sufficient evidence of what the law of Jersey required for a valid marriage): *OBP*, 11 January 1869. In the event these points were not addressed.

[40] The case had been due to be argued before that court a couple of weeks after the trial, but was postponed at the request of counsel for the prosecution, who claimed that they needed more time to prepare: *The Times*, 25 January 1869.

As was usual, Lush, as the judge who had presided over the original trial, was one of the five-member panel.[41] He explained that his direction to the jury had effectively prevented them from considering the likelihood of Alexander being dead.

The discussion before the court accordingly focused on the implications of the presumption of death that applied where a person had not been heard of for seven years.[42] Did this mean, as counsel for the prosecution argued, that there was a corresponding presumption that a person was living up until the seven years had expired? Or, as Eliza's counsel contended, was there simply no presumption at all as to the date of death? And even if there was, would the presumption in favour of innocence take precedence?

In the view of Sir Fitzroy Kelly, the Chief Baron, the point to be decided was of 'such very great importance' that the Court should not give its opinion immediately.[43] The following week the judges reassembled, with Lush delivering the judgment of the court: his own original direction to the jury had been wrong. It was, as he now explained, down to the prosecution to prove that the first spouse was alive at the date of the second wedding, this being 'purely a question of fact'.[44] He went on to explain that the seven-year defence sanctioned a presumption that a person who had not been heard of for seven years was dead,[45] but it did not justify the converse presumption that a person who *had* been seen or heard of within the previous seven years was alive. Even evidence that the first spouse had been seen shortly before the second wedding was not necessarily conclusive. The weight to be given to such evidence would depend on the circumstances, for example whether he was in good health or in 'a dying condition'. Since the direction to the jury had been wrong, Eliza's conviction had to be quashed.

There was still the question of whether the £300 per year settlement that William had made on Eliza back in 1865 could be set aside. This finally came before the Vice Chancellor's Court in early June 1870, as *Lumley v Desborough and others*.[46] As the name of the case indicates, this was not just a dispute between William and Eliza, but also the trustees of the settlement, including – once again – Lawrence Desborough. The *Daily Telegraph and Courier* reminded its readers of the complex history of the parties and sardonically predicted that the case 'will probably last some days'.[47]

In the event it did not last that long. Having heard the evidence in support of William's case and the arguments of his counsel, Sir John Stuart simply dismissed

[41] The rest of the panel was made up of the Lord Chief Justice, Byles and Brett JJ and Cleasby B: '*The Queen v Eliza Lumley*', *The Times*, 26 April 1869.

[42] It might seem surprising that this point had never arisen before, but then a case would not have come to trial in the first place without some evidence that the first spouse was still alive at the time of the second marriage.

[43] '*The Queen v Eliza Lumley*', *The Times*, 26 April 1869.

[44] *R v Lumley* (n 34) 198.

[45] By this he did not mean that the seven-year defence rested on a presumption that the first spouse was dead – after all, it was often invoked when they were actually in court. His point was simply that if seven years had elapsed and nothing more had been heard of the first spouse, they could be presumed to be dead.

[46] 'Law Intelligence', *London Evening Standard*, 2 June 1870; *Morning Post*, 2 June 1870.

[47] 'Law Intelligence', *Daily Telegraph and Courier*, 2 June 1870.

his claim without even calling upon the defendants.[48] As he explained, an individual seeking to set aside a voluntary settlement of this kind had to show that it was executed under circumstances that amounted to fraud. The 'mere recital of words of description that turned out to be inaccurate was not enough'. In other words, it was not sufficient for William to provide evidence that Eliza was not his wife: he also had to show that she had believed that she was not his wife at the time that the settlement was made. As Stuart noted, with a perceptible note of weariness, he had 'asked repeatedly' during the arguments for any evidence that Eliza had known her first husband to be alive at that date, and none had been produced.[49]

Not only did Stuart dismiss William's claim, but he also made him responsible for the costs of the case. These amounted to just under £500 – the equivalent of around £60,000 today. As he noted, the circumstances under which William had instituted the suit reflected 'great discredit' on him.[50] William had, after all, been married to Eliza in church and lived with her for 17 years on affectionate terms. The settlement was made at a time when William had left Eliza for another woman. Moreover, he had already been told of the rumours about Eliza's former marriage and could, had he chosen, have made further inquiries.[51]

There was equally little sympathy for William in the press.[52] The *Lady's Own Paper* rejoiced that he had been taught that 'the strong and unscrupulous' were not inevitably allowed to 'ride roughshod' over those whom they had deceived, discarded and sought to crush 'with a heartlessness that would scarcely find a parallel amongst a nation of savages'.[53] *The Echo* similarly referred to his 'incredible meanness' in seeking to revoke the settlement that he had made on Eliza after acknowledging her as his wife for 17 years, noting that this was no more than 'any man – so called – of honour bestows upon a discarded mistress'. In welcoming Stuart's decision, it expressed the hope that William had by this time 'had enough of costs, not to say of law courts'.[54]

This proved to be a forlorn hope.[55] By the end of the month, William had commenced yet another set of legal proceedings – this time seeking a decree of nullity from the Court for Divorce and Matrimonial Causes.[56] His petition declared that he had not lived with Eliza since discovering her to be already married and had refused to recognise her as his wife, whereas Eliza had 'falsely wickedly and maliciously' continued to insist that they were validly married, to his 'great loss injury and prejudice'. To this, Eliza's first response was to deny both that she had been lawfully married to

[48] 'Law Intelligence', *London Evening Standard*, 3 June 1870.

[49] 'Law Intelligence', *Daily Telegraph and Courier*, 3 June 1870. The depositions of the various witnesses, preserved at the National Archives, added little to the evidence that had been given at Eliza's trial. One of Eliza's sisters said that Eliza had told her that Alexander was dead before she married William; another admitted that she had thought that she had seen Alexander on a street in London after 1847 but now thought that she had been mistaken: TNA, C16/509.

[50] 'Law Intelligence', *Daily Telegraph and Courier*, 3 June 1870.

[51] 'Equity Courts', *Daily News*, 3 June 1870.

[52] 'Charge of Bigamy', *Civil & Military Gazette*, 30 June 1870.

[53] *Lady's Own Paper*, 11 June 1870.

[54] '"A Very Bad Figure"', *The Echo*, 4 June 1870.

[55] There was to be further litigation over the costs: TNA, C16/822/S57, *Studdy v Lumley*, petition filed 29 February 1872.

[56] TNA, *Divorce and Matrimonial Causes Files*, J77/104/1594, *Lumley v Victor (falsely calling herself Lumley)*, petition filed 29 June 1870.

Alexander Victor and that he was still living when she married William.[57] Her second response was to retaliate by petitioning the same Court for a divorce on the basis of William's adultery with Ellen, coupled with his desertion of her.[58]

William's written answer to Eliza's petition illustrated that he was more focused on proving her to be in the wrong than on freeing himself from her. One can understand why he continued to deny that he was married to Eliza, and that he had not, therefore, committed adultery. After all, being the guilty party in a divorce suit had a considerable stigma attached to it. But he went further and claimed that if Eliza *was* found to be his lawful wife, she was also guilty of having committed adultery – specifically, 'in public cabs at night' in February and March 1864 with (perhaps inevitably) Lawrence Desborough.[59] If true, that would have been a bar to the Court granting her a divorce. Admittedly, it was not an absolute bar, but the court had been very sparing in exercising its discretion to grant a divorce to an adulterous petitioner. William either overlooked or ignored the fact that preventing Eliza from divorcing him would, if their marriage was valid, mean that they would never be free of each other; since his relationship with Ellen would then be adulterous, he would be equally barred from divorcing Eliza.

So everything came back to the question of whether William and Eliza were validly married. The Judge Ordinary of the Court for Divorce and Matrimonial Causes, James Hannen, having read the statements from the parties and heard from their counsel, directed that the question of fact should be tried by a special jury.[60] On 12 February 1873, that jury, having heard the evidence, found as a matter of fact that Alexander Victor was still alive on the day of William and Eliza's wedding.[61] This being the case, there was no marriage between William and Eliza to be ended by divorce, and it only remained for the Court to issue a decree of nullity.

Even then, the issuing of a decree was suspended, it being suggested that a question of law might be raised as to the validity of Eliza's first marriage to Alexander. This important point had, after all, still not been tested. But on 11 March 1873, Hannen rejected Eliza's application for a new trial on this point and pronounced the final decree of the Court annulling her marriage to William. It had taken almost a decade from the rumours about her first husband having surfaced, but William was finally free to remarry. On 3 June 1873, he obtained a licence, and he and Ellen tied the knot a week later.[62] The 1881 census found them living together in Kent with their son.[63]

From one perspective, it might appear nonsensical that Eliza's marriage to William could be annulled after her conviction had been quashed and after William had

[57] ibid, answer of respondent Eliza Lumley, filed 5 August 1870.

[58] ibid, *Lumley (Elizabeth) v Lumley (William B)*, petition filed 9 August 1870.

[59] ibid, *Lumley v Lumley*, Affidavit of the Respondent William Brownrigg Lumley, 3 September 1870.

[60] ibid.

[61] '*Lumley v Victor, falsely called Lumley*', *Evening Mail*, 14 February 1873; 'The Lumley Divorce Suit', *Western Morning News*, 14 February 1873; 'A Complicated Case', *Bristol Times & Mirror*, 15 February 1873.

[62] Ancestry, *Marriage Bonds and Allegations*, MS 10091/250; London Church of England Parish Registers, P90/JNB/023 (marriage at St John the Baptist, Kentish Town, 10 June 1873). The annulment of his first marriage meant that William was technically justified in describing himself as a bachelor, but it provides a useful reminder of how the marriage certificate doesn't necessarily give the full picture as to an individual's marital history.

[63] TNA, 1881 census: RG11/998, folio 93, p 5.

been held to be responsible for her support. But each court was deciding a different point. In the nullity proceedings, the question was simply whether it was more likely than not that Alexander Victor was still alive when Eliza married William – a lower standard of proof than applied in the criminal courts. And in the Chancery proceedings, the validity of the marriage was simply irrelevant.

In terms of its legal legacy, it was the decision of the Court for Crown Cases Reserved that was of greatest significance. *R v Lumley* established the approach to be taken where the first spouse was known to be alive within seven years of the second marriage.[64] It reaffirmed that the onus was on the prosecution to prove that the first spouse was still alive at the time of the second marriage, rather than on the accused to show reasonable grounds for believing them to be dead.[65] Evidence that the first spouse had been seen shortly before the second marriage could raise an inference that they were still alive when it took place, but the question was purely one of fact for the jury to decide, with no legal presumption either way. All this remains good law today, with *R v Lumley* still being cited in modern criminal law textbooks.[66]

'The Facts are Short and are Clearly Stated in the Case': Henry Willshire, 1881

In 1881, the Court for Crown Cases Reserved was asked to consider whether Henry Willshire should have been convicted of bigamy. The subsequent report starkly summarised the facts that had been presented to the Court:

> In 1864 W married A. In 1868 he was charged with bigamy in marrying B in 1868, his wife A being then alive, and was on such charge convicted. In 1879 he married C, and in 1880, C being then alive, he married D.[67]

The problem was that the second indictment had assumed that the 1879 marriage to 'C' was the legal marriage. But this depended on whether he was still married to 'A' in 1879. This led to some wrangling between counsel as to whether it was up to the prosecution to prove that 'A' had died by 1879 or for the defence to prove that she was still alive. The Common Serjeant decided in favour of the latter, and Henry was duly convicted.[68] Judgment was then respited while the case was referred to the Court for Crown Cases Reserved. The *Illustrated Police News* gloomily predicted that this 'scoundrel' would escape conviction, noting that the legal point 'cannot, in this case unluckily, be designated a quibble'.[69]

This prediction proved correct. Once again, there were competing presumptions at stake: the presumption of Henry's innocence versus the presumption in favour

[64] W Bruce, *Archbold's Pleading and Evidence in Criminal Cases* (London, Sweet, Stevens & Sons, 1871) 887.
[65] Whether having reasonable grounds for believing the first spouse to be dead would be a defence if they turned out to be alive after all was a separate question: see chapter 7.
[66] *Archbold: Criminal Pleading, Evidence and Practice* (Westlaw online edition, 2025), para 31-27.
[67] *R v Willshire* (1881) 6 QBD 366.
[68] *OBP*, 31 January 1881.
[69] *Illustrated Police News*, 12 February 1868.

of the validity of the 1879 marriage. On 5 March 1881, the Court for Crown Cases Reserved held that the question of whether Henry's first wife was alive should have been left to the jury, and Henry's conviction was accordingly quashed.[70]

It is hard to think of any bigamist who was less deserving of such an outcome. Behind the bland initials in the law report lay a whole history of violence and deception (and yet another marriage). There were also certain material facts that had not been brought to the attention of the court. The confident assertion by the Chief Justice, Lord Coleridge, that the facts were 'short and clearly stated in the case' was hopelessly wide of the mark, on both counts.[71]

To understand Henry's astonishing matrimonial career,[72] we need to go back to the beginning. Henry was born in 1843, the son of a farmer named Daniel Wilshin.[73] His first wedding took place in 1864, when he was 21 and his bride, Ellen Earle, just 20.[74] This was to be the only time that Henry provided accurate details to be recorded in a marriage register.

It did not take long for Henry to begin treating Ellen badly.[75] There was an incident a few months after their wedding when he grabbed her by the throat and shook her until she fell to the ground. On another occasion he kicked her so hard that her legs were bruised for weeks. During the early months of 1867, there were several nights when he locked her out of her bedroom, leaving her with nowhere to sleep. He also deprived her of food or other means of sustenance.[76]

Later, Henry was to claim that he had married beneath him. That, however, says more about his aspirations than the reality. Ellen's family was not quite as well-off as Henry's, but her father could still afford to keep a couple of servants. As one newspaper later noted, Ellen was of a 'respectable' family and 'quite the equal' of Henry in terms of her position in the world.[77] Henry, however, clearly wanted to move in more elevated circles. He joined a musical club called 'The Black Lilies', a blackface musical group for well-off young men. It was through this group that he met 17-year-old Ada Mary Susan Leslie. Ada was the daughter of a baronet, the late Sir Norman Leslie, and was due to inherit a considerable sum when she turned 21. Henry, who had assumed the fictitious surname of 'Grantley', represented himself to be a man of property. He even purported to make a settlement on Ada of some £2,000. The wedding took place at St Stephen's, Paddington, on 22 April 1868.[78] An announcement of the event

[70] *R v Willshire* (n 67).

[71] ibid 369.

[72] For discussion of Henry's parallel criminal career of white-collar crime, see GN Woolnough, 'A Victorian fraudster and bigamist: Gentleman or criminal?' (2019) 19 *Criminology & Criminal Justice* 439.

[73] Over his lifetime, Henry was to use multiple different spellings of his surname – Wilshin, Willshire – as well as different aliases. Newspaper reports added further variations, such as Wellsher. For convenience he will be referred to as Henry in the text, but variations in spelling will be noted to assist in tracing him through the different sources.

[74] Ancestry, *London Church of England Parish Registers*, P90/JNB/017 (marriage at St John the Baptist, Kentish Town, 31 March 1864, using the name of Henry Wilshin).

[75] Or, indeed, for him to start engaging in various fraudulent practices: see *OBP*, 18 September 1865.

[76] TNA, *Divorce and Matrimonial Causes Files*, J77/84/802. His cruelty in depriving her of food was also mentioned at his trial for bigamy: 'Heavy Sentence for Bigamy', *Sun*, 9 June 1868.

[77] 'The Recent Bigamy Case', *Isle of Wight Observer*, 30 May 1868.

[78] Ancestry, *London Church of England Parish Registers*, P87/STE/006.

appeared in the *Morning Post* the following day,[79] and the couple set off to the Isle of Wight for their honeymoon.

Within a few days, however, Henry's first marriage had come to light. Ada's friends went after the couple to take her away from Henry. A description of Henry was circulated in the police newspaper *Hue and Cry*, and a few weeks later he was arrested in a public house on the Mile End Road.[80] He had just tuppence on him, and had been hoping for assistance from his friends to help him leave the country.[81] At the Central Criminal Court, he pleaded guilty. The Recorder, commenting that the case displayed 'almost every possible aggravation', sentenced him to five years' penal servitude.[82]

Henry did not serve the full five years of his sentence. Instead, he was released in 1872 on a ticket of leave.[83] In August 1873, he was in the French port of Boulogne, where he met a Mrs Marshall and one of her daughters.[84] Henry's gentlemanly appearance and good manners made a good impression, as did his claim that his father had been a colonel in the 18th Hussars.[85] Upon learning that he was planning to travel along the Rhine, Mrs Marshall entrusted him with some presents for another daughter, Emily, who was at school in Koblenz.[86] Henry delivered the presents, but he also took the opportunity to woo 17-year-old Emily. The pair became engaged when she left school at the end of that year – with, it seems, the consent of her mother. Mrs Marshall then wisely decided that some further inquiries were necessary before the wedding went ahead and, on learning of Henry's history, forbade Emily to marry him.[87] Despite this, the wedding went ahead without her knowledge, at St Marylebone on 5 July 1874.[88]

Once again, the marriage quickly unravelled on account of Henry's behaviour. Emily left him before their first anniversary, prompting him to petition for restitution of conjugal rights.[89] She responded with a petition for divorce on the basis of his adultery and cruelty.[90] The allegations were all too familiar: locking her out of the room, making threats that forced her to sleep in the sitting room for three nights, and threatening to pitch her downstairs. The case took some time to resolve, partly because of Henry's attempts to deny (or alternatively justify) his conduct,[91] and partly because of the

[79] 'Marriages: Grantley-Leslie', *Morning Post*, 23 April 1868.

[80] 'Marylebone: Bigamy', *London Evening Standard*, 21 May 1868.

[81] 'The Bigamy Case: Capture and Committal of Grantley', *Hampshire Advertiser*, 30 May 1868.

[82] *OBP*, 8 June 1868 (Henry Wilshin); 'An Aggravated Case of Bigamy', *Weekly Times & Echo*, 14 June 1868.

[83] The timing of an individual's release depended on their behaviour.

[84] 'Remarkable Romantic Divorce Suit', *Echo*, 29 April 1876.

[85] 'Remarkable Divorce Suit', *Hour*, 29 April 1876.

[86] '*Willshire v Willshire*', *London Evening Standard*, 29 April 1876.

[87] 'Remarkable Divorce Suit', *Hour*, 29 April 1876.

[88] The marriage took place by licence, with Henry describing himself as a bachelor and now spelling his surname 'Willshire'. He also swore that Emily was of age – a misrepresentation which meant that he could be deprived of any financial benefit he had received as a result of the marriage.

[89] TNA, *Divorce and Matrimonial Causes Files*, J77/157/3735, petition dated 13 April 1875.

[90] ibid.

[91] ibid. Henry denied the adultery, but also alleged that Emily's 'wilful misconduct' in leaving him had 'conduced to the adultery (if any)'; he also denied cruelty, but added that if there was any it had been provoked by Emily's 'threats, violence and habitual taunts and irritating language … and her habit of self-pollution' and in any case had been condoned by her.

accompanying disputes over costs.[92] But eventually the decree was granted and made absolute in November 1876.

Given Henry's track record, it might seem surprising that he then managed to go a full three years without contracting any more marriages. The explanation for this restraint is that by December 1877 he was back in prison, having been convicted of perjury and sentenced to 18 months.[93] The perjury was linked to his non-payment of the costs of his divorce from Emily and his complex attempt to try to make it seem that ownership of various items had passed to a third party to avoid them being seized.

In 1879, a few weeks after being released from prison, Henry married Charlotte Lavers.[94] And just a year later, he went through yet another marriage ceremony, with 18-year-old Edith Maria Miller.[95] This time he managed to conceal his bigamy for a little longer, but in January 1881 he was arrested and brought before Southwark police court. He appeared resigned, telling the Inspector, 'Well, I expected as much'.[96] The evidence indicated that he had been splitting his time between Edith and Charlotte. Edith told the court that Henry generally lived with her three days each week, being away on business for the other three, and Charlotte's sister told a similar story of his relationship with Charlotte. Neither made any complaint of Henry as a husband, with Edith confirming that he had always 'behaved very kindly to her'.[97]

By the end of January he was back before the Central Criminal Court – with the results that we have already seen. The real puzzle is why the discussion focused on the question of whether his first wife, Ellen, was dead. She was still very much alive at the time of his marriage to Charlotte in 1879, and also in 1881, when her continued existence was being debated. She wasn't even that far away: the census records her as keeping a lodging house in Down Street, some three miles from the Central Criminal Court.[98] The twist was that she was no longer Henry's wife. While Henry was in prison, she had petitioned for divorce, citing his bigamy and adultery, and also giving evidence of his cruelty.[99] The decree was made absolute on 3 November 1869. As a result, Henry's 1874 marriage to Emily had been valid, and, since this marriage had been terminated by divorce, his 1879 marriage to Charlotte was also valid. So his second conviction for bigamy in marrying Edith had been justified. What makes the outcome of his case even more surprising is that the fact of his divorce from Ellen was a matter of public knowledge even before his trial.[100]

[92] ibid. Henry's failure to pay the £20 per annum that he had been required to pay while the litigation was pending led to the judge ordering that he be committed to prison for six months unless he paid at least £10.

[93] *OBP*, 10 December 1877.

[94] Ancestry, *London Church of England Parish Registers*, P81/STE1/011 (marriage at St Stephen the Martyr, Hampstead, using the name Harley Henry Willshire).

[95] *OBP*, 31 January 1881 (marriage at Trinity Church, Newington, on 23 September 1880, with Henry using the name Harley Willshire).

[96] 'Bigamy', *Southwark Mercury*, 29 January 1881.

[97] 'Career of a Bigamist', *South London Press*, 29 January 1881.

[98] TNA, 1881 census, RG11/96, folio 12 p 17.

[99] TNA, *Divorce and Matrimonial Causes Files*, J77/84/802; '*Wilshin v Wilshin*', *Morning Post*, 1 February 1969.

[100] 'Southwark: An Extraordinary Career', *London Evening Standard*, 25 January 1881; 'A Local Don Juan', *South London Observer*, 26 January 1881.

If the case had gone a different way, Henry would almost certainly have received the maximum sentence of seven years' penal servitude. While such sentences were rarely imposed by this time, his earlier conviction, his class, and his deception of both Charlotte and Edith would have counted against him.

As it was, the 1881 census saw Henry back with Charlotte.[101] But he was not to be with her for long. Within a couple of months of his conviction for bigamy being quashed, he was back at the Central Criminal Court, this time on trial for embezzlement. It was no doubt with a certain amount of satisfaction that the barrister Montagu Williams put the case for the prosecution, given that he had previously appeared for the prosecution at Henry's 1881 bigamy trial and before the Court for Crown Cases Reserved. Henry pleaded guilty and was sentenced to five years' penal servitude.[102]

This time Charlotte did not wait for Henry to be released from prison. With no means of supporting herself, in December 1881 she began a relationship with a man named Benjamin Gosling. It was Henry's turn to petition for divorce.[103] Unsurprisingly, his petition made no mention of his bigamous marriage to Edith or his prison sentence. Equally unsurprisingly, Charlotte chose not to defend the case. No doubt she was keen to be free of Henry, and she had missed her chance to divorce him for his bigamy and adultery.[104]

At the divorce hearing in November 1886, Henry did at least acknowledge that he had been sentenced to penal servitude for embezzlement in May 1881, but claimed to have 'lived happily' with Charlotte up to that date. Mr Justice Butt noted that if Henry had left Charlotte 'intentionally' and 'without excuse', he would have denied him a divorce, but took the view that offending against the criminal law was a different matter.[105] Henry was granted a decree nisi, though without being allowed costs.

But in January 1887 the Queen's Proctor intervened, on the basis that material facts – Henry's bigamous marriage to Edith, and his adultery with her and other women – had not been brought to the knowledge of the court. Henry must have known that there was no point in his trying to counter these (entirely accurate) allegations. The deadline for filing a reply came and went, but Henry made no answer. The decree nisi was duly rescinded on 22 March 1887. The result was that Charlotte remained married to Henry – in law, if not in any meaningful sense.

At least Henry's other wives were free of him. Ellen never remarried but lived with her daughter until her death in 1914. Ada, Henry's second wife, went to India, where she married John Arthur Barlow, an army officer.[106] Emily Sophia, Henry's third wife,

[101] That this was the Charlotte he had married in 1879 – and not yet another woman – is confirmed by the presence of her brother Henry: TNA, 1881 census, RG11/1355, folio 99, p 3.

[102] *OBP*, 2 May 1881.

[103] TNA, *Divorce and Matrimonial Causes Files*, J 77/351/603.

[104] Under the Matrimonial Causes Act 1857, the court could exercise its discretion not to grant a divorce to a petitioner who had committed adultery. In practice, divorces were only granted to adulterous petitioners in three very narrowly defined circumstances during the nineteenth century: see further *Double Trouble*, ch 8.

[105] '*Willshire v Willshire and Gosling*', *Lloyd's*, 7 November 1886; *Reynolds's Newspaper*, 7 November 1886.

[106] Ancestry, *War Office: Records of Officers' Services*, WO 76/181, noting the marriage as taking place at Bangalore on 30 March 1873.

also went to India after her divorce from Henry, marrying there in 1883.[107] Sadly, Edith Maria, the last of Henry's wives, died in 1883, aged just 21.[108]

Henry's case does have implications for the way in which we view the resort to divorce in late nineteenth-century England and Wales, and how it intersected with bigamy. It shows that there is not a neat relationship between the number of divorces and the number of individuals concerned. Henry alone accounted for two divorces and a further unsuccessful petition, two bigamy trials, and one unsuccessful petition for restitution of conjugal rights. Nor was this overlap between divorce and bigamy unique.[109] It is also worth noting that in one respect nineteenth-century wives had an advantage over their modern counterparts. Henry's third wife Emily had been able to petition for divorce within the first year of their marriage,[110] there being then no bar to doing so.[111] Reading divorce petitions like hers, retaining such a bar nowadays seems difficult to justify.

[107] Ancestry, *India, Select Marriages, 1792-1948* (marriage at Saugor, Bengal, on 21 May 1883).
[108] 'Deaths', *Morning Advertiser*, 15 June 1883.
[109] For further examples, see R Probert, *Double trouble: the rise and fall of the crime of bigamy* (London, Selden Society, 2015).
[110] Her petition was filed on 25 April 1875: TNA, *Divorce and Matrimonial Causes Files*, J77/157/3735.
[111] On the time bar, see further chapter 5.

5

The Defence of 'Divorce'

From a modern perspective, it might seem obvious that a person who has obtained a divorce is not guilty of bigamy if they go on to remarry. In 1604, however, this proposition was rather more controversial. To contemporaries, 'divorce' could mean either of two remedies granted by the church courts. One was an annulment declaring that there was no valid marriage to begin with: a divorce *a vinculo matrimonii* ('from the bond of marriage').[1] The second was an authorised separation: a divorce *a mensa et thoro* (literally 'from table and bed', although the more alliterative 'from bed and board' is often used). This could be granted to allow either a husband or wife to live apart from an unfaithful or violent spouse.[2] In other words, divorce in the modern sense of a decree legally terminating a valid marriage did not exist. Just to add to the terminological confusion, not every decree authorising the parties to separate was referred to as a divorce *a mensa et thoro*, and over time divorce *a vinculo matrimonii* came to refer to divorce in the sense with which we are now familiar. For simplicity, then, I will refer to annulments and separation orders, and, except when quoting from primary sources, will use the term divorce only in its modern sense.

One of the primary sources to use the term 'divorced' was the Bigamy Act 1604 itself. Scholars have suggested that it was ambiguous as to which of the two meanings noted above was intended.[3] But the exception in the Act for those 'divorced by any sentence had or hereafter to be had in the ecclesiastical court' sat alongside an exception for those whose former marriage had been declared by the ecclesiastical court 'to be void and of no effect' – that is to say, whose marriage had been annulled.[4] Given this separate provision dealing with annulment, 'divorced' here had to refer to a separation order.[5] In other words, people who remarried after an annulment *or* a separation order were not guilty of the crime of bigamy under the 1604 Act.

[1] This was the sense in which Henry VIII was 'divorced' from Catherine of Aragon, Anne Boleyn and Anne of Cleves: KJ Kesselring and T Stretton, *Marriage, Separation and Divorce in England, 1500-1700* (Oxford, Oxford University Press, 2022).

[2] M Ingram, 'Breaking Vows: Adultery, Marital Ill-Treatment, and Divorce in England, 1450-1650' in JM Ferraro (ed), *A Cultural History of Marriage in the Renaissance and Early Modern Age* (London, Bloomsbury Academic, 2020).

[3] B Capp, 'Bigamous Marriage in Early Modern England' (2009) 52 *The Historical Journal* 537. See also L Stone, *Road to Divorce: England 1530-1987* (Oxford, Oxford University Press, 1990) 306–07, who refers to the 'calculated ambiguity' of the Act.

[4] Bigamy Act 1604, s 3.

[5] See further *Double Trouble*, ch 2.

There was nonetheless an important difference between annulment and separation when it came to remarriage. A marriage after an annulment was valid, for the simple reason that the annulment effectively wiped out the first 'marriage', declaring that it had never existed in the first place. By contrast, a remarriage after a separation order was void, since the first marriage was still ongoing. In the light of this, it might seem odd that a separation order was a defence to a charge of bigamy at all. But from the vantage point of 1604 it made sense. The previous half century had in fact seen considerable debate and uncertainty about the possibility of remarrying after a separation order. As of 1604, it had only just been settled that such a remarriage would not be valid, but there were still plenty who argued that it should be. And bigamy, it may be recalled, was a capital offence. It accordingly made sense to be generous with the provision of defences.

The first two case studies illustrate the debate over the impact of a separation order. Penelope Rich, who remarried in 1605 after her husband obtained a separation order on the basis of her adultery, was never prosecuted. Margaret Porter, who obtained a separation order on the basis of her husband's cruelty, *was* prosecuted, but my reading of her case is that it was the ground on which the separation order was granted that was the issue here. There was also one matrimonial remedy that was not mentioned in the 1604 Act at all – the decree of jactitation. What this was, and how it featured in one of the most spectacular divorce trials of the eighteenth century, is the topic of the third case study, that of the Duchess of Kingston in 1776. Less controversial, although just as unique in its own way, was the 1814 case of John Troop Juert, who was acquitted upon proof that his first marriage had been annulled.

The final four case studies all involve different kinds of divorce – ones obtained outside England and Wales in the cases of William Martin Lolley in 1812 and Earl Russell in 1901, and the changing rules on separation orders and a private Act of Parliament in the 1838 case of Arthur Battersby. And right at the end of our period, in December 2024, the Family Court was faced with the problem of 79 divorces that technically should not have been granted at all. So we will end as we began, with the question of the status of a marriage following a 'divorce'.

Remarrying after a Divorce *A Mensa Et Thoro*: Penelope Rich, 1605

Much has been written about the life of Penelope Rich, née Devereux.[6] She was a lady in waiting to Elizabeth I, an inspiration for various poets, and has been described as 'probably the most famous woman in Elizabethan England apart from the Queen'.[7] My focus, however, is on just one incident in her life – the ceremony of marriage that she went through on Boxing Day 1605, with Charles Mountjoy, just six weeks

[6] See eg S Varlow, *The Lady Penelope: The Lost Tale of Love and Politics in the Court of Elizabeth I* (London, Andre Deutsch, 2007); J Rickman, *Love, Lust and Licence in Early Modern England: Illicit Sex and the Nobility* (Aldershot, Ashgate, 2008) ch 3, who also reviews the extensive literature on Penelope's relationship with Charles Blount.

[7] G Quealy, 'Astrophil's Star: Locating Penelope Rich in the Sidney Constellation' (2023) 41 *Sidney Journal* 23.

after her first husband had obtained a separation order in the church court on the basis of her adultery.[8]

This wedding was clearly in defiance of the canon law of the Church of England. Revised only the previous year, the new canons had made it clear that a separation order did not permit either party to remarry:

> In all sentences pronounced only for divorce and separation *a thoro et mensa*, there shall be a caution and restraint inserted in the act of the said sentence, that the parties so separated shall live chastely and continently; neither shall they, during each other's life, contract matrimony with any other person. And for the better observation of this last clause, the said sentence of divorce shall not be pronounced until the party or parties requiring the same have given good and sufficient caution and security into the court, that they will not any way break or transgress the said restraint or prohibition.[9]

Nonetheless, Charles was quite insistent that he and Penelope were entitled to marry. To understand his point of view, we need to look back to the debates and precedents of the previous half century.

Over the course of the sixteenth century, all other Protestant states across Europe – including Scotland – had made provision for marriage to be ended by divorce.[10] During the reign of Edward VI, various reforms had been proposed, but his early death (and the accession of his Catholic half-sister Mary) stymied the possibility of these being enacted. There was, however, the precedent of William Parr, whose remarriage following a separation order had been retrospectively declared valid by private Act of Parliament.[11] There had also been occasional cases where remarriages after a separation order had been implicitly authorised by the Church: that of Sir John Stawell in 1572, who was granted a licence to remarry by the Archbishop of Canterbury, and that of Bishop Thornborough of Limerick, granted a dispensation by the Archbishop of York in the 1590s.[12]

So Charles' argument was not without precedent. Not that he relied on these more recent examples: his 28-page disquisition took the reader back to the Garden of Eden, and then through various Biblical passages on divorce and how they had been interpreted by various learned writers.[13] He was somewhat selective in his citation of legal material, relying on an Act passed during the time of Henry VIII to argue that any marriage not prohibited 'by the law of God' was lawful under English law without

[8] Varlow (n 6) 246; Rickman (n 6) 111.

[9] Canon 107: G Bray (ed), *The Anglican Canons, 1529-1947* (Woodbridge, Boydell & Brewer, 1998) 407. Any church court judge who failed to make the order in the required form was to be suspended from office for a year and any such order would be invalid: canon 108.

[10] R Philips, *Putting Asunder: A history of divorce in Western society* (Cambridge, Cambridge University Press, 1988) 40; S Lettmaier, 'Marriage Formation in Europe from the Late Middle Ages until the Late Eighteenth Century' in R Probert and S Thompson (eds), *Research Handbook on Marriage and Cohabitation* (Cheltenham, Edward Elgar, 2024).

[11] Or, rather, declared valid under Edward, invalid under Mary, and valid again under Elizabeth.

[12] See respectively Sir L Dibdin and Sir C Chadwyck Healey, *English Church Law and Divorce* (London, John Murray, 1912) 84–92; AL Rowse, 'Bishop Thornborough: A Clerical Careerist' in R Ollard and P Tudor-Craig (eds), *For Veronica Wedgwood These: Studies in Seventeenth-Century History* (London, Collins, 1986) 92.

[13] BL Additional MS 4149 fols 306–19.

acknowledging the specific context in which this applied.[14] He also wrote a somewhat fawning letter to James I in which he alternated between arguing that he was justified in remarrying and asking the King's forgiveness for having done so.[15] Here too he was somewhat selective, pleading that Penelope – referred to as simply a 'lady of great Birth and virtue' – had first been pressurised into marrying Robert Rich and then into confessing to adultery with a nameless stranger in order for him to obtain a separation order.[16] As he concluded:

> if before God the want of consent doth make a nullity in marriage and the not performing the duties doth break the conditions of marriage, and ... if a sentence of divorce be a judicial separation not prohibited by the law of God, this lady remaineth divers ways free from her Bond.[17]

Charles' vigorous defence illustrates how the debate about the possibility of remarrying after a separation order persisted even after 1604. It was, however, unpersuasive, and his marriage to Penelope was not accepted as valid.[18] But for present purposes its significance lies in the fact that Penelope was not prosecuted for bigamy.[19] After Charles' death in April 1606, his heir subsequently brought charges against Penelope in the Court of Star Chamber, alleging forgery and fraud.[20] It seems unlikely that he would have foregone the opportunity of prosecuting her for bigamy if this had been an option. The obvious answer is that it was not, and that from the start contemporaries read the 1604 Act as exempting those who were separated by virtue of a divorce *a mensa et thoro*.[21]

An Equally Invalid and Possibly not Bigamous Remarriage: Margaret Porter, 1636

The precise scope of the exception for those who had been 'divorced' came to be tested in the 1636 case of Margaret Porter. Margaret had obtained a separation order on the ground of the cruelty of her husband, Richard Porter. The sentence of the ecclesiastical court contained the usual provision against remarriage. Despite this, six months later Margaret married Thomas Rooke, and found herself indicted for bigamy.

For the Crown, it was argued that Margaret's remarriage was not within the exception envisaged by the 1604 Act: the word '*divorciamus*' had not, it was noted,

[14] The Act cited was the Marriage Act 1540, which dealt with the prohibited degrees of marriage – on which see further the case study of James Chadwick in chapter 3.

[15] BL Lansdowne MS 885 fol 93.

[16] The separation order was indeed based on Penelope's adultery with an unnamed man, but since Charles had been having an affair with Penelope since 1590 and had had five children by her, it was rather disingenuous to imply that the allegations of adultery had been fabricated.

[17] BL Lansdowne MS 885 fol 93.

[18] Rickman (n 6) 130.

[19] T Stretton, 'Marriage, separation and the common law in England, 1540-1660' in H Berry and E Foyster (eds), *The Family in Early Modern England* (Cambridge, Cambridge University Press, 2007) 35 notes that Penelope was not prosecuted for bigamy but not why.

[20] Varlow (n 6) 260; Rickman (n 6) 136.

[21] Other contemporary sources support this: see *Double Trouble*, ch 2.

appeared in the sentence handed down by the ecclesiastical court. It was also argued, more radically, that the term 'divorced' did not include mere separations but was limited to divorces *a vinculo matrimonii*, that is to say, annulments.[22] Against this, Margaret's counsel argued that it was annulments that were improperly termed divorces, and that in this context 'divorced' in the Act meant a divorce *a mensa et thoro*, whether granted on the basis of adultery or cruelty. They acknowledged that the canons had clarified that it was not possible to remarry after a separation order but argued that 'an ignorant woman'[23] could not be expected to know that. In any case, regardless of the validity of the second marriage, they contended that the meaning of the statute was that 'such persons marrying shall not be in danger to be felons'.[24]

The very fact that defence counsel were deployed to argue Margaret's case tells us that there was an important legal issue to be determined. At this time, defence counsel were only permitted to make submissions as to the law, and even this was not common.[25] There had to be what the legal commentator William Hawkins later described as some 'point of law … proper to be debated'.[26] Equally, it is important to read the arguments of counsel through the lens of the adversarial system. Then as now, the desire to win a case might lead counsel to advance all possible arguments, however spurious some of them might be. Viewed as a whole, it seems clear that the key issue being argued was the narrower one of whether a separation granted on the basis of a spouse's cruelty should be treated in the same way as one granted on the basis of their adultery.

There was, after all, some justification for viewing the two differently. Granting a separation order on account of one spouse's cruelty could be justified as being necessary for the other's protection. As one judge commented in a case heard a few years later, it was 'only a temporal separation until the anger past'.[27] But cruelty was not seen as striking at the heart of a marriage in the way that adultery did. Plenty of contemporary commentators continued to argue that adultery should dissolve a marriage,[28] drawing on the Gospel of Matthew, where Jesus responds to the Pharisees' questions by saying that a man who divorced his wife and remarried on any ground other than her 'fornication' would be committing adultery.[29] No one made that argument in relation to cruelty. Besides, adultery had a very clear and obvious definition, whereas cruelty did not.

That Margaret's case was solely about the scope of the exception, rather than any more fundamental question as to whether 'divorced' denoted a separation order, also makes sense of the court's response. The Court of King's Bench did not express any

[22] *Porter's Case* (1636) Cro Car 461; 79 ER 1000.
[23] ibid at 1000–01.
[24] ibid at 1000.
[25] JH Langbein, *The Origins of Adversary Criminal Trial* (Oxford, Oxford University Press, 2003, ppbk 2005) 26.
[26] W Hawkins, *A treatise of the pleas of the Crown: Book II* (London, 1721) 400.
[27] *Williams' case* (1641) March, NR 101; 82 ER 430.
[28] For discussion of contemporary attitudes to female adultery see A Fletcher, *Gender, Sex & Subordination in England 1500-1800* (New Haven, Yale University Press, 1995) 109–10.
[29] Matthew 19:9.

doubts as to the meaning of 'divorced',[30] merely whether Margaret's case fell within the scope of the exception. It noted that 'if this should be suffered, many would be divorced upon such pretence, and instantly marry again, whereby many inconveniences would ensue'. In other words, if Margaret were simply allowed to remarry after obtaining a separation order on the ground of Richard's cruelty, this might open up a route out of marriage for any woman who alleged the same. She was advised 'not to insist upon the law, but to procure a pardon to avoid the danger'.[31]

The word 'pretence' is particularly telling here. It needs to be seen in the context of a long history of judicial scepticism about female claims of male violence. It might suggest that male judges were concerned about women making false or exaggerated claims in order to obtain the sanction of the church courts for their separation and escape conviction for bigamy if they remarried. It might also simply indicate that no degree of violence was deemed a sufficient excuse in these circumstances. To put it more bluntly, this was a case in which the gender of the accused was key. It was, after all, wives rather than husbands who sought separation on the ground of cruelty.[32] Lest that seem unduly cynical, it is worth bearing in mind that 300 years were to elapse after Margaret Porter's case before Parliament legislated to make cruelty a ground for divorce.[33]

Other contemporary cases confirm that there was no question about the effect of a separation order based on a spouse's adultery. Thomas Middleton, whose case was heard at the Newgate Sessions a few months after Margaret Porter's trial, similarly produced a separation order, but his was on the ground of adultery, and it was readily agreed that he had a good defence to the charge of bigamy.[34] A few years later, in the case of one Williams in 1641, it was similarly resolved 'without argument' that a person who had obtained a separation order on the ground of adultery fell within the exception set out in the 1604 Act.[35] While the reports of these cases contain conflicting accounts of Margaret Porter's case,[36] that should not distract from the central point: it was clearly accepted that a person granted a separation order on the basis of their spouse's adultery was not guilty of bigamy.[37]

[30] cf Capp (n 3) 539, whose suggestion that the judges 'admitted that they too were unsure of the statute's meaning' is a very loose and misleading paraphrase of the report.

[31] *Porter's Case* (n 22) 1001.

[32] See eg L Gowing, *Domestic Dangers: Women, Words and Sex in Early Modern England* (Oxford, Clarendon Press, 1996) ch 6.

[33] As a result of the Matrimonial Causes Act 1937. That is not to suggest that wife-beating was accepted: for contemporary examples of condemnation, see Fletcher (n 28) 113; J Bailey, '"I dye [sic] by Inches": locating wife beating in the concept of a privatization of marriage and violence in eighteenth-century England' (2006) 31 *Social History* 273, 278.

[34] *R v Thomas Middleton* (1636) Kel J 27; 84 ER 1066.

[35] *William's case* (1641) March, NR 101; 82 ER 430.

[36] The five-line report of Middleton's case (n 34) suggested that the judges had decided that a divorce *causa sævitiæ* had been 'adjudged to excuse from the statute' in what it referred to as 'Rooke's case'. The slightly longer report of Williams' case (n 35) noted that the judges had resolved that such a divorce was not within the proviso to the statute, although it also reported Heath J as referring to a divorce *causa adulterii* as one *a vinculo matrimonii*. Kesselring and Stretton (n 1) 83 note that '[i]f March's report is accurate, it is astounding: Robert Heath, former attorney general and future chief justice, maintaining that adultery *did* allow full divorce and remarriage'. If this was Heath's view, it was not the general interpretation of the law.

[37] See also Sir M Hale, *Pleas of the Crown* (London, 1677) 104, noting that a remarriage was no felony if it be 'after a divorce, though *a mensa et thoro* only'.

A Decree of Jactitation: The Duchess of Kingston, 1776

In 1744, a wedding took place in the parish of Lainston in Hampshire. The bride was Elizabeth Chudleigh, a maid of honour to the Princess of Wales, and her new husband was Augustus John Hervey. Although the ceremony was conducted by the local rector, the Reverend Thomas Amis, in other respects it failed to comply with the requirements of the canon law, being celebrated without banns or licence in a private chapel late one summer evening.[38] The fact that the marriage had been celebrated so quietly allowed them to keep it a secret, enabling Elizabeth to continue in her role at court while Augustus pursued his naval career.[39]

Within a few years, however, both had regretted their marriage, and Elizabeth had begun a relationship with the Duke of Kingston. By 1768 Augustus was contemplating divorcing Elizabeth by obtaining a private Act of Parliament. To pre-empt this, Elizabeth sought a decree of jactitation. This was a specific action designed to silence one person from falsely claiming to be married to another, its name deriving from the Latin *jactitare*, 'to boast'. There were three possible defences that a respondent could make. First, they could deny that they had ever claimed to be married to the petitioner. Second, they could admit that they had made such a claim but show that the petitioner had acquiesced in them making it. And third, they could seek to establish the veracity of their claim, by showing that a marriage had in fact taken place. Augustus, however, made no defence, and on 10 February 1769, the London Consistory Court duly declared that Elizabeth was free from all matrimonial contracts with him. Less than a month later, on 8 March 1769, she went through a ceremony of marriage with the Duke, by virtue of a special licence granted by the Archbishop of Canterbury.

But when the Duke died in 1773, leaving Elizabeth all his property, his family instigated proceedings for bigamy against her. There might have been difficult questions about where Elizabeth should be tried, had it not been for the fact that Augustus was now the Earl of Bristol. This meant that Elizabeth was a peeress, whichever of her marriages was valid, and so entitled to be tried by the House of Lords rather than in a normal criminal court.[40] On 15 April 1776, Elizabeth pleaded not guilty, arguing that the sentence of the London Consistory Court conclusively determined that she was not married to Augustus and so had been free to marry the Duke. Over the next three days, the most eminent lawyers of the day lined up to argue for or against this proposition.

Those representing Elizabeth argued that the church courts were the proper, indeed the only, forum to decide the validity of a marriage. One acknowledged that marriages might be 'incidentally' determined in the common law courts, but added 'it will not be found, that where the proper forum has given a decision upon the point,

[38] C Gervat, *Elizabeth: The Scandalous Life of the Duchess of Kingston* (London, Century, 2003) 28.

[39] For an account of Elizabeth's colourful life, see E Mavor, *The Virgin Mistress: A Study in Survival: The Life of the Duchess of Kingston* (London, Chatto & Windus, 1964).

[40] *The Trial of Elizabeth, Duchess Dowager of Kingston, for Bigamy* (London, 1776).

the common law courts have ever taken it upon themselves to question the validity of the sentence'.[41] On this basis, as long as a decree of jactitation of marriage was in place, it was conclusive evidence that the parties were not married. Another pointed out that the existence of the decree meant that Augustus could not be obliged to support Elizabeth, and that it would be harsh if the only purpose for which their marriage were to be recognised was to enable her to be prosecuted as a felon. Allegations of collusion between Elizabeth and Augustus were noted but denied; in any case, it was argued, it was for the church courts to investigate and if necessary set aside the decree of jactitation.

On the other side, the Attorney General, Lord Thurlow, launched a full-frontal attack on the authority of the church courts, arguing that decisions 'given by the bishop or his official of his own mere authority in matrimonial causes, have the least pretence of all others to bind or influence any question which may arise afterwards in judicature'.[42] Such pronouncements, he added, punished no crime, tried no right, and had no civil effects, being merely *pro salute animae rei* – a matter of the salvation of the soul. This effectively framed the church courts as operating in a different sphere from the *real* legal system. While Thurlow acknowledged that their decisions would be binding on the parties to them, he rejected the idea that a decree of jactitation could preclude a criminal court from investigating the marriage – especially where, as here, it was alleged to have been obtained by collusion. He also mocked the other side's suggestion that only the church court had jurisdiction to investigate the allegation of collusion, pointing out that the court on which the fraud had been practised, and which had 'overlooked such circumstances as appear on the very face of these proceedings', was hardly the place where one would choose to send the question to be tried.[43] Next up was the Solicitor General, Alexander Wedderburn, who was no less critical of what he termed the 'singular' decree of jactitation. Quoting the very phrase that concluded such decrees – 'as far as yet appears, no marriage is proved' – he argued that the sentence did not even purport to be conclusive and could be reopened at any time if new evidence emerged.[44] As a result, he contended, there was 'no incongruity in supposing that the sentence may stand as between the parties, and yet shall have no conclusion either as to the public, or as to third parties'.[45]

The question was then put to the judges. Their unanimous opinion was that no decree of jactitation could be regarded as conclusive so as to preclude the marriage in question being established in an indictment for bigamy. Such a decree, after all, only proved that it did not appear that the parties were married – which might or might not be true. They also took the view that decisions about criminal liability belonged 'solely and peculiarly' to the common law.[46]

The real business of the trial then began. Thurlow, putting the case for the prosecution, was just as vituperative in his comments on Elizabeth's character as he had been in undermining the role of the church courts. Various witnesses were

[41] ibid 4.
[42] ibid 53.
[43] ibid 60.
[44] ibid 68.
[45] ibid.
[46] ibid 169.

called to give details of the wedding of Elizabeth and Augustus. A former maid, Ann Cradock, confirmed that she had been present at the wedding in 1744 and subsequently seen them in bed together.[47] The court surgeon Caesar Hawkins, who had delivered Elizabeth's child, said that they had acknowledged themselves to be husband and wife to him.[48] And the widow of the Reverend Amis reported that he had told her that he had conducted the ceremony and – even more damningly – that Elizabeth had visited Lainston in 1759 to ask for a copy of the register.[49]

On the final day of the trial, Elizabeth had an opportunity to speak. She continued to plead that credit should be given to a decree of jactitation,[50] arguing that such decrees were 'a more effectual divorce and separation of the parties' than those which had been judged to fall within the exception in the 1604 Act.[51] This was a valid point, given that a remarriage after a decree of jactitation would usually be presumed to be valid, whereas a remarriage after a separation order would not be. She also argued that even if the decree was not binding on other courts, she at least had been entitled to rely on it. She had, as one witness confirmed, consulted a civilian lawyer, who had advised her and the Duke that they could marry following the decree of jactitation. As she concluded, 'a criminal and felonious Intent' had to be proved, and she could not be guilty in 'following the Advice I received, and in doing what in my conscience I thought was an authorized and innocent act'.[52]

Their Lordships took a different view. One after another, 161 peers delivered the simple and stark verdict: 'Guilty, upon my honour'.[53] Only the Duke of Newcastle tempered this by adding 'erroneously, but not intentionally'.[54] No one else made any reference to the issue of criminal intent. This was unsurprising, not least because the facts hardly provided a promising test-case for arguments about intention and conscience. After all, even if Elizabeth had genuinely believed that the decree of jactitation permitted her to remarry, she knew that it had only been granted because key facts had been kept from the London Consistory Court. More fundamentally, the idea that intention might be a necessary component of the offence of bigamy had yet to be established. It was to be almost two centuries before an honest and reasonable belief that one was free to remarry was fully accepted as a defence.[55]

There was a final lengthy debate as to how Elizabeth should be punished. The Attorney General argued that she should be subject to the same punishment as any other convicted bigamist, that of branding.[56] Her defence team pointed out in return that any peer so convicted would not suffer such punishment and argued that as a peeress Elizabeth should be entitled to the same exemption. The latter argument prevailed, and Elizabeth was free to leave, unscathed.[57]

[47] ibid 109–10.
[48] ibid 120.
[49] ibid 131.
[50] ibid 140.
[51] ibid 141.
[52] ibid 142.
[53] ibid 154–56.
[54] ibid 155.
[55] See further chapter 7.
[56] *Trial* (n 40) 160.
[57] ibid 166. On branding as the sole form of punishment at this time, see *Double Trouble*, ch 4. On Elizabeth's subsequent life, see Gervat (n 38).

Given that Elizabeth had clearly gone through two ceremonies of marriage, and given that the Bigamy Act 1604 made no reference to decrees of jactitation in its list of exceptions, it might seem to be obvious that she would (and should) be found guilty. But behind the lengthy arguments in her case was an even bigger debate: the relative authority of the church courts vis-à-vis the secular courts. It was to take another 80 years, but eventually the church courts were to lose jurisdiction over marriage altogether.

In the meantime, however, they still had the power to grant decrees of nullity – which, unlike the decree of jactitation, did ensure that a subsequent remarriage was not bigamous. And this brings us on to our next case study.

A Just-in-Time Annulment: John Troop Juert, 1814

On 12 July 1814, John Troop Juert, alias Charles Cox, was tried for bigamy at the Old Bailey.[58] It was one of the quicker trials to be heard that day. A decree of the ecclesiastical court was produced, which stated that his first marriage had been declared to be 'null and void', and John was 'honorably acquitted'.[59] This was hardly surprising. An annulment effectively wiped out the first marriage, meaning that, in the eyes of the law, it had never existed. Moreover, the Bigamy Act of 1604 had explicitly provided that no felony was committed 'where the former Marriage hath been or hereafter shall be by Sentence in the Ecclesiastical Court declared to be void and of no Effect'.[60] So the real puzzle is why John's case came to trial in the first place.

Digging into the history of John's case soon provided the answer. John had actually been committed for trial five months earlier, in February of 1814.[61] As one report of his trial noted, his case had then been postponed 'to give time for the production of certain documents necessary for his defence'.[62] The word 'production' might suggest that it was just a matter of bringing the relevant paperwork to the court. As it turned out, John had not obtained an annulment of his first marriage before entering into his second. He only sought one after he had been charged with bigamy.

John's first marriage, to a woman going by the name of Amelia Jenkins, had taken place by licence in February 1808.[63] But 'Amelia' was not her real name: she was Martha Kay, and had married in a false name so that she would not lose the payments to which she was entitled as the widow of a naval officer.[64] Given that the marriage was by licence, the fact that she had used a false name was immaterial.[65] But John was only 17 at the time of that first marriage, meaning that he needed parental consent. He was

[58] *OBP*, 6 July 1814; *Morning Chronicle*, 13 July 1814.

[59] *OBP*, 6 July 1814; *Sun*, 13 July 1814.

[60] Bigamy Act 1604, s 3.

[61] TNA, *Newgate Prison Calendar*, HO 77/21, February 1814. He was committed on the oath of the second wife.

[62] *Sun*, 13 July 1814.

[63] Ancestry, *London Church of England Parish Registers* (marriage at St Mary, Newington, 16 February 1808).

[64] *Morning Post*, 12 February 1812.

[65] Using a false name was only material where the marriage was by banns: see R Probert, 'The Judicial Interpretation of Lord Hardwicke's Act of 1753' (2002) 23 *Journal of Legal History* 129.

also illegitimate – meaning that there was, in the eyes of the law, no parent able to give such consent.[66] All this meant that the only person who would have been able to consent to John's first marriage would have been a guardian appointed by the Court of Chancery,[67] and no such guardian had been appointed.

We do not know exactly when John and Amelia/Martha separated.[68] But on 23 November 1812 John went through a ceremony of marriage with Mary Loy at St Margaret's church in Westminster, describing himself as a bachelor.[69] He also gave a different name – that of Charles Cox. This, however, was not due to any attempt at concealment. It appears that he had been re-christened to avoid any ambiguity about his 'true' name. Mary's parents knew of his former marriage, and acted as John/Charles' sponsors at his christening.[70]

In February 1814, however, Mary prosecuted him for bigamy. John put in an affidavit and managed to get his trial deferred.[71] He then petitioned the London Consistory Court for an annulment of his first marriage.[72] But getting an annulment was not something that could be achieved in a matter of days or even weeks. John's trial had to be postponed more than once.[73] During all this time he remained in Newgate gaol.[74]

On 8 July, his case finally came before Sir William Scott at Doctors' Commons. Once it had been established that John had married by licence when he was underage and without the required consent being given, the outcome was inevitable. Scott did note the need for careful consideration where the person seeking to set aside the marriage was the very same person who had obtained the licence in the first place. Nonetheless, given that the 'material facts' had been established, he had no option but to declare the marriage to be null and void.[75]

It was just in time. Three days later, John was finally put on trial for bigamy at the Old Bailey. His case is the only example that I have found of someone accused of bigamy producing a decree of nullity in relation to their first marriage. The reason is a very simple one: an individual would not be committed for trial in the first place if they could produce a decree from the ecclesiastical court confirming that their first marriage had been annulled. Had John obtained an annulment *before* he married Mary, he would have been spared several months in gaol.

[66] See *Horner v Liddiard* (1799) 1 Hag Con 337, 357; 161 ER 573, in which Sir William Scott had held that the 'privilege' of giving consent should not be given to 'those who bear the title of parents not as a title of honour and privilege, but of discredit and disability'.

[67] Clandestine Marriages Act 1753, s 11.

[68] The only child of the couple that I have been able to trace was baptised in December 1808: Ancestry, *Westminster Church of England Parish Registers*, SA/PR/A/3 (baptism of Eliza Amelia Juert, the daughter of John and Amelia Juert).

[69] Ancestry, *Registers and Books of St Margaret's Church, Westminster*, MA/01/03/008. The *Proceedings* recorded the second wife as Mary Lloyd, but the *Newgate Prison Calendar* gave her surname as Loy, allowing the marriage to be traced.

[70] *Morning Post*, 12 February 1812.

[71] TNA, *Newgate Prison Calendar*, HO 77/21, February 1814.

[72] London Archives, DL/C/0574/002-003.

[73] TNA, *Newgate Prison Calendar*, HO 77/21.

[74] TNA, *Metropolitan Police: Criminal Record Office: Habitual Criminals Registers and Miscellaneous Papers*, PCOM 2.

[75] *Juert, otherwise Cox v Kay, otherwise Jenkins*, *Morning Chronicle*, 9 July 1814.

A Scottish Divorce: William Martin Lolley, 1812

In the first decade of the nineteenth century, a steady trickle of English litigants began to seek divorces in the Scottish courts. Some of these litigants had married in Scotland, or had lived there, or were married to a Scot. Others had a more tenuous connection with Scotland, just sufficient to fulfil the requirement of 40 days' residence necessary for the Scottish courts to exercise jurisdiction.[76] Most were women, effectively barred from obtaining a divorce from even the most flagrantly adulterous husband in England. Even the granting of the first Parliamentary divorce to Mrs Jane Addison in 1801 gave little hope that other women would be able to succeed: Jane's husband had run off with her sister, and the incestuous nature of his adultery was a key factor.[77] By contrast, in Scotland, divorce was available to husbands and wives equally, on the grounds of either adultery or desertion.[78]

Such litigants might well have assumed that these divorces would be recognised by English law. After all, Scottish marriages were recognised by English law, even where the parties were not resident in Scotland but had eloped there to take advantage of its more liberal marriage laws.[79] This reflected the general principle that the status of a marriage was determined by the law of the place where it was celebrated. It would have been logical to assume that the same principle would apply to divorces, and that the parties would therefore be free to remarry.

This assumption was to prove ill-founded, as William Martin Lolley found to his cost. His first marriage, to Ann Swaine, had taken place at St Nicholas' church in Liverpool in 1802.[80] Ann was a little older than the 22-year-old William and had already been married.[81] She and William had already had a child together,[82] and several more followed: Sarah in 1803, Charles in 1805, John in 1806, and George in 1809.[83] A final daughter, Ann, must have been conceived in the summer of 1811.[84] But by November that year Ann was petitioning for divorce from the Edinburgh Commissary Court on the ground of William's adultery.

[76] This period created 'a presumptive domicile': see L Leneman, 'English Marriages and Scottish Divorces in the Early Nineteenth Century' (1996) 17 *Journal of Legal History* 225 for a discussion of the evolving case law on this point. As the deputy clerk of the Commissary Court of Scotland noted, some judges were of the view that it was sufficient if the offence – ie the adultery – was committed in Scotland and the party cited resided there, without any previous residence: *R v William Martin Lolley* (1812) Russ & Ry 237; 168 ER 779.

[77] D Wright, '"Well-Behaved Women Don't Make History": Rethinking Family, Law, and History Through an Analysis of the First Nine Years of the English Divorce and Matrimonial Causes Court (1858-1866)' (2005) *Wisconsin Women's Law Journal* 211.

[78] G Black, 'The significance of sex in Scots Civil Law' (2024) 36 *Child and Family Law Quarterly* 321.

[79] *Ilderton v Ilderton* (1793) 2 H Bl 145; 126 ER 476. On the phenomenon of elopements to Gretna Green, see R Probert, *Marriage Law and Practice in the Long Eighteenth Century: A Reassessment* (Cambridge, Cambridge University Press, 2009).

[80] Ancestry, *Liverpool Church of England Parish Registers*, 283 NIC/3/7.

[81] Her marriage to James Swainey had taken place on 28 March 1799 at St Peter's church in Liverpool: Ancestry, *Lancashire, England, Church of England Marriages and Banns, 1754-1936*.

[82] William Martin, born on 2 November 1801 and baptised the following year.

[83] Ancestry, *Liverpool Church of England Parish Registers*, 283-PET-2-13.

[84] She was born in Liverpool on 24 February 1812: Ancestry, *England, Select Births and Christenings, 1538-1975*.

The Commissioners had some reservations about hearing the case, noting that the parties were English and that the marriage had been celebrated in England. Ann was accordingly asked to justify why the case fell within their jurisdiction. The file in the National Records of Scotland contains almost 20 pages of argument on this point. In addition to citing various precedents, it was argued that Scotland was where William had violated his marriage vows, and that to deny Ann the remedy allowed by Scots law would be to allow individuals to commit adultery with impunity. It was also argued that even if William had deliberately chosen to commit adultery in Scotland because of its more liberal approach to divorce, this should not 'contaminate the rights of the innocent party to demand ... redress'. The Commissioners were persuaded to hear the case, and their decree ending William and Ann's marriage was granted on 20 March 1812.[85]

Less than three weeks later, the *Liverpool Mercury* ran a small item noting the decision of the Edinburgh court, adding that the divorce 'enables the parties to marry again'.[86] Four pages later came the announcement that William had already remarried – on 25 March, just five days after the divorce had been granted.[87] He had obtained a licence from the ecclesiastical authorities in Cheshire and married Ellen Hunter in Liverpool.[88]

The months that followed were dogged by problems for William. In June he was declared bankrupt.[89] By July it appears he had lost his home, with an advertisement inviting purchasers for the lease of 'a good Dwelling-House, lately occupied by William Martin Lolley'.[90] And in August he appeared at the Lancaster assizes, charged with bigamy.[91]

To this charge he understandably pleaded not guilty, claiming that he had been validly divorced. Evidence was given of the decree of the Edinburgh Commissary Court, with the deputy clerk of the Court explaining its jurisdiction and manner of proceedings.[92] But Mr Rain, for the prosecution, argued that a Scottish divorce 'was of no validity to authorise a second marriage in England so as to excuse the prisoner from the crime of bigamy'.[93] He also argued that the divorce had been obtained 'under such circumstances of fraud and circumvention practised upon his first wife, and of fraud and imposition upon the Court that pronounced the decree,

[85] National Records of Scotland, Process of Divorce: Mrs Ann Sugden v William Martin Lolley, CC8/6/1470. I am very grateful to Nell Stephenson for visiting the archives on my behalf and photographing the file. See also *Ann Sudgen, otherwise Lolley v William Martin Lolley*, somewhat belatedly reported in (1831) 2 Cl & F 567; 6 ER 1268.

[86] 'Edinburgh Ecclesiastical Court, March 20, 1812', *Liverpool Mercury*, 10 April 1812.

[87] 'Married', *Liverpool Mercury*, 10 April 1812. The announcement of the marriage appeared in several other local newspapers: *Lancaster Gazette*, 11 April 1812.

[88] *Cheshire Marriage Licence Bonds and Allegations*, 24 March 1812.

[89] *Morning Chronicle*, 3 June 1812.

[90] *Liverpool Mercury*, 3 July 1812, 7 August 1812, 21 August 1812.

[91] *Lancaster Gazette*, 29 August 1812.

[92] Relatively little detail about the complex legal arguments appeared in the contemporary newspaper reports: 'Assize Intelligence', *Liverpool Mercury*, 4 September 1812. However, the evidence given at trial was summarised in the law report: *R v William Martin Lolley* (1812) Russ & Ry 237; 168 ER 779. A slightly more detailed version was preserved as a result of William's subsequent request for a pardon: TNA, HO 47/52/9, fols 75–78.

[93] ibid fol 76.

that it could not be set up as a bar to the prosecution'.[94] On this latter point, the key witness was John King, William's former business partner. According to John, William had deliberately set out to goad Ann into divorcing him. Having made a study of Scottish divorce law, John said, William had persuaded Ann to join him on a trip to Edinburgh in November 1811. Once over the border he had begun to behave badly to Ann, while strategically leaving papers lying around that informed her of the options for obtaining a divorce. He had then taken Ann to the theatre. There he had left her 'to go in company with a loose girl of the town', whom he took back to the bar of the inn where he and Ann were lodging, and then to his bed. That had been sufficient to spur Ann into instigating proceedings for a divorce. John also contended that William's defence of the proceedings had been equally strategic, in that he had contested only the allegations that he knew Ann would be able to prove.[95]

All this led the judge at the Lancashire assizes, Mr Justice Wood, to decide that there were two important questions that should be reserved for the consideration of the twelve judges: first, whether a Scottish divorce was a good defence to a charge of bigamy and, if so, whether this specific divorce could be set up as a bar to this prosecution, given the allegations made about William's conduct. In the meantime, a formal verdict of guilty was returned against William, who was to remain in Lancaster gaol.

The twelve judges met in the Exchequer Chamber at Westminster on Saturday, 14 November. As the *Morning Chronicle* reported, various members of the public had assembled in 'eager expectation' of hearing the arguments 'in this very important and novel case'.[96] The identity of the counsel employed in the case was another draw: William was represented by Henry Brougham, a brilliant young advocate known for his dazzling rhetoric (if not for his ability to argue complex points of law).[97]

Rather than focusing on the two points that Wood had referred for consideration, Brougham started with the more far-reaching question of 'whether a decree of divorce by a court of a foreign country could dissolve an English marriage'. He spent two-and-a-half hours trying to argue first that marriages in England were not actually indissoluble, and then that Scottish divorces should be recognised.[98]

The case was then adjourned. When the judges reassembled on the evening of 7 December, Brougham continued to argue that it would be 'absurd' for English law not to recognise the Scottish divorce.[99] He then finally got round to the terms of the 1604 Act, where his argument was simply that the exception for those 'divorced by any sentence in the ecclesiastical court' in the 1604 Act should be interpreted

[94] ibid.

[95] ibid fols 76–77.

[96] 'Law Intelligence', *Morning Chronicle*, 17 November 1812.

[97] M Lobban, 'Brougham, Henry Peter, first Baron Brougham and Vaux' (2021) *Oxford Dictionary of National Biography*.

[98] 'Law Intelligence', *Morning Chronicle*, 17 November 1812.

[99] 'Law Intelligence', *Morning Chronicle*, 14 December 1812. To give an example that illustrates how widely his argument ranged – or, rather, how far he had strayed from the point – he raised the question of what the consequences would be for the parties' property rights, imagining a case in which a husband had remained in Scotland and divorced and remarried several times: if the marriages were to be recognised but not the divorces, he argued, then there might be four wives each claiming a third of the husband's land in dower upon his death – 'a third more than there is of each of them'. It was a memorable point, but hardly relevant.

generously in the context of the criminal law, and should not be limited to the divorces *a mensa et thoro* granted by English ecclesiastical courts. Finally, he addressed the allegations that the Scottish divorce had been obtained by fraud, arguing that no such finding had been made by the Scottish court, and that the divorce should not be set aside.[100] Opposing him was Mr Littledale, who argued at some length that marriage in England and Wales was indissoluble, that the principle of giving effect to the *lex loci* applied only 'as far as not repugnant to our own laws', that 'divorced' did not include a Scottish divorce, and that William was debarred from relying on his own fraud.[101]

These were big questions to decide. And even in the three weeks that had elapsed since Brougham had first addressed the twelve judges, yet another case had come to light. At the start of December, Elizabeth Bowles was examined on a charge of bigamy before the magistrates in Marlborough Street.[102] Having obtained her divorce from her first husband, Henry Alding, in Scotland in 1811,[103] she had married General Bowles in London later that same year.[104] Within a year he was dead, having bequeathed his property to her. The suspicion was voiced that Henry had been persuaded not to contest the divorce 'upon an assurance that he should be permitted to visit his wife, and that they should live together as husband and wife after the General's decease'.[105] In the absence of a decision from the judges on Lolley's case, the magistrate refused to commit Elizabeth for trial.[106]

The judges then gave their opinion. According to the published report, they were 'unanimously of opinion, that no sentence or Act of any foreign country or state could dissolve an English marriage *a vinculo matrimonii*, for ground on which it was not liable to be dissolved *a vincula matrimonii* in England'.[107] The upshot was that William's Scottish divorce was of no effect south of the border, and his conviction for bigamy was confirmed.

The following April, he was brought back before the assizes to receive his sentence. There Mr Baron Thompson sentenced him to the maximum possible – seven years' transportation.[108] This was not altogether surprising. Transportation was becoming the default punishment in cases of bigamy unless there were clear mitigating factors.[109] Yet William's second wife Ellen had known of his prior marriage, and had agreed to marry him on condition that he obtained a divorce, so there was no element of deception here. It seems likely, then, that the harshness of the sentence was motivated by a desire to

[100] ibid.

[101] ibid.

[102] *Bury and Norwich Post*, 2 December 1812.

[103] Leneman (n 76).

[104] The marriage took place at St Pancras Old Church on 17 December 1811, with Elizabeth described as 'single (formerly Eliz Alden, divorced)': FindMyPast, *England Marriages 1538-1973*.

[105] *Bury and Norwich Post*, 9 December 1812.

[106] *Lancaster Gazette*, 5 December 1812.

[107] *Lolley* (n 76) 239.

[108] *Lancaster Gazette*, 3 April 1813.

[109] Of the 18 individuals convicted of bigamy that year, seven were sentenced to transportation. See further R Probert and L D'Arcy-Brown, 'The transportation of bigamists in early nineteenth century England and Wales' (2019) 40 *Journal of Legal History* 223; see also *Double Trouble*, ch 5.

deter others from seeking to follow William's example rather than by the harm inflicted in his specific case.[110]

With no formal legal avenues available to him to appeal against either his sentence or his conviction, William went straight to the top to beg for clemency.[111] In his letter to the Prince Regent, written from the *Portland* convict ship in Langstone Harbour, he presented himself as an inexperienced young man who had 'imprudently formed a connection' with an older woman. That was a familiar enough story. What was more unexpected was his claim that his first marriage was void on account of Ann's first husband still being alive at the time he had married her in 1802. As he explained, he had not previously tried to rely on this fact as he had not been able to obtain formal proof, but his friends had since been able to gather the necessary evidence.[112]

As William admitted, he had 'sought the society of other females' during his marriage, but only because of his indignation at being deceived by Ann and the unhappiness of his home life (an argument that he might well have thought would elicit the sympathy of the Prince Regent). But he pleaded that when he married Ellen, 'he had not the remotest idea that he was violating the laws of the land'. He concluded by expressing his mortification at his current position, 'classed with and surrounded by the most wretched and abandoned of the human Race, whose vicious Habits and general Demeanour are calculated to excite continued Disgust and Horror'. Forty-one Liverpool residents added their signatures to support his plea for a pardon.[113]

In practice, it was not the Prince Regent who scrutinised requests for pardons but rather the Home Secretary acting on his behalf. Lord Sidmouth duly sent all this material on to the judge who had presided over the original trial for review. Wood, however, was unconvinced by the allegations about Ann's prior marriage, commenting that he had 'never heard or had the least intimation of the alleged fact of Ann Swain … having a husband living' when William married her. As he pointed out, had that been proved, he would have directed an acquittal, and any inquiry into the status of the Scottish divorce would have been unnecessary.[114]

That was in June 1813, and there matters seem to have languished for some time. Then in April 1814, Ellen wrote to Lady Sidmouth to beg her to remind her husband of William's case. This, she thought, would result in 'the best of men (who neither intended nor committed a crime)' being 'immediately restored to me and our little family'.[115] 'Immediately' was perhaps over-optimistic. Two months on, and William's case was still being discussed. Lord Eldon, the Lord Chancellor, concurred with Wood's

[110] Elizabeth Bowles was luckier: indicted for bigamy at the Old Bailey just a few days after Lolley was sentenced, she was acquitted when Henry Alding failed to appear in the court (*OBP*, 7 April 1813; *Morning Chronicle*, 14 April 1813).

[111] This was the standard way of seeking a pardon: see JM Beattie, 'The Royal Pardon and Criminal Procedure in Early Modern England' (1987) 22 *Historical Papers/Communications Historiques* 9.

[112] TNA, HO 47/52/9, fols 67–68. William's letter was accompanied by copies of the certificates of the marriage between James Swainey, cooper, and Ann Sugden on 28 March 1799 in St Peter's in Liverpool, and of his own marriage to Ann on 18 July 1802 (fols 61 and 62). There were also sworn statements from his father and sister, and from a witness who had seen James Swainey two years after William had married Ann (fols 63–64).

[113] TNA, HO 47/52/9, fols 67–68.

[114] ibid fol 59, letter from George Wood to Lord Sidmouth, the Home Secretary, 28 June 1813.

[115] ibid fols 65–65, letter from Ellen Lolley to Lady Sidmouth, 2 April 1814.

view that 'much more satisfactory proof' of Ann Swaine's first marriage, and the continued existence of her first husband, ought to be given 'before it could be made the ground of relieving the Petitioner'. He also agreed with Wood that William's conduct was sufficiently 'base' to justify transportation.[116] Despite this, on 13 June 1814, Lord Sidmouth wrote to confirm that William was to be granted a free pardon on account of the 'favourable circumstances' in his case.[117] Two days later, William was finally released from his confinement on the *Portland*.[118]

It was a happy ending for William. But the vague reference to 'favourable circumstances' did little to explain *why* he was pardoned. And the precise scope of what the twelve judges had decided was also surprisingly uncertain, largely due to the fact that the published report did not appear for some time.[119] In the meantime, Lord Eldon had asserted that the judges had 'unanimously decided, that an English marriage could not be anywhere dissolved except by act of the Legislature'.[120] That effectively ruled out recognising any Scottish divorce. He reiterated this almost two decades later, in 1831, when trying to introduce legislation determining what period of domicile in Scotland should be necessary to give the Scottish courts jurisdiction to grant a divorce.[121] Other legal treatises implied that the reason for the non-recognition of William's Scottish divorce was that it had been obtained by fraud.[122]

It was a debate that was to run for some time – not least because the Scottish courts continued to grant divorces in relation to English marriages. In 1817, the Court of Session in Edinburgh confirmed that they had jurisdiction to do so, assuming that the requisites relating to residence, grounds and lack of collusion were satisfied.[123] Leah Leneman has even suggested that the judges of the Court of Session 'may have felt a certain pleasure' in defying the twelve judges in Westminster and 'asserting the independence of the Scottish legal system'.[124]

There was, in any case, a very simple way for those who had obtained a divorce in Scotland to remarry without risk of prosecution for bigamy in England – which was for the ceremony to take place in Scotland.[125] Under the 1604 Act, the English courts only had the power to convict individuals of bigamy where the second marriage had taken place in England and Wales. Bigamous marriages celebrated in Scotland were

[116] ibid fols 69–70, letter from Eldon, 8 June 1814.
[117] TNA, HO 13/25, letter from Lord Sidmouth, 13 June 1814.
[118] TNA, *Portland's Quarterly Account for Year 1814-1816*, T 38/328.
[119] The fact that their Lordships' opinion had not been 'formally declared' was noted by W Russell, *A Treatise on Crimes and Misdemeanors* (London, Butterworth & Son, 1819) 287.
[120] *Tovey v Lindsay* (1813) 1 Dow 131; 3 ER 648, 136.
[121] *Hansard*, HL (series 3) Vol 4, cols 295–96 (24 June 1831).
[122] T Starkie, *A practical treatise of the law of evidence* (London, J & WT Clarke, 1824) 254 ('it was held, that a sentence of divorce from the first marriage, obtained in Scotland by fraud on the part of the husband, would be no bar to a prosecution for bigamy').
[123] *Levett v Levett*, reported in *Morning Post*, 17 January 1817.
[124] Leneman (n 76).
[125] See, for example, the double Wellesley-Paget divorce that had taken place in 1810: Henry Wellesley had obtained a Parliamentary divorce ending his marriage to his wife Charlotte on the ground of her adultery with Lord Paget. Paget's wife Caroline had then obtained a divorce in Scotland on the basis of her husband's adultery. Paget and Charlotte had then remarried in both Scotland and England: R Muir, *Love and Marriage in the Age of Jane Austen* (New Haven, Yale University Press, 2024) 270–77.

a matter for Scottish law.[126] And given that a marriage celebrated in Scotland after a Scottish divorce would have been regarded as valid by Scottish law, there was no risk of being prosecuted for bigamy there either. Only in 1828 was legislation passed allowing individuals to be prosecuted for bigamy regardless of where their second marriage had taken place.[127] But the 1828 Act also made another change, which was to have significant implications for our next case study.

No Defence, and a New Precedent: Arthur Battersby, 1838

On 15 June 1826, the dashing Arthur Battersby married 19-year-old Ann Muckleston in the quiet Warwickshire parish of Wellesbourne. It seemed an entirely suitable match. Arthur had only been known to the family for a few months, but enquiries had elicited that he was a man of good family and had property in Ireland. The announcement that appeared in various London and regional newspapers referred to him as the only son of 'Arthur Battersby, Esq'.[128] Ann's clergyman brother John came from his parish to officiate at her wedding, and her father, the Reverend John Fletcher Muckleston, was one of the witnesses.[129] After the wedding, Arthur and Ann got into the waiting carriage, and set off for London.

Three weeks later, Ann returned to her father's house. The trip to London had been a disaster. While they were staying at Fenton's Hotel, Arthur had been to the opera house, where he had been seen in a state of intoxication, behaving 'indecorously' with the dancers. From there he had gone on to the Saloon in Piccadilly, where he was observed with a prostitute on either side, treating them to champagne. As he later confessed to his surgeon, he had also had sex with a prostitute there, before returning to Ann – to whom he communicated 'a loathsome disease'.[130] The following year, Ann was granted a divorce *a mensa et thoro* on the basis of Arthur's cruelty and adultery. The judge, Dr Jenner, commented that there could be 'no doubt' that she was entitled to such relief, 'for no species of cruelty could be more severe than that which Mr Battersby had inflicted upon his wife'.[131]

In the meantime, Arthur had joined the army. His first employment, as a private in the 1st Regiment of Life Guards, did not last long. He appears on the muster roll for 20 July 1827, a few days after the divorce *a mensa et thoro* had been granted, but the next, for 20 February 1828, notes that he had deserted.[132]

[126] For the very different definition of bigamy in Scotland, see D Hume, *Commentaries on the Law of Scotland, respecting the description and punishment of crimes: Vol 2* (Edinburgh, 1797) ch 10.

[127] Offences Against the Person Act 1828, s 22. See further *Double Trouble*, ch 6.

[128] *The Globe*, 21 June 1826; *London Packet*, 21 June 1826.

[129] Ancestry, *Warwickshire Anglican Registers*, Engl/2/1055, DR 159.

[130] *Battersby v Battersby*, *Globe*, 17 July 1827; see also the *Evidence taken upon the Second Reading of the Bill to dissolve the Marriage of Ann Battersby with Arthur Battersby her now Husband, and to enable her to marry again* (House of Lords, 1840).

[131] *Globe*, 17 July 1827.

[132] TNA, *General Muster Books and Pay Lists, 1st Life Guards, 1818-1830*, WO 12/7, 20 July 1827, 20 February 1828.

A year or so later, he assumed the alias of 'Henry Napier Disney'.[133] Here the trail goes cold for a little while.[134] We pick him up again in 1837 when, under his new alias, he went through a second ceremony of marriage – or, rather, *two* ceremonies – with a young woman named Sarah Ann Stovin. The first of these ceremonies took place on 14 August 1837,[135] without any of Sarah's family being present.[136] Two days earlier, Arthur/Henry had gone to Doctors' Commons to get a marriage licence – swearing on oath that he was of age, and a bachelor, that Sarah Ann was also of age, and that there was no lawful cause to hinder the marriage.[137] Of these, only the first was true. Sarah was only 20, which meant that her father's consent to the marriage should have been obtained. She was also a ward of the Court of Chancery, on account of the considerable property to which she would become entitled upon attaining the age of 21. This meant that the consent of the Court of Chancery should have been obtained, and that Arthur/Henry was guilty of a contempt of court in marrying without its permission.[138] While neither of those facts invalidated the marriage, Arthur/Henry must have thought it prudent to repeat the ceremony after Sarah had come of age. Their second ceremony – again by licence – took place on 18 November, five days after her birthday.[139]

The more fundamental problem, of course, was that Arthur (as I shall call him for simplicity) was still married to Ann. When the news of this prior marriage emerged, Sarah's brother obtained a warrant for his arrest. It took some time to find him, as Arthur had strategically left his lodgings, but on 26 December he met him by chance in the street and called upon a police constable to take him into custody.[140] The following day Arthur was before the Bow Street magistrates, charged with bigamy.[141] Bail was subsequently refused, not least because the magistrate had been informed of his desertion from the Life Guards, and he was committed to Newgate to await his trial at the Central Criminal Court.[142]

[133] This information came from a witness at his trial in 1838, who reported that Arthur had adopted his new name some nine years earlier. He was unable to fill in any other gaps, simply noting that Arthur/Henry 'was doing nothing at that time in town, and I lost sight of him for many years': *OBP*, 29 January 1838.

[134] As noted below, he apparently went on to have a more impressive military career, but I have been unable to verify this.

[135] Ancestry, *Westminster Church of England Parish Registers*, STM/PR/6/32 (marriage at St Michael's chapel, a chapel of ease to the church of St Martin in the Fields).

[136] As Sarah's brother later reported, he had had an interview with Arthur/Henry a couple of days later, having heard rumours about their relationship, but Arthur/Henry had denied that any wedding had taken place: *Morning Herald*, 11 January 1838.

[137] Ancestry, *Marriage Bonds and Allegations*, DL/A/D/008/MS10091/214, 12 August 1837.

[138] He was subsequently served with a writ for contempt of court: *The Standard*, 11 January 1838.

[139] Ancestry, *London Church of England Parish Registers* (marriage at St James' Paddington). She had ceased to be a ward of court on attaining the age of 21: *Sun*, 11 January 1838.

[140] *Morning Herald*, 28 December 1837; *St James' Chronicle*, 28 December 1837; *Morning Advertiser*, 28 December 1837. At the subsequent trial, he gave evidence that Arthur had left Sarah on 29 November: *Evening Chronicle*, 2 February 1838.

[141] *The Standard*, 28 December 1837; *Sun*, 28 December 1837.

[142] *Sun*, 11 January 1838. Arthur was also served with an order requiring him to attend before the Lord Chancellor to answer for his contempt in marrying a ward of court without the consent of the Court of Chancery.

The pre-trial press coverage presented Arthur in a surprisingly flattering light, given that Sarah's wealth might suggest a mercenary motive, and his change of name a calculated deception. The elements of the case that were most widely reported were that he was 'a very fine-looking man', had displayed bravery in the service of the Queen of Spain, and had lost an arm during a battle near St Sebastian.[143] The circumstances under which he had separated from Ann, and his deception of Sarah, were glossed over.

Sarah herself played no part in the proceedings. When questioned by the magistrate as to why she was not present, her brother reported that she had been so affected by the discovery of Arthur's deception that the mere mention of his name 'threw her into fits', but that she was not averse to the prosecution.[144] She had still not recovered by the time of the trial at the end of January. Counsel for the prosecution, one Mr Clarkson, solemnly announced that 'it was not deemed consistent with the safety of her life that she should be produced in court'.[145]

As Mr Clarkson made clear in his opening speech, the fact that a separation order had been obtained was now no defence at all, the law having been 'completely altered' by a new Act of Parliament.[146] This was a reference to the Offences Against the Person Act 1828, which had limited the term 'divorced' to those who had obtained a full divorce 'from the bonds of matrimony'.[147] By this time, divorce in the modern sense was available in England and Wales, if only by the cumbersome and expensive route of a private Act of Parliament.[148]

It was somewhat ironic that Arthur would have had a defence had he remarried immediately after Ann had obtained the divorce *a mensa et thoro*. As he had not, he had to rely on the only other remaining statutory exception – that he had been absent from Ann in the seven years prior to his second marriage, and had had no knowledge of her being alive during that time.

The first part of this was easily established. Ann's own brother said that they had not seen Arthur since 1826. He also pointed out that Arthur could easily have found them if he had made inquiries.[149] Here, however, he was stopped by the Common

[143] *The Examiner*, 14 January 1838; *Weekly True Sun*, 14 January 1838; *The Atlas*, 14 January 1838; *Bell's Life in London*, 14 January 1838; *Freeman's Journal*, 17 January 1838; *Dublin Evening Mail*, 17 January 1838. It appears that Arthur served (as 'Henry Napier Disney') as a captain in the 17th Lancers, in the British Legion of auxiliaries raised to fight in support of the infant Queen Isabella II in Spain's First Carlist War. The battle in which he lost his arm would have been the assault on enemy fortifications west of San Sebastian in May 1836, although there were conflicting accounts of precisely which arm he had lost.

[144] *St James' Chronicle*, 11 January 1838. The magistrate noted tartly that it would make no difference if she were, since the prosecution was 'at the suit of the crown': *Morning Herald*, 11 January 1838. See also *OBP*, 29 January 1838.

[145] *Sun*, 31 January 1838.

[146] *Morning Herald*, 1 February 1838.

[147] See further *Double Trouble*, ch 6. Depending on the interpretation of *R v Lolley* on the recognition of divorces obtained in other jurisdictions, this limited the exception to those who had obtained a private Act of Parliament dissolving their marriage.

[148] The first such divorce was that of Lord Roos in 1670: see R Probert, 'The Roos case and modern family law' in S Gilmore, J Herring and R Probert (eds), *Landmark Cases in Family Law* (Oxford, Hart, 2011). For discussion of the number of Acts passed, see S Wolfram, 'Divorce in England 1700-1857' (1985) 5 *Oxford Journal of Legal Studies* 155.

[149] *OBP*, 29 January 1838.

Serjeant, who made it clear that this was not the issue.[150] The only other witness who could cast any light on whether Arthur knew of Ann being alive was an acquaintance of his, Abraham David Newland, who claimed to have met him in 1835 and 1836 and to have had a conversation with him about Ann. Newland was then subjected to 'one of the most rigid cross-examinations … which was ever heard in a court of justice', lasting more than an hour, although much of this was focused on his subsequent attempts to blackmail Arthur.[151] There was then some further skirmishing between Mr Clarkson and counsel for the defence, a Mr Phillips,[152] about the burden of proof. Here Mr Phillips argued that it would be unreasonable to expect Arthur to make inquiries about a wife who had been divorced from him and whom he had not seen for 11 years.

Finally, Mr Phillips called General de Lacy Evans, under whose command Arthur (as 'Henry Napier Disney') had served in Spain. The General said that he had only known Arthur for some 18 months, but from what he had seen, and the reports he had heard, he 'believed him to be brave as a soldier, humane in disposition, and exemplary in his general conduct'. He was preparing to say more, but Mr Phillips, perhaps conscious that it would be difficult to improve on this glowing character reference, quickly jumped in to thank him for saying all that needed to be said.[153]

The Common Serjeant, having summed up the case, left it to the jury to decide whether Arthur had been aware that Ann was still living when he married Sarah.[154] One reporter was so confident of an acquittal that he did not even wait for the jury to finish their deliberations, and the next day's *Morning Chronicle* reported a verdict of not guilty.[155] The eventual guilty verdict – after the jury had deliberated for an hour and a half – caused a sensation in the court.[156]

On 5 February, Arthur was brought back to court for sentencing.[157] The Recorder commented that the offence was all the greater where it was 'committed by those who had superior knowledge and better judgment'.[158] In this case it had also involved the destruction 'of the peace of a family circle, and, more especially, of the confiding victim, whose agonies could not be imagined, much less described'.[159] Arthur was sentenced to seven years' transportation and conveyed to Australia on the ship *Portsea*.[160]

[150] *Morning Herald*, 1 February 1838; *St James' Chronicle*, 1 February 1838. See further chapter 6 for discussion of the changing views on whether the remarrying spouse had to have used 'due diligence' to try to find their absent spouse.

[151] *London Evening Standard*, 1 February 1838.

[152] Charles Phillips, a barrister whose eloquence had earned him the nickname 'Counsellor O'Garnish'.

[153] *Morning Herald*, 1 February 1838.

[154] *London Evening Standard*, 1 February 1838. At least one juror did not fully understand the judge's summing up and asked if a man was under a duty to make inquiries before remarrying. The Common Serjeant, having checked with the other judges, confirmed that this was not required: *Evening Chronicle*, 2 February 1838.

[155] *Morning Chronicle*, 1 February 1838.

[156] *Morning Advertiser*, 1 February 1838, noting that 'the majority appeared to expect a different return'; *Morning Post*, 1 February 1838; *Leamington Spa Courier*, 10 February 1838.

[157] This took longer than it should have done, owing to the attempts of a barrister to challenge the conviction: *Morning Post*, 6 February 1838.

[158] ibid.

[159] ibid.

[160] *OBP*, 29 January 1838.

This prompted Ann Battersby to try to obtain a full Parliamentary divorce. There was no guarantee that she would be able to do so. The only two women to have obtained a Parliamentary divorce previously, Jane Campbell Addison and Louisa Turton, had both done so by establishing incestuous adultery.[161] There was no precedent for a woman to be granted a divorce on any other ground. Ann's divorce Bill had its first reading in Parliament on 2 March 1840. It was decided that personal service on Arthur could be dispensed with, given that his whereabouts in Australia were unknown.[162] After a few delays, the Bill finally passed through all its stages.[163] On Friday 3 July it was given royal assent, and Ann was finally free.

She lost no time in making use of her new freedom. Ten days later she married a widower, Frederick Cuerton Travers Smyth, Esq, at Narborough in Leicestershire.[164] The marriage register bears no hint of her previous marital history: she simply resumed her maiden name and described herself as a spinster.

Ann's divorce from Arthur also established a new precedent for other wives. Twelve years later, Georgina Hall also succeeded in obtaining a divorce by private Act of Parliament from a bigamist husband.[165] When divorce law was finally reformed in 1857, 'bigamy with adultery' was listed as one of the grounds on which a wife could divorce her husband.[166] And our next case study involved a wife petitioning on that very ground.

Domicile and Divorce: Earl Russell

In February 1890, a grand ceremony of marriage took place at St Peter's church in London's Eaton Square.[167] The bride, Mabel Edith Scott, was bedecked in satin, lace and diamonds and was escorted down the aisle by her mother, Lady Scott.[168] The groom, John Francis Stanley Russell, the second Earl Russell, was, as he later declared, 'passionately in love' with Mabel.[169] A couple of weeks later the couple set off for their honeymoon

[161] Jane Campbell's divorce from Edward Addison, on account of his incestuous adultery with her sister, 1801; Louisa Turton's divorce from Edward Turner, 1831.

[162] All that was known was that he had been alive at the end of 1838, according to the return of convicts made at the end of that year, as confirmed by a certificate from the Home Office: 'Mrs Battersby's Divorce Bill', *English Chronicle and Whitehall Evening Post*, 7 March 1840.

[163] Ann's barrister appeared before the House of Lords on 23 March to set out the facts of the case, but consideration of the bill was postponed (*English Chronicle and Whitehall Evening Post*, 24 March 1840). Eventually, on 2 June, the House of Lords dealt with a whole batch of divorce bills that had been languishing on the list awaiting attention for some time (*Morning Herald*, 6 June 1840). Progress thereafter was brisk, with the Committee stage on 4 June and the third reading the following day: House of Lords, Minutes of Proceedings. Once passed, it was sent to the Commons, which dealt with it more speedily.

[164] The marriage took place by licence: FindMyPast, *Leicestershire Marriages and Banns*, DE1653/14.

[165] Georgina Hall's divorce from Henry Hall, 1850.

[166] Matrimonial Causes Act 1857. For examples of wives petitioning on this ground, see chapters 4, 12 and 13, and see further *Double Trouble*, ch 7.

[167] Ancestry, *Westminster Church of England Parish Registers*, SPES/PR/2/16.

[168] 'The Marriage of Earl Russell', *Pall Mall Gazette*, 6 February 1890. Lady Scott was to play a significant part in the legal disputes that followed.

[169] Earl Russell, *My Life and Adventures* (London, Cassell & Co, 1923) 157.

in Torquay. But the marriage very quickly unravelled, and by May 1890 they were living apart. Apart from a brief reunion a few weeks later, they remained apart.

Over the course of the 1890s, each was to make serious allegations against the other as they sought different legal remedies. Mabel's 1891 petition for judicial separation claimed that Russell had been violent towards her, as well as strongly hinting that he was engaging in a sexual relationship with a young man named Roberts.[170] In April 1894, Mabel petitioned for restitution of conjugal rights,[171] which prompted a counter-petition for judicial separation from Russell on the basis of her cruelty. This eventually went all the way to the House of Lords, which decided that Mabel's conduct towards Russell did not amount to 'cruelty' for these purposes.[172]

Russell then met and fell in love with Mollie Somerville. As he later noted in his autobiography, 'on principle Mollie would not be satisfied without a marriage, but she would be satisfied with an American marriage, even though it would not be binding in England'.[173] The pair travelled out to the United States, and lived in Nevada for the six months necessary to establish residency there for the purpose of obtaining a divorce.[174] On 14 April 1900, both obtained divorces from their respective spouses. The following day they went through a ceremony of marriage.

Back in England, a few weeks later, Mabel petitioned for a divorce, citing Russell's bigamy and adultery.[175] This, of course, rested on the Nevada divorce having no legal effect in England and Wales. At the subsequent hearing, her counsel noted that it was 'immaterial' to prove that there had been such a divorce, given that it would not be recognised by English law.[176] Just a few years earlier, the Privy Council had confirmed that English law would only recognise divorces granted in the jurisdiction where the husband (and by extension the wife) was domiciled.[177] Establishing mere residency for the purpose of being able to take advantage of Nevada's divorce laws fell far short of being domiciled there in the eyes of an English court: after all, Russell had no intention of making Nevada his permanent home.

The result was that Russell was still married to Mabel when he went through the ceremony with Mollie. For the purpose of obtaining a divorce, this was all that was needed to establish 'bigamy', which was defined in the 1857 Act as 'the marriage of any person, being married, to any other person during the life of the former husband or wife'.[178] There was no need to show that the remarrying spouse had been convicted of bigamy, or even that they could have been. The decree *nisi* was granted in March 1901.

[170] 'The Russell Matrimonial Suit', *Morning Post*, 2 December 1891. A Sumner Holmes, '"Don't Frighten the Horses": The Russell Divorce Case' in G Robb and N Erber (eds), *Disorder in the Court: Trials and Sexual Conflict at the Turn of the Century* (Basingstoke, Palgrave Macmillan, 1999).

[171] TNA, *Divorce and Matrimonial Causes Files*, J 77/534/16305.

[172] *Russell v Russell* [1897] AC 395. The allegations made again Russell by Mabel's mother, by contrast, resulted in a successful prosecution for criminal libel and a sentence of eight months' imprisonment.

[173] Russell (n 169) 233.

[174] On the subsequent liberalisation of Reno's residency requirements, see J Scandura, *Down in the Dumps: Place, Modernity, American Depression* (Durham and London, Duke University Press, 2008) 32. Russell (n 169) seems to have confused residency and domicile.

[175] TNA, *Divorce and Matrimonial Causes Files*, J77/695/1144. Mollie's first husband, George Somerville, also obtained a divorce on the basis of her adultery with Russell: *The Times*, 12 December 1900.

[176] *Russell (Countess) v Russell (Earl)*, *The Times*, 29 March 1901.

[177] *Le Mesurier v Le Mesurier* [1895] AC 517.

[178] Matrimonial Causes Act 1857, s 27.

But before the decree was made absolute, Russell was arrested and charged with bigamy. After a brief hearing at Bow Street, he was committed for trial, the Grand Jury at the Central Criminal Court found a true bill, and the proceedings were transferred to the House of Lords for him to be tried by his peers.[179] There his defence team sought to argue that the 1861 Act did not apply to a second marriage in Nevada, on the basis that the reference to 'any second marriage contracted elsewhere than in England or Ireland' must be read as meaning '"elsewhere" within the King's dominions'.[180] This was a somewhat hopeless argument, given how the legislation, and its predecessor in 1828, had consistently been interpreted.[181] Halsbury, the Lord Chancellor, noted that he had consulted the judges and that there was nothing in this point.[182]

Russell accordingly pleaded guilty but was allowed to make a speech. In this he argued that he thought he had acquired a 'proper domicile' in Nevada that allowed him to remarry there.[183] He also claimed that he had wanted to defend Mabel's petition for divorce, and that it was only then that he had been informed that he had not established that his domicile had changed. And he emphasised that he had had no intention of breaking the criminal law, having had 'no idea' that a second marriage overseas was punishable as bigamy in England, let alone one that was 'valid and … undisputed' in the place where it was celebrated.[184]

It is difficult to know how much of this was genuine. Given that Russell had paid Mabel £5,000 to divorce him, it was somewhat disingenuous to claim that he had wanted to defend the suit.[185] He had also known that the Nevada marriage would not be recognised back in England. So the only question is whether he had believed that he was safe from prosecution. He was entirely upfront in his autobiography that the speech he had made was the one he had been advised to make, not the one he had wanted to make. As he added:

> What I should like to have said would have been that as there was no other way of getting rid of this horrible woman to whom I was tied I had adopted what appeared to be the only method for cutting the Gordian knot; that Mabel Edith knew all about the proceedings from the beginning and then my conduct did not harm or injure a single human being, and … that the real reason of my prosecution was merely because I was an unbeliever and a radical.[186]

Russell was sentenced to three months in Holloway, but appears to have served his time in relative comfort.[187] His case provides a reminder of the technicalities underpinning the law of bigamy, and that a person might be validly married in one jurisdiction

[179] Russell (n 169) 281.
[180] *The Trial of Earl Russell (before the King In Parliament)* [1901] AC 446, 448.
[181] On which see *Double Trouble*, ch 6. S Cretney, *Family Law in the Twentieth Century: A History* (Oxford, Oxford University Press, 2003) 804 suggested that Russell was 'probably incorrectly' convicted of bigamy, on the basis that the indictment had not explicitly stated that Russell was a British subject. However, the Court for Crown Cases Reserved confirmed in *R v Audley* [1907] 1 KB 383 that this was not necessary.
[182] *The Trial of Earl Russell* (n 180) 449.
[183] Russell (n 169) 281.
[184] ibid 282.
[185] ibid 279.
[186] ibid 283.
[187] On Russell's various attempts to propose reform, see S Cretney, *Family Law in the Twentieth Century: A History* (Oxford, Oxford University Press, 2003) 204–05.

and a bigamist in another. And once again, it underlines the importance of always reading the statute.

The twentieth century saw divorce becoming both increasingly available and accessible. The grounds for divorce were widened, the range of courts able to grant a divorce expanded, and more generous financial support was made available to help with the costs of the process. Once a divorce could be obtained without needing to show that the other spouse was at fault, the 'need' for anyone to commit bigamy more or less disappeared. But our final case study shows that the grant of a divorce is not always the end of the story.

A Premature Application: 79 Divorced Couples, 2024

In December 2024, the Family Court was faced with the challenge of deciding on the legal status of 79 divorces.[188] Each couple shared the same problem, the original application for divorce having been submitted on the parties' first wedding anniversary – a day too early. Under the current law, no application for a divorce may be made before the expiration of one year from the date of the marriage, which has been interpreted to mean one year and one day.[189] But the error had never been picked up. The applications had all been submitted through the new online divorce portal,[190] checked by staff at the Courts and Tribunals Service Centre, and then considered by a legal advisor who had certified that the applicants were entitled to a conditional order.[191] Such orders had then been made by a district judge, final orders had subsequently been granted,[192] and no fewer than 11 applicants had gone on to remarry new partners. But if their divorce was invalid, then so too was any subsequent remarriage.

It was not the first time that the problem had arisen. Previous judges had held that a decree absolute made after a premature application was automatically void – with the result that the parties were not legally divorced and any subsequent remarriage was also void.[193] But in *The Lord Chancellor v 79 Divorced Couples*, the President of the Family Division, Sir Andrew McFarlane, took a different view.[194] He thought it was 'inconceivable' that Parliament could have intended that a final order made in such circumstances would be void automatically.[195] Such a result would, in his view, 'do damage to the public interest which is in achieving clarity and legal certainty as to the marital status of

[188] *The Lord Chancellor v 79 Divorced Couples* [2024] EWHC 3211 (Fam).

[189] See respectively Matrimonial Causes Act 1973, s 3; *Dodds v Walker* [1981] 1 WLR 1027.

[190] The fact that the online system did not prevent the application from being made was attributed to a 'validation error' (*79 Divorced Couples* (n 188) [10]).

[191] Previously known as a decree *nisi*.

[192] Previously known as a decree absolute.

[193] *Butler v Butler (Queens Proctor Intervening)* [1990] 1 FLR 114; *Baron v Baron (Queens Proctor Intervening)* [2019] EWFC 26.

[194] McFarlane justified this as being necessary to comply with 'the overarching approach to interpretation' where the consequences of failing to comply with a particular statutory requirement are not expressly identified within the statute in question: *79 Divorced Couples* (n 188) [40]. Citing *R v Soneji and another* [2005] UKHL 49 and *R (Majera) v Secretary of State for the Home Department* [2021] UKSC 46, he held that it 'is for the court to seek to discern and then impute an intention to Parliament as to those consequences' ([14]).

[195] ibid [40].

a citizen following the making of an apparently valid final order of divorce'.[196] His decision was that the final orders made in the cases of these 79 couples were merely voidable. This meant that it was possible for any of the 79 couples to apply for their final order to be set aside if they so chose. If they did not, the order would stand, and their marriages would have been legally ended.

Premature applications were to some extent the responsibility of the parties, but the previous decades had seen plenty of other professional errors and official blunders where individuals had been led to believe that they had been divorced. There were examples of solicitors having wrongly told a client that the decree absolute had been granted,[197] or even having forged the documentation.[198] There were also occasional mix-ups at the court that meant the decree absolute was invalid.[199] Even more astonishing was the 'legislative cockup' revealed in December 1987, when it was realised that various amendments to the procedural rules meant that a county court had no jurisdiction to grant a divorce where the case had been transferred to it from the High Court.[200] It was estimated that there might be several thousand such cases, and probably hundreds who had remarried and become 'bigamists'.[201] Parliament quickly passed legislation to validate these decrees retrospectively.[202]

But while 'Xmas Bigamy' made a good headline, it was all but unthinkable that any of the individuals involved would ever have been prosecuted. Ever since the late 1960s, it had been accepted that a genuine and reasonably held belief that a divorce had been granted would be a good defence to a charge of bigamy.[203] So too in the case of the *79 Divorced Couples*; even if the President of the Family Division had decided that the orders that had been made were void, there would have been no question of the 11 individuals who had remarried being prosecuted for bigamy. As such, the case provides a final useful reminder of the difference between an invalid second marriage and a bigamous one.

[196] ibid.

[197] *Western Daily Press*, 1 December 1994.

[198] 'Solicitor forged divorce decree', *The Guardian*, 25 September 1981; *The Guardian*, 11 July 1989; *Daily Mirror*, 25 August 1992; 'Lawyer forged divorce papers', *Daily Mirror*, 16 July 1993.

[199] 'Woman's "bigamy" shock', *Hull Daily Mail*, 9 August 1997.

[200] S Gold, 'Xmas Bigamy' (1987) 137 *New Law Journal* 1199.

[201] ibid; see also 'A bigamy shock for 200 couples', *Daily Mail*, 23 December 1987.

[202] Matrimonial Proceedings (Transfers) Act 1988; for commentary see S Gold, 'Xmas Bigamy' (1988) 138 *New Law Journal* 157; 138 *New Law Journal* 359.

[203] *R v Gould* [1968] 2 QB 65, discussed in *Double Trouble*, ch 10, and noted in chapter 7.

6

The Defence of Seven Years' Absence

Before 1604, anyone whose first spouse had simply disappeared was in a difficult position when it came to forming a new relationship. There was no legal procedure by which they could have their absent spouse declared dead and ensure that any subsequent marriage would be valid. If the left-behind spouse waited a decent interval to remarry and the first spouse was never heard of again, then it was likely that their second marriage would be presumed to be valid, should the question ever come before the courts. But there was always the risk that the first spouse would turn up – in which case the second marriage was void and the remarrying spouse at risk of punishment in the church courts.

When bigamy became a felony punishable by death, the stakes were obviously far higher. So it is understandable that the 1604 Act explicitly dealt with those who remarried after a lengthy period of absence but whose first spouse then turned out to be alive. It is worth setting this provision out in full, despite its somewhat clunky wording, because the phrasing makes it clear that there were in fact two quite distinct defences. The Act exempted anyone:

> whose husband or wife shall be continually remaining beyond the seas by the space of seven years together, or whose husband or wife shall absent him or herself the one from the other by the space of seven years together, in any parts within his Majesty's dominions, the one of them not knowing the other to be living within that time.[1]

In other words, one defence arose where the absent spouse was overseas for seven years, regardless of whether the remarrying spouse knew them to be alive during that time. The other, where the absent spouse was not overseas, depended on the remarrying spouse not actively knowing the absentee to be alive during that time. In both cases the second marriage was still nevertheless void, and any children born to the couple would be illegitimate, but the remarrying spouse was not guilty of the crime of bigamy. It was a vital safety valve when a conviction could mean the death penalty.

Over the following two centuries, the second of these two exceptions was invoked more often than the first. The case of Lucy Ahier is the only one I have traced where counsel for the defence tried to make the case that the absent spouse had been overseas. And when the law was reformed in 1828, the two exceptions became one. The new provision only exempted those 'marrying a second time', whose spouse 'shall have been continually absent from such person for the space of seven years then last past, and

[1] Bigamy Act 1604, s 2, discussed further in *Double Trouble*, ch 2.

shall not have been known by such person to be living within that time'.[2] This meant that showing that the other spouse had been absent overseas for seven years was no longer sufficient in itself. Wherever in the world the other spouse might be, any news from or of them would negate any defence – or require another seven years' wait before any remarriage.

As a result, all the other case studies in this chapter focus on the exception that required both absence and absence of knowledge. The examination of Jane Scott in 1665 hinted at how this exception operated. It was for the accused to show that their first spouse had been absent for seven years, and not everyone was able to satisfy the court on this point. But once they had done so, it seems from the 1714 case of Dorothy Poppleton that the onus shifted to the prosecution to show that the accused had known their first spouse to be living during that period.

The nineteenth century then saw that being called into question. To help understand the subtle shifts in the interpretation of the separation defence, I have included a case study of one influential legal work, *A Treatise of the Pleas of the Crown*, written by the barrister (and later MP) Edward Hyde East. His criticisms of the 1604 Act shaped both the 1828 Act and the way in which the separation defence was subsequently interpreted. His question as to whether the remarrying spouse had to exercise due diligence and make active inquiries was echoed in the 1840 case of Peter Cullen. After several convictions, the question was referred to the Court for Crown Cases Reserved. In 1856, in the case of Mary Briggs, it confirmed that it was not sufficient to show that the accused could have discovered that their first spouse was still alive. Nine years later, in the case of John Curgenven, it went further and held that the onus was on the prosecution to prove that the remarrying spouse had known that their first spouse was alive. Perhaps surprisingly, this was the case whether the remarrying spouse was the one who had been left (who could quite reasonably be assumed to have no knowledge of where their spouse had gone or who to ask) or the one who had left (who would at least know where they had left their family as a starting point for inquiries).

New questions continued to arise in the twentieth century, this time about the meaning of 'marrying a second time' and the implications for those who had gone on to marry a third, fourth, or even fifth time. Here again we have an example of a court coming to one conclusion about what this meant – in the case of Thomas Treanor – only for a differently constituted court to reach a different conclusion a decade later in the case of John Taylor.

I have also included one fictional example, partly because 'Enoch Arden' became a convenient shorthand to denote an absent spouse who made an unexpected return and partly because of the intriguing possibility that it influenced the judges' thinking in the case of John Curgenven, decided just a year after Tennyson's poem was published.

As well as tracing the evolution of the separation defence, the case studies in this chapter also show the varying contexts in which it was used. There were enforced absences where one spouse was serving in the army or navy. There were cases of abandonment, where one spouse had simply walked out on the other, and others where the separation appears to have been consensual. Overall, those who relied on the separation

[2] Offences Against the Person Act 1828, s 22.

defence(s) were generally in a much humbler sphere of life than those who argued that they had been 'divorced'. There are no members of the aristocracy in this chapter, nor anyone whose name is likely to be familiar to anyone outside the pages of old legal treatises. Ascertaining their back story is generally a matter of piecing together fragments of information, and some characters simply fade from the picture after the trial.

'She Never did Meet with Anyone who could Certainly Assure Her that He was Alive': Jane Scott Alias Hunter, 1665

In 1651, Jane Simpson married a soldier named Stephen Hunter at Warwick parish church. Given his occupation, they had not been able to spend much time together, and 'did not dwell together at one time above the space of six days'. Stephen then 'went again to his colours', returning to the garrison at Carlisle, some 200 miles to the north.[3] The execution of Charles I two years earlier had not brought peace to the nation. Oliver Cromwell had invaded Scotland in 1650, and in July 1651 he and Major-General John Lambert had won a major battle against the Scots near Stirling.[4] Since Cromwell deployed most of the English army in his subsequent march on Perth, it would have been surprising if Stephen had not been involved in the action.

Whatever the reason for his continued absence, Jane did not hear from Stephen for three or four years. She then wrote to his commanding officer, 'to be satisfied, whether he was dead or alive'. Stephen in fact turned out to be alive, and came south to see Jane. But once again, it proved to be a brief visit: he stayed 'but one night' and then returned to (or at least towards) Scotland. That was the last she saw or heard of him. As she emphasised, she had received no tokens or letters from him during the time he was absent, 'viz seven years', and had not met anyone who 'could certainly assure her that he was alive'. In around 1664, she went through a second ceremony of marriage with one John Scott in the parish of Holm Cultram in Cumberland.

We know about Jane's two marriages because in November 1665 she was questioned by the local Justice of the Peace about the circumstances surrounding her marriage to John Scott. Given that it is very rare for any records of such examinations to survive from this period, this is a particularly valuable document, short and scrappy though it is.

It is also a tantalising one. For one thing, we don't know why Jane was being examined in the first place. The National Archives had indexed her case as being one of bigamy, but other similar cases turned out upon investigation to be about questions of settlement or just happened to mention a marriage.[5] It is possible that Stephen had just turned up: Jane was recorded as saying that she had not seen him for 'about seven years

[3] TNA, ASSI 45/7/2/124.

[4] M Kishlansky, *A Monarchy Transformed: Britain 1603-1714* (London, Penguin, 1997) 200.

[5] The index to the Northern Circuit's criminal depositions and case papers was compiled by an independent researcher some years ago. Other examples of cases from this period that were indexed as bigamy included ASSI 45/5/3/3 (a document certifying that a particular couple had married) and ASSI 45/4/3/6, the examination of the wife of another man who had joined the Parliamentarian army and gone into Scotland, where he was subsequently buried.

before this day'. All we can say is that the phraseology of her answers suggests she was having to defend herself against a suspicion that her second marriage was bigamous.

As such, her case provides a helpful introduction to two key elements of the seven-year defence. First, the 1604 Act made it clear that the absence of the first spouse had to be continuous, 'by the space of seven years together'.[6] Stephen's brief reappearance in around 1654 or 1655 (judging from Jane's recollection) would have reset the clock, meaning that she would have had to wait for seven years to elapse from the day he again left before she might marry without committing a crime. Jane's evidence also brings out the subtle but important difference between, on the one hand, having grounds to believe that one's spouse had died, and, on the other, not knowing them to be alive. If Jane was having to defend herself against a charge of bigamy, there was no need for her to show that she believed Stephen was dead; it was sufficient that she had no positive knowledge that he was alive.

The record of Jane's examination concluded with a stock phrase – Jane 'further sayth not' – and there are no records to tell us what happened next. It may be that the magistrate who examined Jane was satisfied that there was no case against her and that she was not committed for trial. But for the first definite example of an acquittal on the basis of seven years' separation, we need to fast forward half a century.

'The Evidence did not Come Up to Prove that She Knew He was Alive': Dorothy Poppleton, 1714

In June 1714, Dorothy Poppleton stood trial for bigamy at the Old Bailey. The *Proceedings* gave no details of where or when either of the weddings had taken place. Since Dorothy denied the first wedding but admitted the second, the focus was on establishing the former. It was noted that 'about 18 years past she lived with and owned[7] the said Peter Douglas alias Jougla, to be her husband for about six or seven years, and he her as his wife'.[8] The court heard evidence that this Peter Douglas was still living, and that he had 'but lately gone beyond the Sea'. But given that 'the evidence did not come up to prove that she knew he was alive, or conversed with him for seven years last past', the court took the view that 'she was not guilty of felony within the statute'.[9]

While we only have a short summary of Dorothy's case in the *Proceedings* to go on, it does add several points to our understanding of the seven-year defence. First, the specific wording that 'the evidence did not come up to prove that she knew' indicates that the onus was on the prosecution to prove that Dorothy knew Peter to be alive during that period.[10] Second, and even more importantly, Dorothy's case shows very clearly that the seven-year defence was not based on a presumption that the first

[6] Bigamy Act 1604, s 2.
[7] ie acknowledged.
[8] *OBP*, 30 June 1714.
[9] ibid.
[10] The idea that the remarrying spouse needed to show that they had used due diligence to find out what had happened to their first spouse appears to have been a nineteenth-century innovation: see further the work of East and the case study of Peter Cullen, discussed below.

spouse had died – Peter, after all, was still known to be alive at the time of her trial.[11] In fact, unless evidence was provided that the first spouse was alive at the time of the second wedding, a defendant would be entitled to an acquittal even if less than seven years had passed since they had last seen them.[12] Finally, as the court reminded Dorothy, successfully using the seven-year defence did not validate the second marriage. So long as Peter was alive, she was not free to remarry, and her second marriage was void. As a result, her second husband – the Reverend Michael Malard – was 'at liberty to marry when and whom he pleases', as he was told by the judge. Whether he wished to do so is another matter.[13]

Dorothy's case might appear to be just a run-of-the-mill application of the seven-year separation defence. What made it special was how rarely this defence was successfully pleaded. Perusing the *Proceedings* for the eighteenth century, the only other was of one Edmund Elgar, in 1744, who had remarried over 13 years after his first wife Mary had left him.[14] His case serves to illustrate how the reasons for the absence of the first spouse were irrelevant to the question of whether the defence applied: one witness noted that Mary had left Edmund because of his 'keeping company' with other women, while another, forced to admit that Mary had herself remarried, retorted that it was only after Edmund had 'used and abused her so barbarously'.[15] In other words, the remarrying spouse could have driven their first spouse away by their bad behaviour, but as long as they had not seen or heard of them in seven years, they would still have a good defence to a charge of bigamy.

Even so, nobody else managed to avail themselves of this defence. John Watch's attempt to do so failed in 1776 because he had received news that his first wife had remarried – after he had been separated from her for seven years, but crucially before he had remarried.[16] He might well have assumed that he was similarly justified in remarrying, but the fact he knew she was alive reset the clock to zero. There was also Joshua Holmes in 1761, who claimed that after not hearing from or seeing his first wife for seven years, he 'thought the law would not prevent my marrying another woman'.[17] This, however, was contradicted by the evidence that only five years had elapsed between his first and second marriages.

In fact, in most of the cases that came before the Old Bailey during the eighteenth century, the shortness of the period between the two marriages would have prevented the accused from relying on the seven-year defence. Of the 185 cases for which the dates of both marriages can be traced, 59 per cent had occurred within seven years of each other. Given that very few couples parted on their wedding day, fewer still would

[11] This is worth noting given the mistaken assumption that the seven-year defence rested on the presumption that the first spouse had died: see further *Double Trouble*, ch 2.

[12] See eg *OBP*, 14 January 1732 (Mary Stackhouse, acquitted; the *Proceedings* did not give the details of her two marriages but they took place less than five years apart, in 1724 and 1729, at St Paul's Covent Garden and the Fleet respectively: FindMyPast, Boyd's Marriage Index; TNA, RG7/569); *OBP*, 5 July 1749 (Rebecca How, acquitted).

[13] For the story of what happened after Dorothy's trial, which attracted a surprising amount of controversy, see ch 13.

[14] *OBP*, 28 July 1744.

[15] ibid.

[16] *OBP*, 12 July 1776.

[17] *OBP*, 6 May 1761.

have been separated for seven years. And even if they had been, there was always the risk that someone would be able to show that there had been some communication or knowledge of the other being alive during that time. All this explains why Dorothy Poppleton's acquittal was such a rarity.

But there was, as we have seen, a second seven-year exception that only required proof of absence – which is the subject of our next case study.

'My Husband was Gone Abroad': Lucy Ahier, 1800

In May 1800, the arrest of Lucy Ahier on a charge of bigamy attracted the attention of the press. The fact that she was, as several journalists noted, young, attractive and 'very genteel' may have had something to do with the level of interest in her case.[18] Having been brought before the Lord Mayor at the Mansion House, she was committed to the Old Bailey.[19]

On the day of her trial, the court was 'uncommonly thronged with ladies'.[20] Evidence was given of Lucy's marriage to cabinet-maker Joshua Ahier in Bristol in March 1791,[21] and of her having gone through a second ceremony with James Thomas, at St Botolph Aldgate in London in November 1798.[22] The witnesses had each been at one of the ceremonies. One confirmed that Lucy had described herself as a widow when she married James. The other, however, had seen Joshua 'yesterday and to-day', so there was no doubt that he was alive – although as Lucy's legal spouse he was unable to give evidence against her.

Cross-examined by Lucy's counsel, Mr Knapp, as to whether Joshua had ever been out of England, one witness replied, reasonably enough, that he did not know, and, when pressed as to whether he had ever *heard* that Joshua had been abroad, replied more firmly, 'I never did; I always understood that he was in England, and not out of England'. It was the same story with the other witness. He had heard that Joshua had 'gone as a soldier' but had no knowledge of his being abroad. He also stated, in response to a question by Knapp, that he had seen Lucy with Joshua at 'the latter end of 1791, or the beginning of 1792, I cannot say which'.[23]

These questions indicate the line of defence that Knapp was trying to establish. As explained above, the 1604 Act had exempted anyone whose first spouse 'shall be continually remaining beyond the seas by the space of seven years together'.[24] The

[18] *Sun*, 29 May 1800; *Oracle*, 29 May 1800; *Morning Herald*, 11 June 1800; *Observer*, 15 June 1800.

[19] *Lloyd's Evening Post*, 21–23 May 1800. One report claimed that she had eloped from her second husband and returned to her first husband in Bristol, 'from whence she was brought, by virtue of a warrant, to London': *London Packet*, 21–23 May 1800. The suggestion about her eloping from her second husband is hard to square with the evidence that he had already been parted from her by his family – on which see further below – but it is entirely plausible that she had returned to Bristol.

[20] *Oracle*, 29 May 1800.

[21] Ancestry, *Bristol Church of England Parish Registers*, P/St M/R/3/B (marriage at St Michael the Archangel, Bristol, 8 March 1791, Joshua Ahier to Lucy Norton).

[22] Ancestry, *London Church of England Parish Registers*, P69/BOT2/A/013/MS09944/006 (banns book) and P69/BOT2/A/01/MS 9230/6 (marriage register), both recording her surname as Hayers.

[23] *OBP*, 28 May 1800.

[24] Bigamy Act 1604, s 3.

leading legal commentators of the day had interpreted this as providing a defence based on absence alone, regardless of whether or not the remarrying spouse knew the absent spouse to be alive during that time.[25] But Knapp was precluded from saying this expressly. The reason for this was that the status of defence counsel was still somewhat ambiguous.[26] They were not permitted to make opening or closing speeches to the jury. All they could do was examine (and cross-examine) witnesses, and try to make their point clear through the phrasing of their questions.[27] And Knapp's questions had elicited information that was entirely unhelpful to Lucy: not only had one witness denied any knowledge of Joshua having been abroad, but at least one had also suggested that less than seven years had elapsed between him separating from Lucy and her marriage to James. Knapp had no way of challenging that evidence, and he might have worried that a follow-up question would elicit even more unhelpful information.

By contrast, counsel for the prosecution was subject to no such limits on speechifying, and Mr Raine made full use of this privilege. He sought to depict Lucy as an artful young woman who had inveigled 'an inexperienced young man' into an unsuitable marriage.[28] James, he told the court, came from a respectable family in Bristol, where his father was a merchant. Lucy had, he claimed, represented herself as a widow, despite knowing full well that her first husband was still alive, and 'unhappily had influence enough' to persuade James to marry her. His family had, however, made inquiries, discovered that Joshua was still living, and intervened to detach James from 'such an unfortunate connexion'.[29]

When called upon for her defence, Lucy told a very different story. Dressed in black, she delivered her speech with much hesitation, in a 'faint and tremulous' voice that was scarcely audible in the court.[30] She claimed that Joshua had left her some eight-and-a-half years earlier, and that she had believed him to be dead. She also explained that her acquaintance with 'young Mr Thomas' had come about quite by chance. She had apparently been sitting in her parlour with a lady when James had passed the house with another gentleman.[31] The latter being acquainted with the other lady, both came into the house. But when the other gentleman went away, James had stayed with her.

The circumstances of how they had met were, from a legal perspective, entirely irrelevant. But the little detail about their first meeting taking place in her private parlour rather than in a public space helped to create an alternative image of Lucy as a modest young woman who had been sought out by a stranger.[32] If Lucy's account

[25] E Coke, *The third part of the Institutes of the laws of England concerning high treason, and other pleas of the crown, and criminall causes* (London, 1644) 89; Sir M Hale, *Pleas of the Crown* (London, 1677) 104.

[26] JH Langbein, *The Origins of Adversary Criminal Trial* (Oxford, Oxford University Press, 2003, ppbk 2005).

[27] JM Beattie, 'Scales of Justice: Defense Counsel and the English Criminal Trial in the Eighteenth and Nineteenth Centuries' (1991) 9 *Law and History Review* 221.

[28] His words were not recorded in the *Proceedings* but were reported in the press: *Sun*, 29 May 1800; *General Evening Post*, 27–29 May 1800.

[29] ibid.

[30] *Oracle*, 29 May 1800; *Sun*, 29 May 1800; *General Evening Post*, 27–29 May 1800.

[31] The language of 'lady' and 'gentleman' was Lucy's own: given Lucy's own social status as a wife of an artisan, these terms did not necessarily denote that those concerned were members of the social elite.

[32] Contrast the case of Maria Edkins, heard at the Old Bailey a few years earlier, where the evidence was that the accused, described as 'a person of easy virtue', had met her second husband in the street: *Lloyd's Evening Post*, 17–19 September 1794.

is to be believed, James was completely bowled over by her at this first meeting: as she reported, he told her that 'he had taken such a liking to me, that he could not be happy without he had me'. Her coy response was that this was 'extraordinary', given that they were strangers to each other, but her evidence indicated that she had not been averse to hearing more: 'I told him to consider, and to call upon me again the next evening.'[33]

At some point – whether at this first meeting or later is unclear from her account – she told James that she was a poor woman, and that his friends might not approve of him marrying her, and, more importantly, that she had been married, but her husband was 'gone abroad' and she believed he was dead. Nonetheless, James had persisted: 'he paid his addresses to me, several times, and at last he said, if I would not have him, he would not see the light of another day.'[34] The clear message was that she could not be blamed for succumbing to his 'ardent passion' for her.

Unfortunately, we only have Lucy's word for any of this. She called no witnesses to corroborate any of her statements.[35] As a result, we cannot know whether she was telling the truth, or simply presenting a version that she hoped would play well with the court. If the latter, it was a cleverly crafted performance, both in its delivery and its content.

Summing up the evidence for the jury, the Recorder noted that the proof that Joshua had been out of the country for seven years – which 'seemed to be the ground assumed by the prisoner as an excuse for her conduct'[36] – rested solely on Lucy's own word, as no other evidence had been offered. In his view, 'the prosecutor had fully made out his case'.[37] Even so, the jury took some time to consider their verdict. They eventually returned a verdict of 'guilty', but recommended Lucy to mercy 'on the ground of her probably imagining that her first husband was dead'.[38] Lucy was sentenced to three months in prison.

Lucy's case was the first where the prosecution deliberately portrayed the second husband as young and inexperienced – which is no doubt why she took such pains to present herself as the pursued rather than the pursuer. The last decades of the eighteenth century had seen judges beginning to differentiate between different kinds of bigamy. Put bluntly, it was all about the sex, specifically whether the second spouse had lost their virginity as a result of being duped into a bigamous union. And with the passage of new legislation in 1795, sentences had become much harsher. Three of the previous four men convicted of bigamy at the Old Bailey had been sentenced to seven years' transportation. But, as Lucy's case shows, by 1800 bigamy by a woman was

[33] *OBP*, 28 May 1800.

[34] ibid.

[35] *Sun*, 29 May 1800; *General Evening Post*, 27–29 May 1800.

[36] The 'seemed' and 'assumed' here are interesting: none of the reports mention Lucy claiming that Joshua had been overseas for seven years; perhaps the judge had heard something that the reporters had not, or perhaps he was just drawing inferences from Knapp's line of questioning.

[37] *Sun*, 29 May 1800; *General Evening Post*, 27–29 May 1800. Again, the fact that we are reliant on newspaper reports for what the Recorder said reflects a major deficiency with the *Proceedings*.

[38] *Sun*, 29 May 1800; *General Evening Post*, 27–29 May 1800. As this indicates, this was not a defence at the time: on which see further chapter 7.

regarded as far less serious than bigamy by a man. The harm done to a second husband, even a young and inexperienced one, was simply not the same.[39]

Lucy's is also the only trial I have traced where the case for the defence was that the first spouse had been overseas for seven years.[40] And it was around this time that questions were beginning to be raised as to why this should be a defence at all. Here we need to turn to a publication that was to play a key role in the evolution of the seven-year defences.

'Whether the Party be not Bound to Use Reasonable Diligence to Inform Himself of the Fact': East's *Pleas of the Crown*, 1803

A Treatise of the Pleas of the Crown, by Edward Hyde East, was the first of a new generation of textbooks on criminal law. It sought to discuss and analyse the law rather than simply setting out a collection of often quite random points.[41] In writing it, East drew on both his 17 years' experience as a barrister and his study of private collections of cases. That said, given the rarity of cases in which the seven-year defence was raised, it was unlikely that he would have come across one either in his practice or in his readings. So he was very much arguing from first principles: what the law should be, rather than what it was.

From the perspective of 1803, the defence that the other spouse had been overseas for seven years seemed inexplicable. No one had been executed for bigamy within living memory, so having a generous set of defences was no longer quite as critical. In addition, the courts had begun to take the view that bigamists who deceived their second spouse should be punished more harshly.[42] Against that background, it was understandable why East thought it was 'extraordinary' that a person should have a defence to a charge of bigamy if they knew that their first spouse was still alive and that the second marriage was therefore void.[43]

In his view, it would have been 'more reasonable' to make the absence of the first spouse overseas simply 'prima facie evidence of their death'.[44] This, however, suggests

[39] On the changing attitudes and punishment, see further *Double Trouble*, ch 5, and R Probert and L D'Arcy-Brown, 'The transportation of bigamists in early nineteenth century England and Wales' (2019) 40 *Journal of Legal History* 223.

[40] It is possible that this was the defence in the case of Harriet Wilmot, who was acquitted at the Hampshire assizes in 1820. The *Hampshire Telegraph*, 24 July 1820, stated that her first marriage had taken place 17 years earlier and that her first husband had left her three years later and 'went abroad'. Harriet had then waited seven years before remarrying. However, the newspaper also noted that she had 'supposed he was dead'. There may also have been other cases that never came to trial because the magistrates were satisfied that the exception applied and decided not to commit the individual for trial, but newspaper searches did not yield any examples.

[41] KJM Smith, *Lawyers, Legislators and Theorists: Developments in English Criminal Jurisprudence, 1800–1957* (Oxford, Oxford University Press, 1998) 3.

[42] See further *Double Trouble*, ch 5.

[43] EH East, *A Treatise of the Pleas of the Crown: Vol 1* (London, 1803) 466.

[44] ibid 466.

he thought that this is how the other seven-year defence operated – in other words, that 'not knowing the other to be living' actually meant 'assuming the other to be dead'.

East accordingly went on to raise the question of whether a separated spouse who did not know where the other spouse was needed to do more than just sit things out for seven years before remarrying. As he pondered:

> Whether the party be not bound to use reasonable diligence to inform himself of the fact; and still more, whether if he neglect or refuse to avail himself of palpable means of acquiring such information, he will stand excused? are questions which I do not find anywhere touched upon; but which seem worthy of mature consideration.[45]

It was unsurprising that East had not found anything on these questions. If the seven-year defence had been based on the presumption that the first spouse had died, then it would have been perfectly reasonable to expect the other to try to verify this before remarrying, and to have to show that they had made such inquiries as they could. But as we have seen, the defence was only needed where there was evidence that the first spouse was still alive, and the onus of proof was on the prosecution to prove that the accused knew this. So, on the basis of how the law operated in 1803, the answers to East's questions were – no, there was no requirement to 'use reasonable diligence' to find out whether the other spouse was still alive; and yes, they would still have a defence even if they had failed to do so.

Matters might have ended there. But East's influence developed over the years. He was elected to Parliament in 1823, and was serving as an MP during the rush to codify the criminal law in the 1820s.[46] The Offences Against the Person Act 1828 included a provision repealing the 1604 Act and setting out a new definition of the offence of bigamy. This took on board East's criticism of the seven-years-overseas defence.[47] From 1 July 1828, the location of the absent spouse was irrelevant: the remarrying spouse only had a defence if they had not known them to be alive in the previous seven years.[48]

In the meantime, no judge appears to have picked up on East's speculation as to the need to make reasonable inquiries before remarrying. The year after his treatise appeared in print, one John Martin was acquitted at the Old Bailey after giving evidence of his 32-year absence from his first spouse.[49] As John explained, his marriage to Margaret Coghlan had taken place in Ireland in 1771, but two years later he had been ordered to Plymouth, and had gone from there to America for 11 years, where he 'continued in his Majesty's service all the war'. Upon returning home in 1784, he had been informed by Margaret's relatives that she was dead. Even then, another 19 years had elapsed before he remarried. Yet despite this lengthy separation, John could easily have found his first wife if only he had tried – his second wife, it turned out,

[45] ibid 467.

[46] For details of East's election and Parliamentary career, see DR Fisher (ed), *The History of Parliament: the House of Commons 1820-1832* (Cambridge, Cambridge University Press, 2009). On East's own role in bringing about reform, see further *Double Trouble*, ch 6.

[47] The marginal notes to the bill referenced his textbook in explaining the removal of the exceptions: Bill No 21, 3 March 1828.

[48] Offences Against the Person Act 1828, s 22.

[49] *OBP*, 11 April 1804.

had done precisely that after their wedding. As she told the court, she had not believed the rumour that John had been married before, and so went to Ireland herself to satisfy herself as to the truth. In other words, if the law *had* required due diligence on the part of the remarrying spouse, John might well have been convicted.

'It had not been Shewn …': Sarah Horsfield, 1837

In February 1837, a woman named Mary Ayton brought a prosecution against Sarah Horsfield for bigamy. The two women were rivals for the affections of John Sutcliffe, a private in the Carabiniers. John had paid his addresses to Mary, had arranged for the banns to be put up for their marriage, and persuaded her to accompany him to Sheffield, where they had lived together for some time.[50] Mary then had the mortification of discovering that John had gone through a ceremony of marriage with Sarah, who was unflatteringly described by one newspaper as 'advanced in life'.[51]

The marriage between John and Sarah had taken place at Sheffield Cathedral on 30 January 1837, with Sarah using the surname Platts and describing herself as a spinster.[52] Platts was not Sarah's original surname, but rather that of the man she had lately been living with.[53] As the name by which she was known at the time, it was fine for the banns to be called in the name of Sarah Platts.[54] The more fundamental problem was that Sarah was not a spinster. Twenty years earlier she had married one Joseph Horsfield, and he was still alive in January 1837.[55]

But the fact that Sarah had been cohabiting with a different man before her bigamous marriage – and, according to one report, keeping a 'disorderly house' – was irrelevant to the question of whether she had a defence. There was no requirement for her to have spent the seven years chastely waiting for Joseph's return. As her counsel told the jury, 'it had not been shewn' that Sarah had known anything of her first husband being alive within the seven years prior to her second marriage.[56] Sarah was duly acquitted.

The very fact that Sarah's counsel, a Mr Wortley, was able to address the jury in this way hints at how the law had changed since Lucy Ahier's case. The previous year, Parliament had passed legislation removing the restrictions on what defence counsel could do: for the future, they, like prosecution counsel, would be able to make opening and closing speeches and address all that had been alleged against the defendant.[57] Mr Wortley certainly seems to have made full use of this new freedom. As the local newspaper reported, as well as contesting her guilt, Sarah's counsel pointed out

[50] 'Sheffield Intermediate Sessions', *Sheffield Independent*, 4 March 1837.
[51] 'Bigamy', *Sheffield Independent*, 25 February 1837. According to the *Criminal Registers*, she was aged 38 at the time of her trial: TNA, HO 27/54, p 513.
[52] Ancestry, *Parish Registers*, PR138/3/33.
[53] 'Sheffield Intermediate Sessions', *Sheffield Independent*, 4 March 1837.
[54] The name by which the banns were to be called was the name by which the individual was known in the community: see further chapter 8.
[55] Ancestry, *Parish Registers*, PR87/3/7 (marriage at Rotherham Minister on 2 December 1816).
[56] 'Sheffield Intermediate Sessions', *Sheffield Independent*, 4 March 1837.
[57] Trials for Felony Act 1836, s 1.

that the prosecution 'had not been instituted by any relative aggrieved by the second marriage', noted that it 'did not appear to have been contracted from any mercenary or improper motives', and rounded off with a fine rhetorical flourish by protesting 'against the arm and sword of justice being made the weapons of revenge'.[58]

The suggestion that Mary had been motivated by 'revenge' was good rhetoric. Whether or not it reflected the reality is another matter. She may well have hoped that establishing the invalidity of John's marriage to Sarah would pave the way for him to make good on his promise of marriage to her. If this was her motivation, she was to be disappointed: no subsequent marriage has been traced for them.

Sarah's case provides a good example of the complex emotional tangles that might lie behind an individual's decision to bring a prosecution, as well as illustrating the changing role of defence counsel. It was also one of a small flurry of cases on the seven-year defence in the late 1830s – all of which accepted that the onus was on the prosecution to show that the accused knew their first spouse to be alive, and that there was no need for the accused to show that they had made inquiries.[59] But that was about to be called into question, as our next case study will show.

'The Whole of those Seven Years': Peter Cullen, 1840

On the night of 2 August 1840, Peter Cullen, an actor at the Surrey Theatre, went into the Coach and Horses public house in Lambeth. There he got into a somewhat acrimonious discussion with an Irishman named James Brennan, who responded to Peter's claim to be half Irish by calling him a 'damned imposter'. When Peter left the pub, James followed him with a poker that he had taken from the kitchen, and struck him across the head. Had it not been for the hat that Peter was wearing, he would probably have been killed; as it was, the flesh was cut open to the skull, Peter was rendered unconscious, and for a week or so 'his life was despaired of'.[60]

The possibility that this attack had a longer-term impact on Peter's memory was to form a central part of his defence at his subsequent trial for bigamy. At the time of the attack, Peter was lodging at the house of Jane Bristow, a widow with four children. As Jane later recalled, 'after that illness he paid his addresses to me'.[61] When she asked

[58] *Sheffield Independent*, 4 March 1837.

[59] This was the subject of debate in the case of Arthur Battersby, alias Henry Napier Disney, in 1838: see 'Central Criminal Court: Charge of Bigamy', *Evening Chronicle*, 2 February 1838, and see further chapter 5. *R v Disney* was cited in the case of William Watson at the Devizes assizes, in support of counsel's claim that 'as the prisoner had not been proved to have been aware of his first wife being living within seven years, he could not be convicted'. Mr Baron Parke agreed that this was 'conclusive' and directed the jury to acquit William: 'Assize Intelligence', *London Evening Standard*, 15 August 1838. See also 'Cheshire Assizes', *Chester Chronicle*, 13 April 1838 (William Ridings' first wife had absconded 14–15 years before and he had not heard of her since, acquitted); 'Extraordinary Case of Bigamy', *Bradford Observer*, 19 April 1838 (Hull quarter sessions, Martha Norton had remained single for 8½ years after her first husband had left her, hearing nothing of him, acquitted).

[60] 'Central Criminal Court', *Globe*, 19 August 1840; 'Violent Assault', *Sun*, 19 August 1840. James Brennan plays no further part in this story, but readers may like to know that he was convicted of wounding with intent to do grievous bodily harm at the Central Criminal Court and sentenced to transportation for 12 years: *OBP*, 17 August 1740.

[61] *OBP*, 14 December 1840.

him about the rumours that he had been married previously, Peter told her that he had not seen his wife for nearly eight years and believed her to be dead. This was good enough for Jane, and the pair were married on Monday, 16 November at St George's in the East, with Peter describing himself as a widower.[62]

It proved to be an exceptionally short-lived marriage. Three days after the wedding they had an argument, and Peter turned Jane's 14-year-old daughter out of the house. The following day he asked Jane for various papers relating to the substantial sum of money that she held on trust for her children and told her that he had only married her for her money.[63]

Jane's oldest son, William, then (somewhat belatedly, one feels) made inquiries into Peter's first marriage. Together with Peter's brother, he went to St Mary's Whitechapel. There, in its marriage register, they found an entry for Peter's marriage to Mary Ann Mitchell on 23 February 1824. And later that day they met with Mary Ann herself, who was still employed as a tailoress in the same place as when she married Peter.[64] The ease with which they found her showed that Peter could also have done so, had he tried.

On Saturday morning, just five days after his marriage to Jane, Peter was brought before the Union Hall police court in Southwark.[65] By this time, Jane seems to have decided that she wanted nothing more to do with him: when he stretched out his hand towards her, she refused to take it.[66] Peter protested his innocence, initially claiming that his first marriage was 'illegal' and had been annulled,[67] and then (via his solicitor) that he had been underage when it took place, and that he and Mary Ann had separated by mutual consent eight years earlier.[68] The magistrate, however, took the view that the evidence was sufficient to commit Peter for trial.[69]

At the Central Criminal Court in December 1840, the key witness for the prosecution was a woman named Mary Bridge, who had been at Peter's first marriage. She confirmed that he and Mary Ann had separated around 1827 or 1828 but – crucially – added that she had seen them together in the summer of 1834, walking in Whitechapel.[70] If true, that meant Peter had known Mary Ann was alive within seven years of his second marriage.

In response, Peter's counsel, Montagu Chambers, sought to argue that Mrs Bridge's evidence could not be relied upon, and that Peter had been continually absent from

[62] Ancestry, *London Church of England Parish Registers*, P93/GEO/051.

[63] 'Central Criminal Court', *Morning Post*, 17 December 1840.

[64] 'Union-Hall', *Globe*, 21 November 1840; *Morning Post*, 25 November 1840.

[65] 'Union-Hall', *Globe*, 21 November 1840.

[66] 'Charge of Bigamy, in the Theatrical World', *Weekly Chronicle*, 22 November 1840; 'Union-Hall', *Weekly Dispatch*, 22 November 1840.

[67] 'Union-Hall', *Morning Post*, 25 November 1840; 'Union-Hall', *London Evening Standard*, 25 November 1840; 'Charge of Bigamy Against An Actor', *Weekly True Sun*, 29 November 1840. These accounts also reported him as claiming that he had told Jane everything prior to their marriage and that the only reason he was being prosecuted was because of a dispute over the money.

[68] 'Union-Hall', *Morning Chronicle*, 2 December 1840, *Morning Post*, 2 December 1840. By 'underage', he meant under 21; since the marriage was by banns, his claim that it was void was a non-starter: on which see R Probert, 'Control over Marriage in England and Wales, 1753-1823: The Clandestine Marriages Act of 1753 in Context' (2009) 27 *Law and History Review* 413.

[69] 'Union-Hall', *Morning Chronicle*, 2 December 1840.

[70] *OBP*, 14 December 1840.

his wife for more than seven years before he remarried. No fewer than seven men and women with whom Peter had lodged over the previous seven years came forward to say that no wife had lived with him or even visited him during that time. Three of his fellow actors at the Surrey Theatre similarly confirmed that they had not even known that he was married.[71]

By way of a fallback, Chambers also argued that, even if Peter had been in contact with his first wife in 1834, the blow to his head had impaired his memory. He submitted that if at the time of the second marriage Peter had not known that his first wife had been alive during the preceding seven years, 'he would be within the protection of the proviso'.[72] His argument here was not that Peter had forgotten that he was married, but simply that he 'might … have forgotten the period when he last saw his wife, and might have imagined that a much longer period had elapsed'.[73]

Two of Peter's fellow actors confirmed that they had noticed a significant change in him since his head injury. As one, a Mr Saville, put it, 'his memory has been very indifferent, and he has been flighty, and it has been remarked by us that there has been a great alteration in him'.[74] Under cross-examination, however, Saville had to admit that Peter had been back at the theatre three weeks after his accident and had continued to play his most celebrated role, that of 'Blueskin' in *Jack Sheppard*.[75] This part involved singing a ditty called 'Jolly Nose', a paean to the benefits of heavy drinking, a detail that prompted some laughter in the court. When pressed as to whether the injury Peter had received would prevent him from knowing whether he had seen his wife five years earlier, the most Saville would say was that 'it might affect him as to the date'.[76]

Summing up the case for the jury, Mr Justice Patteson made it clear that the question was not what Peter had known at the time of the second marriage. The 1828 Act had exempted those who remarried after their first spouse had been 'continually absent' from them for the preceding seven years, but only if they had not known them to be living 'within that time'.[77] This, he said, meant that the remarrying spouse 'must have been ignorant during the whole of those seven years' that the other spouse was alive.[78] It was not sufficient to show that they did not know that their first spouse was still alive at the time of their second marriage.

The question came down to a simple one of fact: did the jury believe Mrs Bridge's evidence that she had seen Peter and Mary Ann walking together in Whitechapel in 1834? If they did, then that concluded the case, as Peter had known his wife was alive within seven years of his second marriage. Patteson also explained to the jury that even if they did not believe Mrs Bridge, and accepted that Peter had been separated from his first wife for more than seven years, then Peter was not necessarily entitled to an acquittal. Instead, a further question would arise as to whether Peter had 'to prove that he used due diligence to ascertain whether his wife was living before he contracted a

[71] ibid.
[72] *R v Cullen* (1840) 9 Car & P 681; 173 ER 100.
[73] 'Central Criminal Court', *Morning Post*, 17 December 1840.
[74] *OBP*, 14 December 1840 (evidence of Edmund Faucit Saville).
[75] ibid.
[76] ibid.
[77] Offences Against the Person Act 1828, s 22.
[78] *R v Cullen* (n 72) 684.

second marriage'. His phrasing hinted that there was some uncertainty as to whether this did need to be proved. But – somewhat frustratingly – he deferred giving the jury any direction as to the law on this point until they had made up their mind about Mrs Bridge's evidence.

Having consulted, the jury decided that they believed Mrs Bridge's evidence, and that the seven-year defence consequently did not apply. The judge sentenced Peter Cullen to six months in prison, which he served in Surrey county gaol.[79] We will come back to what happened to him shortly, once we have taken a look at the legal significance of his case.

The decision in *R v Cullen* curtailed the emerging idea that an individual should only be convicted of bigamy if they had an 'evil intention' – what lawyers call *mens rea*. This element of the crime had been laid out by a judge at the Liverpool assizes some five years earlier,[80] and the late 1830s had seen a few individuals being acquitted on the basis that they had believed their first spouse to be dead. While Mr Justice Patteson had not directly discussed the issue of mistaken beliefs of this kind, his reading of the 1828 Act left little room for such a defence. As he noted, when explaining why Peter's lack of knowledge that his first wife was alive had to extend across the full seven years they were apart:

> If it had been meant that he should not, 'at the time of such second marriage,' know that the first wife was alive, it would have been easy to make use of these words, and they would have been used instead of the words that are employed.[81]

In Patteson's view, the men who wrote the 1828 Act had never intended that the remarrying spouse could walk free simply because they did not know when they remarried that their first spouse was still alive. After *R v Cullen*, it was to be some time before the idea re-emerged that a genuine but mistaken belief in the death of the first spouse might be a defence to a charge of bigamy.

Peter's case also seems to have given rise to a new assumption – that those seeking to rely on the seven-year defence *did* need to show that they had tried to find out if their first spouse was still alive – despite that point never having been decided. The onus of proving this fell, naturally, to the defence. At the Suffolk assizes in August 1843, the judge took the view that the onus was on Thomas Hayward to show at least some evidence that he did not know his first wife – whom he had left – to be alive.[82] The 73-year-old Thomas, who had last seen his first wife in 1828 and had waited until June 1843 to remarry, was unable to produce any such evidence – resulting in his being convicted and sentenced to three months in prison.[83] Conversely, when Mary Simmons was acquitted at the Lancashire assizes in 1847, it was noted that she had no means

[79] *OBP*, 14 December 1840; TNA, 1841 census, HO107/1065, Book 12, folio 12, p 6.

[80] See chapter 7 for this case and subsequent developments.

[81] *R v Cullen* (n 72) 684.

[82] 'Suffolk Summer Assizes', *Ipswich Journal*, 12 August 1843.

[83] See also the conviction of Francis Owen despite his counsel pointing out that he had been separated from his first wife for eight years and there was no evidence to show he knew of her existence, the judge having taken the view that the burden of proof rested with the defence: 'South Lancashire Assizes', *Manchester Courier*, 23 August 1845.

of ascertaining whether her 'disreputable' first husband was still alive.[84] The following decade, the point was stated even more explicitly at the trial of John Smith at the Central Criminal Court, when the judge was reported as commenting 'that for the parties not to have seen each other for seven years was not enough, they should use diligent inquiries as to whether each other were still living, and then they would escape the penal consequences of the act'.[85]

So, *R v Cullen* was a pivotal case in the most literal sense, the point at which the law took a distinctly different turn. From the perspective of the evolving law of precedent, it might seem odd that it had such an influence. After all, decisions of judges sitting in the Central Criminal Court had no greater weight than those of any other assize judge: they were not binding precedents that had to be followed, just evidence of practice. But *R v Cullen* acquired greater currency by its inclusion in a series of law reports then being compiled by two barristers named Frederick Carrington and Joseph Payne, which in turn led to it being regularly cited in the burgeoning number of criminal law textbooks of the day.[86]

Contemporary developments in communication and information systems may also have made judges in the 1840s more receptive to the idea that individuals should make some inquiry as to the fate of their first spouse before marrying a second. The year of Peter Cullen's trial had seen the launch of the Uniform Penny Post, which made sending a letter between any two places in Great Britain both affordable and convenient.[87] The advent of centralised civil registration in 1837 had also made it far easier to ascertain if a spouse had died in England or Wales.

Even so, the idea of needing to exercise due diligence does not appear to have won universal acceptance. There were other cases where an individual was acquitted, as before, simply because there was nothing to show they had known their first spouse to be alive in the seven years before the second marriage.[88] Other cases never even came to trial.[89] The few textbook writers who explicitly acknowledged the debate simply noted that the point remained unsettled.[90]

[84] 'Bigamy', *Manchester Courier*, 21 April 1847; 'South Lancashire Summer Assizes', *Manchester Courier*, 14 August 1847; 'Lancashire Summer Assizes', *Liverpool Mercury*, 17 August 1847.

[85] 'Central Criminal Court', *Daily News*, 18 August 1854.

[86] T Starkie, *A practical treatise of the law of evidence, and digest of proofs, in civil and criminal proceedings: Vol III*, 3rd edn (London, V&R Stevens and GS Norton, 1842) 1527; JF Arnold, *The justice of the peace and parish officer: Vol IV*, 5th edn (London, Shaw & Sons, 1855) 51; J Jervis and WN Welsby, *Archbold's Pleading and evidence in criminal cases*, 14th edn (London, H Sweet, V&R Stevens and GS Norton, 1859) 756.

[87] Previously, postal charges had been paid by the recipient, who could refuse to accept them, and varied according to the weight of the letter: L Woodward, *The Age of Reform, 1815-1870* (Oxford, Oxford University Press, 1962) 48.

[88] See eg 'Charge of Bigamy', *Norwich Mercury*, 31 March 1849 (Norfolk assizes, Thomas Butterfield acquitted, there being 'no evidence to show that the prisoner had heard from his first wife for a period of seven years'); 'Assize Intelligence', *Hereford Journal*, 10 April 1850 (Monmouthshire assizes, James Armstrong similarly acquitted, with the judge emphasising that the onus was on counsel for the prosecution to 'show that the prisoner was aware his first wife was in existence, that they had attended the same parties, met in some place or other').

[89] See eg 'Charge of Bigamy', *Manchester Times*, 15 January 1853, where it was successfully argued that Harriet Collier's case was not one that should be sent to trial, given the seven-year defence and her desire to return to her legal husband.

[90] B Boothby and L Temple, *A synopsis of the law relating to indictable offences*, 2nd edn (London, Wm Maxwell, 1854) 47 ('whether the party setting up the defence of absence for seven years is bound to show that he has used reasonable diligence to inform himself of the fact, seems not to be settled').

Before we go on to see how this point was subsequently resolved, let us return to see what happened to Peter. From a modern perspective, one of the most striking aspects of his case is the complete absence of any arguments about his mental capacity. After all, he had been knocked unconscious by a serious head injury and barely survived. Admittedly, given the multiple excuses proffered by Peter and his counsel, and Jane's claim that he had avowedly only married her for her money, it would be easy to dismiss the idea that he had lost his memory as yet another thin excuse. In any case, any impairment he had suffered clearly fell far below the level needed to establish insanity (particularly given the evidence that he had continued to act at the Surrey Theatre after his accident). While it was possible for a jury to return a verdict of 'not guilty by reason of insanity', this required evidence that the accused was 'totally deprived of his understanding and memory and doth not know what he is doing, no more than an infant, than a brute, or a wild beast'.[91]

But his after-story does suggest that he may well have experienced long-term problems. In March 1843, he was charged with creating a disturbance at a lodging house, and it was noted that his mental state had worsened since his imprisonment.[92] He was admitted to the Christ Church workhouse in Southwark the following day, classified as 'insane' and sent on to an asylum.[93] He died at the Surrey County Lunatic Asylum two years later.[94]

'They Must be Taken to have Found that She did not know': Mary Briggs, 1856

On 30 March 1856, an umbrella maker living in Bury St Edmunds sent a letter to a friend in Cambridge:

> Dear friends i tak this opertunity of riting to you hoping to find you in Goad health as it leaves us at present thank the lord fo it my friends i wish to let me Now what the misses brothers name is or what name was the woman that he wass married to i meane John that used to do the work for Grany burell as we used to call her i am giving to understand the woman that lived with George whipps has got married to a engineer on the raily on wednesday last; wee are told that shee was Johns wife and if shee iss or if hee can know it that shee is hiss wife hee can come to thiss town and have all expences paid and 5 pounds gave him the moment he comes heere Shee left George whipps and has taken 150 pounds a way with her and has got married. their is 50 pounds of furniture she hat got and John can claim every thing shes has got rite to me by return of post to No 41 bridewell lane bury st Edmons suffolk Yours truly till Death, James GROGAN.[95]

[91] These were the words of Mr Justice Tracey in the 1724 trial of Edward Arnold for shooting at Lord Onslow, as reported by TB Howell, *A Complete Collection of State Trials and Proceedings for High Crimes and Other Misdemeanors: Vol XVI* (London, 1812) 765 and quoted in other contemporary textbooks such as WO Russell, *A Treatise on Crimes and Misdemeanors*, 2nd edn (London, Butterworth and Son, 1826) 9. Cullen's case just predated the decision of the House of Lords in *R v M'Naghten* (1843) 10 Cl & F 200; 8 ER 718.

[92] 'Union Hall', *Morning Post*, 16 March 1843.

[93] Ancestry, *Workhouse Admission and Discharge Records, 1764-1921*, SOBG/101/14.

[94] GRO, death certificate of Peter Anthony Cullen, death registered on 6 January 1845.

[95] 'Bigamy', *Bury and Norwich Post*, 23 July 1856.

The woman whose name James was hoping to learn was Mary Riggle, who had married John Briggs at Alconbury in January 1844 and left him within a few months. Her second marriage, to William Cooper, had taken place at St Paul's church in Cambridge on 27 March 1856 – some three days before James had written his letter.

Mary's case provides a striking example of how community knowledge of who was married to whom could lead to a bigamous marriage being speedily detected.[96] Bury St Edmunds lies around 28 miles to the east of Cambridge, and Alconbury around 23 miles to its north-west. The Cambridge wedding had been authorised by a common licence, so there had been no public calling of the banns. Yet news of it had clearly filtered back to those who knew Mary from Bury St Edmunds almost immediately. All it took was one person who knew of her prior marriage in Alconbury to set matters in train for her prosecution. By mid-April she had been arrested, charged and committed to the assizes.[97]

The press coverage hints at a degree of sympathy for Mary, despite her complex relationship history (and the fact that she had appropriated John's watch and various other items when she left him). John was unflatteringly described in the *Cambridge Independent Press* as a 'withered, hard-featured old man', and noted to be some 32 years older than the still 'blooming' Mary. The writer clearly thought that it was hardly a surprise that such a May-to-December match did not prosper. It was also noted that John had 'never thought it worth his while to fret or even run after his youthful bride'.[98]

At the Cambridge assizes in July, Mary's counsel, a Mr Power, similarly adopted the tactic of implying that John was really the one to blame. Nothing, he said, could have been easier than for John to take legal steps to reclaim his wife. Since he had not done so, and it was not shown that Mary knew he was alive, 'was it, then, unreasonable for her to marry Cooper?'[99]

Mr Justice Coleridge frankly acknowledged that he had never come across such a case before, and went off to consult with Lord Campbell (his fellow judge at the assizes) as to the correct approach to be taken. Upon his return, he directed the jury that there were two questions for them to consider: first, whether they thought that Mary knew that John was still alive, and, if not, whether they thought that she could have found out 'by the exercise of reasonable diligence'.[100] If the answer to either question was yes, they should find Mary guilty of bigamy. The verdict of the jury was that there was no evidence that Mary had known that John was still alive, but that she did have 'the means of ascertaining' this.[101]

Coleridge was clearly still uncertain as to whether this was the right approach, since he decided that the question needed to be referred to the Court for Crown Cases

[96] It also provides a good example of the level of financial support available to those bringing the prosecution: on which see further R Lamont, 'The Crown against …: The Victim and the State in the Pursuit of Criminal Prosecution, 1840-1985' in S Walklate and P Cox, *Victims Access to Justice: Historical and Comparative Perspectives* (London, Routledge, 2022).

[97] 'Bigamy', *Cambridge Independent Press*, 12 April 1856.

[98] 'Bigamy Extraordinary', *Cambridge Independent Press*, 12 April 1856.

[99] 'Cambridgeshire Summer Assizes', *Cambridge Independent Press*, 26 July 1856.

[100] As reported by Coleridge to the Court for Crown Cases Reserved: *R v Mary Briggs* (1856) Dears & Bell 98; 169 ER 933.

[101] 'Cambridgeshire Summer Assizes', *Cambridge Independent Press*, 26 July 1856.

Reserved in London. Five judges sat to hear the case in November 1856. It was clear from the questions that they posed to Mr Power, appearing once again for Mary, that they held quite differing views as to what the law was, or should be.[102]

Eventually, though, all five agreed that Mary's conviction had to be quashed, if only because the jury had not found explicitly that Mary had known John to be alive. But even on that simple point they all had their say, and subtly different takes on the evidence. Chief Baron Pollock thought that the jury 'must be taken to have found that she did not know'.[103] Coleridge himself delivered a rather bewildering speech in which he tried to disguise his disagreement with the more senior judge and provide a different rationalisation for the jury's decision:

> With respect to the interpretation put upon the finding of the jury by the Lord Chief Baron, it does not seem to me that the jury have said that the prisoner in point of fact did not know, and I do not think they meant to say that, but rather, on the contrary, that she probably did know, though the evidence was not quite sufficient to warrant them in finding that she did.[104]

He compromised by agreeing that the finding of the jury was 'imperfect', an opinion which was echoed by Willes.[105] Mr Baron Bramwell then suggested that all the jury had said was that they could not say that she did not know, and Watson concurred (though with whom or what is unclear).[106]

While their decision was a positive outcome for Mary, it was singularly unhelpful in terms of offering guidance for the future. Pollock certainly made it clear that he was opposed to the idea of asking whether someone had the means of finding out whether their first spouse was still alive, pointing out that if that was the test, then 'there would be no limit to the inquiry; one man may have the means of knowing what passes in another town, while another may not have the means of knowing what takes place in the next street'.[107] But none of the other judges commented on this point. And the most fundamental question of all – whether the onus was on the prosecution to prove knowledge, or on the remarrying spouse to prove their lack of knowledge – was left open.

The press drew their own conclusions as to the significance of the decision:

> The upshot of this would seem to be, that if a woman run away from her husband, or a husband run away from his wife, and go far enough to be out of the way of hearing whether he or she is alive or dead for seven years, she or he is then at liberty to marry again; for the act is perfectly silent as to which must be the deserting party, and requires nothing but the facts of absence and ignorance.

In the meantime, what had happened to Mary? Back in July, at the conclusion of her trial, Coleridge had emphasised that she was not the wife of William Cooper, and her acquittal did nothing to change that.[108] The following census found her back with

[102] *R v Mary Briggs* (n 100).
[103] ibid 102.
[104] ibid 103.
[105] ibid.
[106] ibid.
[107] ibid 102.
[108] 'Cambridgeshire Summer Assizes', *Cambridge Independent Press*, 26 July 1856.

her lover George Whipps, with an additional couple of children.[109] But they were never able to marry: her legal husband John Briggs lived on to the hale old age of 84, dying only in 1880.[110]

'If You could Tell Her You had Seen Him Dead …': Tennyson's Enoch Arden, 1864

In 1864, Alfred Tennyson published his best-selling poem *Enoch Arden*. Set a hundred years earlier, and in an unnamed fishing port, it involves the entwined lives of Enoch, Annie Lee and Philip Ray. As children, they play at 'keeping house', with Enoch and Philip each taking it in turn to be the 'master' but occasionally arguing over the length of their tenure, and Annie trying to keep the peace by saying that she 'would be little wife to both'. Once they reach adulthood, Enoch and Annie marry, leaving Philip with a 'lifelong hunger' in his heart. The next 'seven happy years' bring Enoch and Annie two children. But the family's fortunes then take a turn for the worse, and Enoch decides to take a job as boatswain on a ship bound for China, allowing him to sell his fishing boat to meet the family's immediate needs and with the hope of 'returning rich'.

But he does not return. As the years pass, Annie's poverty forces her to accept support from Philip, who has continued to love her and becomes a second father to her children. After 10 years have passed, Philip begs Annie to marry him, arguing that it is 'beyond all hope, against all chance' that Enoch can still be alive. Even then, Annie asks for another year, and then makes further excuses. Eventually she consults her Bible for guidance, lighting on the words 'Under the palmtree'. That night she dreams of Enoch sitting under a palm and believes it to be a sign that he is in Heaven. She finally agrees to marry Philip, and they are married in the same church where she had married Enoch some 20 years earlier. Even then, it takes the birth of their child for Philip to become her 'all-in-all' and her doubts and fears to be allayed.

At this point in the poem, we finally discover what has happened to Enoch – a shipwreck on the homeward voyage, from which he is, after many years, eventually rescued. Browned, silver-haired, bowed and broken, he returns home unrecognised to hear of Annie's remarriage. His main thought is to 'look on her sweet face again/ And know that she is happy'. He manages to observe Annie, his now 'tall and beautiful' children, the new babe on Annie's knee and 'that other, reigning in his place', and 'the warmth, the peace, the happiness' that emanates from them all. He creeps away, resolved never to let her know that he is still alive.

He does, however, ask his landlady Miriam whether Annie has any fear that her first husband is still alive. Miriam confirms that she does, and that 'if you could tell her you had seen him dead … that would be her comfort'. He resolves – and at this point the reader may lose some sympathy for him – that he will arrange for word to be sent to her

[109] TNA, 1861 census, RG9/1141, folio 80, p 26 (with Mary being described as George's housekeeper).
[110] TNA, 1861 census, RG9/973, folio 41, p 20; 1871 census, RG10/1525, folio 38, p 16; Free BMD, Huntingdon RD, Q1 1880.

after his death, so that she may know that he 'loved her to the last'. On his death-bed, he asks Miriam to tell Annie, his children, and even Philip that he died blessing them.

> So past the strong heroic soul away
> And when they buried him the little port
> Had seldom seen a costlier funeral.

Some reviewers thought Enoch's a 'touching story', depicting a 'deep and holy love', and a 'sublime act of self-sacrifice'.[111] Others were less impressed by his actions. One thought that it was 'improbable and unnatural' that a God-fearing man like Enoch would stay silent, thereby allowing 'the woman he loved to live in a state of concubinage, thus sharing his wife's sin, by permitting it'.[112] And an even more hostile review in *The Athenæum* pointed out that Enoch's concern for Annie's peace of mind was entirely undermined by the arrangements that he makes to inform her of his death:

> Honesty and law are both against Enoch in his silly deed; and no artifice of eloquence and imagery can hide the flaw in his proceedings. The poet means that his conduct shall appear brave; in truth, it appears to be that of a dastard .... He does not shield the inconstant woman. He betrays her. By his babble to the landlady, he tells all the world that Philip and Annie are not man and wife.[113]

Had Enoch really wanted to put Annie's mind at rest, he could have invented some story of his own death – backdating it to before her wedding to Philip and the birth of their child. Given that no one has recognised him – even Miriam needs some persuading that he is who he says he is when he finally reveals his identity to her – this would have been easy enough to do.[114] As it is, Annie now knows that her marriage to Philip is void, and their child illegitimate. And although she is now free to remarry Philip legally, this will not legitimate their child. Enoch's funeral is 'costly' for his family in more ways than one.

While some reviewers referred to Annie as a 'bigamist', albeit an 'innocent' one,[115] others took pains to explain that the length of the separation, and her lack of knowledge that Enoch was still alive, would have meant that she was not at risk of prosecution.[116] But such assessments were far easier to make with the benefit of an omniscient narrator describing the innermost thoughts and feelings of the parties. Read against the legal framework, the poem posed an important question: in the age of the postal service

[111] See, respectively, 'Tennyson's "Enoch Arden"', *Carlisle Journal*, 26 July 1864; 'The Laureate's New Work', *Birmingham Daily Post*, 9 August 1864; 'The Literary Examiner', *The Examiner*, 13 August 1864.
[112] WH Ainsworth, 'Enoch Arden' (1864) 132 *The New Monthly Magazine* 462, 463.
[113] 'Literature', *The Athenæum*, 13 August 1864.This point is also made by A Humphreys, '*Enoch Arden*, the Fatal Return, and the Silence of Annie' (1992) 30 *Victorian Poetry* 331.
[114] This, admittedly, was not the solution advocated by the reviewer in *The Athenæum* (n 113) who would have preferred to see Enoch drown himself.
[115] *Bath Chronicle*, 4 August 1864.
[116] WE Baxter, 'Tennyson's "Enoch Arden": Bigamy and Desertion' (1864) 143 *Notes and Queries* 256. One well-informed reviewer even pointed out since Annie's remarriage must, according to the timescale of the poem, have taken place before 1828, the mere fact of Enoch's absence overseas would have been sufficient for her to have a defence under the law as it then stood, regardless of whether she knew him to be alive or not: 'Literature', *Illustrated Times*, 20 August 1864.

and the telegraph, would a modern-day Annie Arden be able to *prove* that she had no knowledge of her absent spouse?

'It is Contrary to the General Spirit of the English Law that the Prisoner should be Called on to Prove a Negative': John Curgenven, 1865

On 1 September 1852, John Curgenven married his cousin Charlotte Langdon Curgenven at St Symplorian's church in the Cornish village of Veryan.[117] The marriage seems to have run into difficulties early on. Charlotte had accompanied John to Ireland, where he had a post as a coastguard. But upon arriving at his house, she discovered another woman already living there. John apparently expected Charlotte to tolerate him conducting an adulterous relationship in their marital home. But when the situation came to the knowledge of the officer in charge of the coastguard station, he required the other woman to leave. The 'enraged' John blamed Charlotte and began ill-treating her. His violence eventually forced her to leave.[118]

John was then posted to Portsmouth, and sent for Charlotte to join him there. But his former paramour was still on the scene, and his conduct towards Charlotte had by no means improved. Even so, Charlotte remained in Portsmouth until March 1853, when John was ordered on to *HMS Princess Royal* and set off to the Crimean War. She then returned to Veryan, and from that time there was no correspondence between them.[119]

John returned to England after the war, but not to Charlotte, who was still in Veryan.[120] In July 1862, he married 19-year-old Eliza Hardy at East Portlemouth in Devon, representing himself as a widower.[121] A subsequent promotion took him to Mullion in Cornwall, just 20 miles from where Charlotte was living, and the truth came out. He was charged at the Truro magistrates' office and committed for trial.[122]

Given the lapse of time between the two marriages, and the lack of communication between John and Charlotte during his absence overseas, John's counsel sought to argue that there was no case to answer. Citing *R v Briggs*, he argued that the onus was on the prosecution to prove that John had known Charlotte to be living within seven years of his marriage to Eliza. After consulting with his fellow judge, Mr Justice Willes took the view that the appropriate course was to ask the jury if they believed that John 'was in bona fide ignorance of his wife's existence during that seven years'. If so, John would be

[117] Ancestry, *Cornwall Parish Registers, 1538-2010*. I have used the spelling of John's name that appears in the parish registers, save when citing the law report that misspelt it as Curgerwen.
[118] 'Charge of Bigamy', *West Briton and Cornwall Advertiser*, 4 August 1865.
[119] ibid.
[120] TNA, 1861 census, RG11/2307, folio 106, p 9. Had he returned, he would have found an addition to the household – a daughter, Sophia, born in 1857, but no mention was made of this at his trial.
[121] Ancestry, *Devon Anglican Parish Registers*; 'Bigamy – Important Legal Question Reserved', *Falmouth Packet*, 5 August 1865.
[122] 'Bigamy', *West Briton*, 21 July 1865.

entitled to an acquittal. But, as he added, 'my learned brother thinks that if they find a verdict adverse to the prisoner, the point raised is of such importance that I should reserve it'.[123]

The discussion as to the point of law and what precisely they had been asked to decide seems (understandably) to have gone over the heads of the jury, who, after a short consultation, came back and said that they had found John guilty. Willes had to explain again that all he was asking them to decide was what John had known. To this the foreman replied bluntly, 'As he lived in a neighbouring county, we think he ought to have known it'.[124] Upon Willes reframing the question for a third time, the foreman finally said that the view of the jury was that John had known Charlotte was alive.[125]

It was accordingly decided that John's case should be referred to the Court for Crown Cases Reserved to decide the legal point.[126] Did the burden of proof lie on the accused to prove that they had not known their first spouse to be alive in the seven years prior to their remarriage? Or was it for the prosecution to prove that the accused *had* known? The decision of the five judges was delivered by Chief Baron Pollock.[127] He observed that the term 'burden of proof' was an 'inconvenient one, except when a person is called upon to prove an affirmative'.[128] He noted the view expressed by Charles Sprengel Greaves, a distinguished legal writer and the editor of the influential treatise *Russell on Crimes*, that the burden of proof lay on the prisoner. Nonetheless, as he explained, the view of the Court was that 'it is contrary to the general spirit of the English law that the prisoner should be called on to prove a negative'.[129] John's conviction was accordingly quashed.

John's case was the first to be included in the series of law reports dedicated to the decisions of the Court for Crown Cases Reserved and published under the aegis of the newly established Council of Law Reporting. Legal commentators quickly updated their textbooks to clarify that it was now for the prosecution to prove that the accused had known their spouse to be alive in the seven years preceding the second marriage.[130]

No mention was made of John's appalling treatment of Charlotte, with Mr Justice Willes simply referring elliptically to 'some disagreement' between them. It was, admittedly, irrelevant to the legal point. But the very fact that it was irrelevant underlines how the seven-year defence was morally neutral. A violent adulterer like John Curgenven who had abandoned his first wife was in the same position as a spouse who

[123] 'Bigamy – Important Legal Question Reserved', *Falmouth Packet*, 5 August 1865.

[124] ibid.

[125] 'Bigamy – Important Legal Question Reserved', *North Devon Journal*, 10 August 1865.

[126] Incidentally, the case as stated by Willes to the rest of the court made it sound as if he had identified John's case as a suitable test case to establish where the burden of proof lay – something that certainly did not come across in the contemporary account of the trial.

[127] The other four were Piggott B, Shee and Montague Smith JJ, and Willes himself.

[128] *R v John Curgerwen* (1865) LR 1 CCR 1, 1.

[129] ibid.

[130] JF Stephen, *Roscoe's Digest of the Law of Evidence in Criminal Cases*, 7th edn (London, Stevens and Sons, 1868) 319; JB Maule (ed), *Burn's Justice of the Peace and Parish Officer*, 30th edn (London, H Sweet, 1869) 452.

had been abandoned: all that mattered was what the prosecution could show they had known.[131]

The fact that John and his second wife Eliza had lived together until the time of his arrest might suggest that this was a stable second marriage that would survive the trial. Eliza even gave evidence that John had treated her kindly.[132] But by the time of the next census, she had reverted to her maiden name and to her former role as a servant.[133]

'It Means "a Second Time"': Thomas Treanor, 1940

In 1938, Thomas Treanor was charged with two counts of bigamy. His first marriage, to Bridget Treanor, had taken place in Belfast back in 1916. As she told the court, he had left her almost immediately, briefly returning once the First World War was over and then leaving her again.[134] Since then she had neither seen nor heard of him. He, however, claimed to have had news of her in 1922, when her brother had come up to him in a street in Dublin and told him that she was dead.[135] Eight years later, in 1930, he went through a second ceremony of marriage with Lilian Anderson in Oxford, presenting himself as a single man. They lived together 'on and off' for some years, but in 1936 he left her.[136] His third marriage, to Kathleen Davis, took place in Chichester in 1938, with Thomas assuming the surname of McAvoy. This relationship lasted only a couple of months before he left her.[137]

Counsel for the prosecution expressed scepticism about Thomas' claim that Bridget's brother had informed him of her death – not just because Bridget was still very much alive, but also because Thomas had made no further inquiries of anyone as to her fate. Rather than trying to make a case that he had believed Bridget to be dead, Thomas' counsel rested his defence on the fact that more than seven years had elapsed between that alleged conversation and Thomas' second marriage, and that there was no evidence that he knew her to be alive during that time.[138]

At his subsequent trial at the Sussex assizes in December, Thomas initially pleaded not guilty. Counsel for the prosecution acknowledged that they were unable to prove that he had heard anything of his wife in the seven years preceding his second marriage. But he contended that the exception in the statute did not extend to a *third* marriage.

[131] For another vivid example of this, see the case of Joseph Evans, acquitted at the Bristol assizes in 1880, who had also behaved very badly to his second wife, spending her money, bringing prostitutes into their home, and threatening her with violence: 'Singular Charge of Bigamy', *Bristol Mercury*, 23 September 1880; 'Singular Case of Alleged Bigamy', *Western Daily Press*, 2 November 1880.

[132] 'Bigamy – Important Legal Question Reserved', *Western Morning News*, 4 August 1865.

[133] TNA, 1871 census, RG10/2102, folio 13, p 17.

[134] 'Belfast War-Time Marriage: Said to Have Been Others: Newry Woman Tells of First', *Belfast Telegraph*, 26 August 1938.

[135] 'Double Bigamy Charge Against Former Bognor Man: "Did Not Recognise First Wife"', *Bognor Regis Observer*, 31 August 1938.

[136] 'Soldier Charged at Chichester: Not Guilty Plea: Committed to Assizes for Trial', *Portsmouth Evening News*, 25 August 1938.

[137] 'Chichester Story of Three Marriages: Alleged Bigamy and Larceny', *Hampshire Telegraph*, 26 August 1938.

[138] 'Double Bigamy Charge Against Former Bognor Man: "Did Not Recognise First Wife"', *Bognor Regis Observer*, 31 August 1938.

Otherwise, he argued, it would be possible 'for a man to go up and down the country ruining women' once seven years had passed without word of his legal wife.[139] The judge, Mr Justice Atkinson, agreed, but thought that the question was one that should be referred to the Court of Criminal Appeal. Thomas accordingly pleaded guilty to bigamy in marrying Kathleen in 1938.

The Court of Criminal Appeal took the view that Thomas had been rightly convicted of bigamy on account of his third marriage. In the words of the Lord Chief Justice, Lord Hewart:

> when the expression 'marrying a second time' is used it means 'a second time' and is not to be artificially expanded into meaning 'a second or subsequent time'. If it had been the intention of the Legislature to extend the effect of the proviso not merely to any second marriage strictly so called, but to any second or subsequent marriage, nothing could have been easier than to say so. This proviso, in our view, means not one word more than it says.[140]

It was a remarkably literal interpretation of the legislation, and one that immediately provoked some concern as to its potential implications. At the hearing of the appeal, Thomas' counsel had pointed out that a strict numerical approach would preclude a man from relying on the seven-year defence if he had been lawfully married twice before (a scenario that Hewart had dismissed as 'unlikely', despite the number of people who did in fact lawfully marry more than once). Subsequent commentators also pointed out that a too-literal interpretation of any references to a second marriage would also criminalise anyone who had been lawfully *divorced* twice before.[141] It did not take long before a different interpretation was adopted.

'He Searched for Perfect Wife': John Taylor, 1950

In March 1950, John Taylor pleaded guilty to two counts of bigamy at the Central Criminal Court. This rather downplayed his matrimonial career. He had met his first wife, Alice, at a dance in Dover in August 1925 and they had married a few months later. Three months later he had left her.[142] His second marriage, in 1927, was much longer-lasting: he was with Phoebe for 17 years and had eight children with her. After that, marriages three, four and five followed in relatively quick succession, to Marjorie in 1942, Lilian in 1946 and Olive in 1948. He was engaged to a sixth woman when he was arrested.[143]

The reason why he was charged with only two counts of bigamy, rather than four, is that he had *already* been tried and acquitted for the 1927 and 1942 marriages, although

[139] 'Double Bigamy – Law and Second Marriage – The Seven-year Proviso' (1939) 103 *Justice of the Peace & Local Government Review* 1, 12.

[140] *R v Thomas Joseph Treanor* (1940) 27 Cr App R 35, 37.

[141] 'Criminal Law: Bigamy, the Second Marriage' (1939) 58 *Law Notes* 80.

[142] 'Marriage certificate, But No Trace of Wife Or Witnesses', *Maidstone Telegraph*, 24 November 1944. Alice herself remarried 12 years later, believing John to be dead, which meant that she was in no danger of being prosecuted: 'He Searched for Perfect Wife', *Daily Express*, 24 March 1950; 'Wife is in no danger of law', *South London Observer*, 24 March 1950.

[143] 'He Searched for Perfect Wife', *Daily Express*, 24 March 1950.

not in that order. In 1944, he had been tried for bigamously marrying Marjorie while married to Phoebe, but his defence counsel produced the certificate of his first marriage to Alice. This was sufficient to acquit him of bigamy in marrying Marjorie, on the basis that Phoebe was not in fact his legal wife; but in the absence of any witnesses to that first marriage, it was not sufficient to charge him with bigamy in marrying Phoebe.[144] Another prosecution was then brought against him, charging him with bigamy in marrying Phoebe while married to Alice, but that too failed to result in a conviction.

At the Central Criminal Court in 1950, then, the best that his counsel could do was to portray John as 'seeking the perfect wife'.[145] The Recorder, unimpressed, commented that John's matrimonial affairs were 'too extensive to be believed', and sentenced him to prison for four years for marrying Lilian in 1946 and Olive in 1948.

It was one of the longest sentences handed down that year. The Home Office's official statistics recorded just four of the 279 individuals convicted of bigamy that year receiving a sentence of more than three years.[146] John subsequently applied for leave to appeal against his sentence. The question was then raised as to why he had not invoked the seven-year defence in relation to his 1946 and 1948 marriages, given that he had not seen his legal wife Alice since 1927. The reason, of course, was the ruling in *R v Treanor*,[147] which made it clear that the seven-year defence could only be invoked for a second marriage, and not any subsequent ones. John was given leave to appeal against his conviction so that *Treanor* could be considered by the full court of seven judges.

They were unanimously of the view that the decision in *Treanor* was wrong. The Lord Chief Justice, Lord Goddard, delivered the judgment of the court and held that it was 'obvious' that the defence applied 'however many times the ceremony of marriage had been gone through'.[148] John's conviction was accordingly quashed. Nonetheless, Goddard did not mince his words in expressing his opinion of John's conduct:

> This man would not have been given leave to appeal against his sentence if he had been properly convicted. A more persistent bigamist one cannot imagine. He is a danger to women – a scoundrel – and the case has no merits at all.[149]

In John's case, it was purely a matter of chance that he had not been convicted of bigamy in relation to his 1927 marriage – for which he would have had no defence. But the result of the decision in *R v Taylor* was that, once seven years had passed without news of the legal spouse, an individual could effectively go through as many wedding ceremonies as they chose without ever being guilty of bigamy. As Glanville Williams noted, while the decision in *R v Taylor* was 'undoubtedly right as a matter of law', this was 'a serious lacuna'.[150]

[144] 'Marriage certificate, But No Trace of Wife Or Witnesses', *Maidstone Telegraph*, 24 November 1944.
[145] 'He Searched for Perfect Wife', *Daily Express*, 24 March 1950.
[146] Home Office, *Criminal Statistics: England and Wales 1950* (Cmd 8301, 1951) Table V.
[147] *R v Treanor* (n 140).
[148] *R v Taylor* [1950] 2 KB 368, 372.
[149] 'Bigamy Appeal Judges Free "Scoundel"', *Evening News*, 22 May 1950.
[150] G Williams, 'Bigamy and the Third Marriage' (1950) 13 *Modern Law Review* 417.

According to a report in the *Daily Mail*, John was planning to make full use of this 'lacuna', saying that he hoped his next wedding would be in a church and that wife number six 'must be medium height, fond of entertainment, fond of pleasure, aged about 25'.[151] By July, he had made his selection. In an interview with the *Sunday Mirror*, the woman in question – who had known John for just three weeks – declared her intention to be 'the last Mrs Taylor'. The interviewer left them sitting hand in hand, throwing the newspaper cuttings of John's trial into the fire, and expressing the hope that they would be married by Christmas once their respective divorces had come through.[152]

[151] 'Man who knows all about women', *Daily Mail*, 23 May 1950.
[152] 'The Cook With Five "Wives" Is Ready to Marry Another', *Sunday Pictorial*, 30 July 1950.

7

Accidental Bigamy: Mistaken Beliefs

How should the law treat 'accidental' bigamy – where someone has remarried in good faith, genuinely but mistakenly believing that they were free to do so? The most obvious example is where a person has received information leading them to believe that their spouse has died and remarries, only for the first spouse to make an unexpected reappearance. The Bigamy Act 1604 did not address this particular scenario, and neither did the subsequent Offences Against the Person Acts of 1828 and 1861. Over time, some scholars and judges took the view that criminal responsibility required a 'guilty mind', or *mens rea*, and that those who remarried in good faith would have a defence despite this not being explicitly stated. Others, by contrast, argued that the statutory seven-year defence precluded any such general defence applying to bigamy cases.

The case studies in this chapter trace how certain kinds of mistaken beliefs came to be a defence to a charge of bigamy. It was a relatively late development. Our first case study dates only from 1835, there being nothing in the reports of cases from the seventeenth or eighteenth century to suggest that any kind of mistaken beliefs were a defence to a charge of bigamy at that time.[1] Moreover, the influence of this first case, which saw Eliza Greenwood being acquitted, was to prove short-lived. Two decades later, the compelling case of Susannah Anderson might have proved a successful test case had it not been for counsel's decision not to offer any evidence against her.

The 1860s and 1870s saw renewed debate as to whether a belief in the death of the first spouse was a defence, with different judges coming to different conclusions. It was not until 1889 that the point was finally settled, in the case of Martha Tolson, and some defendants, like Sidney Rayment in 1907, were still convicted where they had no reasonable grounds for their belief. The early years of the twentieth century then saw new questions arising as to whether a genuine belief in the invalidity of the first marriage, or that a divorce had been granted, would also be a defence, as explored in the case studies of Peter Thomson and Thomas Wheat respectively.

While there are more-or-less equal numbers of men and women within these case studies, their stories were very different. Women were more likely to have been left by their husband, more likely to claim that they had believed him to be dead, and more

[1] There were occasional cases where the accused claimed to have believed that the first spouse was dead, but this only succeeded as a defence if combined with the absence of that spouse for at least seven years. As we shall see, in *R v Tolson* (1889) 23 QBD 168, a number of judges argued that a mistaken belief in the death of the first spouse must have been a defence in earlier centuries, but this was based solely on their unwillingness to believe that someone in that position could have been sentenced to death for remarrying, rather than on any actual authorities.

likely to be acquitted. Men were more likely to claim that they had believed their first wife was already married, and more likely to be convicted.

Underpinning the human stories in this chapter is a bigger story about the evolution of legal doctrine – not as an abstract intellectual process, but as one that is profoundly affected by the individuals involved. Different judges had different views, not just on the substantive law but on how far previous decisions (even their own) should be regarded as binding. Much also depended on judges' decisions as to which cases should be referred upwards for a point of law to be resolved. As we shall see, there was nothing particularly special about the case of Martha Tolson, but how her case became the leading legal authority on the role of *mens rea* in bigamy cases is a fascinating story in its own right, showing how the compelling narrative presented to the Court for Crown Cases Reserved only emerged over time.

'Bigamy, Being a Felony, Implies an Evil Intention': Eliza Greenwood, 1835

Towards the close of 1834, Eliza Greenwood received an unexpected visit from the cousin of her husband William. Eliza had not seen William for some months: he had deserted her earlier that year, leaving her with one child and another on the way.[2] William's cousin now told her he had heard that William had drowned when crossing the Mersey after watching a prize fight.[3] Two boats had set off from Rock Ferry after the fight, overladen with passengers, and had been swamped by the waves. Only a handful had been able to swim to safety. It was the biggest loss of life that the Mersey had seen for several years.[4]

William's name did not appear either in the lists of those who had been saved, or of those who were known to have perished. That, however, was unsurprising, given the scale of the tragedy, and the uncertainty as to who had been on the boats in the first place.[5] Together with her sister Esia, Eliza went to Liverpool to try to ascertain what had happened to William.[6] The information that she received in response to her inquiries led her to believe that he was dead, and upon returning to Manchester she went into mourning for him.[7]

The following March, Eliza, describing herself as a widow, married widower John Heaton at Manchester's Collegiate Church.[8] John knew all the circumstances

[2] 'Charge of Bigamy Against a Female', *Manchester Courier*, 16 May 1835. According to the later reports, he had deserted her just after they had gone through a ceremony of marriage at Manchester Collegiate Church on Easter Sunday. This was in fact their second marriage ceremony. The first had taken place a year earlier, but it had then transpired that Greenwood was not his real name and the ceremony was repeated.

[3] ibid; see also 'Bigamy', *Halifax Express*, 27 August 1835.

[4] 'Awful Loss of Life', *Liverpool Mercury*, 21 November 1834; 'Dreadful Accident on the River Mersey: Upwards of Thirty Lives Lost', *The News*, 23 November 1834.

[5] See eg 'The Late Melancholy Accident at Liverpool', *Morning Chronicle*, 20 November 1834, which predicted that the exact number of those who perished would never be ascertained.

[6] 'Liverpool Assizes', *Liverpool Standard*, 21 August 1835.

[7] 'Bigamy', *Halifax Express*, 27 August 1835.

[8] Ancestry, *Manchester, England, Marriages and Banns, 1754-1930* (marriage 18 March 1835).

of Eliza's first marriage, and shared her belief that William was dead. Much to their astonishment, less than two months later William reappeared and demanded that Eliza return to him.[9] The sight of him caused Eliza so much agitation that she fainted.[10]

Eliza was taken into custody. The magistrates, upon hearing her story, expressed the view that she would have a good defence to a bigamy charge, but that she still had to stand trial.[11] Her case came before Sir Nicholas Conyngham Tindal at the Liverpool assizes a few months later. Here the same evidence was presented as to William's extended absence from Eliza, the information she had received as to his death, and the inquiries she had made.[12] After a short consultation, the jury acquitted Eliza – who promptly burst into tears of relief.[13]

Eliza's relief was understandable. Despite the magistrates' reassurance that she had a good defence to the charge, it was far from being a foregone conclusion that she would be acquitted. Over the decades, there had been plenty of defendants who had claimed to have believed that their first spouse had died. But such a belief had been no defence unless it was combined with the absence of the first spouse for seven years or more.[14] From the late eighteenth century, those who had remarried more swiftly could expect a reduced sentence, at least where they had had good reason to believe that their first spouse had died.[15] But Eliza's case was the first occasion on which anyone had been acquitted solely on account of that belief.

So what lay behind this change? None of the local newspapers who reported Eliza's trial gave any details about the judge's direction to the jury. But according to one contemporary legal writer, Tindal had expressly instructed the jury that bigamy, 'being a felony, implies an evil intention'.[16] In other words, *mens rea* – a guilty mind – was an essential component of the crime; the accused had to have known that what they were doing was wrong. In Tindal's view, such 'evil intention' was lacking where the accused had believed their first spouse was dead.

This makes Eliza's case even more significant, as it was the first time this particular idea had been applied to bigamy.[17] And Tindal, the Chief Justice of the Court of

[9] 'Charge of Bigamy Against a Female', *Manchester Courier*, 16 May 1835.

[10] 'Bigamy', *Liverpool Albion*, 25 August 1835.

[11] 'Charge of Bigamy Against a Female', *Manchester Courier*, 16 May 1835. Bail was accepted.

[12] 'Liverpool Assizes', *Liverpool Standard*, 21 August 1835.

[13] 'Bigamy', *Halifax Express*, 27 August 1835.

[14] As we have seen, the seven-year defence did not *require* the accused to show that they had believed their first spouse to have died, but the two issues often became conflated in practice: see eg *OBP*, 27 October 1790 (Elizabeth Cooper); *OBP*, 11 April 1804 (John Martin). The only individual to be acquitted where less than seven years had elapsed between the two marriages was Elizabeth Copman in 1716. Before she remarried, she had not heard from her first husband, a sailor named William Burkitt, for four years and had been told that he was dead: *OBP*, 6 September 1716. However, from the short report in the *Proceedings*, it is not clear whether there was any evidence that the first husband was in fact alive at the time of the second marriage.

[15] See eg *OBP*, 6 July 1803 (Matthew Banks, received a letter telling him his first wife was dead; one month); *OBP*, 4 December 1805 (Jane Butt, witness noted report that her first husband was dead, seven days); *Morning Post*, 14 August 1809 (Surrey assizes, Philip Facey received the 'mild' sentence of a month in prison and a fine of one shilling, the judge observing that 'the extent of his offence was that he had acted with too little caution in not making more accurate inquiries after his first wife').

[16] WM Hindmarch *A supplement to Deacon's Digest of the criminal law of England* (London, 1836) 506.

[17] Earlier examples can be found of defendants framing their defence in terms of their lack of intention to commit a crime (see eg the case of the Duchess of Kingston, discussed in chapter 5, and Henry Hall's claim that he had remarried in 'perfect innocence', having been informed of the death of his first wife by

Common Pleas, was an influential figure. The previous year, in a case of a fatal stabbing, he had directed the jury that if the accused had inflicted the wound 'under a provocation so recent and so strong' that he was not 'master of his own understanding', the offence would be manslaughter rather than murder.[18] A decade later, he presided over the trial of the delusional Daniel M'Naghten (who had shot and fatally wounded a man, believing him to be the Prime Minister, Robert Peel) and subsequently delivered the common-law judges' decision on the general principles to be applied in such cases.[19] But whereas Tindal's comments on provocation still continue to be cited today,[20] and while the M'Naghten case provided the foundation for the law on criminal liability in cases of insanity, no one today has heard of Eliza Greenwood. So why did her case have so little impact?

One reason is that it was never picked up by contemporary law reporters, the only reference to it being a brief discussion in a textbook by William Matthewson Hindmarch.[21] Clearly some lawyers had read Hindmarch's account, since there were a couple of further acquittals based on the accused's mistaken belief in the death of their first spouse. At the York assizes in 1836, Mr Justice Coleridge directed the jury to acquit James Hall, who had remarried after receiving a letter informing him that his first wife was dead.[22] William Platt, tried at the Leicestershire assizes the following year, had also had good reason to believe that his first wife was dead. They had married back in 1804, but she had run off with a 'conjuror' a few months later. Over the years she had made various reappearances to demand maintenance from William. The last of these occasions was in 1817, after which she had headed to America (with the conjuror in tow). A report then circulated that both had drowned, and some five years later, having heard nothing further, William remarried. After setting all this out, his counsel asked the judge whether there was a case to go to the jury, and the judge agreed that William should be acquitted.[23]

But this approach was to prove short-lived, largely because of a change in the way in which the seven-year defence was interpreted. Following the case of *R v Cullen* in 1840,[24] the idea took hold that even those who had heard nothing from their first spouse for seven years should make inquiries before they remarried. This was obviously difficult to reconcile with the idea that a belief in the death of the first spouse should be a defence even if seven years had *not* passed. At his trial for bigamy in 1847, Edward Calvert claimed to have been informed on good authority that his first wife was dead.

his father-in-law: *OBP*, 19 February 1806). However, such claims had not prevented them from being convicted (and, in Henry's case, sentenced to a year in prison, the crucial conversation with his father-in-law having taken place only after his second marriage).

[18] *R v George Hayward* (1833) 6 Car & P 157; 172 ER 1188, 1189. The jury in that case decided that there was no such provocation.

[19] *R v Daniel M'Naghten* (1843) 10 Cl & F 200; 8 ER 718, 719; R Moran, 'The Modern Foundation for the Insanity Defence: The Cases of James Hadfield (1800) and Daniel McNaughtan' (1985) 477 *Annals of the American Academy of Political and Social Science* 31.

[20] J Horder, 'Provocation and loss of self-control' (1992) 108 *Law Quarterly Review* 191; *R v Smith (Morgan James)* [2001] 1 AC 146; *AG for Jersey v Holley* [2005] 2 AC 580.

[21] Hindmarch (n 16).

[22] 'Yorkshire Assizes', *Sheffield Independent*, 16 July 1836.

[23] 'Assize Intelligence: Midland Circuit', *Morning Chronicle*, 23 March 1837.

[24] On which see further chapter 6.

The judge imposed the 'light' sentence of three months' hard labour on the basis that there was no 'ill motive'.[25] The clear message was that the lack of any such motive was only a mitigating factor, not a defence. In essence, then, things were back to where they had been before Eliza's case, except that the seven-year defence was potentially now harder to establish.[26]

Nor was there anyone to pursue the idea that bigamy required an 'evil intention'. Hindmarch's textbook was soon out of date, and he turned his attention to patent law rather than criminal. No other textbooks made any mention of Tindal's direction to the jury in Eliza's case. Most did not even mention the possibility of a genuine belief in the death of the first spouse being a defence to a charge of bigamy. And Tindal himself died in 1846 without having had the opportunity to try another such case.[27]

As a result, anyone who remarried within seven years was running the risk of being prosecuted for bigamy if it turned out that their first spouse was still alive, whatever rumours had been circulating as to their death. But as our next case study shows, there were ways of ensuring that they were not convicted.

'If the Prisoner had Transgressed the Law She had Inadvertently and but Barely Done So': Susannah Anderson, 1858

Susannah Anderson had good reason to believe that her husband John was dead. The pair had married in 1847, but the marriage got off to a rocky start. Twice they separated and then reunited. They were still together – just – when the 1851 census was taken on 30 March 1851, lodging with the tailor with whom John was serving his apprenticeship.[28] But before April was out, Susannah had decided that she had had enough and refused to live with John any longer.[29] From December 1852 she heard nothing of him. It was rumoured, however, that he had enlisted in the 46th Regiment, in which two of his brothers were already serving, and had gone to war in the Crimea.[30] In February 1855, John's cousin, avidly scanning the newspaper reports of the casualties, spotted the name of Private John Anderson of the 46th Regiment among the many who had died at Florence Nightingale's hospital at Scutari.[31] Believing this to be her cousin, she took the newspaper to Susannah to share the news.

[25] 'South Lancashire Spring Assizes', *Manchester Courier*, 15 December 1847. See also 'Yorkshire Winter Jail Delivery', *York Herald*, 23 December 1848 (Leonard Robinson, had been informed that his first wife had died of a fever, 14 days).

[26] See eg 'South Lancashire Spring Assizes', *Liverpool Mercury*, 31 March 1843 (Hannah Braidley, convicted despite her first husband having been imprisoned 7–8 years earlier for striking her and her 'never having heard anything about him' since, six weeks).

[27] 'Death of Lord Chief Justice Tindal', *The Examiner*, 11 July 1846.

[28] TNA, 1851 census, HO107/1760, folio 693, p 46.

[29] 'Extraordinary Case of Bigamy', *Cambridge Independent Press*, 31 October 1857.

[30] ibid.

[31] Her source was the *Dispatch*, but the same information appeared in 'Deaths at Scutari', *Morning Herald*, 8 February 1855.

Susannah did not immediately assume that the man who had died was her husband. She made inquiries of John's friends, and then wrote to the War Office with a detailed description of him. They confirmed that John had died, and sent her the pay that had been due to him. Susannah also received financial support from the Patriotic Fund, again with the support of the War Office.

In September 1856, 21 months after John's supposed death, Susannah married John Carr at Holy Trinity in Cambridge, the same church where she had married her first husband.[32] Their daughter, Kate Annie, was born the following summer.[33] But then John Anderson arrived back in Cambridge. The rumours as to his having enlisted in the army were completely false. He had never even left England, having been working as a tailor in London. As the local newspaper sarcastically commented, instead of wielding a sword, he 'had only been plying the needle'.[34]

Upon his return, John was immediately informed of Susannah's remarriage. He did not seem unduly concerned, and it was a week before he even asked as to where she was living. But by the end of October, Susannah had been brought before the police court and charged with bigamy.

After the magistrates had heard all the evidence, Susannah's lawyer urged them to dismiss her case, on the basis that she had believed John Anderson to be dead when she married John Carr. The prosecution, however, argued that the magistrates had no discretion in the matter and had to send Susannah for trial, where it would be for the jury to deal with the question of whether she was guilty of the offence. The magistrates agreed with the latter view, and Susannah was committed for trial. The editor of the local newspaper roundly condemned John's actions and expressed the wish that he could be prosecuted instead of Susannah.[35]

At her trial at the Cambridgeshire assizes the following March, counsel for the prosecution did not press the case against Susannah. Quite the reverse: he told the court that 'it was impossible not to see that if the prisoner had transgressed the law she had inadvertently and but barely done so'.[36] As a result, he took the view that justice would best be served by offering no evidence against her. The judge, Mr Justice Wightman, gave this his approval, noting that the case was such that Susannah would only receive a nominal sentence if she was found guilty. All that was left for defence counsel to do was to hope that steps would be taken to ensure the protection of Susannah and her property from John.[37] The jury's verdict of 'not guilty' was 'received with rapturous applause'.[38]

[32] FindMyPast, *Cambridgeshire Marriages* (marriage at Holy Trinity, 23 September 1856).

[33] FreeBMD, Chesterton Registration District, Q3 1857.

[34] 'Extraordinary Case of Bigamy', *Cambridge Independent Press*, 31 October 1857.

[35] ibid, repeated in 'Extraordinary Case of Bigamy', *Morning Herald*, 2 November 1857; *Standard*, 2 November 1857; *Patriot*, 6 November 1857.

[36] 'Bigamy', *Cambridge Independent Press*, 20 March 1858.

[37] This was an allusion to the possibility of making an order protecting the assets of a deserted wife under s 21 of the Matrimonial Causes Act 1857 (on which see chapter 8). Susannah was eventually granted such an order in January 1860, John having disappeared again after her trial ('Sessions and Police Intelligence', *Cambridge Independent Press*, 14 January 1860). In the subsequent census, she was described as a 'proprietor of houses', heading an all-female household consisting of her young daughter, widowed mother and a servant, her second husband having sadly died before her trial (TNA, 1861 census, RG9/1026, folio 40 p 3).

[38] 'Bigamy', *Cambridge Independent Press*, 20 March 1858. Again, the decision was widely reported: see eg 'Singular Case of Bigamy', *Lady's Newspaper and Pictorial Times*, 20 March 1858; 'A Curious Case of Bigamy', *Shields Daily Gazette*, 25 March 1858; 'An Inadvertent Act of Bigamy', *Fife Herald*, 1 April 1858.

The reaction to Susannah's acquittal was an indication that the law governing bigamy was out of step with public opinion. While she was no doubt delighted at the outcome, she must have had months of worry waiting for her trial, particularly if she had read newspaper accounts of other bigamy trials where individuals had been convicted despite their genuine and entirely reasonable belief that their first spouse had died.[39] Besides, there was something distinctly unsatisfactory about the fact that her acquittal was only due to the forbearance of counsel.

From a legal perspective, Susannah's case was a missed opportunity. Had she been convicted, it would have been the perfect test case to refer to the Court for Crown Cases Reserved. While our next case study was responsible for putting the issue of intention under renewed scrutiny, it was a much weaker case.

'Who Says that?': Mr Baron Martin and the Problem of Precedent, 1862 and 1872

Sarah Hannah Swain was only 14 when she married labourer James Turner in September 1854 – younger than most brides, but still two years older than the minimum age for marriage at the time. Exactly when James left her is unclear, but it seems likely that he was with her until at least 1858, when their daughter Mary Ann was born.[40] At the time of the 1861 census, Sarah, still only 21, had returned with Mary Ann to live with her family in the Fenland village of Wisbech St Mary.[41] Four months later she went through a ceremony of marriage with Frederick Lister, describing herself as a widow.[42] But James Turner was still alive, and before the year was out he had charged her with bigamy.[43]

At her trial at the Cambridgeshire assizes in 1862, the clerk for the parish of March was able to give evidence of both ceremonies – both having taken place in the same church. He also told the court that he had believed James to be dead at the time of Sarah's second ceremony, but – when cross-examined by Sarah's counsel – was not willing to say that this was the general belief in the parish.[44]

The statement that Sarah had made before the magistrates was also produced. In this, she too said that she had believed James was dead. He had apparently told her that

[39] Contemporary cases included that of Emma Nicholson, convicted at the Yorkshire assizes in November 1857 and sentenced to four months' imprisonment despite having been informed that her first husband had died ('Local Intelligence', *Sheffield Independent*, 7 November 1857; 'Yorkshire Winter Gaol Delivery', *York Herald*, 12 December 1857).

[40] The birth of Mary Ann Turner was registered in the final quarter of 1858, in the registration district of North Witchford: Free BMD.

[41] TNA, 1861 census, RG9/1047, folio 66, p 3. The Swain household, headed by Sarah's widower father Joseph, was a complex one, with Sarah's grandmother acting as housekeeper, along with several younger siblings and a lodger. Sarah herself was described as a 'visitor' and Mary Ann as Joseph's niece.

[42] The announcement of the wedding appeared in the *Cambridge Independent Press*, 10 August 1861.

[43] *Cambridge Chronicle*, 14 December 1861; *Peterborough Advertiser*, 14 December 1861.

[44] 'Bigamy at March', *Cambridge Independent Press*, 22 March 1862; see also *Peterborough Advertiser*, 22 March 1862. Another local newspaper, the *Cambridge Chronicle*, 22 March 1862, reported him as saying that there was a 'general belief' at March that James Turner was dead but that does not appear in any other reports.

he was going to Clenchwarton, some 20 miles to the north, telling her that she should 'walk the streets' if she wanted money.[45] Since his departure he had only sent her three letters and she had not heard of him for at least a year.[46] Although none of this put James in a good light, it was hardly the strongest of evidence on which to found a belief in his death.

Nonetheless, at this point in the proceedings, Sarah's counsel, a Mr Naylor, asked the judge whether he regarded the second marriage as 'felonious'. Mr Baron Martin's response was an unwelcome and uncompromising 'Yes'.[47] Somewhat downcast, Mr Naylor concluded that it would be 'useless' for him to continue. But Martin jocularly told him, 'you can try your hand at it' – while reminding him that 'the law says that a husband or wife must not be heard of for seven years to justify a second marriage'.[48]

Naylor did his best. Even so, in his summing up, Martin strongly hinted that the evidence was insufficient to show that Sarah had honestly believed that James was dead, noting that 'beyond the mere belief of one witness called, they had nothing but the prisoner's statement'.[49] Yet he left open the possibility for the jury to decide in Sarah's favour by concluding that 'if they believed' she had married Frederick honestly believing James to be dead, then she would not be guilty of the offence with which she was charged.[50] And the jury, ignoring Martin's hints about the thinness of the evidence, found Sarah not guilty.[51]

At this point Sarah fades out of our story.[52] But her case – unlike that of Eliza Greenwood nearly three decades earlier – did make it into a set of criminal law reports.[53] Over the next few years, *R v Turner* was regularly cited by counsel claiming that a genuine belief in the death of the first spouse was a defence to a charge of bigamy.

Judicial reactions to this were, however, somewhat mixed. At the 1870 trial of Emma Georges Dixon, the citation of *Turner* was sufficient to change the judge's mind and convince him that this was a defence.[54] The following year, at the Derbyshire assizes, Mr Baron Cleasby added an additional nuance by directing the jury that Frederick Horton must also have had 'fair and reasonable grounds for believing' his wife to be dead.[55] The jury, however, was unconvinced that this was the case, and Frederick was convicted.

Other judges simply refused to follow *Turner*. At the Manchester assizes in 1872, counsel for Ann Gibbons tried to argue that she had a *bona fide* belief that her first

[45] *Peterborough Advertiser*, 22 March 1862.

[46] *Cambridge Chronicle*, 22 March 1862; 'Bigamy at March', *Cambridge Independent Press*, 22 March 1862.

[47] *Cambridge Chronicle*, 22 March 1862.

[48] 'Bigamy at March', *Cambridge Independent Press*, 22 March 1862.

[49] *Cambridge Independent Press*, 22 March 1862.

[50] ibid.

[51] They may well have taken the view that it was very unlikely that anyone would be so foolish as to remarry in the same church if they had not genuinely believed they were free to do so.

[52] All attempts at tracing her proved fruitless: her second husband had gone to London within a few months of their wedding, the Swain household had broken up by the time of the 1871 census, and Turner is an unfortunately common surname.

[53] *R v Turner* (1862) 9 Cox CC 145.

[54] 'Trial for Bigamy – Not Guilty', *Alnwick Mercury*, 13 August 1870; see further chapter 13.

[55] *R v Horton* (1871) 11 Cox CC 670; 'Charge of Bigamy', *Nottinghamshire Guardian*, 10 March 1871; 'Trial for Bigamy', *Reynolds's Newspaper*, 12 March 1871.

husband was dead. In her case, however, there appears to have been nothing to suggest that he had died other than the fact that nothing had been heard from him for several years. Mr Justice Brett, having consulted with his fellow judge Mr Justice Willes, held that a *bona fide* belief that the husband was dead was no defence unless the seven years had elapsed, and refused to have the point referred to the Court for Crown Cases Reserved on the basis that the point was 'quite clear'.[56] And in the case of *R v James Chappell Bennett*, Lord Justice Bramwell was still more strident, explaining that 'I cannot, and never do, recognise as a defence such a ruling as my brother Martin laid down in *Reg v Turner*'.[57]

These, of course, were just the cases that made it into the law reports. Those cases whose details were only reported in the newspapers demonstrated a similar diversity of approach to the question of whether a *bona fide* belief in the death of the first spouse was a defence. All this left the law in a considerable state of uncertainty, since a decision reached at one assize court was not binding on a judge at a later assize.[58] If, over time, a whole series of cases were all decided in the same way, then it would be difficult for a judge to justify diverging from that pattern. But a single case – or even a couple of cases – was not determinative. And conflicting cases were no help at all.

All this must have made it very difficult for counsel, especially given the unpredictability as to which judge would be hearing which cases. But Mr Thomas, representing Daniel McKoy at the Winchester assizes in 1872, was probably more confident than most when he cited Cox's report of *R v Turner*. The judge's reaction was almost certainly not what he had expected:

> The Judge: Who says that? – Mr Thomas said the name of the Judge was not given. (Laughter.) – The Judge: You must find that out. (Renewed laughter.) – After some conversation, the Judge said the only defence to an indictment of this kind was the absence of the woman for seven years, or information of the death.[59]

The jury duly convicted Daniel. The judge said that he would 'look into' the case that Mr Thomas had cited, and, if he had 'any doubt' about the law, would have Daniel's case referred to the Court for Crown Cases Reserved. But he did not hold out much hope that this would happen, saying 'he had no doubt now'.[60]

The reason why this was so surprising, and why this exchange prompted such mirth in court, is that the judge was Mr Baron Martin, who had of course been the judge in *R v Turner* – as Cox's report of the case stated quite clearly. It seems unlikely that he had simply forgotten his direction to the jury, even if it had been 10 years earlier. It may be that he had never intended to lay down the ruling that the report of the case had captured: after all, his comment in Daniel's case now drew a subtle but important

[56] *R v Gibbons* (1872) 12 Cox CC 237, 238. See also *R v Moore* (1877) 13 Cox CC 544, in which Mr Justice Denman asked the jury to say whether they thought Emma Moore 'reasonably believed her first husband to be dead before she married again' without expressly directing them that this was the law, and then decided not to refer the case for the consideration of the Court of Crown Cases Reserved as Emma would only have received a nominal punishment if she had been found guilty.

[57] (1877) 14 Cox CC 45.

[58] WHD Winder, 'The Rule of Precedent in the Criminal Courts' (1941) *Journal of Criminal Law* 242.

[59] 'Hampshire Lent Assizes', *Hampshire Telegraph*, 9 March 1872.

[60] ibid.

distinction between the accused *believing* in the death of their first spouse and having specific, if erroneous, information from someone else. But it is also possible that Martin was simply averse to the idea of being held to a specific rule derived from an earlier decision, even one of his own. He had, after all, previously questioned the value of precedent in criminal law, asking, 'what would be the consequence of permitting the criminal law of this country to depend upon reasonings and criticism such as may be found in the reports of these cases?'[61]

Such views were, however, increasingly out of step with the time. In an era of more systematic law reporting, and with a concomitant increase in the citation of authorities, any conflicts between judges were now more obvious, and more problematic. The conflicting decisions on whether a genuine belief in the death of the first spouse amounted to a defence were flagged up by Sir James Fitzjames Stephen in his 1883 *History of the Criminal Law of England*.[62] And in his capacity as a judge, Stephen identified our next case study as a suitable test case to resolve the uncertainty.

'Undoubtedly a Principle of English Criminal Law': Martha Ann Tolson, 1889

On 11 September 1880, a teenaged girl named Martha Ann Penrice married John Henry Tolson in Cumberland's Whitehaven registration district.[63] The pair were still together when the census was taken the following year, living in the village of Distington, around four miles north of Whitehaven town.[64] But at some point after this, John left Martha, subsequently heading to America.[65] Having heard nothing from him, Martha agreed to marry Thomas Harrison, a miner from the same village. Their wedding took place at Whitehaven register office on 10 January 1887, with Martha describing herself as a widow.[66] John, however, was still very much alive, and made a most unwelcome reappearance some months later.[67]

[61] Copies of the Lord Chancellor's 'Letter to the Judges', quoted by P Handler, 'Judges and the criminal law in England 1808-61' in P Brand and J Getzler (eds), *Judges and Judging in the History of the Common Law and Civil Law: From Antiquity to Modern Times* (Cambridge, Cambridge University Press, 2012) 149.

[62] J Fitzjames Stephen, *A History of the Criminal Law of England: Vol 2* (London, Macmillan, 1883) 117–18.

[63] TNA, ASSI 51/45.

[64] TNA, 1881 census, RG11/5182, folio 92, p 18.

[65] Those who are familiar with the facts of *R v Tolson* (n 1) may be thinking that my account does not tally with what was stated in the case report. As will become clear, the story of Martha Ann Tolson is a multi-layered one in which the changes to the way in which her story was told are part of a bigger story about the selection and presentation of test cases. In what follows, I have given the details only as they emerged or could be verified from external sources.

[66] Certified copy of an entry in the register of marriages in the Registration District of Whitehaven, issued by the GRO, 11 March 2025. The marriage was authorised by a superintendent registrar's certificate, which would have required a notice of the intended marriage to be displayed in the register office for 21 days before the marriage could take place.

[67] According to a later report, he turned up – with a sense of dramatic timing worthy of a modern soap opera – at Christmas 1887: 'A Singular Bigamy Case', *Lancashire Evening Post*, 7 July 1888. That, however, is somewhat difficult to reconcile with the fact that Martha did not appear before the magistrates until the following April.

As a result, Martha – still only 25 – was brought before Whitehaven Police Court to be charged with bigamy. The summary that appeared in the two local newspapers which reported the case noted that:

> We understand that Tolson had been away, and after a lapse of two years he went to America. Mrs Tolson, as years rolled by, heard no tidings of him, and being under the impression that he was dead, she accepted an offer of marriage by Harrison.[68]

Bail was accepted, and Martha was bound over to appear at the next assizes.

The case came before Mr Justice Stephen at the Cumberland assizes in July 1888.[69] Addressing the Grand Jury, he explained that Martha's first husband had 'gone to America, and was absent for five or six years, and was currently reported to have been drowned'.[70] However, as he added, it 'had never been exactly determined' whether an individual who remarried within seven years of their spouse's departure, mistakenly believing them to be dead, would be guilty of bigamy. But as long as they were satisfied that Martha had married twice, they would be bound to find a true bill against her. Martha was accordingly put on trial.

Stephen's reference to an absence of 'five or six years' made it seem that Martha might have only narrowly missed being able to take advantage of the seven-year defence. How it fitted with the original claim that John had only gone to America two years after leaving Martha was not entirely clear. But during the course of the trial, the details as to John's departure, rumoured fate, and unwelcome return, became decidedly more specific. It was stated that he had set off for America with his brother on 13 December 1881, without giving any indication of where he was headed.[71] A rumour had then arisen that he had drowned while on his way to America. And upon his return, he had, so it was claimed, brought with him a woman with whom he had been living.

After hearing the evidence, Stephen directed the jury 'that a belief in good faith and on reasonable grounds in the death of one party to a marriage was not a defence' if the remarriage had taken place within seven years. The jury duly found Martha guilty, but added that they thought she had believed that her first husband had drowned. Stephen agreed, with his statement that she was 'morally as innocent as any man or woman in the court' being greeted with applause. He sentenced her to a single day in prison, counting from the start of the assizes, resulting in her immediate release. And he declared his intention to have the case referred to the Court for Crown Cases Reserved to decide whether she was even legally guilty of bigamy.[72]

By the time Martha Tolson's case came before the Court for Crown Cases Reserved in November 1888, it was attracting national rather than just local interest.[73] 'Is Martha

[68] 'Alleged Bigamy By A Distington Woman', *Carlisle Journal*, 27 April 1888; *West Cumberland Times*, 28 April 1888.

[69] TNA, ASSI 51/45.

[70] 'Cumberland Assizes: Yesterday's Trials', *West Cumberland Times*, 7 July 1888.

[71] This was the date given in various newspaper reports of her trial: 'Cumberland Assizes: Yesterday's Trials', *West Cumberland Times*, 7 July 1888; 'Cumberland Summer Assizes: Charge of Bigamy', *Carlisle Journal*, 10 July 1888.

[72] 'Cumberland Assizes: Yesterday's Trials', *West Cumberland Times*, 7 July 1888.

[73] 'An Important Law Case', *Kerry Evening Post*, 24 November 1888; 'Interesting Point in a Bigamy Case', *Kirkintilloch Herald*, 28 November 1888.

Ann A Bigamist: A Romantic Story', asked the headline in the *Empire News*.[74] Most commentators were sympathetic to Martha's plight. Only the *St James' Gazette* struck a discordant note, demanding, 'will anything make women of the lower classes believe that a missing husband is nevertheless a husband?' In its view, such a woman was 'going into a state of concubinage' and her children would be 'bastards'.[75] But that of course rather missed the key difference between being unsure as to one's husband's whereabouts and having good reason to believe he was dead.

The story as presented to the Court for Crown Cases Reserved shifted once again. John had, it was claimed, 'deserted' Martha – a more loaded term that carried a clear message as to who was at fault. It was also stated that Martha and her father had made inquiries 'and learned from his elder brother and from general report that he had been lost in a vessel bound for America, which went down with all hands on board'.[76]

In short, the story had evolved from John having gone to America two years after separating from Martha and her having received no news of him, to him having left for America as early as 1881 and there being rumours that he had drowned, and then to her having made specific inquiries of him via his family and being told that the ship on which he was travelling had sunk. Of course, it is possible that new facts emerged as the proceedings progressed. But there is no obvious reason why that should have been the case. It seems far more likely that the subtle shifts in the story were a deliberate strategy to craft a good test case and ensure that Martha's belief in her first husband's death appeared reasonable as well as genuine.

After Martha's case had been presented to five judges of the Court for Crown Cases Reserved, the importance of the legal point at stake was deemed to require the presence of the whole court, and the case was adjourned. Some commentators were impatient with the law's delay. The *Sporting Chronicle* derided the idea that five judges were not sufficient to decide what to them seemed so obvious a point. In its view, five geese 'could have decided it in five minutes', there being 'surely no doubt of Mrs Tolson's innocence of bigamy'. It suggested that the only question left to decide must be 'whether Mr Tolson deserves to be hanged for turning up again where he was so evidently not wanted'.[77]

But at least some of the 14 judges who sat to hear the case in January 1889 disagreed. Mr Justice Manisty, with whom Pollock, Field, Huddleston and Denman all agreed, maintained the view that the 'plain language' of the statutory seven-year defence precluded any additional defence based on a *bona fide* belief in the death of the first spouse.[78] In his view, it was up to Parliament to change the law if it saw fit.

The majority, however, took the view that an honest and reasonable belief in the death of the first spouse was a defence to a charge of bigamy, and that Martha's conviction should be quashed. Four judges – Wills, Cave, Hawkins, and Stephen himself – delivered judgments giving varying reasons for this. Four other judges agreed with

[74] 'Is Martha Ann A Bigamist: A Romantic Story', *Empire News*, 25 November 1888.

[75] *St James' Gazette*, 26 November 1888.

[76] These were the details recorded in the official law report (*R v Tolson* (n 1)) and were widely reported in the newspapers at the time: *Leeds Mercury*, 26 November 1888.

[77] *Sporting Chronicle*, 27 November 1888.

[78] *R v Tolson* (n 1) 196.

them – or rather, one agreed with Wills, two agreed with Cave, and one agreed with Stephen.[79] The final judgment was delivered by Coleridge, the Lord Chief Justice. In it he dithered and changed his mind, eventually coming down on the side of the majority.

Key to Coleridge's change of mind was Cave's explanation of how a defence based on an honest and reasonable belief in the death of the first spouse could be reconciled with the seven-year defence. As Cave pointed out, once it had been established that the first spouse had been absent for seven years, it was irrelevant that the accused had no reasonable grounds for believing them to be dead; it was for the prosecution to prove that the accused knew them to be alive.[80] He contrasted this with the much harder task of proving facts from which a jury 'may reasonably infer that she honestly and on reasonable grounds believed her first husband to be dead before she married again'. Having such a limited defence, he thought, was entirely consistent with the existence of the 'wider and more easily established defence' that was available after seven years had passed.

So, Cave was being very careful to emphasise that the belief in the first spouse's death had to be *reasonable*. If the facts before them had been different – if, say, the case had proceeded on the basis that Martha had known that John had not gone to America until 1883, and had merely heard nothing more of him rather than being told his ship had sunk – it would have been far harder to claim that she had reasonable grounds for believing him to be dead.

In other words, there was nothing special or unusual about the facts of Martha's case to justify a change in approach. It was not even a matter of being the right case at the right time. It was simply a good enough case, the facts of which could be subtly massaged to make it the right case. Given that the court was split 9–5, it is not fanciful to suggest that the changes to Martha's story did make a difference.

But what is particularly interesting about the judgments delivered by Wills, Cave, Hawkins and Stephen is that they did not even acknowledge that accepting an honest and reasonable belief in the death of the first spouse as a defence *was* a change in approach. Early in his judgment, Wills asserted that it was '[u]ndoubtedly a principle of English criminal law' that 'ordinarily speaking a crime is not committed if the mind of the person doing the act in question be innocent'.[81] And Cave, Stephen and Hawkins all argued that this principle of *mens rea* had always applied to the offence of bigamy. All three laid considerable stress on the harsh punishments meted out to those guilty of bigamy in earlier centuries and even, at least potentially, under the 1861 Act. Their argument was that, since Parliament could never have intended that a woman who remarried in the honest belief that her first husband was dead, but without waiting for the statutory seven years, would be sentenced to death or to a lengthy period of penal servitude, such a belief must, perforce, have been a defence.

[79] Wills, with whom Charles agreed, highlighted the 'cruel injustice' (177) of exposing a person to criminal penalties for remarrying if they had believed their first spouse to be dead, especially where the evidence would have been sufficient for the spouse's estate to be distributed; Cave, with whom Day and Smith agreed, focused primarily on the relationship with the seven-year defence, as did Hawkins; Stephen, with whom Grantham agreed, devoted most of his judgment to discussion of the broader issue of *mens rea*.

[80] *R v Tolson* (n 1) 183.

[81] *R v Tolson* (n 1) 171–72.

Such backwards reasoning is obviously problematic. In terms of actual cases, their citations went back no further than that of Sarah Turner in 1862. It is true that no one was sentenced to transportation or seven years' penal servitude after they had shown that they had good reason to believe that their first spouse had died. But they were still convicted. Similarly, it could be claimed that no one was sentenced to death in the seventeenth century after they had shown that they had good reason to believe that their first spouse was still alive – but that is only because there is no case where any such belief was discussed.

So the reasoning of the judges – that an honest and reasonable belief in the death of the first spouse must always have been a defence – was simply not borne out by the evidence. But it reflected the story these judges wanted to tell about the idea of *mens rea*. They garlanded their judgments with references to the legal luminaries of the seventeenth century – Coke, Hawkins and Hale. Stephen even managed to work in the *Leges Henrici Primi*, a legal treatise dating from the early twelfth century. None of this material related to bigamy, but it all helped to create an impression that the criminal law was based on principles with a pedigree.

At this point, let us return to Martha herself. Writing in the mid-twentieth century, one legal scholar voiced the suspicion that the outcome might well have been different had she not been 'more sinned against than sinning'.[82] There were, however, certain telling facts that were not discussed at any stage of the proceedings, though they must have been known to at least some of those involved at the time. No mention was made of Martha's daughter Hannah, who had been born in the first quarter of 1882. At first sight it seems odd that this detail was omitted – after all, being left without support while heavily pregnant would surely have increased sympathy for Martha. There was, however, a *second* daughter, Sarah, who had been born in June 1884.[83] Either Martha herself had 'sinned' by having a child by another man while John was away, or the original report that John had not left for America until 1883 was true, and Martha had remarried after less than four years.

Whatever the truth of Martha's marital history, her case does at least appear to have had a happy-ever-after ending. In 1891, she and Thomas Harrison were living together with her two daughters from her marriage to John Tolson and their two-year-old son – named, perhaps surprisingly, John. Ten years later another two children had been added to their family.[84] The 1911 census recorded that they had been married for 24 years – which they clearly dated from their bigamous 1887 ceremony.[85] With John Tolson still alive, there was no prospect of them being able to remarry legally.

But *R v Tolson* did at least mean that those who had reasonable grounds for believing that their first spouse had died could remarry without committing bigamy. In the decade that followed, around one-tenth of all cases tried at the Central Criminal Court involved the accused claiming that they had believed their first spouse to be dead. Some would have been entitled to an acquittal even before *Tolson*, on account of the

[82] CHS Fifoot, *Judge and Jurist in the Age of Victoria* (London, Stevens & Sons Ltd, 1959) 131, 133.
[83] Sarah's existence was discovered from the 1891 census. Her birth was registered by Martha, with no details of the father being given.
[84] TNA, 1891 census, RG12/4311, folio 96, p 4; 1901 census, RG13/4890, folio 27, p 4.
[85] TNA, *Census Returns of England and Wales, 1911*, RG14.

length of time since they had seen or heard from their first spouse. But there were still a number who were acquitted who might well not have been, had it not been for the case of Martha Ann Tolson.[86]

'Sid, I Think it Now Time to Let You know that I am Still Alive': Sidney Rayment, 1907

In 1907, 22-year-old hall porter Sidney Rayment was charged with bigamy. Only a couple of years separated his two marriages, the first, to Mary Maude Horn, having taken place in December 1903, and the second, to Fanny Ayre, in December 1905. And Mary, it appeared, had lived with him until as late as June 1905. But according to Sidney's defence counsel, Mary had left a note on the mantelpiece, written in red ink, saying, 'Do not look for me. I have gone to do away with myself.'[87] Sidney, he claimed, had made inquiries about Mary 'in every direction he could think of' and had heard rumours that she had killed herself, albeit 'nothing definite'.[88]

But at the Central Criminal Court, Vincent Horn, one of Mary's brothers, giving evidence for the prosecution, claimed that the note had said something altogether different: 'You have told me to go so often I have now taken you at your word. I can work for my living.'[89] He painted a picture of an abusive marriage, with Sidney drinking too much and ill-treating Mary, knocking her about and on one occasion threatening her with a carving knife. Vincent had been in a good position to observe his sister's marriage, as he had lodged with them while he was working alongside Sidney as a porter. He had continued to work with Sidney after Mary had left – but Sidney, he claimed, had never asked him what had happened to Mary.

Nor had Sidney been honest with his second wife. As Fanny Ayre told the court, she had only met him in July 1905, after Mary had left. At that time she was working as a barmaid, but she gave this up to take a position as a housekeeper to a lady living in the block of flats where Sidney worked. By October they were walking out together, and before the wedding they had started living together.[90] Only after the ceremony did she hear that he had been married before, and even then Sidney had insisted that his first wife was dead.

Sidney himself gave evidence on oath.[91] He was a little vague about the precise language of the note that Mary had left him, but detailed the various efforts that he had made to find her. But the fact that he had described himself as a bachelor when he

[86] See further *Double Trouble*, ch 8.

[87] 'Charge of Bigamy', *Morning Advertiser*, 19 January 1907.

[88] 'Charge of Bigamy', *Islington Gazette*, 21 January 1907; 'Charge of Bigamy', *St Pancras Chronicle*, 25 January 1907.

[89] *OBP*, 28 January 1907.

[90] In various newspaper reports of Sidney's trial, it was stated that Fanny's friends had 'practically compelled' Sidney to marry her on account of her 'condition': see eg 'Bigamy Charges: "Thought His Wife Was Dead": Old Bailey Trials', *The People*, 3 February 1907. This might imply that Fanny was noticeably pregnant, which would in turn indicate that their relationship had started some time earlier. However, no mention was made of them having had a child together.

[91] This was still something of a novelty, only having been a possibility since the Criminal Evidence Act 1898.

married Fanny somewhat weakened his claim that he had believed Mary had drowned herself. And upon being cross-examined, he admitted that he had received a second letter from Mary in July 1905.[92] This had been unambiguous: 'Sid, I think it now time to let you know that I am still alive, for which no thanks are due to you. I absolutely refuse to live with you any more.' She had asked him to send her linen on to her mother's home in Greenwich, there being one or two items that she needed. As he acknowledged, this 'did not look much like committing suicide.'

The Recorder stated that he was 'absolutely horrified' by the suggestion that Sidney might have a good defence to the charge of bigamy. As he noted:

> The law used to be that, there was no defence to bigamy except absence for seven years, but the judges on the question being referred to them decided that, if a jury should come to the conclusion that there was good ground for believing that death had occurred, that might constitute a defence. It was, however, never contemplated that a man should act as prisoner had done and marry six months after his wife had left him, describing himself not as a widower but as a bachelor.

Unsurprisingly, the jury convicted Sidney.[93] He did, however, receive only the nominal sentence of two days (without hard labour). The judge, noting that 'the object of the statute was to prevent innocent and virtuous women being entrapped', pointed out that as Fanny had been living with Sidney before the so-called marriage, 'she had sustained no injury in that way'.[94]

Fanny herself had spoken warmly of Sidney, telling the court that he had been a 'kind and good' husband to her and that she was 'very fond' of him. Sadly, this was not to be a case of an enduring second marriage: by the 1911 census Fanny was living with her brother's family, describing herself as a widow, and Sidney had gone to Australia.[95]

In the meantime, questions had arisen as to whether the principle established in *R v Tolson* applied to other kinds of mistaken belief, as our next case study will discuss.

A Mistaken Belief that the First Marriage was Invalid: Peter Thomson, 1905

In October 1905, a police constable arrived at the home of Peter Thomson to arrest him for failing to comply with a court order requiring him to pay 10 shillings per week

[92] On the removal of the accused's former immunity from cross-examination as a result of the 1898 Act, see D Bentley, 'Acquitting the Innocent. Convicting the Guilty. Delivering Justice?' in J Rowbotham and K Stevenson (eds), *Behaving Badly: Social Panic and Moral Outrage – Victorian and Modern Parallels* (Aldershot, Ashgate, 2003) 22.

[93] They had made up their mind as to his guilt much earlier, asking the Recorder if it was necessary for them to hear any more of the case: 'Bigamy Charges', *Morning Advertiser*, 30 January 1907.

[94] *OBP*, 28 January 1907.

[95] TNA, *Census Returns of England and Wales, 1911*, RG14; UK Outward Passenger Lists, 7 January 1910.

towards the support of his wife Ada.[96] In response, Peter declared, 'She is no wife of mine; this is my wife.' Annie, the wife to whom he was referring, ran upstairs to get their marriage certificate to prove that she and Peter had married at the Edmonton register office in April 1903. But the constable still took Peter into custody – together with the marriage certificate, so that Peter could also be charged with bigamy.[97]

There was no doubt that Peter and Ada had gone through a ceremony of marriage at the Wandsworth register office in 1892. But when Peter appeared before the Central Criminal Court in the November of 1905, his defence was that he had believed his first marriage to Ada to be void. The basis for this belief was a conversation with Ada's sister, in which she had told him that Ada's first husband was still alive.[98] Ada's brother, called as a witness for the defence, confirmed that Ada had married a man named Jack Turner in 1887. According to another witness, who had lived next door to Peter and Ada after their 1892 wedding, Ada had said that Jack had been compelled to leave the country, and, when the worse for drink (which apparently was quite often), had 'cried and said she wondered where Jack was'.

Unusually, the jury were unable to agree on a verdict and were discharged.[99] The following session, Peter was back before the Court, with a new jury.[100] Much the same evidence was given as previously. This time, however, the Common Serjeant seems to have been more explicit in his direction to the jury,[101] telling them that they could only acquit Peter if they were satisfied that the first wife's first husband was in fact still alive when Peter married her, or 'that he believed the first husband was alive after making all proper and reasonable inquiries'.[102] As he explained:

> What are proper and reasonable inquiries depend on the importance of the step about to be taken. If you are going to take a step which is very important, it is not enough to act upon rumour; very serious inquiries must be made. If the step you are going to take is marriage, it is clear that a man ought to make most careful inquiries, not to act on someone saying that the previous husband may be alive. He must do his best to learn whether his first marriage was valid or not.[103]

The jury found Peter guilty – unsurprisingly so, there being no evidence that he had made any such inquiries.[104]

Peter's case did at least indicate that an honest and reasonable belief in the invalidity of the first marriage *could* be a defence. But the Common Serjeant's direction was

[96] For the original order, made by the Brentford magistrates, see 'Police Court', *Middlesex Independent*, 23 September 1903. Under the Summary Jurisdiction (Married Women) Act 1895, magistrates had the power to order a husband to pay his wife a sum of up to £2 per week by way of maintenance if certain conditions were met, for example if he had deserted or assaulted her, or if his cruelty or wilful failure to support her had led her to separate from him. On such powers, see S Cretney, *Family Law in the Twentieth Century: A History* (Oxford, Oxford University Press, 2003) 444–45.

[97] 'Charge of Bigamy', *Middlesex Independent*, 14 October 1905; *OBP*, 13 November 1905.

[98] *OBP*, 13 November 1905.

[99] 'Jury Disagree in Bigamy Charge', *Lloyd's Weekly Newspaper*, 19 November 1905.

[100] *OBP*, 11 December 1905.

[101] According to 'Jury Disagree in Bigamy Charge' (n 99), at the close of the first trial he had simply told the jury that the onus was on Peter to prove that his first marriage was invalid.

[102] *R v Peter Thomson* (1905) 70 *Justice of the Peace* 6, 7.

[103] ibid.

[104] *OBP*, 11 December 1905. He was, however, only sentenced to a week in prison.

only reported in the *Justice of the Peace*, and was not picked up by textbook writers. A decade and a half later, counsel for Henry Connatty had to convince the Recorder that such a belief was a defence, rather than simply something that might mitigate the offence. Once convinced, the Recorder directed the jury that they should acquit Henry if satisfied that he 'bona fide believed that his first or legal marriage was invalid' and had 'made careful inquiries' that justified this belief.[105] Again, however, the jury were not satisfied, and Henry was convicted.[106] And across the twentieth century, this continued to be a theme: the defence being accepted in principle, but not made out in practice.[107]

Peter's case also shines light on how some individuals might display quite unconventional attitudes to the importance of being legally married to the person they were living with. Peter, it seems, was happy to continue living with Ada despite being told of her prior marriage not long after their 1892 wedding. He even made a will in her favour in 1902, before they parted on account of a quarrel.[108] But the evidence given at his trial suggests that Ada's sisters did not want her potential bigamy to be known: Peter and Ada's gossipy neighbour reported on a conversation in which one sister had told Ada that she would 'look very funny' if her first husband were to turn up, prompting another to tell her to 'Hold your tongue … you fool'.[109] This neighbour had subsequently caustically commented to Ada that Peter 'is no more your husband than I am, from the conversation I have heard'.[110] Peter's second wife Annie had initially refused to marry him, on the assumption that he was married to Ada, telling him that she 'did not want to enter into anything like that'; only when he told her that his first marriage was void did she agree. Here, then, in one single case we have a whole range of attitudes to cohabitation outside legal marriage, but at least among the women it was a source of criticism and concern rather than acceptance.

A Mistaken Belief that a Divorce had been Granted: Thomas Wheat, 1921

The marriage of Thomas Allsop Wheat and Florence Daybell proved to be one more casualty of the First World War. The pair had married at St Phillip's church in Nottingham in 1911 and had two children together, Florrie and Anne, born in 1911 and 1914. Thomas had then joined the army in 1914, serving with the Royal Engineers. While he was away, Florence had gone to live with another man, described by Thomas's step-brother as a 'poacher'.[111]

[105] *R v Connatty* (1919) 83 *Justice of the Peace* 292, 293.

[106] In Henry's case there was no doubt that his first marriage was valid. He had married Jane Burns on the assumption that she was a widow, only for her (supposed) husband to turn up. Henry then left Jane and remarried, but then discovered that Jane had never been married to her first husband at all; *Connatty* (n 105); 'A Complicated Story', *The People*, 16 March 1919.

[107] See *R v William Dolman* (1949) 33 Cr App R 128 and *R v King* [1964] 1 QB 285, discussed in *Double Trouble*, ch 10.

[108] *OBP*, 13 November 1905.

[109] ibid.

[110] ibid.

[111] 'Bigamy Charge at Alfreton', *Alfreton Journal*, 20 August 1920.

Thomas investigated the possibility of obtaining a divorce. In 1919, he was found to be eligible to bring proceedings under the Poor Persons' Procedure, and in May solicitors were assigned to him.[112] It was still necessary for him to pay for some of the out-of-pocket expenses, amounting to £14.[113] After some delay he did so, and in April 1920 his solicitors confirmed that they could now proceed and would 'lose no time' over his petition.[114] As that phrase hinted, no petition had actually been filed at this point.[115]

In the meantime, Thomas had begun a new relationship with Marian Stocks. He was living at her parents' house, and Marian was taking care of his two children. Sometime in June 1920, Thomas sent a telegram to his solicitors to enquire about the progress of the divorce proceedings. On 1 July, he received a brief and ambiguous reply, which read simply, 'We have your telegram and hope to send you papers for signature in the course of a day or two.'[116]

On 21 July, Thomas and Marian went through a ceremony of marriage at the Nottingham register office, with Thomas describing himself as a 'bachelor' rather than divorced. That could simply have been because he did not want to admit to having been divorced. But it could also indicate that he knew that he was not. Another indication that the pair were trying to avoid attention was their choice of the more expensive superintendent registrar's licence – which removed the need for a notice of their marriage to be displayed in the register office and allowed the wedding to go ahead after a single day had elapsed.[117]

Within the month Thomas and Marian had been arrested. At the committal hearing before the Alfreton magistrates in August 1920, there was no mention of Thomas being under any misapprehension as to his marital status.[118] Nor did any of the witnesses report that Thomas had told them that he was divorced. The only evidence about the progress of the divorce proceedings came from the police sergeant who had arrested Thomas and Marian. According to his account, Thomas had, on being charged with bigamy, admitted that it was true. He had added that he had begun divorce proceedings against Florence in 1918 when on leave and that he had received 'several letters' about them. Marian, whom the sergeant had charged with aiding and abetting, had also admitted that she had known Thomas to be married when they began 'to keep company', but that she had believed he had got his divorce by the time they married.[119]

When their cases came before the Derby assizes later that year, Thomas appeared in court wearing his war medal and was said to be suffering from shell-shock. There was clearly considerable sympathy for him – as the headline chosen by one local newspaper

[112] The Poor Persons' Procedure was the successor to the old *in forma pauperis* procedure. Under it, litigants with capital of up to £50 (and in exceptional cases £100) were eligible for assistance, although in 1920 the requirement that they should also be earning less than £2 (or exceptionally £4) per week was added.

[113] 'Man Who Thought He Was Free: Appeals Against a Sentence For Bigamy: Divorce Error', *Globe*, 31 January 1921.

[114] *R v Wheat and Stocks* [1921] 2 KB 119.

[115] No petition has been traced at the National Archives.

[116] *R v Wheat and Stocks* (n 114) 120.

[117] These details were ascertained by obtaining a copy of the marriage certificate from the GRO.

[118] 'Bigamy Charge at Alfreton', *Alfreton Journal*, 20 August 1920.

[119] 'Not Divorced: South Normanton Miner Charged With Bigamy', *Derbyshire Courier*, 21 August 1920.

made clear, billing him as a 'Wronged Husband'.[120] Thomas declared that he had inferred from the solicitors' letters that a divorce had in fact been granted. It was accordingly argued by his counsel, Norman Birkett, that Thomas, being illiterate, had formed the 'honest belief' that the divorce had been granted, and that this was a 'complete answer' to the charge against him.[121]

That raised two questions. Did Thomas have such a belief? And if he did, was it the 'complete answer' that Birkett claimed? The case of *R v Tolson* had established that an honest and reasonably held belief in the *death* of the first spouse would be a defence to a charge of bigamy. But did the reasoning in that case apply equally to an honest and reasonably held belief that a divorce had been granted?

With no authorities directly on point, Mr Justice Sankey thought that the matter needed to be referred to the Court of Criminal Appeal. He accordingly asked the jury if they thought that Thomas had believed in good faith and on reasonable grounds that there had been a divorce. They took the view that yes, he had. Sankey then directed the jury to find Thomas guilty on the basis that this was no defence and referred the matter to the Court of Criminal Appeal for the legal point to be resolved. In the meantime, he sentenced Thomas and Marian to a single day in prison.[122]

Upon their appeal, the Lord Chief Justice agreed that the legal point was an important one that needed to be decided before a 'fuller court'.[123] The story that was eventually told to the five-strong Court of Criminal Appeal was subtly different again.[124] Birkett gave the impression that the marriage had needed to take place quickly, describing Thomas as sending an 'urgent' telegram to the solicitors on finding that Marian 'was about to become a mother'.[125] But given that their daughter was not born until the end of January 1921, some seven months after Thomas had sent the telegram, their wedding could not have been quite as urgent as this implied.[126]

Birkett also said that it was Marian who had conducted the correspondence with the solicitors on Thomas' behalf. This was consistent with his claim that Thomas was illiterate, but it did not tally with what Marian was reported to have said at the time of her arrest. Finally, he claimed that Thomas had gone to a friend on receiving the letter from the solicitors 'and, clapping his hands, said: "Thank God my divorce has gone through." The friend said in evidence that Wheat's heart was full of joy.' Various newspapers also reported his claim that Thomas had thought that he could be divorced just by signing some papers because he 'had been told that at the local market' (a claim that apparently provoked some laughter in the court).[127]

[120] 'Wronged Husband: New Bigamy Defence at Derby', *Derby Daily Telegraph*, 11 November 1920.

[121] 'Imaginary Divorce: Curious Defence in South Normanton Bigamy Case', *Derbyshire Courier*, 13 November 1920.

[122] 'Wronged Husband: New Bigamy Defence at Derby', *Derby Daily Telegraph*, 11 November 1920. The novelty of the legal point meant that the case was picked up by newspapers around the country.

[123] 'A Bigamy Appeal: Important Point in Derbyshire Case', *Derby Daily Telegraph*, 20 December 1920; 'A Point To Be Argued: Sequel to a Nottingham Bigamy Case', *Nottingham Evening Post*, 20 December 1920.

[124] *R v Wheat and Stocks* (n 114). The judges were Avory, Bray, Greer, Salter and Shearman JJ.

[125] ibid 135.

[126] The date of their daughter's birth was given in the 1939 register: TNA, *1939 Register*, RG101/6177E.

[127] '"Divorce" By Signing a Few Papers: Five Judges Ponder Over Man's Curious Idea: "Told At The Local Market"', *Evening News*, 31 January 1921. The unlikelihood of this being an option may be less evident

Despite Birkett's best efforts, the appeal judges were unsympathetic. Mr Justice Avory, delivering the decision of the court, stated their view that there was no evidence on which the jury could have found that Thomas or Marian 'believed in good faith on reasonable grounds' that Thomas had been divorced. Even more significantly, they held that such a belief would in any case not be a defence to a charge of bigamy, although it might 'afford good reason for the infliction of a nominal punishment'.[128]

Most of the newspapers simply reported the outcome without commentary.[129] Within legal circles, however, the decision in *Wheat* was criticised for its strict stance on the issue of *mens rea*. One legal commentator described it as 'a blunder in the development of our jurisprudence'.[130] One has to wonder whether the Court of Criminal Appeal might have taken a different approach if they had been convinced that Thomas' belief was both genuine *and* reasonable. The case of Wilfred Markwick at the Essex assizes two years later might have provided a better test case. Markwick's claim that he had genuinely believed that his decree nisi had been made absolute was credible, given that proceedings had been instigated in India, where the process was different. He had even shown the documents relating to his divorce proceedings to the registrar on giving notice prior to his second marriage. And he and his second wife – 'a woman of the highest respectability' – had separated upon learning that their marriage was not valid. As the judge noted, he had 'no felonious intent at all'.[131] But in the light of *Wheat*, that could not be accepted as an excuse.[132] It took another four-and-a-half decades before the Court of Appeal finally decided that an honest and reasonable belief that a divorce had been granted was a defence to a charge of bigamy.[133]

At the same time, as the Attorney General had pointed out in his submissions in *Wheat*, there was a key difference between the genuine uncertainty that might exist as to whether the first spouse had died and the 'fact of divorce' – something which was 'capable of precise ascertainment'.[134] He also told the court how those accused of bigamy were now 'constantly' raising the defence that they had believed a divorce had been granted.[135] The line taken by the Court of Criminal Appeal sent a message that those involved needed to wait for confirmation that they were free to remarry rather than jumping to conclusions. As another contemporary commentator

to modern readers, used to divorces being granted without any need to attend court, but this was clearly unimaginable in 1921.

[128] *R v Wheat and Stocks* (n 114) 125.

[129] '"Reasonable Belief": No Defence to a Charge of Bigamy', *Westminster Gazette*, 14 February 1921 'Novel Bigamy Point: Belief In Divorce No Excuse, Says Appeal Court', *Daily Herald*, 15 February 1921; 'Man Who Thought He Was Divorced: Not A Defence To A Bigamy Charge', *Daily Chronicle*, 15 February 1921; 'Bigamy Law: Necessary to be Sure of Divorce Before Remarrying', *Daily News*, 15 February 1921; 'Bigamy Appeal: Important Decision Against Nottingham Man: Not Divorced', *Nottingham Journal*, 15 February 1921; 'Divorce Assumed: Couple Who Married Because They Thought Man Was Free', *Daily Mirror*, 15 February 1921; 'Derby Assize Appeal Case: Man Who Thought He Was Divorced', *Alfreton Journal*, 18 February 1921.

[130] 'Presumption of Divorce' (1921) 65 *Solicitors Journal* 321, 321.

[131] *Essex Chronicle*, 2 March 1923.

[132] There was at least a happy sequel: Wilfred was, despite his conviction, able to obtain a divorce, and he remarried his second wife legally: *Evening Telegraph*, 18 July 1924; FreeBMD, 1st quarter, 1925.

[133] *R v Gould* [1968] 2 QB 65; see further *Double Trouble*, ch 10.

[134] *R v Wheat and Stocks* (n 114)122.

[135] 'Derbyshire Bigamy', *Derby Daily Telegraph*, 31 January 1921.

noted, 'a decision in favour of the appellants would have opened the door to all kinds of abuses by the classes which now flock to the Divorce Court'.[136]

It seems that Thomas never made it to the Divorce Court. Nonetheless, he remained with Marian. The 1921 census captured them living together in Nottingham, with his two children from his first marriage, her young daughter, and their new baby.[137] The family was still together when the 1939 register was taken.[138] And when Thomas died in 1947, Marian was granted a pension as his widow.[139] There is no evidence that they ever remarried.

[136] 'Bigamy and "Mens Rea"' (1921) 56 *Law Journal* 74.
[137] TNA, 1921 census, RG15/15735.
[138] TNA, *1939 Register*, RG101/6177E.
[139] TNA, Ministry of Pensions, *Pension Ledgers and Index Cards*, 187/0993/WHA-WHE.

8

Blundering in the Shadow of the Law

There was, and remains, a subtle but crucial distinction between mistakes of fact and mistakes of law. As we saw in the previous chapter, the courts gradually accepted that certain mistaken beliefs – that the first marriage had been ended by death or divorce, or had never been valid in the first place – would, if honest and reasonable, constitute a defence to a charge of bigamy. But these were all categorised as mistakes of fact – what one twentieth-century judge summarised as 'a fact affecting [the defendant's] matrimonial status, which, if true, would make his second marriage lawful and innocent'.[1] Mistakes as to the law, by contrast, were not accepted as a defence. So, for example, those who thought that a separation agreement ended the marriage or that living apart from their spouse for seven years allowed them to remarry were still guilty of bigamy despite their genuine belief that they were acting within the law.

I have termed such mistaken beliefs 'blundering in the shadow of the law'. The term 'bargaining in the shadow of the law' was first coined by American scholars in the 1970s to refer to the impact of legal rules and norms on the way in which couples negotiated their post-divorce finances and childcare arrangements outside the courtroom.[2] Substituting 'blundering' for 'bargaining' emphasises how these bigamists lacked the necessary legal knowledge to navigate their way to a second marriage without exposing themselves to prosecution. Nonetheless, they were still operating in the 'shadow' of the law, because their mistaken beliefs can be traced back to specific legal rules.

A parallel can be drawn with the emergence (and persistence) of the 'common law marriage myth' in modern-day England and Wales. Although this is a myth that was generated by misunderstandings, it was not completely unfounded. The emergence of the myth can be traced very precisely to the way in which various legal developments benefiting cohabitants were reported in the 1970s. That decade saw new rights being accorded to cohabitants, both by Parliament and in the courts. The extent of these new rights was often exaggerated by the press, and even by some legal commentators, implying that their effect was to give the 'common law wife' the same rights as a legal wife. By the end of the decade, the myth was firmly established, and subsequent attempts to dislodge it had only a limited effect.[3] Even as late as 2018, a national-level study showed

[1] *R v Gould* [1968] 2 QB 65, 76.

[2] RH Mnookin and L Kornhauser, 'Bargaining in the Shadow of the Law: The Case of Divorce' (1979) 88 *Yale Law Journal* 950.

[3] I have traced the history of the myth (and the reasons for its persistence) elsewhere: see R Probert, 'Common law marriage: myths and misunderstandings' (2008) 20 *Child and Family Law Quarterly* 1; R Probert, 'Why do couples still believe in common law marriage?' [2007] *Family Law* 403.

that almost half of the population – and over half of cohabitants – thought that 'couples who live together for a period of time have a common law marriage which gives them the same rights as married couples'.[4]

From this we can take two key points. First, we should not be surprised by individuals holding tenacious, if erroneous, views about their right to remarry, especially at a time when levels of literacy were lower and sources of accessible information far fewer. Second, given that no one would attribute modern misunderstandings to an 'alternative plebeian subculture', we need to be very careful about attributing past misunderstandings to supposed 'customs'.[5]

The case studies in this chapter take various mistaken beliefs and show how each had its root in a specific (and often quite reasonable) misunderstanding of the law rather than some alternative subculture. Some of these misunderstandings were rooted in the general law of marriage and the successive Acts governing bigamy. Katharine Edwards was far from being the only person to believe that an unconsummated marriage was not valid, and so not binding on her. In the case of James Keen, it was argued that his first marriage had been compelled by the parish and was not in his real name. And the seven-year defence was responsible for many inadvertently bigamous marriages, as individuals mistakenly thought that the mere absence of the other spouse for that period was a defence.

Other mistaken beliefs emerged at different times as the law developed or changed. William Beard was one of the first to claim that he thought a separation agreement allowed him to remarry, a misunderstanding that can be traced to the developing law on such agreements. William Tompkins, remarrying in 1861, was under the equally mistaken impression that an order granted under section 21 of the Matrimonial Causes Act 1857 was a divorce. Maria Waulby, on the other hand, was caught out by a change in the law, believing that her first marriage was void.

Of course, a more cynical view of these individuals' claims would be that they knew full well what the law was and were merely trying to come up with an excuse after they had been caught. But they were not alone in their misunderstandings. In short, we should take seriously the possibility that they were just 'blundering in the shadow of the law'.

'Never Bedded': Katharine Edwards, Alias Watkins, 1678

In 1678, a young woman named Katharine petitioned King Charles II in anticipation of her impending trial for bigamy. As she explained, at the age of 12 she had been forced by her mother to marry William Edwards, who had only been after her money, but she was

[4] A Barlow, 'Modern Marriage Myths – the dichotomy between expectations of legal rationality and lived law' in R Akhtar, P Nash and R Probert (eds), *Cohabitation and Religious Marriage: Status, Similarities and Solutions* (Bristol, Bristol University Press, 2020).

[5] For the argument that there were various 'customs' that individuals relied on to legitimise separations and new relationships in the eyes of their local community, see J Gillis, *For Better, For Worse: British Marriages 1600 to the Present* (Oxford, Oxford University Press, 1985) 209–18. For analysis of the problems with his sources, see R Probert, 'Approaching sources critically: Challenging myths in the standard narratives' in R Auchmuty, C Derry and D Wright (eds), *Research Handbook on Gender, History and Law* (forthcoming).

subsequently 'importuned by Charles Watkins to disown and revoke the said marriage, which he and several of her friends advised she might easily do, in regard she never had bedded with the said Edwards'.[6] Still aged only 16, she had married Charles, only for her aggrieved first husband to have her arrested; as she concluded, he 'intends to prosecute her at the next assizes at Carmarthen for her life'. All these factors – her age, the advice she had received, and the risk of being sentenced to death if convicted – strongly suggest that she had genuinely believed that she was free to remarry. Happily, the King was sympathetic, and Katherine was duly reprieved and pardoned.[7]

Nor was Katherine's an unreasonable misunderstanding of her legal position. The canon law held that a marriage was voidable if one of the parties was physically incapable of consummating it. In such a case, either party was able to obtain a decree of nullity. At the time, such an annulment operated retrospectively, rather than just prospectively, with the formal sentence declaring that the marriage had been void from its inception.[8] It is easy to see how this combination of factors could give rise to a belief that a marriage was only valid if it had been consummated, and that couples who had not had sex were not bound to each other. After all, a remarriage after a first void marriage was perfectly legal without the need for any sentence from an ecclesiastical court.

It was a misunderstanding that recurred over the centuries. At the Old Bailey, there was a whole run of cases in the 1720s and 1730s where women claimed that one or other of their marriages had never been consummated and so was no marriage at all. One, Elizabeth Thorn, claimed her second husband as her 'lawful' one, telling him, 'You know that I was never bedded by John Howell, and therefore he's no Husband to me'.[9] Mary Picart was even more vehement in her protests that she only had one husband:

> Vat signifie de Parsoon, and de Ring, and all de Ceremonie, vy dat no make de Husband, dare be no Husband, no Vife, till dey go to Bed togader. But Monsieur Benchain, he no do vid me in de Bed, he do nothing in de Varld; – noting but de Ceremonie; – vy den dat be no Husband.[10]

The fact that both women were acquitted – along with a third, Elizabeth Hutchinson, whose first husband had similarly been 'taken from her within two hours'[11] – may well have encouraged others to make similar claims.[12] But these acquittals would

[6] FH Blackburne Daniell (ed), *Calendar of State Papers Domestic: Charles II, 1678 With Addenda, 1674–9* (London, 1913) 27–28.

[7] ibid 93.

[8] See eg the declaration made in the case of *Kingsman, formerly Maunsell, falsely called Tenducci v Tenducci* on 28 February 1776 to the effect that the ceremonies in question 'were from the beginning and are absolutely null and void to all intents and purposes whatsoever by reason of the impotency of … Ferdinando Tenducci': H Berry, *The Castrato and His Wife* (Oxford, Oxford University Press, 2011) 191.

[9] *OBP*, 6 September 1732. The claim did have a degree of plausibility, as the wedding took place when her first husband was an apprentice and she was a servant and they had no opportunity to set up home together as husband and wife.

[10] *OBP*, 30 June 1725. The statements in this case were set out in an approximation of a foreign accent, although exactly what accent is debatable. The non-consummation of the marriage was due to lack of opportunity rather than incapacity, Mary's relatives having arrived on the scene shortly after the ceremony had taken place to tell Philip Bouchain that Mary was already married. As Philip somewhat sadly recounted, 'me vas force to go to Bed vid mine self'.

[11] *OBP*, 26 February 1724.

[12] See eg *OBP*, 17 July 1728 (Mary Northorp, who claimed that her first husband had left before the ceremony was complete and she had 'never Cohabited with him as a Husband', although in this case there was 'good Evidence to the contrary'.

have been based on the absence of proof of the marriage, not the fact it had not been consummated.[13] Allegations that a couple had married clandestinely could be given credibility by evidence that they had set up home together and that others had assumed they were married. In the absence of such evidence, they were likely to acquitted unless there was other evidence of the ceremony. So although it might appear that those whose marriages had not been consummated were more likely to be acquitted, this was a matter of correlation rather than cause.

Examples of individuals claiming that they believed they were entitled to remarry if the first marriage was not consummated also occurred in the nineteenth century. Elizabeth Shaw ran away from Charles Shields within hours of their wedding and married James Brooker four days later, claiming that her first marriage was 'of no force in as much as it had not been consummated'.[14] There was a somewhat complex back-story to this. Elizabeth had in fact been engaged to marry James, and the banns had already been called for their wedding, but Charles persuaded her to marry him while James was away.[15] At the subsequent Surrey assize, the judge bluntly told her that she was wrong in supposing that her first marriage was not binding and sentenced her to six months in prison.[16] Men, too, sought to rely on the non-consummation of the first marriage when explaining why they had believed themselves entitled to remarry.[17] At the Old Bailey in 1828, Onesiphorus Frederick put in a written defence explaining that his first wife Mary Jolly had refused to go home with him after their wedding in 1823 'and had never once cohabited with him', and that he had been informed that their marriage was null and void.[18] A few years later, John James Frasser displayed great (if misplaced) confidence that he would not be convicted on account of his first marriage not having been consummated.[19]

The twentieth century saw changes to when a non-consummated marriage could be annulled, with the other spouse's wilful refusal to consummate the marriage being added to the list of grounds.[20] As a result, more unconsummated marriages were potentially voidable. There appears to have been some sympathy for James Napier Thompson Holmes, whose case came before the Court of Criminal Appeal in 1950.

[13] This was explicitly stated in the case of Mary Picart, with the *Proceedings* noting that she was acquitted on account of there 'not being a legal Proof of the second Marriage': *OBP*, 30 June 1725.

[14] Ancestry, *London Church of England Parish Registers*, P92/CTC/028 (marriage at Christ Church, Southwark, 23 February 1815) and P92/GEO/179 (marriage at St George the Martyr, 27 February 1815). Elizabeth's comments were reported by James' father at the hearing before the magistrates ('Curious Case of Bigamy', *Morning Chronicle*, 4 April 1815) and confirmed by a friend who had been present at both ceremonies (*Globe*, 31 July 1815).

[15] *Public Cause*, 2 August 1815.

[16] 'Bigamy', *Morning Post*, 31 July 1815; *St James' Chronicle*, 1 August 1815; TNA, *Criminal Registers*, HO27/11, p 370. The case revealed another legal misunderstanding: the prosecution was brought by the father of the first husband, who assumed that this would have the effect of dissolving her marriage to his son. The judge had to explain that he had been mistaken as to the law, and that the prosecution would 'affirm' the first marriage, rather than dissolving it: 'Bigamy', *Morning Post*, 31 July 1815.

[17] See also *OBP*, 17 February 1819 (John Dayer); 'Surrey Sessions', *The Standard*, 13 April 1831 (James Obee).

[18] *OBP*, 23 October 1828. The jury found him guilty but recommended mercy, and he was sentenced to just two months in prison.

[19] 'Bigamy', *Morning Chronicle*, 6 September 1833.

[20] Matrimonial Causes Act 1937, s 7.

James, who had originally been sentenced to a year in prison, was given an absolute discharge to enable him to remarry his second wife as soon as possible. His first wife had confirmed that their marriage had never been consummated, and Lord Goddard, the Lord Chief Justice, commented that James could have applied for a decree of nullity if he 'had been better advised'.[21]

Separation Agreements: William Beard, 1800

At the Old Bailey in 1800, 54-year-old William Beard asserted that his second wife was his 'lawful' one as he and his first wife had 'agreed to part'.[22] This was not an excuse that carried any weight: the jury found him guilty, and the judge sentenced him to seven years' transportation. From the short report in the *Proceedings*, William's case is not promising material for a case study. But it is a useful starting point for discussion as the first example I have traced of a bigamist arguing that he believed he was entitled to marry on account of an agreement with his first spouse.[23]

This was not, it should be noted, the first example of someone accused of bigamy claiming that they had made an agreement with the first spouse. But in earlier cases such claims had not been accompanied by any suggestion that the agreement permitted a legal remarriage. At the 1748 trial of John Collins, for example, a letter was produced by his second wife Elizabeth Watkins. It addressed her as his 'dearest wife', assuring her that 'the other is, by agreement, to me no more, than one that I never saw' and that he regarded himself as 'being more than divorced from her, in the sight of the Almighty'. The invocation of the 'Almighty' was significant: as Elizabeth told the court, John had acknowledged that 'he knew it was against the laws of the land' but claimed that it was 'not against the law of God'.[24] Whatever the Almighty might have thought of it, the judge agreed that the remarriage was illegal, and John was convicted. Some decades later, John Augustus Thomas Rayner cross-examined his sister-in-law with the intent of confirming that a deed of separation had been executed between him and his first wife, although his actual defence was that he had believed her to be dead.[25] And as late as 1793, William Turnbull and Sarah Hemmings were clearly aware that their agreement to part did not allow them to remarry, despite the bonds they had signed, since they asked the clergyman who had married them to deny any recollection of doing so.[26] In other words, in none of these cases did the accused seek to argue that they were entitled to remarry, and in some we have clear evidence that they knew that the law did not permit it.

[21] 'Jailed man told "Go and marry"', *Daily Herald*, 20 June 1950.
[22] *OBP*, 28 May 1800.
[23] Other cases followed: see eg *OBP*, 15 September 1825 (Sydney Frederick Reed 'put in a written Defence, stating that an agreement to separate had been drawn up between him and his first wife, after which he considered himself at liberty to marry'); *The London Dispatch and People's Political and Social Reformer*, 18 June 1837 (Robert William Arnell 'said that he had a deed of separation drawn up between his first wife and himself, and he therefore considered himself perfectly at liberty to marry again').
[24] *OBP*, 6 July 1748.
[25] *OBP*, 15 September 1790.
[26] *OBP*, 29 May 1793. He refused: see *Double Trouble*, ch 4.

So, why might William Beard possibly have been labouring under a misunderstanding that an agreement with his first wife *did* permit him to remarry? Here we need to delve into the complex law governing separation agreements.

On the face of it, the belief that a private separation agreement allowed the parties to remarry was completely at odds with the law. Indeed, such an agreement did not even allow the parties to separate. The remedies that were available in the ecclesiastical courts until 1857 (and in the Divorce Court after that date) assumed that husbands and wives had an obligation to live together, at least as long as both observed the duties inherent in marriage. Separation from an adulterous or cruel spouse could only be authorised by means of a divorce *a mensa et thoro* (renamed 'judicial separation' in 1857). Those who separated from their spouse without such justification could be compelled to return. At least until the mid-eighteenth century, such a return might be ordered by the church courts as part of their office jurisdiction – that is to say, as part of their remit to ensure good order within the community, and without either party requesting it. Refusals to return could be punished by penance and ultimately by excommunication. After that date it was down to the other spouse to seek an order for restitution of conjugal rights. Here again a refusal to return could be sanctioned by punishment – with the threat of excommunication being replaced by the possibility of imprisonment from 1812 until 1884.[27] All this meant that the parties could not simply agree to separate, and any agreement to this end would not be recognised. From the perspective of the church courts, any contract in which the parties had agreed to separate was deemed contrary to public policy and therefore void.

Yet the church courts were not the only ones to adjudicate on separation agreements that were brought before them. Such agreements, or at least the more formal ones drafted by lawyers, tended to do much more than simply provide for the parties to separate. The detail focused on the financial arrangements – for example the level of maintenance that the husband would provide, and a commitment by the wife's trustees to indemnify the husband for any debts that the wife might accrue.[28] Such terms would not be litigated in the ecclesiastical courts, but in the Court of Chancery and the King's Bench respectively. And in a case from 1792, the Court of Chancery had decreed that a separation agreement *was* enforceable insofar as the husband could be required to pay the agreed maintenance.[29] It was only a small step from understanding that certain terms of a separation agreement were legally enforceable to a misunderstanding that *all* of them were, including the agreement to live apart.

This is not the place to trace all the twists and turns in the development of the law governing separation agreements.[30] Nor is it necessary to my central point: once a

[27] Matrimonial Causes Act 1884.

[28] S Staves, *Married Women's Separate Property in England, 1660–1833* (Cambridge, MA, Harvard University Press, 1990) 163. The 1756 separation agreement between Richard Warren and his first wife Frances was in this form: he agreed to allow her £3 18s per year, 'he to be clear of any debts she should contract, and Thomas Butler to pay to [Richard] the money again, if he the said [Richard] should pay any debts that Frances his wife should contract': *OBP*, 20 October 1756.

[29] *Guth v Guth* (1792) 3 Bro CC 614; 29 ER 729.

[30] For an excellent discussion of the legal rules, see M Parker, 'The draft Nuptial Agreements Bill and the abolition of the common law rule: "swept away" or swept under the carpet?' (2015) 27 *Child and Family Law Quarterly* 63. See also O Anderson, 'State, Civil Society and Separation in Victorian Marriage' (1999) 163 *Past and Present* 161 on the broader social context.

misunderstanding takes hold, it is difficult to dislodge. But it is worth noting one mid-nineteenth century decision that appears to have fuelled the belief that a separation agreement legitimated a subsequent remarriage. In 1848, the House of Lords confirmed that the financial terms of a separation agreement could be enforced.[31] From this point, there does appear to have been an increase in bigamists explaining that they had believed they could legally remarry where there had been an agreed separation, or where their first spouse had given them permission.[32]

Time and again, judges wearily tried to explain that, whatever the nature of the agreement, it conferred no right to marry.[33] There were also regular reminders in the press that a separation agreement did not prevent the parties from being prosecuted for bigamy. From the 1850s on, publications such as *Reynolds's Newspaper* and *Lloyd's Weekly Newspaper* included advice columns that responded to readers' questions. Although some of their answers were a little opaque in the absence of the original query, the warning given in this 1852 example could not have been clearer: 'R.B. A bond of separation does not constitute divorce, and by marrying again you will be committing bigamy.'[34] Yet we know from the persistence of the common law marriage myth that even government-funded information campaigns have only a limited effect in dislodging entrenched beliefs.

Caught Out by a Change in the Law: Maria Waulby, 1822

On 30 August 1822, 16-year-old Maria Hopwood left her parents' house in Hull in a horse-drawn carriage, to be married to a tailor named John Waulby in the nearby town of Beverley.[35] As the marriage was by licence, and took place without her father's consent, it would have been void under the provisions of the 1753 Act. Four years later, still only 20, she went through a second ceremony of marriage with Abraham Capes at Sutton in Holderness. They made no attempt to conceal the fact, with an announcement of the wedding appearing in the local newspaper.[36] But less than two months later, she was on trial for bigamy at the York assizes.

As fate would have it, Maria's first marriage had in fact taken place during a brief window when the 1753 Act was in abeyance. The perception that individuals were strategically using the annulling provisions of that Act had led to its repeal by the Confirmation of Marriages Act 1822, passed in July of that year. This new Act also set out a more demanding set of provisions that required couples to provide supporting evidence of their names, ages, and places of residence before banns could be called or a

[31] *Wilson v Wilson* (1848) 1 HLC 538; 9 ER 870, dismissing the husband's appeal from the Vice-Chancellor's 1845 decision.

[32] For the different types of agreements that might underpin such misunderstandings, see the case studies in chapter 10 and *Double Trouble*, ch 7.

[33] See eg 'South Lancashire Assizes', *Manchester Courier*, 19 August 1846; 'St Austell – Charge of Bigamy', *Royal Cornwall Gazette*, 16 October 1857.

[34] 'Notices to Correspondents', *Reynolds's*, 14 November 1852. For similar examples, see *Reynolds's*, 6 March 1853, 15 January 1854, 24 July 1881, 4 September 1881.

[35] 'Singular Case of Bigamy', *York Herald*, 7 April 1827.

[36] *Hull Packet*, 27 February 1827.

licence issued.[37] But these provisions were only to come into effect on 1 September 1822 – two days *after* Maria's marriage.

The prosecution argued that Maria's first marriage was valid, and her second therefore bigamous. Their reasoning was that, with the 1753 Act having been repealed, the validity of the marriage had to be tested by reference to the law prior to that Act, when lack of parental consent did not invalidate a marriage. The judge agreed, and directed the jury to find Maria guilty.

She was, however, permitted to go free, upon entering into recognizances for her appearance at the next assizes, while the matter was referred to the judges for consideration. They confirmed that Maria's first marriage was valid, and her second therefore bigamous and void.[38] Even so, Maria was sentenced to just 14 days in prison, an exceptionally light sentence for that period.[39] It was easy to see how she had been caught out by a change in the law.

A Parish Marriage, and the Wrong Name?: James Keen, 1834

At the Central Criminal Court in 1834, James Keen was indicted for bigamy. At first sight his case appeared to be a particularly bad one: his first marriage had taken place in February 1833 and his second at Easter 1834, with him using a different surname each time. But his second wife, Martha Griffiths, gave evidence that she had known of his first marriage, telling the Old Bailey that it was 'a parish marriage' and that he had used his 'real' name when he married her. She also said that she had sought advice before marrying James:

> I went to Mr. Rogers, who is called a wise man, in Pratt-street, and consulted him about marrying the prisoner – I stated to him all that I knew about the first marriage, and about his real name being Keen; and in consequence of what he told me, I married the prisoner, and did not know I was doing wrong.[40]

Even if the parish authorities had compelled James to marry his first wife – which the witnesses for the prosecution strenuously denied – it would not have excused his second marriage. Nor, in the circumstances, would his use of the name Williams, rather than Keen, made his first marriage void. But it is nonetheless easy to see why those involved might believe otherwise.

James' was far from being the only case where it was alleged that the first marriage was the result of pressure from the parish rather than the free consent of both parties.[41] James Knight, convicted at the Sussex assizes in 1813, had been forced to marry his

[37] So demanding, indeed, that they proved impracticable to implement and were quickly repealed in March 1823: see R Probert, *Marriage Law and Practice in the Long Eighteenth Century: A Reassessment* (Cambridge, Cambridge University Press, 2009) 307–09.

[38] *R v Maria Waully* (1827) 1 Moody 163; 168 ER 1226; (1827) 1 Lewin 23; 168 ER 945.

[39] Only John Kelly received a lighter sentence – a one shilling fine – that year. Indeed, in the 22 previous years, over 94% of those convicted received harsher sentences.

[40] *OBP*, 15 May 1834.

[41] See also the case study of Josiah Thornton in chapter 9.

pregnant first bride, but left her as soon as the ceremony was over and never cohabited with her.[42] John Lovell Woodcock similarly pleaded in his defence that his first marriage was 'compulsory',[43] while William Grainger told the magistrates that he did not consider himself married to his first wife, the marriage having been 'a parish affair'.[44]

It had long been accepted that duress was a ground for an annulment. Some legal writers went further and took the view that a marriage entered into without the full and free consent of the parties was automatically void.[45] The main problem was that establishing duress required it to be shown that there had been 'some danger of death, or else bodily torment and distress'.[46] Being locked up for refusing to marry the woman who was carrying one's child did not meet this high threshold. Even in the late twentieth century, judges were still of the view that a man who married under threat of prosecution would not be able to rely on such threats to annul the marriage unless they arose from 'some external circumstance' for which he was not responsible.[47]

What about Martha's second claim, that James' first marriage was not in his 'real' name? Here again there was a kernel of truth. Between 1753 and 1822, marrying without 'due publication' of banns invalidated the marriage. Having the banns called in a completely false name, or in a variation that was so significant as to disguise the identity of the individual in question, was deemed to be no publication at all, and any resulting marriage was equally void.[48] When the law was revised in 1823, however, it was provided that a marriage would only be void if both parties 'knowingly and wilfully' married without due publication of banns.[49] In other words, there were cases where using the wrong name did invalidate the marriage, but it all depended on the circumstances.

Such legal niceties were, perhaps unsurprisingly, not always readily understood. One particularly strong example of a bigamist who had not intentionally flouted the law is Sidonia Gant, convicted at the York assizes in 1838. Sidonia was a teenager at the time of her marriage to John Sanderson. She was also unable to write, simply making her mark next to her name in the marriage register. Believing that the erroneous spelling of her surname as 'Gaunt' invalidated the marriage, she refused to live with John unless he married her again.[50] He in turn refused to so, and around seven weeks later she went through a second ceremony of marriage with Charles Rodgers.[51]

[42] 'Circuit Intelligence', *Sun*, 19 August 1813.

[43] 'Lincolnshire Assizes', *Lincoln, Rutland and Stamford Mercury*, 20 March 1829.

[44] 'Union Hall', *The Standard*, 18 September 1833.

[45] J Ayliffe, *Parergon juris canonici anglicani* (London, 1726) 361 stated unequivocally that 'matrimony contracted through any menace or impression of fear is null and void ipso jure'.

[46] ibid 362, repeated by T Poynter, *A Concise View of the Doctrine and Practice of the Ecclesiastical Courts in Doctor's Commons*, 2nd edn (London, 1824) 138.

[47] *Buckland v Buckland (otherwise Camilleri)* [1968] P 296, 301; see also Law Commission, *Report on Nullity of Marriage* (Law Com No 33, 1970) para 65, discussing when certain threats might be regarded as 'legitimate'. For discussion of the evolving law in this area, see D McClean and M Hayes, 'But I Didn't Really Want To Get Married' in S Gilmore, J Herring and R Probert (eds), *Landmark Cases in Family Law* (Oxford, Hart, 2011).

[48] Probert (n 40) 291.

[49] Marriage Act 1823, s 22. For examples of marriages being annulled on that basis, see *Wiltshire v Prince* (1830) 3 Hagg Ecc 332; 162 ER 1176; *Tongue v Allen* (1835) 1 Curt 38; 163 ER 13; *Brealy v Reed* (1841) 2 Curt 834; 163 ER 601; *Orme v Holloway* (1847) 5 Notes of Cases 267; *Tooth v Barrow* (1854) 1 Sp Ecc & Ad 371; 164 ER 214; *Wormald v Neale and Wormald* (1868) 19 LT 93.

[50] 'Town Hall', *Sheffield Independent*, 7 July 1838.

[51] Ancestry, *Parish Registers*, PR87/3/13 (marriage at Rotherham Minster on 18 June 1838).

But her conviction clearly convinced her that her first marriage was valid after all, since it was to John that she returned after serving her sentence.[52] In other cases, wives had believed their husband's story that the marriage was invalid on account of the wrong name being used. This happened to Elizabeth Friend, then just 15, whose first husband turned her out of the house a few weeks after their wedding and who went on to remarry four years later.[53]

Just to add to the complexity, there was also the question of what name *should* have been used. The 'real' name was not necessarily the name in which a person had been baptised, but rather the name by which they were known within the community. This brings us back to James Keen – who, it turned out, had good reason to use the name of 'Williams': his mother's maiden name was Keen, but his father's name was Williams, and his parents had only married after his birth. As his brother-in-law explained, he had known him by the name of Williams for about seven years, and by the name of Keen for four or five months.[54]

In the circumstances, then, James' first marriage was valid, and he had no defence to the charge of bigamy. He was convicted and sentenced to six months in prison. The report in the *Morning Chronicle* left its sympathies in no doubt by adding the touching detail that he had leaned over the dock to kiss Martha goodbye, with Martha standing on tiptoe 'to receive the tender salute'.[55] Such reports reflected the increasing criticism of parish officials who 'arranged' marriages for pregnant paupers, and the practice ceased. After 1834, the occasional examples of parish-instigated marriages that surfaced in bigamy cases were all ones that had taken place in earlier decades.[56]

'Economic Divorce': William Tompkins, 1861

In July 1861, a 50-year-old butcher's labourer named William Tompkins went through a ceremony of marriage with widow Elizabeth Bayliss. The census taken earlier that year had recorded William as lodging with Elizabeth at her home in Cardigan Street in Oxford, along with her four children from her first marriage.[57] Both knew that his first wife Charlotte, whom William had married back in 1836, was still alive. But something had happened that made them believe that they could get married. Just a few months earlier, a local paper had reported Charlotte's successful application for an order

[52] TNA, 1841 census, HO107/1335, Book 5, folio 15, p 27.

[53] 'Bigamy', *Leeds Mercury*, 23 March 1839. She too was convicted, but the 'great extenuation' meant that she only received a sentence of 14 days.

[54] *OBP*, 15 May 1834.

[55] 'Bigamy', *Morning Chronicle*, 17 May 1834.

[56] See eg *Woolmer's*, 7 July 1838 (Henry Willie, first marriage in 1811); *Lane v Goodwin* (1843) 4 QB 361 (George Rudman, first marriage in 1814).

[57] TNA, 1861 census: RG9/896, folio 96, p 36. A small slash mark before William's name confirms that he was considered as forming a separate family unit from Elizabeth and her children. The 1861 census distinguished lodgers from boarders who were part of the household: E Higgs, *Making sense of the census: the manuscript returns for England and Wales, 1801–1901* (London, HMSO, 1989) 59. As this indicates, it cannot be assumed that 'lodger' was a coded way of referring to a cohabitant (on which see further R Probert, '"A Banbury Story": cohabitation and marriage among the Victorian poor in "notorious Neithrop"' (2012) 19 *Cake and Cockhorse* 2).

protecting her property from William.[58] According to *Jackson's Oxford Journal*, William, 'misconstruing the law, considered that he was thereby put in the position of a divorced man as effectively as it was possible for some Cresswell Cresswell to place him'.[59] William and Elizabeth certainly made no attempt to conceal their marriage, with the wedding taking place in their local church of St Paul after banns had been published,[60] and the pair being congratulated by their friends. Less than two months later, however, William was before the Oxford City Court, charged with bigamy.[61]

William's misunderstanding was understandable. The order that Charlotte had obtained was something of a novelty, having only been available for a few years. It was one of the many innovations introduced by the Matrimonial Causes Act 1857. Under section 21, wives who had been deserted by their husbands 'without reasonable cause' could apply to the local magistrates' court for an order protecting any property they had acquired by their own industry, or by inheritance.[62] The result of the order was to treat the wife as though she was single at least so far as this property was concerned. This, along with the fact that the 1857 Act had also introduced the possibility of obtaining a divorce from a court, was apt to cause confusion.

Whether William had actually deserted Charlotte was another matter. It was subsequently claimed that it was Charlotte who had left him. She may, of course, have had good reasons for doing so. Judges in the Divorce Court were subsequently to develop the concept of 'constructive' desertion, recognising that one spouse might have been driven to leave the matrimonial home on account of the other's behaviour.[63] But that was still in the future when Charlotte applied for her order. The fact that her application was successful tells us more about the absence of procedural safeguards than about William's behaviour.[64]

Of course, the issue of who had left whom made no difference to whether William was guilty of bigamy. At his subsequent trial at the Oxfordshire assizes in March 1862, William simply pleaded guilty.[65] But the claim that it was Charlotte who had left him was one of the mitigating circumstances eloquently argued by his counsel – along with William's belief that a section 21 order had the same effect as a divorce, and the fact that Elizabeth had not been 'imposed on' by any deception on William's part.[66] Elizabeth herself was called and confirmed that she knew about Charlotte but had seen the statement in the Oxford paper and thought that William had therefore 'got rid' of her.[67] The judge, Mr Justice Crompton, was clearly keen to ensure that others did not make the

[58] 'Petty Sessions', *Oxford Journal*, 4 May 1861.

[59] 'Charge of Bigamy', *Jackson's Oxford Journal*, 28 September 1861. Sir Cresswell Cresswell was the judge appointed to preside over the new Divorce Court.

[60] Ancestry, *Anglican Parish Registers*, PAR212/1/R3/2.

[61] 'Charge of Bigamy', *Jackson's Oxford Journal*, 28 September 1861.

[62] For a superb analysis of s 21, see J Aston and O Anderson, *Deserted Wives and Economic Divorce in 19th-Century England and Wales: For Wives Alone* (Oxford, Hart, 2024). The Divorce Court also had the power to grant s 21 orders but in practice the majority were made by magistrates.

[63] On the development of the concept of constructive desertion, see R Probert 'The Double Standard of Morality in the Divorce and Matrimonial Causes Act 1857' (1999) 28 *Anglo-American Law Review* 73; Aston and Anderson (n 62) 86.

[64] On the lack of procedural safeguards, see Aston and Anderson (n 62) 82.

[65] 'Oxfordshire Assizes', *Banbury Advertiser*, 6 March 1862.

[66] 'Oxfordshire Lent Assizes', *Jackson's Oxford Journal*, 8 March 1862.

[67] 'Oxfordshire Lent Assizes', *Oxford Chronicle*, 8 March 1862.

same mistake, saying that 'it ought to be known that orders of the kind alluded to only treated women as single women with respect to their property',[68] and warning that those who remarried were, like William, liable to prosecution.[69] Even so, he thought that a 'slight' punishment would suffice, given that this was not a case of deception.[70] William was duly sentenced to three weeks' imprisonment with hard labour.[71]

Crompton's comments did little to dispel the misunderstandings about the effect of section 21 orders. One handbook advising magistrates as to their powers even set out the provisions of section 21 under the misleading title 'Divorce'.[72] And the risk of misunderstandings leading to bigamous remarriages was exacerbated by the sheer number of section 21 orders being made. Jennifer Aston and Olive Anderson have calculated that, between 1858 and 1893, 'at the very least 19,000 and probably over 20,000 orders for economic divorce were made'.[73] Of course, many if not most of those obtaining such orders would have understood their limits, and others may well have had no wish to remarry. Nonetheless, over the next few decades, there was a steady trickle of cases coming before the assizes where one or other of the spouses had misunderstood the effect of the order and remarried, only to find themselves on trial for bigamy.[74] But with the passage of further legislation enabling married women to own and control property, there was no longer the same need for a section 21 order, and the numbers dwindled away, to around a couple of dozen a year by the start of the twentieth century.[75] At least one source of confusion had been removed.

'A Common, Though Very Vulgar and Absurd, Belief'

In December 1872, the *Leeds Mercury* ran a piece commenting on the prosecution of several bigamists from Preston at the recent Liverpool assizes. Noting that Lancashire, like Yorkshire, had 'customs and traditions', it hinted that the men in question had been influenced by a 'popular delusion' that a couple simply had to separate and 'after a certain number of years, apparently seven' would be free to marry again. It also expressed some cynicism as to whether there might be some wilful self-delusion in the case:

> It is so easy to convince men who have set their minds upon doing a certain thing that it is lawful to do it, that there need be no wonder that husbands and wives who wish to remarry

[68] 'Oxfordshire Lent Assizes', *Jackson's Oxford Journal*, 8 March 1862.
[69] 'Oxfordshire Lent Assizes', *Oxford Chronicle*, 8 March 1862.
[70] ibid.
[71] TNA, *Criminal Registers*, HO27/132, p 401. It would have been a month, but he had already been in prison for a week awaiting trial: 'Oxfordshire Lent Assizes', *Jackson's Oxford Journal*, 8 March 1862. He and Elizabeth remained together until his death: TNA, 1871 census, RG10/1441, folio 79, p 48; Ancestry, *Anglican Parish Registers*, PAR197/1/R5/1 (burial of William Tompkins at St Barnabus, 30 April 1871).
[72] GC Oke, *The Magisterial Synopsis: a Practical Guide for Magistrates, their Clerks, Attorneys and Constables*, 7th edn (London, Butterworths, 1860) 916. This was repeated in subsequent editions.
[73] Aston and Anderson (n 62) 102.
[74] 'Lancaster Spring Assizes', *Lancaster Gazette*, 9 March 1872 (Joseph Irvin, three months' imprisonment); 'A Humorous Bigamy Case', *Lancaster Gazette*, 24 February 1872, 'Lancaster Spring Assizes', *Preston Chronicle*, 16 March 1872 (George Pilkington, five months' hard labour); 'A Day's Imprisonment for Bigamy', *Penny Illustrated Paper*, 2 February 1878 (Thomas Kelsall, one day, having already been in prison for three months awaiting trial); 'Stafford Summer Assizes', *Birmingham Daily Gazette*, 19 July 1880 (Edward Jearum, one week's imprisonment).
[75] Aston and Anderson (n 62).

before they are free to do so should yield ready assent to a common, though very vulgar and absurd, belief like that which has taken root in Preston.[76]

It concluded, however, on a more positive note, commenting that after the warning given by the judge, 'we shall probably hear no more of any such defence for bigamy'.[77]

If nothing else, this article provides a good example of why it is vital to look at local reports of any case wherever possible, rather than at those written by journalists relying on (at best) second-hand reports. There *had* been a clutch of bigamists from Preston at the Liverpool assizes. Each had been sentenced to three months' imprisonment on account of various mitigating circumstances, but the presiding judge, Mr Justice Mellor, had warned that he would not be so lenient if future cases came before him. No mention was made by any of the accused, their counsel, or the judge, of any belief that it was possible to marry after a period of seven years' separation.[78]

As we shall see, there were plenty of others who did. But for the moment I want to focus on the decision of the *Leeds Mercury* to frame the belief in the right to remarry after seven years as a 'custom' – and the significance of a Yorkshire paper making such claims about those living in Lancashire. In this context, attributing beliefs to 'custom' or 'tradition' was a coded way of implying a certain backwardness. This can be seen even more clearly in an Irish case at the Leinster assizes in 1891, when Mr Justice Murphy seems to have taken a particular delight in turning the tables on English assumptions of superiority. Before him was Rowland Haigh, whose first marriage had taken place in Huddersfield in 1880 and who was accused of bigamously marrying Mary Walker at Killaloe in 1891. Upon being informed that there was a 'superstition' in England – or at least in Bradford and Huddersfield – that couples who had been separated for seven years could marry again, Murphy opined that it 'must be a very barbarous country'.[79] According to another report, in sentencing Rowland, he also expressed his regret that the serious crime he had committed had arisen 'from being brought up in a country so involved in darkness and bewilderment as to the laws of marriage', and added that 'whatever superstition there might be about Bradford and Huddersfield, it was certain that it did not exist in that backward place called Killaloe'.[80] As the *Huddersfield Chronicle* noted, '[r]arely have the tables been so completely turned upon what we consider enlightenment and in favour of those we believe to be less advanced'.[81]

We should be wary, then, of claims that certain beliefs were a matter of 'custom' – especially in the case of this particular belief, for which there was a far more obvious explanation. As we have seen, each successive piece of legislation dealing with bigamy

[76] 'A Bigamous City', *Leeds Mercury*, 16 December 1872.

[77] ibid.

[78] According to one local newspaper, Mellor did remind those in front of him that 'though a man was deserted by his wife he was not at liberty to infringe the law by marrying again': 'Liverpool Assizes', *Liverpool Weekly Mercury*, 14 December 1872. Others did not even report this point: *Liverpool Weekly Courier*, 14 December 1872; *Liverpool Albion*, 14 December 1872.

[79] 'Assize Intelligence: Leinster', *Freeman's Journal*, 7 December 1891.

[80] 'An Irish Judge on the English Marriage Laws', *Manchester Evening News*, 7 December 1891; 'An Irish Judge on English Superstition', *Evening Chronicle*, 7 December 1891.

[81] *Huddersfield Daily Chronicle*, 11 December 1891. The Lancashire press also seem to have relished the opportunity to emphasise the barbarism of their traditional rivals: see eg 'Curious Bigamy Trial: The Barbarity of Yorkshiremen', *Lancashire Evening Post*, 8 December 1891; 'Superstition in Yorkshire In Regard to the Marriage Laws', *Lancaster Gazette*, 9 December 1891.

from 1604 onwards had included a seven-year defence, and every year there were cases around the country where it was successfully invoked.[82] Other contemporary commentators explicitly referred to the statute as the origins of these misunderstandings. As the *Bristol Mercury* commented in 1856:

> It is a vulgar and very dangerous error to suppose that any term of absence of one of two persons married will, while that party is living, permit of the other marrying again. This misconception, but too fatally prevalent among the lower classes, has arisen from a clause in the statute relating to bigamy, the 9 Geo. 1V., c. 31, s. 22, which provides that no punishment therein enacted shall extend to any person marrying a second time, whose husband or wife shall have been continually absent from such person for the space of seven years then last past, and shall not have been known by such person to be living within that time.[83]

As with the common law marriage myth, it did not seem to matter how often judges tried to remind those in front of them of what the law actually said.[84] Time and again, those accused of bigamy – and sometimes the second spouse as well – said that they thought those who had been separated for seven years were free to remarry.[85] At the Yorkshire assizes in 1837, Isabella Robinson stated that 'it had been told her, that when she had been seven years from her husband, she was at liberty'.[86] Similarly, in 1881, the second wife of James Joseph Richardson said that she did not know that it was wrong for them to marry, given how long James had been separated from his first wife, adding that 'several people told me that I could marry him'.[87]

But given the statutory seven-year defence, it was hardly unreasonable – and certainly not absurd – for these individuals to make the mistake of believing that separation for that period would be a defence, or even that a remarriage would be valid. After all, exactly the same mistake appears in some modern academic sources.[88] Once again, we do not need to invent a custom to explain a simple legal mistake.

[82] See chapter 6.

[83] 'Prolonged Absence No Leave For A Second Marriage', *Bristol Mercury*, 26 July 1856.

[84] For attempts by judges to correct misunderstandings about the seven-year defence, see eg 'Assize Intelligence', *Daily News*, 19 August 1846; 'Latest Assize News: Shrewsbury: Regina v Ann Hitchcock – Bigamy – Absence for Seven Years', *Lloyd's Weekly Newspaper*, 23 March 1851; 'Cornwall Summer Assizes', *Royal Cornwall Gazette*, 4 August 1854.

[85] 'Bigamy at Weymouth', *Western Gazette*, 24 July 1868 (William Keats, had been living apart from his first wife for more than 10 years); 'Bigamy at Hull', *Hull Packet*, 23 April 1880 (Walter Greenwood, separated for seven years, judge thought it 'probable' that he was labouring under the misapprehension that he was free to marry).

[86] 'Bigamy', *Sheffield Independent*, 14 January 1837. See also 'Bigamy Charge: Two "Wives" Give Evidence at Stourbridge', *Birmingham Gazette*, 22 March 1930 (second wife of Samuel Hipkiss).

[87] 'Alleged Bigamy By A Holbeck Man', *Leeds Mercury*, 28 October 1881. See also 'A Miner Charged With Bigamy', *Sheffield & Rotherham Independent*, 7 December 1881 (second wife of David Sherborn told the magistrates that she had known that he was already married but had thought he was free to marry again 'as he had been separated from his wife over seven years').

[88] See eg T Gilfoyle, 'The Hearts of Nineteenth-Century Men: Bigamy and Working-Class Marriage in New York City, 1800–1890' (1994) 19 *Prospects* 135, 139, claiming that '[a]s early as the 17th Century, English civil law allowed desertion to be regarded as dissolving the marriage. Common law further recognized the right of remarriage when one spouse was absent without news for seven years.'

9

Brief and Broken Marriages

Bigamy is sometimes presented as simply being an extra-legal solution to marital breakdown at a time when divorce was not available.[1] As we shall see in the chapters that follow, matters were rather more complicated: marital breakdown was not the only reason for someone to commit bigamy, and a bigamous marriage did not necessarily mean that the first marriage had broken down. And 'marital breakdown', as this chapter will show, encompassed a wide range of circumstances.

Of course, it is often impossible to know exactly why a particular marriage had broken down. There were plenty of cases, at least from the early nineteenth century onwards, where the accused sought to explain their actions by reference to the first spouse's behaviour, but their allegations were not always corroborated by others.[2] And within any marriage, there may well be a whole host of unseen factors that make it difficult to say definitively that one spouse was responsible for its breakdown. But inferences can be drawn from examining how the first marriage came about, how long the couple were together, and details of their shared life.

Some broken marriages never existed in any meaningful sense. Thomas Terraux's wife left him immediately after their impulsive wedding, Josiah Thornton's second marriage took place just two days after his first, and Eliza Ann Dent was quickly separated from her first husband when it was discovered that he already had a wife. In other cases, by contrast, the first marriage had subsisted for some time before something happened to precipitate a separation. George Harrower's first wife was confined as a lunatic, Benjamin Griffiths' wife cheated on him with his nephew, and Emily Scully was deserted by her first husband and left without any support for herself and their three young children. There were also some cases where it does seem to have been the behaviour of the bigamist that led to the breakdown of the marriage. Harry Lloyd Bickerstaffe was quick to absolve his wife of any blame for their separation and his subsequent bigamy, and Mabel Violet Bell had already left her husband for one man before she committed bigamy with another.

[1] See eg B Capp, 'Bigamous Marriage in Early Modern England' (2009) 52 *The Historical Journal* 537, 545, suggesting that the majority of bigamists were 'people moving on from an old or failed relationship, and hoping to make a permanent commitment to a new partner'; P Sharpe, 'Bigamy among the Labouring Poor in Essex, 1754–1857' (1994) *Local Historian* 139, 140 ('a bigamous marriage was either an accident or a divorce substitute').

[2] See *Double Lives*, ch 7, for analysis of how allegations about the breakdown of the first marriage increasingly featured in bigamy trials.

The Madness of the First Spouse: George Harrower, 1816

In 1794, Captain George Harrower married Mary Usher in Bombay. Over the next few years, George spent much of his time at sea, shuttling between India and China, with occasional visits to England.[3] Of Mary we know very little, except that she suffered from some hereditary mental illness which developed around 1801.[4] According to George, she was seen by various medical practitioners, who declared that her illness was incurable.[5] After various arrangements for her care had been tried without success, George placed her in the care of one of her relations in India, one Thomas Cook. In November 1811, he wrote to Thomas to explain how Mary should be managed:

> She is turned, and of course any person speaking to her in a determined way, will make her obedient. When she used to be in those heats, I found by telling her to obey, and threatening to put her into the room, that she did obey. It will be necessary sometimes to put her into the room when she is obstinate. As to her habits of cleanliness, she does not like to bathe; but you must make her. She was one of the most cleanly women living; but her habit is quite altered now, as is herself.[6]

He asked Cook to 'pay particular attention' to Mary and to write to him twice a year to let him know how she was doing. The chaplain of the Presidency of Bombay, the Reverend Arnold Burrowes, subsequently reported that he had seen Mary in 1813, noting that she was not 'raving', but acknowledging that she was a 'lunatic'.[7]

George had no legal means of freeing himself from Mary. If he could have proved that she had been insane at the time of their marriage, then this would have been a ground for declaring his marriage to be void.[8] But insanity that developed after the marriage was not a ground on which a marriage could be annulled.[9] Nor was insanity a ground for divorce, even by the exceptional route of a private Act of Parliament.[10]

In 1812, George returned to England for good and purchased the lease of a property in Hertfordshire. He had become acquainted with the Giblett family, and was attracted to one of the daughters, Susannah. According to Mr Giblett, George asked his permission to marry Susannah after spending only a few days in her company. Mr Giblett was somewhat astonished at so sudden a proposal but told George that he had no objection

[3] *Bombay Courier*, 22 March 1800; *Madras Courier*, 26 November 1800; *Government Gazette*, 20 December 1804; *Calcutta Gazette*, 6 June 1805; *Globe*, 8 October 1805; *Bombay Gazette*, 17 January 1810; *Madras Courier*, 8 May 1810.

[4] This, at least, was what George wrote in his account of events (G Harrower, *The Refuter Refuted* (London, 1816) 53, 57), in response to his father-in-law's allegation that George himself was responsible for Mary's malady (P Giblett, *A Refutation of the Calumnies of George Harrower, Lately Convicted at The Old Bailey Sessions, on a Charge of Bigamy* (London, 1816)). As the titles of their respective pamphlets indicate, there were a lot of allegations and counter-allegations in this case.

[5] ibid 53.

[6] *OBP*, 14 February 1816.

[7] The term 'lunatic' was used to denote those who were periodically insane.

[8] S Lettmaier, *Spouses, Church, and State* (Tübingen, Mohr Siebeck, 2025) 276–77.

[9] Although inferences about an individual's mental state at the time of the marriage could be drawn from evidence of insanity during the marriage: E Foyster, *The Trials of the King of Hampshire: Madness, Secrecy and Betrayal in Georgian England* (London, Oneworld Publications, 2016).

[10] Incurable insanity only became a ground for divorce in 1937: *Double Trouble*, ch 9.

if Susannah wished to marry him.[11] On 20 October, George and Susannah married at St George's Hanover Square, with George describing himself as a bachelor.[12]

This should perhaps have rung some alarm bells, as the family were aware that George had been married before but were under the impression that his first wife was dead.[13] The following year, Mr Giblett received two anonymous letters stating that George's wife was in fact still living in Bombay. He attached little credit to them, especially when George alleged that they were 'the vile attempt of some miscreant to ruin him', and threw them into the fire.[14] But he then received a visit from the Reverend Burrowes, who confirmed that the story was true.[15] George still continued to protest his innocence, but when he failed to bring forward the promised proofs, Mr Giblett informed Susannah of the allegations against him. He begged Susannah to leave George until the matter was resolved, explaining to her how her actions would be viewed if she continued to live with him knowing him to be the husband of another woman.[16] Susannah did return to the family home for a short time but, convinced of George's innocence, soon made her escape to rejoin him.

George and Susannah left England for France, where they were to remain for some months.[17] But after they returned to England, George was finally arrested and brought before the magistrates at Bow Street.[18] Evidence was given of his prior marriage, and that Mary was still living, but Susannah was still adamantly opposed to the prosecution. On George being committed for trial, she fainted, and, on recovering, begged to be allowed to accompany him to Newgate prison while he awaited his trial. This being refused, she 'cried vehemently', and it was with difficulty that she was removed from the building.[19]

At his trial, George continued to maintain that it was all a conspiracy against him, this time blaming his father-in-law. In a lengthy statement, he detailed the various financial dealings between him and Mr Giblett. Mr Baron Richards reminded the jury that both the identity of the prosecutor and the motivations for the prosecution were irrelevant, and that the only question they had to decide was whether George was legally married to Mary when he married Susannah. Even so, the jury took half an hour (rather longer than in most trials) to decide that George was guilty, and strongly recommended him to mercy. The sentence of six months was relatively merciful by the standards of the day, given how many other bigamists were being sentenced to seven years' transportation at this time.

Mr Giblett then published a lengthy refutation of the claims that George had made about their financial dealings,[20] prompting an even lengthier response from George. After around 50 pages on the finances, George eventually got round to the question of

[11] Giblett (n 4) 5. George, it should be noted, vehemently denied that any such conversation had ever taken place but did not provide any alternative account of when Susannah agreed to marry him: Harrower (n 4) 12.
[12] Ancestry, *Westminster Church of England Parish Registers*, STG/PR/7/12.
[13] Giblett (n 4) 6–7.
[14] ibid 9–10.
[15] ibid 11–12.
[16] ibid 13.
[17] According to George, this was Susannah's idea: Harrower (n 4) 50.
[18] 'Bow Street', *Public Ledger and Daily Advertiser*, 29 January 1816.
[19] 'Examination at Bow Street of Captain Harrower for Bigamy', *Morning Chronicle*, 5 February 1816.
[20] Giblett (n 4).

whether he was guilty of bigamy. His claim was that he had believed, and still believed, that Mary was dead. He asserted that he had received news of her death 'from many respectable individuals', including a medical practitioner who had seen her in India.[21] He suggested that Mr Cook might have pretended that Mary was still alive so that he could continue to be paid for her care, and had passed off a different woman as Mary when the Reverend Burrowes came to visit in 1813. And he ridiculed the idea that the Reverend Burrowes could be certain as to Mary's identity:

> I know he swore so; but how Mr Burrowes, who only professes to have seen the late Mrs Harrower twice in his life, once when he christened her, in the earliest stages of infancy, and again in the bloom of youth, can, after a lapse of fifteen years, take an oath that he perfectly recollects her, is to me totally incomprehensible, especially when she had for the last twelve years of that period been afflicted with a severe mental derangement, which must have greatly altered her appearance.[22]

George even blamed his father-in-law for his unsuccessful defence, claiming that he would have been acquitted if he had challenged the evidence rather than being distracted into 'a portraiture of the deception of his conduct, the baseness of his designs, the infamy of his actions [and] the degradation of his character'.[23]

Here it should be noted that amongst all the copies of the letters that George included in his pamphlet, there was not a single one informing him of Mary's death. The only letter that he quoted was one that he had written himself, telling a friend that 'poor Mrs H is no longer in this world'.[24] His account also lacked both logic and chronology, since on the very page where he was claiming to have believed that Mary was dead, he simultaneously accused Mr Giblett of knowing that she was alive at the time that he was paying his addresses to Susannah, the implication being that Mr Giblett had cynically allowed his daughter to enter into a marriage that he knew to be void just to get his hands on George's money.[25]

All this made it somewhat difficult to credit George's account of events. Yet right at the end of his pamphlet he made a passionate plea that even if Mary was still alive, he had done everything for her that could be expected. His final words were ungrammatical and spiked with too many exclamation marks, but came from the heart:

> If I were guilty, the crime could not but be pronounced venial! For a long period of time, had my first wife been deranged! Situated as she was her circumstances were not injured! Her prospects were not clouded! Her feelings were not wounded! Her happiness was not destroyed! While the heroic constancy, the tender sensibility, the warm affection of her I have now married; which induces her to love me still more for the persecution I have undergone![26]

In the circumstances, it was impossible not to have sympathy for George, even if he did know that Mary was still alive. And public opinion was clearly on his side. 'Never', opined the *Morning Post*, 'was there less ground for a prosecution.'[27] When his father-in-law left

[21] Harrower (n 4) 50.
[22] Harrower (n 4) 57.
[23] ibid 73.
[24] ibid 18.
[25] ibid 50.
[26] ibid 85–86.
[27] *Morning Post*, 29 January 1816.

the court after George's conviction, he and a witness were hooted by the crowd.[28] Later that year, the press gleefully reported that Mr Giblett had himself been committed to Newgate, for bankruptcy.[29] If, as the *Newgate Calendar* claimed, he did indeed occupy the very same apartment that his son-not-quite-in-law had done, the reversal of fortune would have been complete.

Meanwhile, there was a happy ending for George and Susannah, reported to be 'living happily in retirement in Scotland'.[30] Three children were born to them over the years that followed. In February 1828, George wrote to the King to beg for a Royal pardon so that he might be 'restored in all things to what he has lost by reason of such conviction'.[31] The reason behind this belated request was that Mary had now died, and he and Susannah had remarried legally. It was noted in his favour that his case had not been an aggravated one. But across its cover in the National Archives there is a scrawled note: 'No ground for such pardon – refused.'

A Compelled First Marriage: Josiah Thornton, 1829

Josiah Thornton holds the record, so far as I am aware, for the shortest gap between his two marriages. On 11 July 1829, he married Anna Knowles in Matlock parish church. Two days later, he went through a second ceremony of marriage with Hannah Pearson at Manchester Collegiate Church.[32] But Anna and her friends were already on his tail, and he was arrested in Stockport before the week was out. On 18 July, he was committed for trial at the next assizes – prompting the droll observation by the *Chester Chronicle* that he was 'thus a bachelor, twice a husband, and a prisoner with the prospect of a long sea voyage, in the short space of one week!'.[33]

The journalist who penned the *Chronicle*'s account had clearly just seen it as a funny story and had been unable to resist larding it with arch literary, legal and cultural allusions. In his account, Josiah was a 'gay Lothario' and Anna 'the fair forsaken "Maid of Derby"', whose pursuit of her husband was because 'love and a crown no rivalship will bear'.[34] Hannah, less flatteringly, was one of 'the Lancashire witches' whose 'spells' Josiah had been 'unable to resist', and the second marriage was 'contrary to the statute in that case made and provided' – this being a then-familiar phrase found in indictments for bigamy.

Newspapers around the country repeated this amusing take on events.[35] But the report in the local *Stockport Advertiser and Guardian* hinted at a more serious

[28] *Bury & Norwich Post*, 21 February 1816.
[29] *Morning Post*, 6 December 1816.
[30] *Morning Post*, 6 December 1816.
[31] TNA, HO 17/107/174.
[32] Ancestry, *Manchester, England, Marriages and Banns, 1754-1930 (Cathedral).*
[33] 'Bigamy Extraordinary: A good week's work', *Chester Chronicle*, 24 July 1829. The allusion to him facing a 'long sea voyage' was an allusion to the (very real) risk of transportation.
[34] These were, respectively, a character in Nicholas Rowe's 1703 play *The Fair Penitent*, the subject of a folk song, and the opening line of John Dryden's poem *Thesaurus Dramaticus*.
[35] *London Evening Standard*, 27 July 1829; *Evening Mail*, 27 July 1829; *Star*, 27 July 1829; *Morning Advertiser*, 27 July 1829; *New Times*, 27 July 1829; *St James's Chronicle*, 28 July 1829; *Manchester Mercury*, 28 July 1829; *London Packet*, 29 July 1829; *Stamford Mercury*, 29 July 1829; *Sheffield Independent*, 1 August 1829; *Yorkshire*

story behind Josiah's two marriages. As it noted, 'some very severe and unpleasant reflections were thrown out during the investigation, touching the conduct of the overseer and constable of Matlock'. The first marriage, it was alleged, had taken place 'through some disgraceful stratagems of these persons, whilst Thornton was in a state of intoxication'.[36]

At the subsequent Chester assizes in September 1829, Josiah, the alleged Lothario, was revealed to be an 18-year-old lad.[37] Anna, meanwhile, was no 'maid': as a result of 'keeping company' with Josiah, she had become pregnant.[38] This had in turn led to her being removed to her parish of settlement in Matlock, where she had given birth to Josiah's son in early June. And Hannah was a young woman to whom he had been paying his addresses for some time. The banns had already been called for their wedding.[39] Indeed, it was the news that Josiah was due to marry Hannah that had spurred the parish officials of Matlock into action; if Anna remained unmarried, the upkeep of her illegitimate child would be their responsibility. They had accordingly had Josiah arrested, procured a licence for his marriage to Anna, and, before the ceremony, gave 'two or three drops of rum' to 'keep up his spirits'.[40] The cross he made next to his name in the marriage register looked distinctly drunken.[41]

None of this was any defence to the charge of bigamy. Despite one ecclesiastical judge having suggested that intoxication could vitiate an individual's consent to a marriage,[42] there is no evidence of any marriage ever being annulled on that basis. And there were plenty of individuals who had been convicted of bigamy despite having consumed quite staggering amounts of alcohol.[43] Nor was the pressure placed on Josiah by the parish to marry Anna regarded as sufficient to constitute duress.[44] The judge described his case as an aggravated one, and Josiah was sentenced to two years' imprisonment with hard labour.[45] Certain sections of the press were markedly more sympathetic. The *Morning Chronicle* thought that the blame lay squarely with the practice of forcing men into marriage; individuals should, it thought, 'be left spontaneously to contract that tie, and free from all other bias than their own inclinations'.[46]

Gazette, 1 August 1829; *Leicester Chronicle*, 1 August 1829; *Durham County Advertiser*, 1 August 1829; *Nottingham Journal*, 1 August 1829; *Birmingham Journal*, 1 August 1829; *Westmorland Gazette*, 1 August 1829; *Macclesfield Courier and Herald*, 1 August 1829.

[36] 'Bigamy', *Stockport Advertiser and Guardian*, 24 July 1829.

[37] *Chester Chronicle*, 4 September 1829.

[38] The term 'keeping company' seems to have been used to denote a range of relationships, from couples who were simply walking out together to full-blown sexual relationships, as here.

[39] Ancestry, *Manchester, England, Marriages and Banns, 1754-1930 (Cathedral).*

[40] *Standard*, 5 September 1829.

[41] Ancestry, *Derbyshire, England, Church of England Marriages and Banns*, D 1847 3/3.

[42] *Sullivan v Sullivan* (1818) 2 Hag Con 238; 161 ER 728.

[43] *Double Trouble*, ch 3.

[44] See further chapter 8.

[45] *Chester Chronicle*, 4 September 1829; TNA, *Criminal Registers*, HO 27/37, p 79. It could have been worse. Three years later John Pearmain was sentenced to seven years' transportation at the Essex assizes, having married two women three days apart, with the judge reportedly describing his case as the worst he had ever encountered on account of his 'deliberate seduction of two women at the same time': *Leicester Chronicle*, 2 June 1832.

[46] *Morning Chronicle*, 8 September 1829.

An Already Married First Husband: Eliza Ann Dent, 1843

In the spring of 1843, the Welsh town of Monmouth was transfixed by the arrest and trial of 24-year-old Eliza Ann Dent on a charge of bigamy. It was rare enough for its assizes to have any cases of bigamy to deal with, there having been only eight prosecutions between 1805 and 1842. And the circumstances surrounding Eliza's case were, as one local newspaper commented, 'so singular as to appear more like the work of a highly wrought imagination than a tale of reality'.[47]

It had all started back in 1834 when 18-year-old Richard Stanley Wall, the newly appointed organist of Monmouth parish church, noticed that 14-year-old Eliza Ann Morgan had a very fine voice, and persuaded her father to allow her to join the choir.[48] Two years later, Eliza gave birth to Richard's child. The next few years saw her shuttling back and forth between different locations. She left her father's house and for some months lived with Wall in Bristol. Upon him promising to marry her, she returned to Monmouth, but her father thought it best to keep her away from Richard, and sent her to Newport, some 20 miles distant. Here she established a business as a dressmaker until illness forced her to return home to Monmouth again in 1839.

At this time, a troop of the 12th Lancers was quartered at Monmouth, part of a larger military force stationed there to deal with the Chartist uprising. A private named Edward Dent was billeted with Eliza's father in the Golden Ball public house. Edward took a shine to Eliza, and proposed marriage. Eliza's father, perhaps despairing as to whether Richard would ever make good on his promises, prevailed upon Eliza to accept Edward's proposals. The wedding took place by licence in Monmouth parish church on New Year's Day 1840.[49]

According to Eliza's counsel at her subsequent trial, Richard then told her that Edward was already married with two children and swept her off to Bristol, her new husband 'not having touched her person, nor consummated the marriage'.[50] Richard's story was subsequently confirmed when a woman claiming to be Edward's wife turned up in Monmouth, upon which Edward beat a hasty retreat.

Eliza and Richard then lived together in Bristol for a time before Eliza obtained employment in London.[51] Richard followed her there, and on 4 July 1842 they married in the St Pancras register office.[52] After the ceremony, Eliza remained in London while Richard returned to Monmouth. She then discovered that Richard was paying his addresses to another woman, took a mail coach to Monmouth, and headed for the church where Richard was playing the organ at the evening service. With a fine dramatic instinct, she 'stood as an apparition before him', demanding whether he had forgotten

[47] 'Singular Case of Bigamy', *Monmouthshire Beacon*, 25 March 1843.

[48] The facts are largely taken from the report of Eliza's trial in the local newspaper, verified wherever possible from other sources: 'Extraordinary Charge of Bigamy', *Monmouthshire Merlin*, 8 April 1843. The report of the case in Carrington and Kirwan's collection only covers a small part of what was said, but this tallies exactly with the local report.

[49] Ancestry, *Monmouthshire Baptisms, Marriages and Burials, Monmouth St Mary*, p 31; TNA, ASSI 5/163/10.

[50] 'Extraordinary Charge of Bigamy', *Monmouthshire Merlin*, 8 April 1843.

[51] 'Singular Case of Bigamy', *Monmouthshire Beacon*, 25 March 1843. Richard was recorded as living with his family in Monmouth at the time of the 1841 census.

[52] TNA, ASSI 5/163/10.

his promises to her.[53] He denied that he had any plans to marry anyone else. But Eliza, having received further evidence of Richard's matrimonial intentions, showed their marriage certificate to the family of the woman in question. She then threw herself on the parish, and the authorities immediately took action against Richard to require him to support her financially.

Richard's brother Frank then applied for a warrant for Eliza's arrest for bigamy.[54] On 21 March, she made her appearance before the crowded police court.[55] Richard somewhat reluctantly gave evidence but declined to answer whether he was aware of Eliza's prior marriage to Dent or where he was on 1 January 1840. Public sympathy was clearly with Eliza: it was reported that a subscription had been set up to pay the expenses of her defence, including the cost of bringing witnesses from Scotland to prove Edward's first marriage.[56] In the meantime, bail was granted, and Richard was dismissed from his role as organist.[57]

At the assizes in April 1843, the speech by Eliza's counsel, one Valentine Lee, was a tour de force of impassioned rhetoric. He responded with righteous indignation to the suggestion by Richard's brother that the prosecution had been instigated to rid the family of a 'disreputable person', proclaiming that he would 'prove to the Jury that a more profligate, a more disreputable, a more abandoned wretch never wore the shape of man than he of whom this woman was the victim'.[58] After all, he demanded, who was it who had 'polluted' Eliza's mind and 'degraded' her person? None other than the person who 'has now the meanness, the baseness, the matchless perfidy, to put forward his brother to stigmatise her in the place of her birth and before the world as disreputable'. He then launched into the whole history of the relationship between Eliza and Richard. At this point, counsel for the prosecution intervened to ask whether the back story was relevant to the case before the court, but the judge overruled his objection, and Mr Lee continued to expound on Richard's 'malignancy'.

More to the point, he also produced witnesses to Edward Dent's first marriage, which had taken place before a minister in the latter's house in Leith, a mile or so from Edinburgh, in 1828. (Edward, incidentally, does not come out of this story well either. These two women described his bride as a respectable young girl whom he had induced to leave home to follow his regiment. They had played a much bigger role than simply being witnesses to their marriage, having been the ones who insisted he marry her in the first place.)

The only remaining question was whether Edward's 1828 ceremony was a valid marriage according to the law of Scotland. Wherever one of the marriages in question had taken place outside England and Wales, evidence of the law of the country in question

[53] 'Extraordinary Charge of Bigamy', *Monmouthshire Merlin*, 8 April 1843.

[54] 'Singular Case of Bigamy', *Monmouthshire Beacon*, 25 March 1843; 'Extraordinary Charge of Bigamy', *Hereford Times*, 25 March 1843; *Morning Chronicle*, 28 March 1843.

[55] TNA, ASSI 5/163/10.

[56] 'Singular Case of Bigamy', *Monmouthshire Beacon*, 25 March 1843. She did have a legal adviser at the hearing before the mayor, but his main (and entirely hopeless) line of defence seems to have been that the register office ceremony was not a real wedding and that it was necessary to prove that the wedding was conducted by a clergyman.

[57] *Berrow's Worcester Journal*, 30 March 1843.

[58] 'Extraordinary Charge of Bigamy', *Monmouthshire Merlin*, 8 April 1843.

was always required. The person called upon to provide such evidence was one Alexander Gibbon, a Monmouth resident who had been born and educated in Scotland and had lived there until he was 20. After expressing some diffidence about his qualifications to comment on the law of Scotland, 'not being a lawyer by profession', he explained that couples could either be married by a clergyman of the Church of Scotland or by acknowledging themselves 'as man and wife' in the presence of witnesses.[59] Cross-examined, he confirmed that he had never heard of weddings being performed in the Kirk itself, and that no certificate was required or given. Counsel for the prosecution did make a faint protest as to Alexander's competence, but the judge, Mr Justice Wightman, was happy to accept his evidence. Once it had been established that Edward was already married at the time he went through the ceremony with Eliza, their marriage was void, meaning that she had been free to marry Richard. The jury was directed to acquit Eliza, and their verdict of 'not guilty' was received with loud applause.[60]

For lawyers, the main interest of Eliza's case lay in the question of what qualification someone needed to have in order to give credible evidence of the law of another country. Barristers Frederick Carrington and Andrew Kirwan included *R v Eliza Ann Dent* in their contemporary collection of law reports for just that reason. Those who have read their report, shorn of any of the background detail about Eliza's two marriages, may well have thought that accepting the evidence of someone who had no legal qualifications or connection with the law was a shockingly casual approach. The following year, the Lord Chancellor declared that the approach taken in Eliza's case did not represent the law, and in subsequent cases the expectations of witnesses giving such evidence were noticeably higher.[61] But given the circumstances of Eliza's case, it is entirely understandable why the judge was willing to accept the word of someone less qualified.

Non-lawyers may be more interested in what happened to Eliza and Richard. Despite all the twists and turns of their relationship, they stayed together. Judging from where their children were born, they moved around quite a lot, with a daughter being born in Yorkshire in 1849 and a son in Lancaster some years later. But the 1851 census found them back in Bristol, and in 1852 the *Monmouthshire Beacon* published a letter from Richard addressed to 'the Clergy, Gentry, and Inhabitants of Monmouth', in which he thanked them for the kind reception he had received during his recent stay in the town.[62] Having tested the water, they finally returned to Monmouth together – a decade after they had hit the headlines.[63]

An Adulterous First Spouse: Benjamin Griffiths, 1850

In October 1849, Benjamin Griffiths appeared before the Handsworth magistrates, charged with having left his children to be supported by the nearby parish of Wednesbury. In his defence, it was argued that his wife Mary Ann had left him some

[59] ibid; *R v Eliza Ann Dent* (1843) 1 Car & K 97; 174 ER 729.
[60] 'Assize Intelligence', *Hereford Times*, 8 April 1843.
[61] *The Sussex Peerage case* (1844) 11 Cl & F 85; 8 ER 1034, 1053; *R v William Povey* (1852) Dears 32; 169 ER 625.
[62] TNA, 1851 census, HO107/1953, fol 155, p 57; *Monmouthshire Beacon*, 11 September 1852.
[63] *Monmouthshire Beacon*, 11 February 1854, recording the birth of their daughter there.

four years earlier, prompting him to place his two children in the care of one Ann Cuxon. He had left Ann money for their care when he travelled to America, and had also remitted money to her while he was there. Mary Ann, however, had apparently taken her children away from Ann and asked the parish overseers for money for them, subsequently receiving four shillings each week for their support. Benjamin was accordingly discharged and left the court 'hand in hand' with his children. But he did not get far. He was immediately arrested by sub-inspector Dew and charged with having bigamously married Ann.[64]

At the Staffordshire assizes the following spring, Benjamin gave his account of his actions in a 'straightforward and artless manner'.[65] He explained that he and Mary Ann had lived together for three years after their wedding in 1840 but that he had then learned that she had been having sex with his nephew under their roof. She had admitted this, and he had then separated from her, taking their two eldest children. They had gone to live in Birmingham, and his marriage to Ann had taken place in 1847, just before he set out for America.[66]

The judge, Mr Baron Platt, asked whether Benjamin and Ann had been living together 'on comfortable terms' up to the time of the trial. This was confirmed by Ann's brother. According to the report in the local *Staffordshire Advertiser*, Platt then expressed the view that it was a 'cruel' prosecution, and 'an abominable perversion of the law, which was intended for the protection of women who had been seduced by men into an illegal marriage'.[67] Legally, of course, there was no doubt as to Benjamin's guilt, and the jury found him guilty. But Platt's view as to Benjamin's moral guilt was reflected in the sentence: a fine of a single shilling.[68]

Such a lenient sentence was sufficiently unusual for the case to attract attention nationally as well as locally.[69] And there was a degree of inflation in the language used by reporters, depending on how distant they were from the events described.[70] Other Midlands-based newspapers had Platt saying that the object of the law against bigamy was 'to protect the second female from living in a state of unconscious prostitution'.[71] This was essentially what the *Staffordshire Advertiser* had said, just in slightly more graphic language. But in the various London-based papers that took up the story, the focus was very much on the bad behaviour of the first wife. Platt was reported as saying that the prosecution was 'evidently only instituted by the parish authorities as a kind of screw to compel an honest hard-working man to support a prostitute wife'.[72]

[64] 'Singular Charge of Neglecting to Maintain a Family and Subsequent Charge of Bigamy', *Daily News*, 1 October 1849.

[65] 'Singular Case of Bigamy', *Birmingham Journal*, 16 March 1850.

[66] Ancestry, *Birmingham Church of England Parish Registers*, Archive Roll M86 (marriage at St Peter and St Paul, Aston Juxta Birmingham).

[67] *Staffordshire Advertiser*, 16 March 1850. Given the differing reports as to what Platt actually said, it is important to note that this was not reported as direct speech.

[68] TNA, *Criminal Registers*, HO27/94, p 99.

[69] In the previous 45 years, only one other convicted bigamist had been fined: Mary Parkinson in 1847.

[70] The report in the other local newspaper, the *Wolverhampton Chronicle and Staffordshire Advertiser*, 20 March 1850, was identical to that in the *Staffordshire Advertiser*.

[71] 'Singular Case of Bigamy', *Birmingham Journal*, 16 March 1850; 'Bigamy', *Worcestershire Chronicle*, 20 March 1850.

[72] *Morning Chronicle*, 16 March 1850; *Standard*, 16 March 1850; *London Evening Standard*, 16 March 1850; *Evening Mail*, 18 March 1850. This was the version that was then picked up and reported by other newspapers around the country: 'The Biters Bitten', *Liverpool Mercury*, 19 March 1850; 'Disgraceful Prosecution', *Bristol Times and Mirror*, 23 March 1850; 'A Parish Prosecution!', *Leicestershire Mercury*, 23 March 1850.

Since all these reports appeared on the same day, and all the statements attributed to Platt are compatible with the facts of the case, as well as with each other, he might well have said all these things.[73] Equally, he might not. The shift of focus to the bad behaviour of the first wife reflected the story that reporters now wanted to tell: how the lack of access to divorce was driving poor men whose wives had cheated on them to commit bigamy.[74] Newspapers around the country published Benjamin's story under the headline, 'A Case for Divorce'.[75] Most vehement of all was the *Liverpool Mercury*, which cited Benjamin's case as yet another example of the 'wickedness' of a system that 'compels an injured husband to submit to the contamination of the legal society of an adultress, or to expend the sum of three or four thousand pounds in obtaining a release from the odious ligature which binds him to infamy', and called for the law to be reformed.[76]

Benjamin's case is less well known that that of his near-contemporary Thomas Hall.[77] But it was Benjamin's case, rather than Thomas', that should be seen as marking a turning point in the punishment of bigamy. While no other judges were quite as lenient as Platt,[78] there was a noticeable rise in the use of nominal sentences of a week or less after Benjamin's case. In the five years between Thomas' case and that of Benjamin, just eight bigamists had received such a sentence. In the five years that followed, it was 46 – considerably more than in the previous 45 years put together.[79]

Even so, nominal sentences remained relatively rare. Benjamin had been particularly lucky that his case was heard by Platt. The other three bigamists tried in Stafford that March were less fortunate. The weight of business at the assizes had meant that other judges were pressed into service to hear criminal cases. George Smith came before Mr Justice Patteson and was sentenced to three months.[80] Richard Harrington pleaded guilty before Mr Sergeant Allen and was sentenced to four months.[81] The fourth case, that of Edward Davis, had some similarities with that of Benjamin. His first wife had also left him for another man, and his second confirmed that Edward had behaved kindly to her, and that she had no wish to prosecute him. The one difference was that the latter, who was just 19, had also given evidence that Edward had represented himself to her as a single man. Allen accordingly told Edward that the conduct of his first wife was 'no apology for his marrying a young woman, and probably ruining her', and sentenced him to eight months.[82]

[73] He was reported as making similar comments in other cases: see eg *Lancaster Gazette*, 16 August 1851, reporting him as handing down a sentence of just two days' imprisonment to Richard Brocklebank at the Lancashire assizes on the basis that he had 'married a profligate woman, with whom he was not bound to live'.

[74] See *Double Trouble*, ch 7.

[75] *Sheffield Independent*, 23 March 1850; *Manchester Times*, 23 March 1850; *Hull Advertiser*, 29 March 1850.

[76] 'The Law of Divorce', *Liverpool Mercury*, 26 March 1850.

[77] It did, however, become entwined with it. In 1857, *The Times* published a scathing attack on the law of divorce which included an account of an address by Maule J to an unnamed bigamist who was imprisoned for just one day, this event supposedly happening on the Oxford circuit: 'The Law of Divorce', *The Times*, 27 January 1857. This seamlessly blended Maule's 1845 peroration on the law of divorce with the location of Benjamin's case and the sentence handed down to another cuckolded bigamist: see R Probert, '*R v Hall* and the changing perceptions of the crime of bigamy' (2019) 39 *Legal Studies* 1.

[78] Just one other bigamist was fined in the next five years: Catherine Appledore.

[79] Between 1805 and 1849, just 30 bigamists were sentenced to a week or less.

[80] TNA, *Criminal Registers*, HO27/94, p 98.

[81] TNA, *Criminal Registers*, HO27/94, p 98.

[82] *Staffordshire Advertiser*, 23 March 1850; TNA, *Criminal Registers*, HO27/94, p 98.

That, however, brings us back to a key ambiguity in Benjamin's case. His second wife Ann did not appear to give evidence, either before the magistrates or at the assizes. And no evidence was given as to whether she knew Benjamin was a married man at the time that they went through the ceremony together. She obviously knew that Benjamin had been married before, but she might have thought that he was a widower, as he claimed to be in the marriage register. And while Platt's comments certainly give the impression that she had not been 'seduced', this might simply have been a reference to the fact that she was not a young girl but a mature widow with two children. All this suggests that we should be careful about claiming Benjamin as an 'honest' bigamist.

Whatever the circumstances under which they had wed, Benjamin and Ann remained together after his conviction, at least in the short term. At the time of the 1851 census, their household – in the delightfully named Paradise Place, off Guildford Street in Birmingham – included Ann's daughters from her first marriage, together with Benjamin's two children from his marriage to Mary Ann, 9-year-old Catherine and 8-year-old Thomas.[83] Perhaps for the sake of appearances, Benjamin and Ann were claiming to be husband and wife. Ten years on, however, Benjamin was recorded as a lodger, with no sign of Ann or his children.[84]

A Holiday Romance: Thomas Du Terreaux, 1858

In 1853, 16-year-old Jane Kennerley was on holiday in the Welsh seaside resort of Aberystwyth. On the morning of 15 October, she left the house at around seven o'clock. There was nothing unusual in this, and her family presumed that she had gone for her usual morning walk. A little over two hours later, she returned and confessed, in tears, that she had in fact got married by licence at the parish church of Llanbadarn Fawr, a mile or so away.[85]

Her mother and step-father were aghast, especially when inquiries revealed that her new husband, Thomas, was a 36-year-old French teacher – far from a suitable match for Jane, whose father had been a gentleman of property. There was nothing that could be done to annul the marriage; although Jane had claimed to be 21, neither that misstatement nor the lack of parental consent had any impact on its validity. Nonetheless, her family decided that it would be best if Jane never saw Thomas again, and sent her to the continent, where she spent the next two or three years.

What Thomas thought of this is unknown. But on 24 April 1858, he went through a ceremony of marriage in London with a woman named Ann Butcher. Six months later, Jane petitioned for divorce, citing Thomas' bigamy and adultery. The adultery with Ann was alleged to have taken place at the White Horse Hotel in Ipswich, as well as at Bungay and other places.[86] One does have to wonder if there had been any collusion between Thomas and Jane to enable them to end a marriage that had never had a

[83] TNA, 1851 census, HO107/2058, folio 809, p 37.

[84] TNA, 1861 census, RG9/2154, folio 51, p 3.

[85] Ancestry, *Cardiganshire Baptisms, Marriages and Burials*, marriage register for Llanbadarn Fawr, p 16.

[86] TNA, *Divorce and Matrimonial Causes Files, Du Terreaux v Du Terreaux*, J77/13/D14. This is the same White Horse Hotel famously depicted in Dickens' *Pickwick Papers*.

chance. The timing of his bigamous marriage is certainly suggestive, just a few months after the Matrimonial Causes Act 1857 had come into force. The detail of his adultery being committed in a hotel was also suspiciously convenient, there being employees who could give evidence that Thomas and Ann had slept there together.

When the case came before the full court of three judges,[87] the main issue was whether Jane had 'wilfully separated' herself from Thomas.[88] If they had decided that she had done so, they could have denied her a divorce. In the event, the judges decided that Jane's separating from Thomas could be regarded as reasonable, on the basis that she 'must, from the circumstances of the case, have been entrapped into the marriage'.[89] Their marriage was accordingly dissolved.

This brings us on to the even more remarkable epilogue. On 9 July 1859, Thomas sought a licence to marry Ann legally.[90] The 1861 census shows them living together in London with a four-month-old baby daughter, named Marianne – born a comfortable year or more after their second wedding.[91] Ten years later they were in Ipswich with three more daughters.[92] They may never have even realised that their second marriage was no more valid than their first. The 1857 Act allowed either of the parties to appeal within three months of the court's decision. Once those three months were up, if no appeal had been made, it was lawful for the parties to remarry. But, as the Act made clear, 'not sooner'.[93] With his second wedding to Ann taking place within that three-month window, Thomas was not free to marry, and their second marriage was also technically bigamous.

But there was little likelihood of Thomas being prosecuted for either of his bigamous marriages. Even if the divorce was not collusive, there were other reasons why Jane's family might not want to instigate a prosecution. There were facts in Jane's life that they would not want to come to light. The 1861 census shows Jane living with her mother, her brother and her son, five-year-old Louis William Kennerley.[94] Had the court been aware of the existence of Louis – proof that Jane herself must have committed adultery – it would have denied her the divorce.

As it was, Jane was now free to remarry. And on 20 June 1861, she did so. Her second husband was the far more socially acceptable William Frederick Dennis (Esquire), and the wedding took place at the fashionable church of St George's Hanover Square.[95] Between them they had so many names that the clerk was barely able to fit them all into the space provided in the register book, with Jane's surname of 'Du Terreaux formerly

[87] There was nothing unusual in this. Prior to 1860, all divorce cases had to be heard before three judges: the Judge Ordinary, plus any one of the Lord Chancellor, the Lord Chief Justice of the Court of Queen's Bench, the Lord Chief Justice of the Court of Common Pleas, the Lord Chief Baron of the Court of Exchequer, or the Senior Puisne Judge for the time being of any of the three last-mentioned courts: Matrimonial Causes Act 1857, s 8.

[88] This was one of the discretionary bars to a divorce, as set out in s 31 of the Matrimonial Causes Act 1857: see further *Double Trouble*, ch 8.

[89] *Du Terreaux v Du Terreaux* (1859) 1 Sw & Tr 555; 164 ER 857.

[90] Ancestry, *London and Surrey, Marriage Bonds and Applications*, DL/A/D/009/MS10091/236/003.

[91] TNA, 1861 Census, RG9/6, folio 65, p 19.

[92] TNA, 1871 Census, RG10/1756, folio 177, p 3.

[93] Matrimonial Causes Act 1857, s 57.

[94] TNA, 1861 Census, RG9/2220, folio 78, p 10.

[95] Ancestry, *Westminster Church of England Parish Registers*, STG/PR/7/51.

Kennerley' appearing rather squished. As that indicates, her earlier marriage was fully acknowledged, with a cramped note at the bottom of the page recording that her previous marriage had been dissolved on her petition. This detail was key to her being able to remarry in church: the 1857 Act had allowed clergy to refuse to conduct the marriage of any person who had *been* divorced, but not that of the person who had *obtained* the divorce.[96] That such remarriages were still a novelty was reflected in the description of her as a 'spinster'. Alas, Jane's second marriage did not turn out well either. The following year, she was petitioning for divorce again, this time on the basis of William's adultery and cruelty.[97]

The case of *Du Terreaux v Du Terreaux* does not hold a prominent place in legal history, but it shows that what was reported during a divorce was not always the full story: there was certainly adultery, and possibly collusion. It also illustrates how individuals could be tripped up by the complexities of the new law: Thomas is one of the very few individuals in England and Wales to go through two ceremonies of marriage with the same person, both of which were bigamous. And Jane was probably the first woman in England and Wales to obtain *two* divorces. Such was the chain of events sparked by a holiday romance in Aberystwyth.

Alcohol and Violence: Harry Lloyd Bickerstaffe, 1860

In November 1859, an announcement of the wedding of the Reverend Harry Lloyd Bickerstaffe to Anna Maria Campbell appeared in various national and local newspapers.[98] It had been a quiet ceremony in the village of Bartlow in Cambridgeshire, the only guests present being Anna's brother Archibald and her sister Isabella.[99]

It was not the wedding that Anna had planned. Three weeks earlier, 60 guests had assembled in Brighton, but the wedding had to be cancelled when Harry failed to show up. When Archibald subsequently confronted him, he had apparently made the excuse that, as a clergyman, he had not wanted a big wedding. A quieter wedding 'more befitting a minister' had therefore been arranged.[100]

Harry's failure to turn up for his own wedding was not the only hint that he might not be the most reliable of husbands. He had also lost his job. Back in April 1859, when he had first met Anna, he had been employed as a curate by the Reverend Henry Blancker, the rector of Thursley, near Godalming in Surrey. Within a few months, however, he had fallen off the wagon both literally and metaphorically, taking a tumble from the rector's

[96] Matrimonial Causes Act 1857, s 57.

[97] TNA, *Divorce and Matrimonial Causes Files*, *Dennis v Dennis*, J77/14/D67.

[98] *The Times*, 11 November 1859; *British Standard*, 11 November 1859; *Derbyshire Advertiser and Journal*, 11 November 1859; *Cambridge Chronicle and Journal*, 12 November 1859; *Cambridge Independent Press*, 12 November 1859; *Norfolk Chronicle*, 12 November 1859; *Derby Mercury*, 16 November 1859; *British Ensign*, 16 November 1859; *Derbyshire Courier*, 19 November 1859; *Bucks Herald*, 19 November 1859.

[99] 'The Rev. Mr. Bickerstaffe and His Two Wives', *Leeds Times*, 21 January 1860.

[100] Quite why they had hit upon Bartlow is unclear, but that may have been the point. The marriage register described both as resident there, but it could at most have been the 15 days required by statute before a licence could be granted.

coach while drunk.[101] As a result, he been dismissed from his curacy and asked to leave the rectory. Henry had strongly advised Anna to break off her engagement to Harry, but she had not heeded him.

Thirteen days after the wedding, Anna's brother Archibald came to Cambridge, where Harry and Anna were spending their honeymoon. There he confronted Harry, accusing him of having a previous wife who was still alive. Harry denied this, insisting that although he had previously been married, his first wife was dead. He then contradicted himself, admitting that she was still alive. Indeed, he made such contradictory statements that Archibald began to suspect that he might not be quite sane.[102] At the very least, Archibald thought it best for Anna to separate from Harry until the question of his prior marriage had been investigated.[103]

Harry then went on the run. A warrant was issued for his arrest,[104] and his description was circulated in the police magazine *Hue and Cry*.[105] Towards the end of December, details of the search also began to appear in the press, describing Harry's appearance ('juvenile and somewhat effeminate'), attire ('a black wide-awake hat, and grey plaid thrown over his shoulders') and habits ('partial to public houses').[106] Early in January 1860 he was finally arrested at the Bee Hotel in Abergele, near Rhyl in North Wales. He had been staying there but had been unable to pay his bill, prompting its owner to send for the police – to whom Harry had admitted that he was wanted on a charge of bigamy.[107]

He was then brought back to Leeds. Even before his formal examination before the magistrates, the newspapers were providing details of his career and the breakdown of his first marriage.[108] It was a sad tale of an apparently initially happy marriage that had disintegrated into alcohol addiction and violence.

Harry had met his first wife, Miss Elizabeth Mona Brougham Drew, in 1850, while studying for holy orders at St Bees Theological College in Cumberland. Mona, as she was known, was the daughter of the rector of Youghal in Cork, and she and Harry married there in 1851 after a 12-month courtship.[109] Harry was then appointed as curate at Thornes, near Wakefield, where their first child, Harry Roger Drew, was born in October 1852.[110] At this stage there was nothing to indicate any problems. But money was almost certainly tight: an advertisement for a curate at St Andrew's Ancoats, Harry's next posting, offered a stipend of just £100 per year.[111] It was not much to support a wife and a growing family – a second son, Pierce, having been born in 1854.

[101] 'Capture of a Clerical Bigamist', *Leicestershire Mercury*, 24 January 1860.
[102] 'The Clerical Bigamist at Leeds', *Sheffield Daily Telegraph*, 24 January 1860.
[103] Deposition by Archibald Campbell, *Divorce and Matrimonial Causes Files*, J77/3/B75.
[104] 'Clerical Bigamist in Leeds', *Leeds Mercury*, 24 December 1859.
[105] This was a magazine that was published twice weekly with details of 'wanted' individuals: 'Scotland Yard Journalism: How the Police Communicate with One Another', *Answers*, 19 July 1890.
[106] 'Clerical Bigamist in Leeds', *Leeds Mercury*, 24 December 1859; 'A Clergyman in the "Police Gazette"', *Leeds Evening Express*, 24 December 1859; 'A Clerical Bigamist', *Leeds Times*, 24 December 1859.
[107] 'Apprehension of a Clergyman Charged with Bigamy', *Leeds Intelligencer*, 14 January 1860.
[108] Some of these details later turned out to be untrue – for example the claim that Archibald had met with Harry's father prior to the wedding – and had to be retracted: 'The Clergyman Charged with Bigamy', *Leeds Intelligencer*, 21 January 1860. The summary that follows has been verified from other sources.
[109] The wedding had taken place according to the rites of the United Church of England and Ireland.
[110] 'Births', *Cork Examiner*, 11 October 1852; Ancestry, *Yorkshire Parish Records*, WDP80/1.
[111] 'Births', *Liverpool Albion*, 11 December 1854.

In May 1855, Harry was appointed to the stipendiary curacy of the new parish church of St Clement in Chorlton-cum-Hardy, then just outside Manchester.[112] But by this time, he had already begun to ill-treat Mona. As she subsequently noted, he had taken to drinking and had struck her on numerous occasions.[113] A third son arrived in 1856.[114] In 1858, they moved on again, this time to Headingley in Leeds, where their fourth son was born.[115] Harry, now without any employment, was dependent on the sums received from his father and father-in-law. He was, however, still drinking. In January, a particularly violent assault on Mona forced her to take refuge with a neighbour.[116] Harry then abandoned his family, his next post being with the Reverend Henry Blancker in Surrey – with the results that we have already seen.

Perhaps the only aspect of Harry's story that puts him in a good light is his willingness to accept the blame for the breakdown of his marriage. He made no attempt to excuse his actions. Before the magistrates, his solicitor noted that the newspapers had reported that 'quarrels or bickerings' had taken place between Harry and Mona, and that Harry wanted to set the record straight. Harry then told the court that he wished to exonerate Mona from any blame, 'if any has been ascribed to her', emphasising that he alone was to blame.[117]

At the Yorkshire assizes two months later, Harry pleaded guilty to bigamy. The judge, Mr Justice Blackburn, was unsparing in his comments. He told Harry that his offence was of a most aggravated nature, given his clerical status, his education, and his knowledge that his first wife was still alive. It was, in his view, a 'deep injury' to Anna and 'an outrage to society'.[118] He sentenced Harry to penal servitude for three years.[119]

Harry's case provides a useful reminder that the term 'marital breakdown' covers a wide spectrum of behaviour and that the spouse who went on to commit bigamy might well be the one to blame for the breakdown of the first marriage. Unlike Benjamin Griffiths, Harry had no grounds to divorce Mona, but his behaviour did give her grounds to divorce him. On 13 March 1860, just after Harry had been sent to prison, Mona filed her petition, citing his adultery, cruelty and bigamy.[120] Harry made no defence, and the decree *nisi* was granted in July 1861, with Mona being granted custody of their three surviving children.[121]

[112] 'Diocese of Manchester', *Manchester Courier*, 26 May 1855.

[113] TNA, *Divorce and Matrimonial Causes Files*, J77/3/B75.

[114] Roger Bickerstaffe, baptised at Poulton-le-Sands on 12 May 1856: Ancestry, *Lancashire Anglican Parish Registers* Pr 3274/1/1.

[115] Francis Browning Bickerstaffe, baptised at St Michael Headingly on 13 April 1858: Ancestry, *Yorkshire Parish Records*, RDP39/4.

[116] Various newspapers reported this as having occurred in January 1859, but Mona herself gave the date of this as January 1858 (TNA, *Divorce and Matrimonial Causes Files*, J77/3/B75).

[117] 'The Rev. H.L. Bickerstaffe, The Clerical Bigamist', *Harrogate Herald*, 26 January 1860; see also 'The Clergyman Charged with Bigamy', *Leeds Intelligencer*, 28 January 1860; 'Committal of a Clergyman for Bigamy', *Leeds Times*, 28 January 1860.

[118] 'Yorkshire Spring Assizes', *Leeds Mercury*, 13 March 1860; 'Bigamy by a Clergyman', *Sheffield Daily Telegraph*, 13 March 1860. The *Leeds Evening Express*, 17 March 1860, reported this as an offence against 'public decency, religion, and morality'.

[119] TNA, *Criminal Registers*, HO 27/127, p 246.

[120] TNA, *Divorce and Matrimonial Causes Files*, J77/3/B75.

[121] '*Bickerstaffe v Bickerstaffe*', *Globe*, 20 July 1861. She eventually remarried Charles Brent at Grendon, 19 April 1870: Ancestry, *Northamptonshire, Church of England Marriages, 1754–1912*, Ref 141p/8.

Harry did not serve his full term of three years' penal servitude. His good behaviour while in prison meant that he earned an early release,[122] and on 19 November 1862 he remarried Anna legally in the Warwickshire town of Kenilworth.[123] Sadly his story does not have a happy ending. Six years later, his name was in the newspapers again, this time reporting his sudden death at Caen in Normandy from the effects of a severe fall.[124] Anna never married again.[125]

'For the Sake of the Children': Emily Scully, 1881

In 1872, Edward Scully and Emily Brown married in Bristol. Three children were born to them over the next few years, the last in 1879. But very shortly after this, Edward deserted his family. He headed off to America, leaving Emily with the children and three weeks' rent owing.[126]

For a few months, Emily tried to support herself and her children by working in a cloth factory. This was probably the Great Western Cotton Works in Bartons Hill, which by this time had around 1,000 employees, three-quarters of whom were female. The textile industry was a major employer of women at this time, both married and single.[127] But while being married was no bar to engaging in paid employment, married women with young children faced obvious challenges in doing so full time. Even working full time, Emily would not have been earning very much. The poor rates of pay at the Great Western Cotton Works had prompted the workers to go on strike several times during the 1870s.[128]

In August 1880, Emily married Robert Medway, a cabinet maker. Edward then made an unwelcome reappearance and informed the police. Indicted for bigamy at the Bristol assizes the following year, Emily's statement was simply, 'What I did I did for the best; for the sake of the children.'[129] While she had no one to defend her, even counsel for the prosecution acknowledged that it was a 'very sad case'.[130] Robert did try to argue that he and Emily had thought Edward was dead before they married. No evidence was tendered to substantiate that claim, which was at odds with the fact that Emily had reverted to her maiden name and described herself as a spinster when remarrying.

[122] Successive quarterly returns recorded his behaviour as 'VG': TNA, *Convict Hulks, Convict Prisons and Criminal Lunatic Asylums: Quarterly Returns of Prisoners*, HO 8/148 (June 1861), HO8/151 (March 1862), HO8/152 (June 1862). A licence was granted for his release on 30 August 1862 TNA, PCOM 3/113/11749.

[123] Ancestry, *Warwickshire Anglican Registers*, DRO 101. Harry described himself as a bachelor, which explains why he was able to remarry in an Anglican parish church. The Matrimonial Causes Act 1857 had allowed Anglican clergy to refuse to conduct the remarriage of any person who had been divorced.

[124] 'Bickerstaffe', *Derbyshire Advertiser*, 24 December 1868.

[125] She died at Sidmouth in 1883, leaving a substantial personal estate of £5,445: *Calendar of the Grants of Probate and Letters of Administration made in the Probate Registries of the High Court of Justice in England.*

[126] 'Painful Case of Bigamy', *Western Daily Press*, 8 February 1881.

[127] X You, 'Women's labour force participation in nineteenth-century England and Wales: evidence from the 1881 census enumerators' books' (2020) 73 *Economic History Review* 106.

[128] M Richardson, 'The Maltreated and the Malcontents' (Bristol, Bristol Radical History Group, 2016) chs 9–10.

[129] *Bristol Mercury and Daily Post*, 12 February 1881.

[130] ibid.

In any case, as the judge pointed out, such a belief was no defence to a charge of bigamy.[131] Emily was duly convicted and sentenced to a month in prison.[132]

Emily's story, lacking the drama of other contemporary cases, attracted little attention in the press beyond a few local newspapers.[133] It was, after all, nothing out of the ordinary for a woman accused of bigamy to have a sad story of abandonment to tell. But that is precisely what makes her story important. It illustrates three distinctive features of trials featuring female bigamists: their desertion and often ill-treatment at the hands of their first husband, the idea that they had married for the sake of the children, and their relatively lenient treatment.

Desertion featured heavily in the stories told by female bigamists. Searching local newspapers for 1880 and 1881, another 33 bigamy trials involving women were traced. Of these 33, seven said that their first husband had left them,[134] another three had left on account of his violence,[135] and one said that he had forced her to become a prostitute and abused her when she did not bring enough money home.[136] Over the decades, many more women had similar stories to tell. Some were in a pitiful condition: Martha Midgely's second husband told the court that she had been in a 'very destitute and emaciated condition', her body being covered with sores, which he attributed to the 'brutality' of her first husband, who had 'driven her out to be a houseless and a homeless wanderer'.[137] Others had no means of supporting themselves. Martha Reeves had been left 'without anything' by her first husband,[138] while Jane Moore, acknowledging her second marriage, said 'I had to marry [him] or starve'.[139]

The needs of the children also featured far more strongly in bigamy trials where it was the wife who was on trial. Maria Dickinson had heard nothing from her first husband for some time, and her two children were in 'the greatest distress' when she remarried.[140] James Cotton left his wife Mary with four children and her blind mother dependent upon her for support.[141] Elizabeth Singleton, convicted in 1868, said that she had not been supported by her first husband for 11 years, and had remarried to support her two children.[142] Male bigamists, by contrast, were far less likely to claim that they

[131] On the different views on this point, see chapter 7.

[132] TNA, *Calendar of Prisoners*, HO140/53.

[133] In addition to those already cited, the *Western Gazette*, 11 February 1881 and the *Bridgend Chronicle*, 11 February 1881 both briefly noted Emily's conviction and sentence.

[134] 'Bigamy Cases', *Manchester Courier*, 20 January 1880 (Betsy Smith); 'Singular Charge of Bigamy', *Manchester Courier*, 27 January 1880 (Mary O'Leary); 'Bigamy', *Coventry Times*, 7 July 1880 (Jane Walker); 'Sentence for Bigamy', *Liverpool Daily Post*, 27 July 1880 (Margaret Thelwall); 'Painful Case of Bigamy', *Newcastle Courant*, 21 January 1881 (Sarah Jane); 'Singular Bigamy Case', *Shields Daily Gazette*, 15 March 1881 (Mary Hall); 'Denbighshire Assizes', *North Wales Chronicle*, 23 July 1881 (Emma Hindley).

[135] 'Bigamy at Hull', *Leeds Mercury*, 27 January 1880 (Mary Hamilton); 'Charge of Bigamy at Pontypridd', *Western Mail*, 8 July 1880 (Rachael Batt); 'Yorkshire Assizes', *York Herald*, 21 July 1881 (Mary Ann Lee).

[136] 'Bigamy at Hanley', *Staffordshire Sentinel*, 11 December 1880 (Lucy Ann Hodgkiss).

[137] 'Bigamy at Oldham', *Manchester Courier*, 29 March 1856.

[138] 'Charge of Bigamy at Llandaff', *Cambria Daily Leader*, 30 January 1869.

[139] 'Bigamy or Starvation', *Portsmouth Evening News*, 15 May 1901. For examples of other female bigamists framing the choices available to them in similarly stark terms, see *The Journal*, 19 April 1869 (Ellen Edwards).

[140] 'South Lancashire Assizes', *Manchester Courier*, 24 August 1839.

[141] 'Louth: Borough Police Report', *Hull Packet and East Riding Times*, 30 April 1852.

[142] 'Charge of Bigamy Against A Newcastle Woman', *Newcastle Weekly Chronicle*, 21 March 1868; 'Bigamy at Jarrow', *Newcastle Daily Journal*, 13 July 1868.

had married for the sake of their children, but then they were also far less likely to have their children living with them. On occasion, however, a man's children were a factor in a second marriage. The second wife of William Barber said that she had married him, despite knowing he already had a wife, because his children were neglected.[143]

As in Emily's case, it was quite often the first husband who prosecuted. Some judges took a dim view of their actions. At the Lancaster assizes in 1880, the judge described Betsy Smith's first husband as a 'vindictive scoundrel' for prosecuting her, especially as he had also committed bigamy. Betsy he regarded as merely 'foolish', telling her to go home to her second husband.[144] But there were plenty of other cases where it was the second husband who brought the prosecution. Some, like the second husband of Louisa Akehurst, had been unaware of the prior marriage before they married.[145] Others, like Mary Hamilton's second husband, had known of it but now wanted to be rid of their bigamist spouse.[146]

Analysis of sentencing patterns indicates that judges were generally sympathetic to the plight of any female bigamist who had been abandoned by their first husband, even where she had not been honest with her second. The judge who sentenced Emily described her one-month sentence as 'lenient',[147] but seven of the other eight women whose husbands had left them received an even lower sentence.[148] The only one to receive a higher sentence was 41-year-old Margaret Thelwall, whose second husband was only 22.[149] It is possible that the speed with which Emily remarried counted against her.[150]

In his comments on Emily's behaviour, however, the judge was far less sympathetic than his claim of leniency might suggest:

> If you had attended to what was said to you when you were at church (if you went there) when the ceremony was gone through, you would have known what a very serious thing it was. You have made an excuse for which there seems to be some foundation, that your real husband treated you with unkindness. But I am surprised to think that a modest woman should on that account go and marry another man. It might have been a reason for your not living with your husband; but not for your marrying another man. You must be aware that to marry another man and to go to his embraces, was no other than if you had gone to any man in the street.[151]

[143] 'Bigamy', *Manchester Evening News*, 15 September 1869.
[144] 'Bigamy Cases', *Manchester Courier*, 20 January 1880.
[145] *OBP*, 14 September 1891.
[146] 'Bigamy at Hull', *Leeds Mercury*, 27 January 1880. For other examples of prosecutions by second husbands, see 'A Disgraceful Bigamy Case', *Sheffield Daily Telegraph*, 21 August 1880 (Ann Elizabeth Scrowston).
[147] 'Bigamy Through Cruel Desertion', *Bristol Mercury*, 12 February 1881.
[148] TNA, *Calendar of Prisoners*, HO140/52 (Jane Walker, two weeks); HO140/53 (Emma Hindley, 10 days); HO140/53 (Sarah Jane, one week); HO140/53 (Mary Hall, recognizances of £20); HO140/50 (Betsy Smith, recognizances of £2). Mary O'Leary was acquitted by virtue of the seven-year defence: 'Singular Charge of Bigamy', *Manchester Courier*, 27 January 1880.
[149] TNA, *Calendar of Prisoners*, HO140/50 (three months).
[150] See also the case of Ann Holmes, who was sentenced to three months despite having been beaten, half-starved, and abandoned by her first husband, her second marriage having taken place just three days after her first husband had left her: 'Bigamy by a Woman', *Liverpool Shipping Telegraph*, 27 November 1868; 'Committal for Bigamy', *Liverpool Weekly Courier*, 28 November 1868; 'Charge of Bigamy', *Liverpool Daily Post*, 19 December 1868.
[151] 'Bigamy Through Cruel Desertion', *Bristol Mercury*, 12 February 1881.

Despite such a moral dressing-down, Emily remained with Robert. Their union was to prove far more durable than Emily's legal marriage.[152] But despite having married for the sake of her children, Emily did not get to keep them with her. The 1881 census recorded them living elsewhere in Bristol with Edward, his new 'wife' Esther and a new baby half-brother.[153]

An Elopement and a Wartime Bigamous Marriage: Mabel Violet Bell, 1917

The case of Mabel Violet Bell, tried at the Central Criminal Court in 1917, was in many respects a classic wartime bigamy. Her bigamous marriage, to a Lieutenant Ernest Ashcroft, had taken place in 1915. Following his death, she had claimed a pension as his widow – which had ultimately led to her prosecution. The story behind this, though, was far more complex than that of those whose first marriage had broken down under the stresses and strains of war.

Mabel's first marriage, to Edward Nevinson Bell, had taken place in the village of Chalynch in Somerset back in 1909.[154] The ceremony was conducted by Edward's father, the Rector of Charlynch, and from the report in the local newspaper, it appears to have been a very happy occasion, with the couple receiving presents from the inhabitants of their respective parishes 'and the sincere good wishes of everybody … for their happiness and prosperity'.[155] They set off for their honeymoon in Paris, and then on to Burma, where Edward was employed as a member of the Indian Civil Service.[156]

Out in Burma, Edward's career flourished. Also living out there was one Captain Clement Gascoyen Ransford. At some point a relationship began between him and Mabel. By March 1912 Mabel had left Edward and was living with Clement. The pair came back to England together in 1912 when Clement transferred to the South Staffordshire Regiment, with Mabel passing as his wife.

In 1914, when war broke out, Clement went to the Western Front. He was reported missing on 26 October 1914. Mabel inquired as to whether she was entitled to any pension but was told by the War Office that she was not eligible. Although arrangements had been made for separation allowances to be payable to the dependants of unmarried soldiers as early as November 1914,[157] the rules on pensions were stricter.

For a while Mabel supported herself by running a teashop in Aldershot.[158] But a few months later, in May 1915, she went through a ceremony of marriage with Lieutenant Ernest Ashcroft, using the name of 'Mavais Violet Ransford'. Their wedding

[152] William and Emily were traced in the 1881 census (TNA, 1881 census, RG11/2475, folio 38, p 2) and again in the 1891 census, this time with three daughters, plus 19-year-old Edward from her first marriage (TNA, 1891 census, RG12/1960, folio 102, p 27).

[153] TNA, 1881 census, RG11/2478, folio 83, p 5. No marriage record has been found for James and Esther.

[154] Ancestry, *Somerset Parish Records, 1538-1914*, D\P\chlch/2/1/5.

[155] 'Marriage', *Taunton Courier*, 29 September 1909.

[156] ibid; TNA, *Divorce and Matrimonial Causes Files, Bell v Bell*, J 77/1248/8035.

[157] *Separation Allowances for Dependants of Unmarried Soldiers (or Widowers) During the War*, Departments of State and Official Bodies, 17 November 1914.

[158] 'An Officer's Widow: Charges of Bigamy and Fraud', *Pall Mall Gazette*, 11 January 1917.

took place by licence at a church in Aldershot.[159] Three days later, Ernest was sent out to France, where he was killed in action in September 1915. In November, Mabel made a statutory declaration that she had been lawfully married to Ernest, and had not remarried, and was granted a gratuity of £140, together with a pension of around £8 per week.[160]

Her bigamy might never have come to light if her first husband had not come back to England. But in January 1916, Edward left India on leave and arrived in London, with the intention of finally seeking a divorce from Mabel.[161] Whether he knew of her bigamous marriage to Ernest does not appear from his petition, which simply noted her adultery with Clement. As he noted, his solicitors 'experienced great difficulty in obtaining the necessary evidence of identity', and his petition was not filed until 23 May.[162] He then had to seek leave to proceed without formally naming Clement as the co-respondent; this was eventually granted, but only after an appeal.[163] All this took time. On 5 October, he wrote to the court to ask if his hearing could be expedited as he had been recalled to Burma and was due to leave on 26 October 1916; as he noted, it was uncertain whether his case (number 234 in the undefended list) would otherwise be heard in time.[164] The case came before Mr Justice Shearman on 23 October, Edward and his witnesses gave their evidence, and the decree *nisi* was granted.[165]

Mabel made no effort to defend the divorce, or even to file an answer. But she clearly knew that the case was happening, as a newspaper cutting of the proceedings was found in her lodgings at Aldershot after she had left.[166] This proved to be her undoing. Her landlady realised that Mabel had not in fact been validly married to either of her assumed husbands and reported her to the authorities. Mabel then found herself facing charges of bigamy, perjury, and obtaining a widow's pension and gratuity from the War Office by false pretences.[167] The prosecution, like a number of others involving fraudulent financial claims, was instigated by the Director of Public Prosecutions.[168]

At the Bow Street magistrates, one additional detail did emerge that put her actions in a somewhat different light. Upon being arrested she had apparently claimed that she had written to Edward in India 'time after time, and got no reply', leading her to assume that he was dead.[169] That said, even if she had believed Edward to be dead at the time she married Ernest, she *had* known he was alive during the time that she was drawing a pension as Ernest's supposed widow, since it was noted at her trial that Edward had been present when the divorce petition was served on her.[170] The result was that she

[159] Ancestry, *Surrey Church of England Parish Registers*, 6927/1/21.
[160] As later revealed at her trial: 'Not a Lieutenant's Widow', *Morning Advertiser*, 14 December 1916.
[161] TNA, *Divorce and Matrimonial Causes Files, Bell v Bell*, J77/1248/8035.
[162] ibid.
[163] ibid; see also 'Divorce Court: A Bridgwater Petitioner', *Bristol Times and Mirror*, 29 July 1916.
[164] ibid.
[165] 'Civil Servant's Divorce Suit', *Evening Mail*, 25 October 1916.
[166] 'Matrimonial Tangle: Charge Against Abbey Wood "Widow"', *Woolwich Gazette*, 19 December 1916.
[167] 'Not a Lieutenant's Widow', *Morning Advertiser*, 14 December 1916.
[168] '"Widow's" War Pension', *Daily News*, 14 December 1916.
[169] 'Charges Against A Woman', *Morning Advertiser*, 29 December 1916. One of the many newspapers that reported her story chose to highlight this claim in its headline: '"I Thought He Was Dead": Charge of Bigamy Against Munition Worker', *Sheffield Daily Telegraph*, 29 December 1916.
[170] 'Abbey Wood Munition Worker's Career: Sent to Prison for a Year', *Woolwich Gazette*, 16 January 1917.

was acquitted of the bigamy charge but found guilty on the other charges and sentenced to 12 months.

Edward's divorce decree was made absolute on 30 April 1917.[171] Mabel was swift to take advantage of this, remarrying less than two months later.[172] Edward, however, never got the chance to remarry. He died at Secunderad in 1918 and was buried in Madras.[173]

[171] TNA, *Divorce and Matrimonial Causes Files, Bell v Bell*, J77/1248/8035.
[172] BMD, 1917 Q2 marriage to Lister Kaye.
[173] Ancestry.com, *India, Select Deaths and Burials, 1719-1948* [online database].

10

Bigamy by Agreement and Double Remarriages

Not every case of bigamy was prompted by one spouse abandoning the other. There were also couples who agreed to part, some even signing a document giving each other permission to remarry. Such documents obviously had no legal force whatsoever, but some individuals certainly believed that they did. There are, of course, obvious difficulties in ascertaining how common such agreed separations were, and how often the parties exercised their supposed right to remarry. They were something of a rarity within the cases that came to trial, but that could of course have been because they were less likely to result in a prosecution. Certainly, within my study of bigamists who were never prosecuted, there were a significant number of cases where both the husband and the wife had remarried.[1] Upon further investigation, however, it turned out that these double bigamies were not so very different from other non-prosecuted cases. Some of those involved simply waited until they were able to satisfy the seven-year defence, while others moved sufficiently far away to be able to remarry without detection. In other words, even if there had been an agreement between the parties, this was not the main reason why they were never prosecuted.

The case studies in this chapter are all ones where one spouse gave permission to the other to remarry or both spouses went on to commit bigamy (or both). John Taylor's first wife gave his second marriage her blessing, and Eliza Corbett was given written permission to remarry by her husband Thomas. The Whitworths signed a document saying that each of them was free to remarry if they so wished, and both ultimately went on to do so, while David and Christian Kemish were witnesses to each other's subsequent remarriage. But there were also cases of double remarriages that involved deception. Such was the case of John Blair Wills and his wife Marian, which could have come straight from the pages of a Wilkie Collins novel, featuring a spell in a lunatic asylum and a cruel deception practised on a vulnerable young woman. And there was also the exceptionally messy case of Thomas Alexander, Ann Alexander and John Wilkinson – the only trial I have traced that involved *triple* bigamy.

[1] R Probert, 'Escaping detection: illegal second marriages and the crime of bigamy' (2022) 6 *Journal of Genealogy and Family History* 27. In total, 74 individuals, just over one-quarter of the email sample, had a spouse who had also remarried.

Bigamy with the Blessing of the First Spouse: John Taylor, 1794

The trial of John Taylor at the Old Bailey in 1794 was remarkable for a number of reasons. Most second wives who gave evidence spoke of how they had been deceived into the marriage and had no desire to remain with a bigamist husband. But John's second wife Sophia, whom he had married in 1790, spoke of him in the warmest terms, and indicated her desire to remain with him. As she defiantly told the court, she considered it a happiness to have known him. She also confirmed that she had known he had a wife living when she married him, and that she nonetheless held herself to be 'sacred, as his wife, as ever'.[2]

Equally unusual was the fact that John's first wife Sarah had given his second marriage her blessing. Admittedly, our information on this point comes from Sophia, Sarah being barred from giving evidence to confirm this directly. But Sarah's willing presence in the court was used by John's counsel, Mr Knowlys, to show 'that she hath approved of it, both by giving them leave, and approving of them since, and has supported them, and loves them both cordially'. Mr Knowlys also elicited, by some delicate questions, that the first marriage had never been consummated due to 'an act of Providence, in the formation of [Sarah's] person'.[3]

So here we have a first marriage that never got off the ground on account of the wife's inability to consummate it,[4] and a second wife who knew all the facts and was willing to stand by her bigamist husband. The sentence was unusually light, just two weeks in prison, a record at the time for the shortest sentence handed down to any bigamist at the Old Bailey.[5] On the face of it, this might well suggest that judges were lenient in cases where the parties were happy with the new arrangement. That was the view of historian Joanne Bailey, who interpreted this as a case of sexual incompatibility and thought that the sentence indicated 'a measure of sympathy' for John.[6] But when we dig a little deeper, a rather different story emerges.

Bubbling beneath this story of love and acceptance was a darker one about why the prosecution had been brought in the first place. John Taylor's prosecutor was one John Pearce – who was under bail to answer a charge of high treason. Both Johns were members of the London Corresponding Society, a working-class organisation founded

[2] *OBP*, 11 November 1794.

[3] ibid.

[4] If what was said about Sarah was true, John would, of course, have been able to obtain an annulment that would have allowed him to remarry legally. There is no indication of why he did not take this course.

[5] That is not saying much, given that all those convicted of bigamy prior to 1779 had either been sentenced to death or branded, but even after this time the most common sentence was a year's imprisonment: *Double Trouble*, ch 4.

[6] J Bailey, *Unquiet Lives: marriage and marriage breakdown in England, 1660-1800* (Cambridge, Cambridge University Press, 2003) 184. A different explanation is offered by J Witte Jr, *The Western Case for Monogamy Over Polygamy* (Cambridge, Cambridge University Press, 2015) 318, who makes the somewhat baffling suggestion that the court 'hung their light sentence on the stated suspicion that the second marriage had not been properly formed'. As usual, the *Proceedings* did not report the Recorder's reasons for the sentence. Nor did it make any reference to any issues regarding the formation of the second marriage.

in 1792 to push for Parliamentary reform.[7] With its championship of Thomas Paine's (to some) dangerously subversive work *Rights of Man*, the Society and its activities had come under suspicion from the English authorities, France's bloody Reign of Terror being still fresh in people's minds. In October 1794, our John Taylor had been a witness at the trial of Robert Watt and David Downie, which had concluded with their execution for plotting high treason.[8] Meanwhile, key members of the London Corresponding Society were awaiting trial. Against this background, Knowlys lost no opportunity to imply that John's bigamy prosecution had been brought for unworthy reasons, mocking Pearce's claim to be acting in the interests of 'public justice' by asking him what other cases he had prosecuted or intended to prosecute. As he sarcastically noted, 'There are a great many bawdy houses, gaming houses. Be so good as to let me see you here every sessions.'[9]

But if Pearce's motivation had been to get John Taylor out of the way before the other members of the Society were due to stand trial, it failed. And this casts a very different light on John's two-week sentence: one Society member's trial for treason began at the Old Bailey just 19 days later, with John, already discharged from prison, being a key witness.[10] In any case, there is no hint of sympathy or approval in the Recorder's comments on the case. He had, after all, forcefully objected to Knowlys referring to John as Sophia's husband.[11] He was also reported as telling the jury that Sophia 'was to be considered in no other view than as a prostitute', and as expressing his surprise that her relations 'should so far forget themselves, as to consent to a union so contrary to every moral, legal and religious precept'.[12] This makes it clear that the lightness of the sentence was not because he thought John's behaviour acceptable, but because Sophia had not been harmed by it.

This was consistent with an emerging trend in bigamy cases in which sentences were determined by the degree of harm that the marriage had caused.[13] If the second spouse was a young and innocent woman who had been deceived into the bigamous marriage, the harm to her was deemed to be far greater than if she had already engaged in sexual relationships outside marriage or knew herself to be entering into a union that had no legal recognition. A wife who was willing to remain with their bigamist spouse after learning that their marriage was void was similarly regarded as suffering less harm than one who was not. In this case, Sophia's declaration that she

[7] EP Thompson, *The Making of the English Working Class* (London, Penguin, 1972, first published 1963) 167–72; E Griffin, *Liberty's Dawn: A People's History of the Industrial Revolution* (New Haven, Yale University Press, 2014) 213.

[8] *The Trials At Large of Robert Watt and David Downie for High Treason At the Session of Oyer and Terminer at Edinburgh … At Which They Were Both Found Guilty and Sentenced to be Hanged, Drawn and Quartered* (Philadelphia, 1794); *The last speech, confession and dying declaration of Robert Watt, wine merchant in Edinburgh; who was strangled and executed at the west end of the Tolbooth there, on Wednesday the 15th of October 1794, for the crime of high treason* (Edinburgh, 1794).

[9] *OBP*, 11 November 1794.

[10] 'High Treason', *Hampshire Chronicle*, 8 December 1794.

[11] *OBP*, 11 November 1794.

[12] *Leicester Journal*, 14 November 1794. It is of course possible that Sophia and her relations believed that John's first marriage was automatically void in the circumstances: see further chapter 8 for similar misunderstandings.

[13] See further *Double Trouble*, ch 5.

had known of John's prior marriage, and intended to continue to live with him, would have led to him receiving a reduced sentence even if his incarceration had not had any wider political ramifications. Had she been deceived into the marriage, John would have received a much harsher sentence, regardless of his first wife having given it her blessing.

Permission to Remarry: Eliza Corbett, 1854

Eliza Corbett's bigamous marriage to Henry Percy seems to have been celebrated with the agreement of (almost) all concerned. Her first marriage, to Thomas Corbett, which had taken place in her home parish of Bromyard, Herefordshire, in January 1845, had swiftly proved a mistake.[14] As one witness later confirmed, they had separated within a year or so.[15] Eliza had been obliged to move back in with her parents, which is where she was living at the time of the 1851 census.[16]

Exactly what happened between Eliza and Thomas was not stated in the accounts of her case. One reported that she was obliged to leave him, another that he left the town and went to reside elsewhere – although he had continued to visit Bromyard on occasion, which removed any possibility of Eliza claiming that she did not know he was still alive.[17] What we do know is that, at some point after leaving Bromyard, Thomas had penned a note agreeing to a separation:

> I, Thomas Corbett, of the parish of St. Martin's, Worcester, do hereby give up, with a very good will, all claim upon Eliza Corbett and her property and estate, personal as well as real, and advise her to marry again. (Signed) THOMAS CORBETT. Witness, Elizabeth Weaver.[18]

'Weaver' was Eliza's maiden name, and the Elizabeth Weaver who witnessed the note was her mother. On 14 July 1853, Eliza went through a ceremony of marriage with Henry Percy, a baker employed by her father, at St Thomas in Birmingham.[19] Describing herself as a spinster, she gave the name 'Eliza Corbett Weaver' – as if, as her lawyer later put it, 'she were remitted to her maiden name, but still had a right to retain that of Corbett'.[20]

A few months later, on Christmas Eve 1853, Eliza was brought before the magistrates in Bromyard, and charged with bigamy.[21] Her counsel pleaded for her to be admitted to bail rather than 'consigned to a dungeon'.[22] While this was a somewhat exaggerated description of the local lock-up, the inspectors of prisons had recently drawn attention to

[14] 'Bigamy', *Hereford Times*, 24 December 1853 (parish clerk of Bromyard giving evidence of having attended Thomas and Eliza's marriage in the parish church on 21 January 1845).

[15] 'Bigamy', *Hereford Times*, 24 December 1853.

[16] 'Charge of Bigamy', *Berrow's Worcester Journal*, 24 December 1853; 1851 census, TNA, HO107/1980, folio 73, p 19.

[17] 'Charge of Bigamy', *Berrow's Worcester Journal*, 24 December 1853.

[18] 'Oxford Circuit', *Morning Herald*, 28 March 1854; 'Assize Intelligence', *Morning Chronicle*, 28 March 1854. The local paper confirmed the details of this: 'Herefordshire Lent Assizes', *Hereford Journal*, 29 March 1854.

[19] Ancestry, *Birmingham Church of England Parish Registers*, Dro 11, Archive Roll M72.

[20] 'Assize Intelligence', *Morning Post*, 28 March 1854.

[21] 'Charge of Bigamy', *Berrow's Worcester Journal*, 24 December 1853.

[22] 'Bigamy', *Hereford Times*, 24 December 1853.

its 'extremely cold cells', so it would not have been a pleasant place to spend Christmas.[23] Bail was granted, and Eliza was bound over to appear at the next Herefordshire assizes – with none other than her own brother, Charles, being bound over to prosecute.

At Eliza's trial the following March, Charles was cross-examined as to his role in the affair. He told the court that he had gone with Thomas to get a warrant for Eliza's arrest, and eventually acknowledged that he had prosecuted his sister 'out of spite'.[24] The signed note from Thomas was put in as mitigation of her offence, with her lawyer claiming that Thomas had himself remarried in the interim.[25] Eliza's mother Elizabeth confirmed that both she and Eliza had believed that the document released Eliza from any obligations to Thomas, adding that she herself had been obliged to pay their rent and taxes as Thomas had never supported them. As the *Morning Post* commented, she 'seemed to speak as if the failure of consideration in maintaining the daughter did really, together with the document, put an end to the marriage'.[26] The judge was less convinced, telling Eliza that 'she must have been aware that such a document could not have been legal', and that 'the act of breaking her marriage vows was a very wicked one'.[27] Even so, he thought that there were some mitigating factors in her case, and sentenced her to a month in prison.[28]

Despite this clear indication that the separation agreement had no legal force, the parties all continued to act as if they were released from their legal ties. Henry, who had stood by Eliza during her trial, proved loyal, with the pair remaining together until Eliza's death 36 years later in 1890.[29]

It was understandable that Eliza's trial was widely reported in the local newspapers. Bigamy trials were something of a rarity in Herefordshire, with its largely rural population. There had only been 11 over the previous half century. But the fact that it also attracted national attention, and was subsequently reported around the country, suggests that it was unusual for other reasons.[30] Within my corpus of 464 trials reported in the newspapers from the 1850s, just 17, less than 4 per cent, involved an agreed separation or the first spouse giving permission for a second marriage. Most of these agreements were relatively informal, as in the case of James Dalton, who reported that his first wife had told him that she would 'never trouble him any more' and that he could get remarried if he wanted, following which they 'shook hands and parted'.[31] Only a handful involved a written agreement. And whatever the nature of the agreement, it did not preclude the first spouse (or indeed anyone else)

[23] *Inspectors of Prisons of Great Britain III: Southern and Western District, Fourteenth Report* (Cm. 1112, 1849) 27.

[24] 'Bromyard – Bigamy', *Hereford Times*, 1 April 1854.

[25] I have been unable to verify whether this was true. At the time of the 1851 census, Thomas was lodging in Worcester with a widow and her daughter (TNA, HO107/2042, fol 467, p 36) but there is no record of a Thomas Corbett having married in that city between then and Eliza's trial.

[26] 'Assize Intelligence', *Morning Post*, 28 March 1854.

[27] 'Herefordshire Lent Assizes', *Hereford Journal*, 29 March 1854.

[28] TNA, *Criminal Registers*, HO27/107, p 373.

[29] In 1861 they were both living with Eliza's mother but by 1881 had their own home: see respectively TNA, RG 9/1827, folio 11, p 16; RG11/2601, folio 13, p 18.

[30] In addition to the reports in the London-based *Morning Post*, *Morning Chronicle* and *Morning Herald*, cited above, see 'Hereford Assizes: Novel Plan of Divorce', *Northern Daily Times*, 30 March 1854; 'Extraordinary Bigamy Case', *Liverpool Mercury*, 31 March 1854; 'Singular Bigamy Case', *Chester Chronicle*, 8 April 1854.

[31] 'Barnsley Petty Sessions', *Sheffield & Rotherham Independent*, 7 April 1855.

from prosecuting. Nor, at least in the case of male bigamists, was it likely to secure a particularly lenient sentence.[32] Agreed separations like Eliza's were not unknown, but they were certainly not the norm, and there was nothing in these reports to suggest that they mitigated the harm of bigamy.

Triple Bigamy: Thomas Alexander, Ann Alexander and John Wilkinson, 1857

Towards the end of 1857, the *Morning Chronicle* reported on a story emerging from the Lambeth Police Court. The escalating headlines – 'Another Extraordinary Case of Double Bigamy', 'Alleged Treble Bigamy', and 'Extraordinary Polygamy' – disclosed what the newspaper justifiably described as 'one of the most extraordinary cases' ever to come to the attention of the police.[33] For once the hyperbole was justified: this was the only example I have found of a husband and wife both being indicted for bigamy alongside the wife's second husband.

The three individuals on trial were Thomas Alexander,[34] his wife Ann, and her second husband John Wilkinson. Their story – a particularly messy one that undermines any neat account of unhappy first marriages and stable bigamous unions – came to light when Ann charged John with bigamy, after he had gone back to his first wife Frances. Although there was no substantial disagreement between any of them on the key facts, it makes sense to tell the story of each in turn, since each put forward a slightly different defence.[35]

It was established that John had married Frances in Bury St Edmunds in 1833.[36] He had been just 20 at the time, and Frances three years younger. Both, it appeared, had soon formed other relationships – leading what was dubbed 'a gipsy life', with both living with other partners.[37] Sometime around 1838 John had met Ann, and they had lived together 'except at intervals'.[38] At some point in the 1840s they had even travelled together to America, but by 1851 they were back in London.[39] There, upon Ann promising to abandon 'her drunken habits', they were eventually married in 1853, with John describing himself as a widower and Ann as a widow.[40] But Ann's 'passion for gin was

[32] See eg 'Liverpool Special Assizes', *Liverpool Mercury*, 14 December 1852 (James Arthur Skerriff, seven years' transportation); 'Bigamy at Bristol', *Bristol Mercury*, 9 April 1853 (John Silvester Terry, eight months); 'Bigamy at Chelmsford', *Essex Standard*, 11 March 1859 (William Gilbert, six months).

[33] 'Another Extraordinary Case of Double Bigamy', *Morning Chronicle*, 26 November 1857; 'Alleged Treble Bigamy', *Morning Chronicle*, 2 December 1857; Extraordinary Polygamy', *Morning Chronicle*, 16 December 1857. More-or-less identical reports appeared in the *Morning Advertiser*, *Morning Herald* and *Morning Post*.

[34] 'Thomas' was the name by which he was indicted, but he also appears as 'John', 'Richard Thomas' and 'Richard William' in different sources.

[35] To minimise repetition, the text synthesises the revelations from the proceedings before the magistrates, which took place over a few weeks, and the subsequent trials at the Central Criminal Court.

[36] Ancestry, *Suffolk, Church of England Parish Registers*, FL541/4/14 (marriage at St James, Bury St Edmunds, 14 September 1833).

[37] 'Alleged Treble Bigamy', *Morning Chronicle*, 2 December 1857.

[38] 'Extraordinary Polygamy', *Morning Chronicle*, 16 December 1857.

[39] TNA, 1851 census, HO107/1491, folio 50, p 9.

[40] Ancestry, *London Church of England Parish Registers*, P89/MRY2/067 (marriage at St Mary, Bryanston Square, Marylebone, 4 October 1853).

too strong to resist'.[41] She broke her pledge – at which point John resumed his relationship with Frances. At the police court, charged with bigamy, John did not seek to deny any of this. He did, however, claim a defence: that Ann was already the lawful wife of Thomas Alexander when he married her.[42]

Ann's marriage to Thomas had in fact taken place in 1840, presumably during one of the intervals when she was not living with John.[43] Here Frances, who as John's legal wife had been unable to give evidence regarding him, proved a key witness.[44] She had seen Ann and Thomas coming out of St Andrew's church on the day of the wedding, arm in arm.[45] They had, however, separated some 12 or 18 months later. The story was continued by Ann, who claimed that she had heard no more of Thomas after this. Her defence was that she had believed him to be dead when she married John in 1853 – a story that was backed up by her mother and another witness.[46]

Less plausibly, Ann also denied knowing that John was married to Frances, and spent much of her time making allegations about Frances's own past. Not, it seems, without cause. Ann alleged that Frances had been living with one Tom Frewatt, before he was sentenced for transportation, and had had a child by him.[47] Frances herself acknowledged, in response to a pointed question from Ann, that she had lived with a man named Joe Stitch for eight years.[48] (Ann also asked Frances if she had lived with one Jem Crummet, another delightfully Dickensian name, but Frances replied that this was none of her business.)[49] And to add an additional layer of complexity, Frances had also been living with John, both before and after he had married Ann. They had been together when Ann had turned up in 1852; this, as she told the court, 'was the cause of our parting, and I told him I never would live with him any more'. But she had gone back to him again in 1856, adding 'we were living together very comfortably, till [Ann] came and gave him into custody'.[50]

The story told by Thomas Alexander was, thankfully, much simpler. He told the magistrates that shortly after his marriage to Ann in 1840 he had discovered her in 'a house of ill-fame', where she was 'in the habit of meeting a gentleman'. This was subsequently corroborated by Frances, who had witnessed the occasion: 'I saw a mob in West Street, and saw Alexander pushing his wife out of a house of ill fame – he said that it was a pretty sight for a husband to see his wife in bed with a man.'[51] Thomas had accordingly left Ann. He knew that she had accompanied John to the US, and assumed that she was unlikely to return – 'knowing her determined propensity for drink', and the cheapness of spirits there.[52] Hearing nothing more from her,

[41] 'Another Extraordinary Case of Double Bigamy', *Morning Chronicle*, 26 November 1857.

[42] ibid.

[43] Ancestry, *London Church of England Parish Registers*, P69/AND2/A/01/MS 6672/9 (marriage at St Andrew Holborn, 14 May 1840, *Richard William* Alexander to Ann Sullivan).

[44] 'Alleged Treble Bigamy', *Morning Chronicle*, 2 December 1857.

[45] *OBP*, 14 December 1857.

[46] It was, however, contradicted by John's brother, a former shopmate of Thomas', who claimed to have told Ann that Thomas was still alive, but in the event nothing turned on this point.

[47] 'Alleged Treble Bigamy', *Morning Chronicle*, 2 December 1857.

[48] *OBP*, 14 December 1857.

[49] ibid.

[50] ibid.

[51] ibid.

[52] 'Extraordinary Polygamy', *Morning Chronicle*, 16 December 1857.

'he concluded she was dead',[53] and in 1850 he married Rebecca Collard Sayers at Faversham in Kent.[54] He had been living there with her until he was brought up to London to give evidence.[55]

At the Central Criminal Court, Thomas pleaded guilty to bigamously marrying Rebecca. Ann, however, was acquitted – not on account of the time that had elapsed since she had seen Thomas, or because of any belief that he was dead, but because John was already married when she went through the ceremony with him. The *Proceedings* made this explicit, with a terse note that the court 'considered that the second marriage would not have been valid, being to a person who was married already, and that, therefore, there was an end of the case'.[56] By the same reasoning, John was also not guilty, and no evidence was offered against him. Nonetheless, the Common Serjeant expressed the view that the conduct of John and Ann had been 'disgraceful' – far worse than that of Thomas, whom he sentenced to just a month's imprisonment.[57]

All of this underscores how guilt and innocence were matters to be determined by the application of clear legal rules, rather than by any sense of moral blameworthiness or of whether bigamy was 'acceptable' or not. But it also illustrates how some of those rules made little sense. Ann and John were far from being the only bigamists to escape conviction on account of the second marriage being void, but their acquittal did highlight the absurdity of applying that principle to cases of double bigamy.[58]

Some readers might see the multiple and interlocking relationships of John, Frances and Ann as proof of a lack of regard for marriage among the London poor,[59] or at least as evidence that cohabiting outside marriage was a feature of life among what one historian has described as that 'minute proportion of the residuum, the dregs of society, which was incorrigibly disreputable'.[60] Yet given the messiness of what had gone before, perhaps the most surprising aspect of this case is the subsequent stability of the parties' living arrangements. After serving his sentence, Thomas Alexander returned to Rebecca, and the pair were living together in Faversham at the time of the 1861 census.[61] John and Frances were also reunited.[62] She had indicated that this was her intention

[53] ibid. Such a belief was, however, no defence at this stage: see chapter 7.

[54] Ancestry, *England, Select Marriages, 1538-1973* (marriage at Faversham parish church, 8 May 1850).

[55] TNA, 1851 census, HO107/1626, folio 365, p 42 (*Richard* Alexander); 'The Case of Treble Bigamy', *Morning Herald*, 8 December 1857.

[56] *OBP*, 14 December 1857. That detail did not appear in the newspapers, which wrongly reported that Ann and John had been acquitted for lack of witnesses to identify them: *Morning Post*, 17 December 1857; *Morning Chronicle*, 17 December 1857; *London Evening Standard*, 18 December 1857.

[57] 'The Treble Bigamy Case', *Lloyd's Weekly Newspaper*, 20 December 1857; *OBP*, 14 December 1857.

[58] See further chapter 3.

[59] For some (largely unevidenced) claims about the extent of cohabitation in this period, see eg R Fletcher, *The Shaking of the Foundations* (London, Routledge, 1988) 144; F Barret-Ducrocq, *Love in the Time of Victoria: Sexuality, Class and Gender in Nineteenth-Century London* (London, Verso, 1991, trans John Howe; original edn 1989) 4; KT Hoppen, *The Mid-Victorian Generation, 1846-1886* (Oxford, Oxford University Press, 1998) 321; M Sweet, *Inventing the Victorians: What We Think About Them and Why We're Wrong* (London, Faber and Faber, 2002) 217. For analysis of such claims and the lack of evidence, see R Probert, *The Changing Legal Regulation of Cohabitation: From Fornicators to Family* (Cambridge, Cambridge University Press, 2012).

[60] FML Thompson, *The Rise of Respectable Society: A Social History of Victorian Britain, 1830-1900* (London, Fontana Press, 1988) 91.

[61] TNA, 1861 census, RG9/526, folio 142, p 19. Thomas died in 1865.

[62] TNA, 1861 census, RG9/331, folio 69, p 33.

at the time of the trial, telling the court that she and John had agreed that they would put themselves 'on the mercy of the law' if Ann came to disturb them again, 'so that we might live comfortably in our old age together'.[63]

'Double Bigamy, Intentional Bigamy, Innocent Bigamy …': John Blair Wills and Marian Wills, 1857

Among the cases of double husband-and-wife bigamy, there are quite a few where one spouse seems more to blame than the other. But nowhere was the gulf in culpability between husband and wife greater than in the case of John Blair Wills and his wife Marian.

It was in the summer of 1850 that Marian Maxwell first came to the notice of her future husband. John Blair Wills was then an 18-year-old medical student, and Marian was a 12-year-old child.[64] Having spotted her in an omnibus, John followed her home. He then sought out her mother and made a formal offer of marriage. This was refused on the basis that Marian was too young, 'and here the matter, at that time, ended'.[65]

Legally, it should be noted, Marian was not too young to get married. Under canon law, the minimum age of marriage had been set at 12 for girls and 14 for boys. Even more shocking to modern eyes, marriages under those ages could be ratified once the underage spouse reached the relevant age. It was not until 1929 that Parliament intervened to create a new statutory minimum age of 16 that applied to both spouses and admitted of no exceptions.[66] That said, early marriages had always been rare. Even in the early 1850s, the number of girls who married under the age of 16 was tiny, under 0.03 per cent of the total.[67] And the *Morning Post* – admittedly viewing matters through the lens of subsequent events – clearly thought that John's behaviour was creepy, referring to him singling out 'a child' out of 'disgusting caprice or passion' and then, 'Thug-like', tailing her to her home.[68]

Five years later, however, John and Marian met again, apparently quite by chance, in the Royal Surrey Gardens.[69] This time Mrs Maxwell consented to John marrying her now 17-year-old daughter, and the ceremony took place at Kennington church on 24 March 1855.[70] John and Marian's daughter Kate was born the following year, on 21 May 1856. Within a few days, however, Marian's mental health took a dramatic

[63] *OBP*, 14 December 1857.

[64] The parish register for St Mary the Virgin in Great Ilford, Essex, records her baptism on 8 March 1838, a month after her birth: Ancestry, *Essex Church of England Parish Registers*.

[65] 'Extraordinary Case of Double Bigamy and Double Marriage', *Morning Chronicle*, 16 November 1857.

[66] On the passage of this legislation, see L Lammasniemi and K Sharma, 'Age of Marriage Act 1929' in R Auchmuty, E Rackley and M Takayanagi (eds), *Women's Legal Landmarks in the Interwar Years: Not For Want of Trying* (Oxford, Hart, 2024).

[67] *Fifteenth Annual Report of the Registrar-General of Births, Deaths, and Marriages in England* (London, HMSO, 1854) 6.

[68] *Morning Post*, 17 November 1857.

[69] 'Extraordinary Case of Double Bigamy and Double Marriage', *Morning Chronicle*, 16 November 1857.

[70] Ancestry, *Church of England Parish Registers*, P85/MRK/022 (marriage at St Mark's church, Kennington).

downward turn, and at the start of August she was admitted to the Bethlem Royal Hospital – the asylum better known as Bedlam.[71]

Any such admission had to be supported by the certificates of two qualified medical practitioners who had examined the patient personally.[72] One doctor recorded that he had been informed by John, the attendant nurse and others that Marian had 'attempted to starve herself, refusing food, asserting that it would poison her'.[73] As he added, he had also 'heard her make use of many expressions quite inconsistent with reason or a right state of mind'. A second confirmed that Marian was refusing to eat, was occasionally violent towards John, and displayed an 'almost total absence of Parental Attachment to her Child'. The notes made upon her admission more starkly described her as 'incoherent and maniacal'.[74]

These were the classic symptoms of what was known at the time as 'puerperal mania'.[75] Marian was most likely suffering from postpartum psychosis. Many of her fellow inmates would have been in a similar position: one doctor who reviewed admissions to the Bethlem Hospital around this time found that 'the most common physical influence which occasioned insanity among women, was unquestionably puerperal', identifying 70 such examples among the 1,058 women admitted.[76] Even so, committal to an asylum was by no means automatic in such cases, with doctors favouring treatment at home wherever possible.[77]

Marian was to remain in the hospital for almost a year. When she eventually left the hospital on 3 August 1857,[78] she was collected by John's older brother, James, and taken to her mother-in-law's house in Clapham. A few days later John summoned Marian to his office in the City – where he informed her that she had no claim on him, as he was already married at the time of their 1855 wedding. Even more shocking was his advice to her – to marry his brother James, who, he claimed, was very fond of her.

Here we need to go back to the prohibited degrees of marriage. By this time, a marriage to a deceased husband's brother was simply void.[79] A marriage to a *living* husband's brother was obviously even more problematic. But if Marian had never been legally married to John in the first place, then there was no bar to her marrying James: the rule that simply having sex with someone brought their relatives within the prohibited degrees had been abolished under Henry VIII.[80]

[71] TNA, *Lunacy Patients Admission Registers*, MH94/16 (admission on 5 August 1856).

[72] The template required by the Lunatic Asylums Act 1853, s 75, specifically required doctors to make clear what they had observed personally and what had been reported to them by others. On the history of such certificates, see FM Sposini, *The Certification of Insanity: Local Origins and Imperial Consequences* (Palgrave Macmillan, 2023).

[73] TNA, *Bethlem Hospital Patient Admission Registers and Casebooks*, CB-069, 1856, p 76.

[74] TNA, *Lunacy Patients Admission Registers*, MH94/16 (admission on 5 August 1856).

[75] I Loudon, 'Puerperal insanity in the 19th century' (1988) 81 *Journal of the Royal Society of Medicine* 76, 78.

[76] JC Bucknill and DH Tuke, *A manual of psychological medicine: The history, nosology, description, statistics, diagnosis, pathology, and treatment of insanity* (Philadelphia, Blanchard & Lea, 1858) 260.

[77] H Marland, 'At home with puerperal mania: the domestic treatment of the insanity of childbirth in the nineteenth century' in P Bartlett and D Wright (eds), *Outside the Walls of the Asylum: The History of Care in the Community, 1750-2000* (London, Bloomsbury, 1999).

[78] Extraordinary Case of Double Bigamy and Double Marriage', *Morning Chronicle*, 16 November 1857.

[79] As a result of the Marriage Act 1835: on which see further chapter 3.

[80] For a particularly good guide to the twists and turns of the legislation passed under Henry VIII, see M Harding, 'The Curious Incident of the Marriage Act (no 2) 1537 and the Irish Statute Book' (2012) 32 *Legal Studies* 78.

On 21 August 1857, just 18 days after leaving hospital, Marian went through a ceremony with James at the register office in Lambeth. The wedding was authorised by a superintendent registrar's licence, which, following certain revisions to the legislation the previous year, now only required one full day's notice and involved no publicity whatsoever.[81] The person giving notice did, however, have to sign a formal declaration confirming that there was no impediment to the marriage and that any necessary consents had been given. Since Marian was still only 20 years old and so legally a minor, James declared that her mother had given her consent to the wedding.[82]

Mrs Maxwell had certainly not given her consent. When she learned of the wedding from Marian, she immediately instituted inquiries. The pair of them went to Somerset House to look for the entry of John's other marriage. They soon found it – but it had taken place in April 1857, *after* his marriage to Marian.[83] So Marian was John's first wife, not his second – which meant that she too had committed bigamy, albeit unintentionally, in marrying James.

James, who had accompanied them to Somerset House, then deserted Marian. The result was that she sought refuge in the Lambeth workhouse – leading the authorities to pursue James to compel him to support his supposed wife. James appeared before the magistrates to deny any responsibility for her, and the whole story then came out. A warrant was issued for John's arrest. In the meantime, James was to be charged with making and signing false declarations to a notice of marriage.[84]

John did not hang around to be arrested for bigamy. By the time his brother was being examined at the Lambeth Police Court, he was already in Liverpool. On 16 November, he met his bigamous wife Ann and her three-year-old son from their train at Lime Street Station and they all boarded the *Great Western*, with John giving the false name of John Goddard to avoid being identified.[85] The ship set sail for New York the following day.[86]

James, who had been allowed bail, subsequently failed to appear in court at the time appointed for the case against him to be heard, and a warrant was immediately issued for his arrest.[87] His mother Janet, who had entered into recognizances on his behalf, had to pay the £80 that was thereby forfeited – equivalent to around £5,000 today.[88] By the end of the month, the press was gloomily predicting that James would not be captured.[89] This fear proved to be well grounded. In the absence of a paper trail, we can only assume that, like his brother, he changed his name to avoid detection and fled the country. His

[81] On these changes, see generally R Probert, *Tying the Knot: The Formation of Marriage, 1836-2020* (Cambridge, Cambridge University Press, 2021) ch 4.

[82] 'Extraordinary Case of Double Bigamy and Double Marriage', *Morning Chronicle*, 16 November 1857.

[83] Ancestry, *London Church of England Parish Registers*, P71/OLA/031 (marriage of John Blair Wills to Anne Good, 28 April 1857, St Olave's Southwark).

[84] 'The Police Courts', *Daily News*, 16 November 1857.

[85] *Illustrated London News*, 28 November 1857.

[86] 'The Police Courts', *Daily News*, 23 November 1857; 'Extraordinary Case of Double Marriage – Flight of One of the Brothers From Liverpool', *Morning Chronicle*, 24 November 1857; *Illustrated London News*, 28 November 1857. This *Great Western* was a 'packet' ship on the transatlantic route between London and New York, operated by the Black Ball Line: a much humbler vessel than the steamship the *SS Great Western* that had been scrapped the previous year.

[87] 'The Extraordinary Case of Double Bigamy – Disappearance of the Accused', *Morning Chronicle*, 19 November 1857.

[88] 'Extraordinary Case of Double Bigamy', *Sunday Dispatch*, 22 November 1857.

[89] 'The Case of Mrs Wills, the Victim of the Double Marriage', *Observer*, 29 November 1857.

death in 1891, at least, was recorded under his true name – in Yarraville, Victoria, on the other side of the world.

There was, understandably, considerable sympathy for Marian. As *The Globe* noted, although she had been guilty of bigamy, 'on the face of the narrative who can accuse her of any offence at all, except the offence of being helpless?'[90] No one seems to have suggested that she should be prosecuted. Instead, efforts were made to assist her. The Royal Benevolent Society provided her with some financial support, including the means to set up a business.[91] The subsequent census found her living with her mother, the pair of them described as dealing in fancy goods.[92]

One notable absence from this household was Marian's daughter Kate. While Marian had been in hospital, her mother-in-law Janet had placed baby Kate with a Mr and Mrs King, a bricklayer and his wife living in Stockwell, paying them a few shillings each week. The Kings subsequently refused to return Kate to Marian, or even, it was reported, to let her see her child, 'except through the window'.[93] Before the Court of Queen's Bench, counsel debated whether this was a contest between Marian and Janet as to who should be entitled to have custody of Kate or whether Janet had simply been acting as her son's agent in placing Kate with the Kings. At a time when paternal rights to custody were more or less absolute, this mattered. Questions were also raised as to whether Marian was fit to have custody of Kate. Counsel for the Kings read out an affidavit in which Mr King claimed that Marian had threatened to murder Kate if she heard her call anyone else 'mother'. Somewhat frustratingly, the report of the case in *The Times* concluded with the judge ordering that the discussion should continue before a judge in his chambers, rather than in open court, and no further records of the proceedings have been traced. But the fact that Kate was not living with Marian at the time of the census a couple of years later suggests that Marian had failed in her attempt to gain custody of her child – yet another indication of how nineteenth-century family law was stacked against wives.

A Double Wedding: David and Christian Kemish, 1859

On 14 September 1857, the village of Fisherton Anger in Wiltshire witnessed a double wedding. Everything appeared to be in order. Banns had been called on the three preceding Sundays. The parish register recorded the marriages of David Kemish, a 32-year-old travelling hawker, to 27-year-old Ann Collins, and of 40-year-old Christian Kemish to 35-year-old John Pitt.[94] David and John were both described as bachelors and their respective brides as spinsters. And each couple acted as a witness to the other's ceremony, with Ann and Christian making their marks next to their names.

But all was not as it seemed. David and Christian were both slightly older than they claimed to be, David being 36 and Christian 48. More fundamentally, both were already

[90] *The Globe*, 17 November 1857.

[91] 'The Case of Mrs Wills, the Victim of the Double Marriage', *Observer*, 29 November 1857; 'In re Kate Marian Wills', *The Times*, 26 November 1858.

[92] TNA, 1861 census, RG9/367, folio 103, p 7.

[93] 'In re Kate Marian Wills', *The Times*, 26 November 1858.

[94] Ancestry, *Wiltshire Church of England Parish Registers*, 1902/18.

married – to each other. The vicar presiding over their double remarriage, Henry George de Starck, had conducted their previous wedding in Fisherton Anger in 1843.[95] And – in a further twist – David's new wife Ann Collins was Christian's daughter by her first husband George, whom she had married back in 1830.[96]

The question of what had happened to George Collins was raised when Christian and David were subsequently charged with bigamy in October 1859. At the petty sessions held at the Town Hall in Southampton, it was elicited from various witnesses that he had been transported to Van Diemen's Land in 1830 on account of his involvement in machine riots.[97] It was argued on Christian's behalf that George might still have been alive in 1843, which would have made her marriage to David that year void; if so, her 1857 marriage to John would be valid – assuming, that is, that George had died in the meantime.[98] And if his 1843 marriage to Christian was void, then David would also have been free to marry her daughter Ann, since the prohibitions on marrying one's wife's daughter only applied to a legal marriage. Simply cohabiting with a woman, or even going through an invalid ceremony of marriage, created no legal impediment. But in the absence of any proof that George was still alive in 1843, the magistrates took the view that the evidence was sufficient to commit both Christian and David for trial at the next assizes.[99]

When David and Christian appeared at the Hampshire assizes the following spring, they simply pleaded guilty, so the question of what had happened to George and whether their 1843 marriage was valid was never put to the test. All that they said in their defence was that they had done it 'for the best', without intending to harm anyone.[100] David was sentenced to two months, and Christian to 21 days.[101] This was more or less to be expected: their mutual knowledge mitigated the harm of the offence, female bigamists almost always received a lower sentence than male bigamists, and 1859 had seen a higher than usual number of bigamists being sentenced to three months or less.[102]

At first sight, the case of David and Christian would appear to be a clear example of a bigamous marriage being accepted by the church and the community, where all parties concerned knew the truth and were happy with the arrangement. After all, here we have two bigamists who married by banns in the same parish where their first marriage had

[95] Ancestry, *Wiltshire Church of England Parish Registers* (marriage at Fisherton Anger, 6 June 1843).

[96] Ancestry, *Anglican Bishop's Transcripts*, 83127/1/6 (marriage at Lockerley on 18 July 1830).

[97] 'Miscellaneous Local News', *Hampshire Advertiser*, 30 October 1858. Further investigation established that George had been convicted on 18 December 1830 and sent to Van Diemen's Land on 2 February 1831: TNA, *Convicts transported*, HO 11/8.

[98] It has been possible to trace George's arrival in Van Dieman's Land in 1831, and his subsequent pardon in 1836: Tasmanian Archives, *Description Lists of Male Convicts, 1831-1833*, CON18-1-6, p 25, convict ship *Eliza*, arriving in Van Dieman's Land on 29 May 1831; http://search.archives.tas.gov.au. Unfortunately, Collins is too common a surname to be sure of his subsequent actions and whether he was still alive in 1843.

[99] Here it should be noted that if Christian had been charged with marrying David while still married to George, it would have been necessary for the prosecution to prove that George was still alive in 1843. However, she was being prosecuted for marrying John while married to David, and it was not necessary for the prosecution to prove that George was dead.

[100] 'Double Bigamy', *Hampshire Chronicle*, 5 March 1859.

[101] TNA, *Criminal Registers*, HO 27/124, p 50.

[102] *Judicial Statistics, 1859 (England and Wales): Part I. Police, Criminal Proceedings, Prisons* (London, HMSO, 1860) 47.

taken place, the same vicar presiding at each, and a relatively light sentence. But a different story emerges when we dig a little deeper into the facts.

It seems far more likely that the by-then 61-year-old Reverend de Starck simply did not remember David and Christian's prior marriage than that he aided and abetted a crime by conducting a double remarriage that he knew to be bigamous. After all, 14 years separated the ceremonies, during which time there had been some 250 marriages at Fisherton Anger. Nor is there anything to suggest that de Starck would have met David and Christian again during that period, for the simple reason that they did not live in his parish. Successive censuses showed them living in Michelmersh, some 16 miles away.

The fact that David and Christian did not live in the parish also explains why no one objected to the banns being called for their 1857 remarriages; presumably no one knew who they were. There had been enough newcomers to Fisherton Anger in the 1850s for the congregation to be unsurprised at not knowing the couples planning to marry there. Indeed, the parish had grown so much that the ancient parish church of St Clement, where David and Christian had wed in 1843, had been dismantled in the early 1850s and replaced by a larger church dedicated to St Paul, a short distance to the north.[103] Moreover, Kemish was a common local surname. And while Christian was a distinctive name, at the time of her wedding to David she had been known as Catharine.[104] Even if the name David Kemish did ring any bells in Fisherton Anger in 1857, there was no reason for anyone to make a connection between the David Kemish and Catharine Collins who had married each other in 1843 and the David and Christian Kemish marrying new partners in 1857.

The revelation of David and Christian's double remarriage was sufficiently remarkable to be reported around the country, in over 100 different newspapers.[105] But the coverage was hardly sympathetic. Much was made of the fact that Christian had had three husbands, implying that her marriage to David had taken place within a short time of George being transported, rather than 12 years later. And the allusions to David taking a 'fancy' to her daughter made the whole arrangement seem very seedy.

Once again, it is important to put the case in its broader context. David and Christian's double wedding was, perhaps unsurprisingly, the only example I have found of a husband and wife each remarrying new partners in the same church on the same day. More significantly, in terms of assessing community attitudes to bigamy, is just how rare it was for *any* bigamous remarriage to take place in the same church as the first legal marriage, especially in rural areas. In urban Manchester, with thousands of weddings taking place at the Cathedral each year, individuals might hope to get away with bigamy.[106] In the countryside, the only cases that took place in the same church were ones where the remarrying spouse had good reason for thinking that they were

[103] 'Fisherton Anger' in E Crittall (ed), *A History of the County of Wiltshire: Volume 6* (London, 1962).

[104] This was the name recorded in the marriage register for both the 1830 and 1843 ceremonies and by which she was known at the time of the 1841 census: TNA, HO107/400, folio 5, p 5.

[105] The following is just a small selection, chosen to illustrate the geographical reach of the story: 'Extraordinary Bigamy Case', *Bicester Herald*, 5 November 1859; *Kent Times*, 6 November 1859; *Walsall Free Press and General Advertiser*, 6 November 1859; *Cornish Times*, 6 November 1859; *Whitby Gazette*, 6 November 1859; *Norfolk Chronicle*, 6 November 1859; *Cumberland and Westmorland Advertiser*, 9 November 1859.

[106] On this see the case study of Thomas Burgess in chapter 2.

entitled to remarry.[107] Within the unprosecuted sample, too, of the 74 cases where both spouses had gone on to remarry, just two husbands did so in the same church, and in both cases their wives had long since departed.[108] Once again, the bigger picture shows how exceptional the individual case actually was.

An Agreed Separation and 'Accidental' Adultery: Edmund Whitworth, 1893

Edmund Whitworth's divorce from his wife Elizabeth has a modest place in legal history as an example of the limited circumstances in which a court would exercise its discretion to grant a divorce to a petitioner who had themselves committed adultery.[109] Today, it is chiefly remembered for the judge's description of Edmund as a 'stupid man' who was 'entirely unable to understand his legal position'.[110]

The wedding of Edmund and Elizabeth Simpson had taken place in 1872, in the parish church of Spotland, a village on the edge of Rochdale.[111] Over the next few years, the couple had five children together. By the 1880s, however, the marriage was clearly in difficulties.[112] In 1883, Elizabeth left Edmund – apparently after he had been drinking for a week – and went to live with another man, one John Clegg.[113]

Edmund asked her several times to return home, but she refused to do so. He also thought about applying for a divorce. But he was persuaded by an acquaintance that this was an unnecessary expense. This individual, a man named Whitehead, suggested that he and Elizabeth could just sign a piece of paper giving each other leave to marry again. When Edmund asked if this would be legal, Whitehead told him that he and his wife had separated in this way. Having spoken to Whitehead's wife and confirmed that she had remarried, Edmund decided to adopt this course. Whitehead's brother John, a pork butcher, wrote out a document for him. This simply stated: 'I agree to separate from my wife, and either of us is at liberty to marry if we please.'[114] Having made one final attempt to persuade Elizabeth to return to him, Edmund showed her this document and she consented to sign it.

Edmund did not act on his new 'liberty' immediately. For the next 18 months he lived alone. But work in Rochdale was slack, and so in 1885 he moved to Halifax, some 25 miles away. There he met Nancy Naylor. Having explained that he was married, but that

[107] See eg the case of Susannah Anderson in chapter 7, who had received news that her first husband had been killed in the Crimea.

[108] See Probert (n 1).

[109] See S Cretney, *Family Law in the Twentieth Century: A History* (Oxford, Oxford University Press, 2003) 167.

[110] *Whitworth v Whitworth and Thomasson* [1893] P 85.

[111] Lancashire OnLine Parish Clerk Project, marriage at St Clement, Spotland, 30 April 1872.

[112] At the time of the 1881 census, Edmund was living with his mother, with Eliza lodging in the house next door: TNA, RG10/4121, folio 54, p 26.

[113] 'Singular Lancashire Divorce Suit: Extraordinary Deed of Separation', *Manchester Courier*, 30 January 1893.

[114] According to the evidence later given by John Whitehead, although he was relying on memory, not having kept a copy: '*Whitworth v Whitworth and Thomasson*', *Evening Mail*, 30 January 1893.

he and his wife had signed a paper that made it legal for him to marry again, they were married in Halifax on 14 August 1885.[115]

It appears that Edmund was a much better husband to Nancy than he had been to Elizabeth. He had given up his 'habits of drunkenness' and the pair lived quietly together for three years, attending a local Sunday school together.[116] But a chance conversation with one of the teachers at the Sunday school then led Edmund to consult a solicitor about his marriage. At this point he learned that the piece of paper he had signed was legally worthless, and that his marriage to Nancy was void.

Edmund and Nancy accordingly separated. He left Halifax for Manchester, where he obtained work, and asked Elizabeth to return to him and 'live the life that they ought to do'.[117] She consented and they lived together for around three months. She then left him again and returned to live with John Clegg in Rochdale. Upon Clegg's death, Elizabeth did not return to Edmund but married a 49-year-old widower named James Thomasson.[118]

At this point, Edmund finally decided to seek a divorce from Elizabeth. Having saved up sufficient funds from his weekly wage of 25 shillings, his petition, filed on 2 August 1892, simply recited the details of his marriage to her, their subsequent cohabitation, and her adultery with James Thomasson starting around 5 November 1891.[119] This date was actually the date on which Elizabeth and James had married, a detail that Edmund failed to mention. Elizabeth did not defend the divorce, but James filed an answer as co-respondent, making it clear that he had not been aware that Elizabeth was a married woman.[120]

Elizabeth's adultery was clear. The difficulty was that Edmund was also guilty of adultery. While this was not an absolute bar to his being granted a divorce, it did mean that the Divorce Court had a discretionary power to refuse to grant one.[121] Over the 35 years that it had been in operation, it had denied divorces to adulterous petitioners in all save a handful of exceptional cases. One category of such cases did involve petitioners who had mistakenly believed that they were free to remarry, for example where they had believed the first spouse to be dead or that the grant of a decree *nisi* terminated a marriage.[122] But would any judge believe that Edmund had genuinely believed that a simple written agreement entitled him to remarry?

The case came before the Divorce Court in January 1893. Edmund gave evidence as to the history of his two marriages, affirming that he had genuinely believed that the

[115] 'Singular Lancashire Divorce Suit', *Manchester Times*, 3 February 1893.

[116] 'Extraordinary Divorce Case: A Singular Document: Bigamy Made Easy', *Sheffield Evening Telegraph*, 30 January 1893.

[117] 'Easy Divorce: A Popular Conception of the Law', *Empire News & The Umpire*, 29 January 1893.

[118] Ancestry, *Manchester, Church of England Marriages and Banns* (marriage at St Chad's Rochdale on 5 November 1891).

[119] TNA, *Divorce and Matrimonial Causes Files*, J77/497/15139.

[120] He had known that she had been married before but was under the impression that her first husband was dead.

[121] Matrimonial Causes Act 1857, s 31.

[122] The other two kinds of case in which a court would exercise their discretion in favour of an adulterous petitioner were where a petitioning wife had been driven into prostitution by her husband or where the respondent had condoned the petitioner's adultery: WNM Geary, *The law of marriage and family relations: a manual of practical law* (London, Adam and Charles Black, 1892) 290.

agreement had left him free to remarry.[123] John Whitehead, the pork butcher who had drawn up the agreement, was initially somewhat cagey when questioned as to his view on the validity of the document, but eventually admitted that he knew that any subsequent marriage would not be legal.[124] But he also confirmed that he had not said this to Edmund, leaving him to 'judge for himself'.[125] Edmund's sister Annie also gave evidence that she and her mother had had a conversation with Nancy Naylor before her marriage to Edmund, during which Nancy had said that she knew Edmund had a paper signed by him and his first wife and that their marriage would be 'all right'.[126] Edmund was then recalled to the stand for a final question and acknowledged that when marrying for a second time he had described himself in the register as a bachelor 'because he was not certain' – an admission that prompted laughter in the court.[127]

Mr Justice Gorell Barnes found it difficult to believe that Edmund had not known that it was necessary to obtain a divorce before remarrying, commenting tartly that it was 'too ridiculous' to think otherwise. But Edmund's counsel, a Mr Priestley, argued that allowances had to be made for 'ignorance' and that his client was a 'perfect fool'. He cited wife sales as another example of a firmly held belief with no legal foundation, pointed to Nancy's apparent belief in the validity of the second marriage, and added that it was 'well known in Yorkshire' that such agreements were thought to be binding.[128]

Gorell Barnes decided to reserve his judgment on the question of whether the divorce should be granted. Over the next few days, various newspapers commented sardonically on the degree of ignorance displayed by the parties in the case.[129] By the time that Gorell Barnes came to deliver his judgment on the following Tuesday, he had come to the conclusion that ignorance was indeed the explanation for Edmund's actions, and that he had acted in good faith. As he said:

> It certainly struck me that there was some difficulty in believing that the petitioner ever honestly thought that what he had done released him from his marriage, so as to entitle him to contract a second marriage. I waited with some anxiety to see what class of man he was, and whether he would strike me as an honest man; and, after hearing his evidence, I have come to the conclusion that he honestly believed his first marriage to be legally dissolved. And my reasons for that are these. He was a man in a humble rank of life; he knew nothing about law – according to his own counsel, he was a stupid man, he was entirely unable to understand his legal position, and he allowed himself to be misled. A proof of that is, that he entered into the second marriage by banns; that he explained the state of the case to his second wife; that as soon as he discovered the second marriage to be illegal he separated from her, and returned to his first wife. It was only in casual conversation that he learned his error – if his wife had

[123] 'Easy Divorce: A Popular Conception of the Law', *Empire News & The Umpire*, 29 January 1893.
[124] He had, as he told the judge in response to a question, read reports of divorce trials: 'Singular Lancashire Divorce Suit: Extraordinary Deed of Separation', *Manchester Courier*, 30 January 1893.
[125] 'Blissful Divorce Ignorance: An Irresponsible Pork Butcher Divorces an Innocent Couple', *Morning Leader*, 30 January 1893.
[126] '*Whitworth v Whitworth and Thomasson*', *Evening Mail*, 30 January 1893.
[127] 'Blissful Divorce Ignorance: An Irresponsible Pork Butcher Divorces an Innocent Couple', *Morning Leader*, 30 January 1893.
[128] 'Divorce By Agreement: Two Marriages Spoiled By A Popular Delusion: A Romance of Rochdale and Halifax', *Yorkshire Evening Post*, 30 January 1893.
[129] ibid.

> not left him again, they would have been living together now; and as soon as she left him he applied to the Court for relief.[130]

On that basis, Gorell Barnes exercised his discretion to overlook Edmund's adultery (and bigamy) and granted the decree *nisi*.

Some of the headlines under which the case was reported – 'Divorce By Agreement' and 'Divorce Made Easy'[131] – gave a rather misleading impression of what it had actually decided. *Whitworth v Whitworth and Thomasson* was also a reminder of the different approach taken in the Divorce Court as compared to the criminal courts. Had Edmund been tried for bigamy, then his ignorance of the law, and of the fact that his informal separation agreement did not allow him to remarry legally, would have been no defence.

[130] *Whitworth* (n 110) 88.
[131] 'Divorce Made Easy: An Extraordinary Case', *Reynolds's Newspaper*, 5 February 1893.

11

Overlapping Relationships, Affairs, and Simultaneous Families

One often overlooked aspect of bigamy is that the second marriage did not necessarily mark the ending of the first. Sometimes this was just a matter of a short-term overlap while the bigamist strung their first spouse along with excuses for their absence, not revealing that they had married again. In other cases, it was the second marriage that proved to be short-lived, with the bigamist returning to their first spouse. And, in some, the bigamist tried to maintain both marriages simultaneously.

The case studies in this chapter represent different variations on this theme. Edward Drane Hannibal was clearly hoping to make a new life with his second wife and was simply trying to conceal his actions from his first wife to avoid being prosecuted. More complex was the case of William Flounders, where the overlap was not between his first and second marriages, but between his second and his third (with the added complication that his relationship with his third wife had begun before he met his second). John Smith Mase and Philip Field each seem to have treated their second marriage as no more than a brief affair (and in John's case, a one-night stand). John Ridiough, by contrast, appears to have entered into his second marriage for purely pragmatic reasons, and never left his first wife, while John Rhodes remained with his second wife for many years, but ultimately returned to his first. Finally, we have the duplicitous Richard Francis Archibald Farquharson. His intentions are more difficult to discern, as for some time he managed to lead a double life, shuttling between one wife in London and another in the country, but he too ultimately remained with his legal wife.

The overlapping nature of these relationships meant that the bigamist was often writing to one or other of his wives, either to reassure them of his love or to make excuses for his absence. Some of their letters were printed in the press when their bigamy came to light, giving us an insight into how they tried to string these women along. The gendered language here is intentional: as readers will have noticed, all these case studies involve male bigamists. That reflects the reality of the cases coming to trial. There were plenty of bigamy trials featuring women who had formed a new relationship while still living with their husband, but such women tended to run away to get married rather than pretending that they had not.[1] There was also the occasional woman who engaged in

[1] See eg the case of Annie Clancy, who took advantage of her husband being away from home for a short while to pack up her clothes and leave town with her lover: 'Elopement, Bigamy, and Robbery', *York Herald*, 25 April 1857.

which we might term bigamy 'holidays', but statistically such cases were far rarer.[2] And I have traced no example of a woman leading a double life and shuttling between two households.

The Travelling Tinker: John Rhodes, 1747

In 1716, John Rhodes, a travelling tinker aged just 16, met Mary Thompson in her hometown of Halifax in the West Riding of Yorkshire.[3] The pair decided to get married – possibly, it seems, on the spur of the moment. As it was Lent, getting married in church would take longer than usual (or require them to pay for a licence to dispense with the calling of banns).[4] Rather than waiting, they went to Bacup in Lancashire, to the house of a Mr Hargrave, whom John described as a 'lawless priest'.[5] As John reported, Hargrave married them 'as he lay in bed' – either he was ill, or John and Mary had arrived rather late in the evening.[6]

John and Mary subsequently lived together in Wakefield. We don't know much about their married life together, except that they had no children, Mary having had a miscarriage. After seven years together, John left Mary and resumed travelling around the country as a tinker. In December 1729, he met and married Mary Harrison – this time in a regular ceremony, with banns being called and the ceremony taking place in the parish church of Bowden in Cheshire.[7] The pair lived together in Warrington in Lancashire and had eight children together.[8] But in the summer of 1746, John left Mary Harrison, then pregnant with their ninth child, and returned to his first wife in Wakefield. Despite his having been away for 23 years, and his acknowledgment that he had married another wife in the meantime, Mary took him back.[9]

John was subsequently committed to York Castle, to be tried at the assizes the following spring.[10] All we know from the surviving record is that he was 'discharged by proclamation',[11] which suggests that no evidence was offered against him. Mary, after all,

[2] For a rare example, see the case of Charlotte Goddard, convicted at the Maidstone assizes in 1858 for marrying soldier James Babington in September 1851. Charlotte had been living with her first husband Henry until the time of this second marriage and immediately returned to him once James was posted overseas with his regiment (TNA, 1851 census, HO107/1631, folio 670, p 30; *Morning Post*, 10 December 1858). She remained with Henry after James' return and returned to him after serving a four-month sentence for bigamy (TNA, *Criminal Registers*, HO27/119 p 314; 1861 census, RG9, piece 540, folio 9, p 11). They were to remain together – so far as can be ascertained from decadal censuses – until Henry's death in 1898 (TNA, 1871 census, RG10/997, folio 93, p 19; 1881 census, RG11/991, folio 91, p 21; 1891 census, RG12/733, folio 117, p 2).

[3] TNA, ASSI 45/23/3/69.

[4] R Probert, *Marriage Law for Genealogists*, 2nd edn (Kenilworth, Takeaway, 2016) 131.

[5] The phrase does not appear to have been a commonly used one, but other examples of its usage suggest that it is more likely that Hargrave was an Anglican minister who had been deprived of his living rather than a Catholic priest.

[6] TNA, ASSI 45/23/3/68.

[7] TNA, ASSI 45/23/3/70.

[8] ibid.

[9] TNA, ASSI 45/23/3/69.

[10] *Newcastle Courant*, 28 March 1747.

[11] TNA, *Gaol book: Northern Circuit: York and Yorkshire*, ASSI 41/4.

would not have been able to give evidence, and with no witnesses and no documentation for that first marriage, in the house of a 'lawless priest' 31 years earlier and 60 miles distant, there was no way for the prosecution to prove that the ceremony had ever taken place.

The case of John Rhodes and his two wives is special as one of the very few from this period where we have the voices of both the accused and their two spouses, albeit filtered through the clerk who wrote their words down. All three appeared before the local Justice of the Peace to tell their story, and, even more unusually, their depositions have survived to the present day. The narrative above is drawn from all three, since their stories were broadly consistent. There were, however, some significant differences in what each chose to say or not say. John was noticeably vaguer on the dates of his two weddings than either of his wives. The timeline in his deposition raised the possibility that he had been separated from his first wife for more than seven years before marrying his second, but this was contradicted by their evidence. John also chose to mention only his two surviving children, omitting any reference to the six who had died. On the other hand, it was John, rather than Mary, who mentioned her miscarriage. We can only speculate that the absence of children may have been a reason for his leaving her.

John's case also helps to illustrate various broader trends. It shows that those living at a distance from London had very limited options for marrying clandestinely: his 34-mile roundtrip from Halifax to Bacup to be married by a 'lawless priest' rather suggests the lack of any closer options. It also shows the importance of mobility in escaping detection: his second wedding took place almost 50 miles from his first wife in Wakefield, and he managed to live with his second wife undisturbed for around 15 years. Had he not returned to his first wife and confessed, his bigamy might never have come to light. That said, distance was no guarantee of escaping detection: looking at cases tried at provincial assizes across the eighteenth century, the average distance between the two weddings was 54 miles, and the median a still substantial 27.5 miles (these two calculations excluding the bigamist whose first marriage took place in Tortola in the British Virgin Islands).[12]

Not everyone would have found it so easy to move as John did. As a tinker, John was able to travel around the country. Others were more tied to a specific location. Almost half of the male population was still employed in agriculture, and agricultural labourers were perhaps the least mobile of any occupational group.[13] Of course, their lack of mobility did not necessarily mean that their marriages were any less likely to break down, but it would certainly have affected the likelihood of them being able to marry bigamously without swift discovery.

[12] Based on a sample of 42 cases tried at provincial assizes for which the locations of both marriages could be ascertained. Cases tried at the Old Bailey were excluded from this sample so as not to skew the result, since here it was far more common for both marriages to have taken place in London.

[13] On patterns of employment, see P Wallis, J Colson and D Chilosi, 'Structural Change and Economic Growth in the British Economy before the Industrial Revolution, 1500–1800' (2018) 78 *Journal of Economic History* 862. While their overall argument points to a significant shift away from agriculture from the start of the seventeenth century, they still estimate that it accounted for 48% of male employment even in the early eighteenth century. On the limited mobility of agricultural labourers, see CG Pooley and J Turnbull, *Migration and Mobility in Britain Since the Eighteenth Century* (London, Routledge, 1998) 53.

A Pragmatic Marriage: John Ridiough, 1831

The case of John Ridiough, tried at the Lancashire assizes in 1831, was unusual in a number of respects. One was the lapse of time between his first wedding, which had taken place in Ormskirk in 1802, and his bigamous wedding to Mary Hunter over 20 years later. Amongst those who stood trial in the 1830s, the average time between the two marriages was under six years.[14] A second unusual element was that it had taken more than seven years for John to be arrested and tried – whereas most stood trial within a year of their bigamous wedding.[15] The reason for this delayed prosecution was that he had never set up home with his bigamous wife Mary. Instead, he had continued to live with his first wife (also Mary) until her death a few months prior to his trial. Only then did he take the second Mary to live with him and 'some party or other' thought it proper to institute a prosecution.[16]

At the trial, Mary told the court that she had been fully aware that John was already married at the time of their bigamous wedding in 1831. They had, however, already embarked on a relationship. She had had two children by him and was expecting a third. As she explained, the magistrates of Ormskirk 'were in the habit of committing single women who had more than one bastard child, but … did not commit those who were married'. She therefore persuaded John to go with her to Liverpool and marry her under the assumed name of 'William Smith'.[17] This had enabled her to return to Ormskirk with a marriage certificate without suspicion falling upon John.

None of that made any difference to John's guilt. The courts had been very clear that using a false name for the second marriage provided no defence to a charge of bigamy, whatever the status of the marriage would have been if it had not been bigamous. But his second wife's knowledge that he was married did at least mitigate his offence, resulting in him receiving the relatively light sentence of two months.[18]

A One-night Stand: John Smith Mase, 1850

In the early months of 1849, Mary Ann Hoy, a 30-year-old lady's maid, was walking back from the City to her residence in Southampton Row when she was accosted by a man, who invited her to take his arm. She refused, and walked on. Undeterred, he followed her, asking if she was married. She refused to answer, telling him 'That is my business'. Still he persisted, asking her to meet him the following evening. Again she declined, and finally reached home.[19]

[14] Based on 73 cases tried at provincial assizes during the 1830s for which the date of both marriages has been ascertained, with the median time between them being 2,219 days.

[15] Based on 80 cases tried at provincial assizes during the 1830s for which the date of the second marriage has been ascertained: 45 were tried within the year, with the median time between second marriage and trial being 277 days.

[16] 'Extraordinary Case of Bigamy', *Preston Chronicle*, 26 March 1831.

[17] ibid.

[18] 'Lancaster Assizes', *Lancaster Gazette*, 19 March 1831 (as John *Widdiough*).

[19] 'Clerkenwell', *London Evening Standard*, 7 March 1850; *OBP*, 8 April 1850.

But the man in question, John Mase Smith, now knew where she lived. A few days later, he called upon her, and told her that he was a widower. Over the next few months, he made many professions of his love for her. He even threatened to destroy himself unless she married him.[20] Eventually she agreed, and their wedding took place on Tuesday 25 September 1849. Within less than 24 hours, however, he had deserted her. As she later recounted, 'he went home with me on the Tuesday night, and left at half-past five o'clock on Wednesday morning'.[21]

Mary Ann subsequently made enquiries as to his whereabouts, and discovered that John was a married man and – even more significantly – that he was still living with his wife.[22] He was arrested in Norfolk, and brought back to London to stand trial. At the Clerkenwell police court, Mary Ann had hysterics upon seeing him again and had to be taken out of the courtroom and revived before she could give her evidence.[23] John's own sister gave evidence of his first marriage, and he was committed for trial.[24]

At John's trial at the Central Criminal Court, the evidence against him was clear, and he was sentenced to a year's imprisonment.[25] His sentence would probably have been even higher had he not returned to his legal wife.[26] Judges always took a dim view of bigamists who had deceived their second wife, especially those who had gone on to abandon her.[27] Those who did so after just one night were treated even more harshly, their actions being viewed as tantamount to rape. As the Chief Baron observed in one such case, by committing bigamy the man had 'obtained by fraud that which would, a few years ago, have caused his life to be forfeited'.[28]

The Evasive Edward Drane Hannibal, 1853

Edward Drane Hannibal was working in Hull when he met Mary Crackles. The letter that he wrote declaring his affection for her was calculated to appeal to her pious nature: he asked her pardon for addressing her, but justified this on the basis that it 'had been ordained by God that man should make the first advance', claimed to belong to the same religious denomination as her, and concluded by saying that he would 'leave it in the hands of the Lord' as to whether she would grant him an interview. After a second letter, Mary eventually consented 'to accept his suit'.[29]

[20] 'Clerkenwell', *London Evening Standard*, 7 March 1850.
[21] *OBP*, 8 April 1850.
[22] 'A Cruel Case of Bigamy', *Lloyd's*, 14 April 1850.
[23] 'Clerkenwell', *London Evening Standard*, 7 March 1850.
[24] 'Clerkenwell', *Morning Advertiser*, 7 March 1850.
[25] *OBP*, 8 April 1850.
[26] See eg William Robert Eastwell, who deserted his second wife within five days of their wedding and was sentenced to five years' penal servitude at the Central Criminal Court (*OBP*, 25 February 1901; *Gloucester Citizen*, 25 February 1901).
[27] See further *Double Trouble*, ch 5.
[28] 'Assize Intelligence', *Morning Post*, 11 March 1857; 'Bucks Lent Assizes', *Bucks Herald*, 14 March 1857, reporting the conviction of Samuel Wilson, who was sentenced to the then-maximum of four years' penal servitude. The allusion to his life being forfeited reflected the fact that rape had, until 1828, been punishable by death.
[29] 'Singular Case of Bigamy', *Daily News*, 15 December 1853.

In the meantime, Edward wrote to his first wife Ellen, whom he had married in Manchester the year before, to tell her that he was planning to travel to America in search of work:

> My dear wife, I write to let you know what I am about doing, as I cannot get employment here, nor anywhere round about here; and, as I have had an offer to go to America by a very respectable man, I have accepted it, and am going to sail on Monday next, from Grimsby Roads, the weather permitting. We expect to be a month on the voyage at this time of the year.[30]

After advising her to go to his family in Ipswich, who would, he assured her, be kind to her, he ended on a reassuring note:

> You must not be cast down about it; bear with it for a time, and I will send for you in the summer. If you wish to write to me again before I leave England, you must do it by return of post, or I shall not receive it. … If you have not time to do so, you may write to the New York post-office, to be left till called for, and I shall get it when I arrive in America. Good bye, and God bless you, and take care of you, my dear wife. I remain your unhappy, but still affectionate husband until death, E. HANNIBAL.

The letter was dated 25 March 1853. Edward did not set sail for America, but remained in Hull, where on 3 June he went through a ceremony of marriage with Mary at Sculcoates church.[31]

Within a couple of months, however, he was arrested and confined to Hull prison to await his trial.[32] During this time, he wrote to both Ellen and Mary. He begged Ellen to get someone to write him a letter stating that she was dead, backdating it to before his second marriage, in order to save him from transportation. He was clearly hopeful that she would do so, writing to Mary that he had 'every hope of being acquitted of the charge against him, and that they could then live happily together'.[33]

Ellen, perhaps unsurprisingly, was unwilling to collude in fabricating evidence to get him off the bigamy charge. The jury found Edward guilty, 'expressing their opinion that the offence was aggravated by being committed under the garb of religion'.[34] While he escaped transportation, he was sentenced to four years' penal servitude – the maximum possible sentence at that time.[35]

The Duplicity of Philip Field, 1858

On 16 July 1858, travellers at Chester railway station witnessed a dramatic scene. As the train from Holyhead drew in, a man put his head out of one of the windows. Seeing a police officer on the platform, he immediately withdrew and jumped out of the carriage on the other side, before the train had even stopped. But the police officer in question

[30] 'The Bigamy case', *Hull Packet*, 12 August 1853.
[31] 'Bigamy at Hull', *Yorkshire Gazette*, 17 December 1853.
[32] 'The Bigamy case', *Hull Packet*, 12 August 1853.
[33] 'Bigamy at Hull', *Hull Packet*, 16 December 1853.
[34] 'Singular Case of Bigamy', *Daily News*, 15 December 1853.
[35] TNA, *Criminal Registers*, HO 27/106, p 396. On the shifts in the potential penalty for bigamy, see *Double Trouble*, ch 8.

was on the look-out, having already travelled to Holyhead and back in search of this particular man. Risking his own life, he chased after him down the tracks and made his arrest. The captured man was Philip Field, a merchant who dealt in china and glass. Accompanying him in the carriage was Mary Ann, a young woman with whom he had recently gone through a ceremony of marriage. And waiting for him on the platform, next to the police officer, was his legal wife Mary.[36]

The following day Philip appeared before the Liverpool Police Court to be charged with bigamy. The *Liverpool Mercury* painted him in an unflattering light, describing him as 'of unprepossessing countenance and figure'.[37] The *Morning Chronicle* was more interested in the 'two unfortunate women' he had married. Both were, as it noted, 'deeply veiled, seeking to screen their grief from the prying eye of the public', although the journalist did later apparently get a glimpse of the 'very handsome little face' of the second wife. It also reported that the two women 'appeared to be on good terms, a community of grief having given them a community of sympathy, which was exhibited in many little acts of mutual attention'.[38]

Over the next few weeks, the facts of the case emerged before the magistrates. Presenting the case for the prosecution, Mr Cobb described it as 'one of the most melancholy ever brought into a court of justice'. He set out the apparently happy history of Philip's first marriage. Philip had married his first wife, Mary Kidger, in 1843, at Carlton in Leicestershire. Two daughters were born to them, in 1850 and 1851, and the family had prospered. In the spring of 1858, however, Philip spotted 18-year-old Mary Ann Thomas on Breck Road in Liverpool, where she was employed as a nurserymaid. Smitten by her appearance, he followed her and struck up a conversation, introducing himself as William Harrison, a commercial traveller, and – crucially – unmarried.[39] Over the weeks that followed they met on several occasions. Philip also began writing to her – initially purporting to be her cousin, in case his letters should be intercepted, but later abandoning this pretence. The one he sent on 9 April was relatively circumspect: addressing her as 'My dearest Polly', it was mainly concerned with the arrangements for their next meeting, although he did slyly drop in hints about what constituted an ideal marriage ('Don't you think that Mrs Nisbett and her husband were a pattern of what married life ought to be? *I do*'). By 23 April he had progressed to calling Mary Ann 'my love', referring to her 'confession' of her love for him, and planning their own marriage:

> Do you feel that all your happiness is centred in me? I must say that I value the love even of a friend; how much more the one I choose for a *life friend*. But don't think, my dear Polly, that I in the least question your attachment. I have been a poor observer if I have not detected, even if I had no confession from you, that you dearly love me. I asked you on Sunday how you knew, that you loved me, and also what love was. I think it is not at all a difficult matter to know when you love. Why do we desire to be near one individual more than another? Is

[36] 'Alleged Elopement and Bigamy by a Liverpool Merchant', *Liverpool Mercury*, 17 July 1858; 'Bigamy and Elopement from Liverpool', *Liverpool Mercury*, 19 July 1858; 'The Extraordinary Case of Bigamy and Elopement from Liverpool', *Liverpool Mercury*, 27 July 1858.

[37] 'Bigamy and Elopement from Liverpool', *Liverpool Mercury*, 19 July 1858.

[38] 'Elopement and Capture', *Morning Chronicle*, 20 July 1858.

[39] ibid; 'The Extraordinary Case of Bigamy and Elopement from Liverpool', *Liverpool Mercury*, 27 July 1858.

> there nothing in a speaking countenance, even without words? Have not even a pair of eyes declared many a love tale? But have not our own hearts unmistakably told us, which is a sufficient judge, for whom it beats? Do I not love the one who is always in my thoughts – one for whom it seems to be that I can only create and maintain my own happiness by making a certain one happy? And could I not possess this dear one, my own life would seem a perfect blank. Without you, my ever dear one, I should see in life nothing worthy of living for. These being truly my own feelings, can you wonder then, when I say how the time seems to lag? How sweetly real, then, will it be when I can press you to my heart and say you are dearly mine for ever.

There was quite a lot more of this duplicitous flannel – concision in writing was not one of Philip's strong points – but he eventually had to stop in order to catch the post and concluded by asking her to 'accept the love and kisses on paper till I can give you some on a more moist substance'.[40]

Having 'secured her affections', Philip took Mary Ann to London. There he obtained a licence to marry her, their wedding taking place at St Bartholomew the Great on 4 May 1858 under his assumed name of William Harrison.[41] After the wedding, the pair stayed in London for another month before travelling to Wales for a few days. From there they went to Seacombe, on the Mersey opposite Liverpool. Here, Philip finally admitted that he was a married man, and left Mary Ann to return to his first wife.

But if Philip had hoped that Mary Ann would not make a fuss, he was sadly mistaken. On 14 June, she penned him a letter that alternated between declarations of love, recriminations, and threats to expose him. In it she revealed that she had been to Liverpool and ascertained his real name and address:

> I have only told it to one, of whose secrecy I can depend on. They must know of it in time, and I am sure nothing will keep them back from punishing you to the utmost of their ability. But do not think I would do you the least harm. God knows that I do love you; but I come again to my position, and most plainly tell you that I have every reason to believe I am in that state which will in course of time prove me to be a mother. Oh, misery of miseries, what can I do, or where can I go? You well know my position in life; you also know my respectability and virtue previous to meeting with you. You know well enough the respectability of my friends. I gave you every information by which you could prove it to your satisfaction. Therefore I must claim my rights, as you cannot restore me to the position you found me. You are and shall be bound to protect me. It is not money that I want. That will not make me happy. I am sure I cannot tell you what I want; but I insist that you come to me in two days from the receipt of this, or it will be worse for you.[42]

Upon receiving this, Philip decided that his best course of action was to return to Mary Ann rather than wait to be exposed. He left her letter for his wife to find, with an accompanying note that, while short by his usual standards, managed to combine

[40] 'The Extraordinary Case of Bigamy and Elopement from Liverpool', *Liverpool Mercury*, 27 July 1858. 'Moist' is not a word that should ever appear in a love letter.

[41] 'Charge of Bigamy', *Daily News*, 19 July 1858.

[42] ibid.

sickening self-pity, vague promises of financial support, avowals of love, and practical advice:

> My ever dear Mary. You will not be very much surprised at me not returning home again at present, when you see the letter I received yesterday from that young lady from London. It was no use; I could not stay. I am going to see if something cannot be done. If not, I shall steer, I think, to either America or Africa. I will let you know about it in due course and then you will be more satisfied. I have paid dearly for my sin. It has indeed been hard for me. But, oh, the deep injury I have done you, who have always been everything to me. You don't know how I love you, still for all. Don't think I am going to make away with the money. I shall at once, health permitting, get to America to try to make more, and some day my dear child M.A. will receive from me. I meant to have brought her likeness with me. I was out this morning. I enclose you a £100 note. Don't think hardly of me. Tell the lads to do the best. Get all the money in, wind up the business. Give my love to all. Tell my father to act kindly to you. Remember me to mother. I must close. Good-bye at present.-Your ever affectionate husband. P. Field. Keep up your spirits.[43]

We have already seen how Philip came to be apprehended at Chester railway station. After his arrest, he admitted that he had 'acted very foolishly, and was sorry for what he had done'.[44] His first wife and her family tried to persuade Mary Ann not to prosecute, promising to arrange employment for her in Leicestershire; she initially agreed, but then changed her mind.

When she was in the witness box, one salient fact emerged that changed perceptions of her as the victim. This was her evidence as to when she had learned that Philip was a married man. Her counsel had been under the impression that she was unaware of this before his arrest at Chester. That she had already learned the truth and was still willing to go away with Philip was a black mark against her – a circumstance which, as the magistrate noted, might well be pleaded in extenuation of his crime.

All this meant that the actual trial attracted far less interest than the proceedings before the magistrates. As the *Liverpool Mercury* noted, the case 'was robbed of much of its romantic interest by the admission of the second wife, at the last examination before the magistrates, that the prisoner told her at Seacombe that he was a married man'.[45] Philip pleaded guilty and was sentenced to three years' penal servitude.[46]

Philip's letters show how he was hoping to use a bigamous marriage as a cover for a brief affair. There is nothing to suggest that he had any real intention or desire to leave his first wife. She, understandably, certainly contemplated leaving him, filing a petition for divorce on 23 December 1858.[47] But there is no evidence that this ever came to a hearing.

Upon his release from Dartmoor prison, Philip returned to Mary.[48] The 1861 census records them living together with their daughter in Everton.[49] But – in a detail that

[43] 'Bigamy and Elopement from Liverpool', *Liverpool Mercury*, 19 July 1858.
[44] 'The Extraordinary Case of Bigamy and Elopement', *Liverpool Mercury*, 31 July 1858.
[45] 'The Extraordinary Case of Bigamy', *Liverpool Mercury*, 4 August 1858.
[46] TNA, *Criminal Registers*, HO27/119, p 98.
[47] TNA, *Divorce and Matrimonial Causes Files, Field v Field*, J77/18/F10.
[48] He was released early on licence on 31 December 1860: TNA, PCOM 3/83/8738.
[49] TNA, 1861 census, RG9/2714, folio 94, p 4.

I hope reflected the changed power dynamics of their relationship rather than just an error by the enumerator – Mary is recorded as being the head of the household. Philip was relegated to the status of 'visitor'.

The Double Life of Richard Francis Archibald Farquharson, 1874

It was some broken crockery – and a distinctive set of initials – that led to the double life of Richard Francis Archibald Farquharson being discovered. He had been renting lodgings in the Wiltshire village of North Bradley, located between Westbury and Trowbridge, his household including his mother, his wife Jessie, and their four children. When their aggrieved landlady sued them for breakages and other damage, the case came before the Trowbridge County Court.[50] Her claim was strongly resisted by her tenants, and the case was dropped. The local newspaper noted that evidence had been given by Mrs Farquharson, the wife of 'Mr R.F.A. Farquharson'.[51]

A copy of the newspaper made its way to the landlord of a hotel in Devizes, some 12 miles away. Shortly afterwards, the landlord received a letter from another Mrs Farquharson. This Mrs Farquharson was living in Stepney and was asking whether there was any news of her husband, one 'R.F.A. Farquharson', not having heard from him for some time. He had previously given her the address of the hotel. The landlord replied to say that he knew nothing of this individual, but helpfully forwarded a copy of the newspaper featuring the Farquharsons' legal affairs.[52]

As a result, the mother of this second Mrs Farquharson, a Mrs Benest, immediately came down from London to investigate. Having tracked Mr Farquharson down to his home, she discovered that he was indeed her truant son-in-law. As might be imagined, 'a painful scene ensued'.[53] Mrs Benest ordered a carriage, commanded Richard to get into it, and took him to the nearest police station, 'loudly upbraiding him all the way'.[54] Upon their arrival there he was understandably reluctant to alight, but Mrs Benest ordered him to do so, and her loud tones attracted a crowd of spectators. As the *Western Gazette* reported, 'as it began to ooze out what his little game had been', the sympathies of those present were very definitely with Mrs Benest.[55] Richard had no choice but to enter the police station.

At the subsequent committal proceedings before the Trowbridge magistrates, the details of his two families emerged. Richard had married Jessie Hooper, the wife with whom he was living in North Bradley, in London in 1865. Details in the marriage register suggest that it was a quiet ceremony, celebrated by licence at St Michael's, Strand,

[50] '*Murphy v Farquison*', *Trowbridge Chronicle*, 27 September 1873.

[51] 'Extraordinary Bigamy Case in Wiltshire', *Bristol Times and Mirror*, 6 October 1873; 'The Extraordinary Bigamy Case', *Trowbridge Chronicle*, 11 October 1873.

[52] 'Extraordinary Bigamy Case', *Western Gazette*, 10 October 1873.

[53] 'Heartless Case of Bigamy in Wiltshire', *Wells Journal*, 9 October 1873; 'Bigamy', *Devizes and Wilts Advertiser*, 9 October 1873.

[54] 'Extraordinary Bigamy Case in Wiltshire', *Bristol Times and Mirror*, 6 October 1873.

[55] 'Extraordinary Bigamy Case', *Western Gazette*, 10 October 1873.

on 26 December. The church no longer exists, but it stood on the corner of Exeter Street and Burleigh Street in Covent Garden, a less busy (and certainly less fashionable) location at the time than today. Neither Richard nor Jessie was a permanent resident of the parish, as evidenced by both giving a hotel as their address at the time. Richard had also used his middle name of 'Archibald' rather than his first name.[56] While this would not have invalidated his marriage, it was another hint that he had something to hide.

At the time of the census taken in April 1871, they were living in Honiton in Devon, with three young sons, in a household headed by Richard's mother Sarah.[57] By this time, however, he had already begun a relationship with Alice Benest. As she told the magistrates, she had met him some seven or eight months before their wedding, which had taken place at West Hackney parish church in early September.[58] This time Richard used the name of Roderick Francis Archibald Farquharson.[59] Between 1871 and 1873 he divided his time between the two households, telling Jessie that he had business in London and Alice that he had business in the country.[60]

Alice had clearly had no idea that Richard was already married.[61] She fainted when he was brought into the waiting room, and again when Jessie arrived. As one local newspaper noted, Alice's case was a 'pitiable one' – not least because she had already had one child by Richard, with another on the way. Her small son had accompanied her from London, and recognised Richard as his 'Papa'. Richard, however, 'took not the slightest notice' either of his child or of the weeping Alice, but spoke only to his 'first love'.[62]

There was, however, a question as to whether Jessie was Richard's first love – or, more pertinently, his legal wife. Alice's mother showed the magistrates a newspaper cutting reporting the wedding of a Captain Archibald Farquharson to a Miss Henrietta Buckley in 1859 – some six years before his marriage to Jessie.[63] When questioned about this earlier marriage, Richard's mother Sarah acknowledged that she had some recollection of it but demanded to know what it had to do with the present case. The bench pointed out that it might be grounds for a second charge of bigamy to be preferred against Richard – at which point she explained that Richard had been divorced from his first wife within the year. In the absence of any proof of the divorce – Sarah's airy claim that it was in 'all the papers' at the time being insufficient to satisfy the magistrates – a sergeant was dispatched to London to investigate the records of the Divorce Court.[64]

It is easy to understand why Sarah chose to be somewhat economical with the truth in setting out the circumstances surrounding this earlier marriage and its ending. In her version of events, Richard had been a 'mere boy of 18' at the time of this first marriage, and Henrietta 'many years his senior'. In fact, Richard had been only a month short of

[56] Ancestry, *Westminster Church of England Parish Registers*, SMBU/PR/2/1.
[57] TNA, 1871 census, RG10/2039, folio 11, p 14.
[58] 'The Case of Bigamy', *Trowbridge Chronicle*, 18 October 1873.
[59] Ancestry, *London Church of England Parish Registers*, P79/WH/022.
[60] 'Extraordinary Bigamy Case in Wiltshire', *Wiltshire County Mirror*, 14 October 1873.
[61] 'Extraordinary Bigamy Case in Wiltshire', *Swindon Advertiser and North Wilts Chronicle*, 13 October 1873.
[62] 'The Extraordinary Bigamy Case', *Trowbridge Chronicle*, 11 October 1873.
[63] 'The Wiltshire Bigamy case: Further Disclosures', *Bristol Times and Mirror*, 9 October 1873.
[64] 'Extraordinary Bigamy Case in Wiltshire', *Bristol Times and Mirror*, 9 October 1873.

his twentieth birthday, and Henrietta had been just 21. Moreover, Henrietta's divorce petition reveals just how badly Richard had behaved. While she was pregnant, Richard had been 'in the habit of frequenting the Turkish Divan in the Haymarket and the Portland Rooms in Foley Street and of meeting and associating with prostitutes there'. In one month alone, he had sex with three different women – and these were just the ones that Henrietta was able to name. She was aware that there were others, noting that at various times and places 'and particularly at Portsmouth … and at Cork' he had committed adultery with other women whose names she did not know. She was also able to establish cruelty: at the time of their marriage he was already suffering from gonorrhoea and infected her with the disease. Their only child was born prematurely and did not survive. The divorce was granted in July 1861, the judge commenting that Richard's conduct had been such 'that it could only be characterized by terms which were hardly fit to be used in public'.[65]

This earlier marriage and divorce explain why Richard's subsequent marriage to Jessie had been celebrated so discreetly, and with Richard using just one of his names. Ever since the Matrimonial Causes Act 1857, clergy had the right to refuse to marry any person who had been divorced on account of their adultery.[66] Richard's adultery had been so flagrant that it is hard to imagine any clergyman aware of the circumstances being willing to conduct his remarriage.

Back in Trowbridge, the details of the earlier divorce satisfied the magistrates that they were not dealing with a multiple bigamist. Even so, bail was set at £500 plus two sureties of £250 each. This Richard was unable to muster. He begged the magistrates to reduce the amount, pleading that his health would not cope with six months' incarceration, but they refused.[67] As the *Western Gazette* noted, he would therefore face the prospect 'of considering his heartless conduct for six months in Devizes Gaol till his trial comes on'. Richard had, it added, been a 'general favourite' in local circles until his bigamy was discovered, but his friends had forsaken him and had 'steadily declined to be responsible for his appearance'.[68] But at least Jessie and Alice had not forsaken him. The *Trowbridge Chronicle* reported that they had obtained permission to visit Richard in his cell, noting tartly that 'the crying, kissing, and caressing of the prisoner by both was something quite tragic'.[69]

Richard's case caused a sensation both locally and nationally. It was unusual for Wiltshire to have *any* cases of bigamy: fewer than 20 had come before its assizes since the start of the century. But the two-timing element meant that it was sufficiently unusual to be reported around the country, with newspapers sagely repeating how it illustrated the adage that truth was often stranger than fiction.[70]

[65] 'Court of Probate and Divorce', *Morning Post*, 22 July 1861.
[66] Matrimonial Causes Act, s 57.
[67] 'The Bigamy Case in Wiltshire', *Swindon Advertiser and North Wilts Chronicle*, 20 October 1873.
[68] 'The Bigamy Case', *Western Gazette*, 24 October 1873.
[69] 'The Case of Bigamy', *Trowbridge Chronicle*, 18 October 1873.
[70] 'Singular Charge of Bigamy', *Monmouthshire Merlin*, 24 October 1873; 'A Gentleman With Three Wives', *Bicester Herald*, 24 October 1873; 'A Strange Case of Bigamy', *Liverpool Weekly Courier*, 25 October 1873; 'A Curious Matrimonial History', *Hull Daily News*, 25 October 1873; 'Charge of Bigamy', *Sheerness Guardian and East Kent Advertiser*, 25 October 1873.

Richard's subsequent trial at the Wiltshire assizes the following April attracted far less interest. Since he pleaded guilty, there were no new revelations to report. His defence counsel did not seek to excuse his actions, telling the court that 'this was a case in which he had felt that no defence could be maintained'.[71] The best that could be said for Richard was that he had co-operated fully with the prosecution since his arrest and that they had 'no desire to press the charge heavily'.[72] When called upon, Richard said he had nothing to say, except to throw himself on the mercy of the court. But the judge, Mr Justice Keating, 'did not consider this was a case in which mercy could justly be extended' as Richard had done a 'grievous wrong'.[73] Richard was duly sentenced to 15 months' imprisonment with hard labour.[74] This was one of the harshest sentences handed down that year, with Richard being one of just nine bigamists nation-wide sentenced to more than 12 months.

Admittedly, it is difficult to feel much sympathy for Richard. Quite apart from his deception of Jessie and Alice, and his appalling treatment of Henrietta, there were other circumstances in his history that do not put him in a good light.[75] During a sojourn in Paris – and in the middle of his divorce from Henrietta – he had paid his addresses to yet another woman, Mary Torrens. Upon it being discovered that he was still married, Mary's uncle, Sir Ralph Anstruther, dashed off a missive to Lord John Russell, the former Prime Minister, asking him to intervene. As he explained, although Mary's mother had been apprised of the circumstances, 'there is reason to fear that she is not inclined to interfere with sufficient energy to prevent her daughter from forming this illicit connection'.[76] Russell duly wrote to the British Ambassador to France, requesting him to 'take such measures as you shall find advisable to prevent the marriage from being solemnized in any English Chapel at Paris'.[77]

So, in a few short years, Richard had been married, attempted bigamy, been divorced, remarried legally, and gone through a bigamous ceremony of marriage. But despite this chequered history, his story had an unexpectedly (and, one feels, undeservedly) happy-ever-after ending. After serving his time in prison, Richard returned to his legal wife Jessie. The 1881 census found them still living in North Bradley – and from the spacing of his growing family one would not imagine that he had ever been away.[78] They remained together until Richard's death in 1912.[79]

Richard's tale indicates some of the challenges for bigamists in juggling two families. Unless the two households were very close by – which brought its own obvious risks of discovery – a bigamist needed to have a plausible reason for being away from each

[71] 'The Wiltshire Bigamy Case', *North Wilts Herald*, 6 April 1874.

[72] ibid.

[73] 'Wilts Lent Assizes', *Reading Mercury*, 4 April 1874. See also 'A Bad Case of Bigamy', *Bristol Times and Mirror*, 30 March 1874.

[74] TNA, *Criminal Registers*, HO27/169 p 190 (as Roderick Francis Archibald Farquharson).

[75] He also got into debt, appearing in the Court for Relief of Insolvent Debtors: *London Gazette*, 3 September 1861. He seems to have had a brief spell of buying and selling horses, and to have moved from hotel to hotel across the south of England as well as in Paris and Naples. By the time he appeared in court, he was described as being 'in no business or profession'.

[76] TNA, PRO30/22/104/72, folios 344–47, letter from Sir Ralph Anstruther, 29 June 1861.

[77] ibid, letter from Lord John Russell to Lord Cowley, 29 June 1861.

[78] TNA, RG11/2052, folio 24, p 7.

[79] TNA, 1891 census, RG12/407, folio 7, p 8; 1901 census: RG13/469, folio 112, p 16; 1911 census, RG14.

home for extended periods of time, and the means to travel easily between them. He also needed to have the financial resources to be able to support two households, and the mental ability to be able to cope with deceiving both wives. Overall, while a handful of nineteenth-century bigamists shuttled between two households, generally for short periods of time, it was only really in the twentieth century that leading a double life became a viable proposition.[80]

Before widespread car ownership, travel opportunities were generally linked to employment. In one example from 1914, the bigamist cycled back and forth between his two wives in north and south London, but his double life only lasted for a few months.[81] Another, in 1916, had a job as a sleeping car attendant on trains between London and Newcastle. This gave him a cast-iron excuse for being absent from home, as well as eliminating the likelihood of chance meetings between his two wives, but after two years of this he gave himself up at the Bow Street Police office.[82] But the occupation that provided the best combination of a cast-iron reason for being away from home overnight, good wages, and the opportunity for travel was that of long-distance lorry driver, with a number of examples cropping up over the course of the twentieth century.[83]

In addition to the logistical challenges of travelling between the two households, there was also the cost. This proved the undoing of some bigamists. One resorted to fraud to support his two households, defrauding his first wife, his son, the Post Office Savings Bank, two other banks, and his employers.[84] A lorry driver who had been maintaining two households for six years was brought to court for falsely claiming benefits, although the police decided not to press bigamy charges against him.[85] Another, who had been maintaining two households 120 miles apart and spending half of each week with each wife, stole a credit card from his second wife and went on a 'spending spree'.[86]

As a somewhat tongue-in-cheek article from 1986 advised, there were certain signs that could alert wives to the possibility that their husband had 'a home from home'. A checklist of questions invited a wife to ask herself how much she knew about her husband's earnings, bank accounts, and will, whether she had met his relatives or work

[80] For earlier examples, see *Manchester Times*, 20 September 1856 (corporal William David, discovered when his wives met at the Salford barracks when both were looking for him); *Nottinghamshire Guardian*, 24 June 1858 (Thomas Johnson, discovered by one wife while out walking with the other); *Manchester Times*, 27 November 1891 (George Ridings, 'never able to give a reasonable account of where he had been').

[81] Quite apart from the sheer effort involved, he found it difficult to maintain both homes on his weekly wage of £2 7s: *The Times*, 5 March 1914; 'Engineer's Double Life', *Lancashire Daily Post*, 5 March 1914. 'Engineer Who Kept Two Homes', *Huddersfield Daily Examiner*, 5 March 1914.

[82] According to the reports in the newspapers, he spent alternate days with each of the women – Hannah, whom he had married in 1899, in Newcastle, and Agnes, whom he had married in September 1914, in Woodford: *The Times*, 19 August 1916; *Chelmsford Chronicle*, 25 August 1916.

[83] For examples, see 'Double Bigamy: Lorry Driver's Two "Brides" in Four Months', *Yorkshire Evening Post*, 11 July 1938; 'It's the End of George's Double Life', *Daily Herald*, 17 June 1953; 'Lorry Driver For Trial on Bigamy Charge: Alleged Admission to Police', *The Times*, 17 February 1956; 'Amorous driver got "married" to three Irenes', *Daily Mail*, 29 March 1972; 'Bigamist had 15 years of "nightmare"', *Wolverhampton Express & Star*, 12 August 1975.

[84] 'Fraud on Wife, Sons, Banks', *Daily Mail*, 18 June 1952.

[85] 'No bigamy prosecution', *Birmingham Evening Mail*, 13 December 1976.

[86] 'Card spree exposes husband's double life: "Wife No 2" tells of bigamy blow', *News and Star*, 7 October 1993.

colleagues, and if she knew where he was when he was away from home.[87] And even if the bigamist had a convincing story that explained their absences from home, was able to maintain both households financially, and allay any suspicions, they were, like Richard Farquharson, only ever one accident away from discovery.

'Please Sort this Matrimonial Story Out': William Flounders, 1966

On 9 January 1965, a young Egyptian woman named Amal Abdel Halim El Said arrived at London Airport.[88] She was seeking to rejoin the man she believed to be her husband, William Flounders, whom she had married in Cairo the year before.[89] He had been sent out to Egypt by his employers and had met Amal sometime in early 1964.[90] In June he had made a declaration that he had become a Muslim, a necessary step before they could marry, and on 15 July 1964 the wedding ceremony took place at the register office. Six weeks later, however, William left Cairo to return to England.[91]

From the multiple letters that William wrote to her from England over the autumn of 1964, Amal would have had no reason to doubt his feelings for her, the validity of their marriage, or that they would one day be reunited. An extract from one written in mid-September gives a flavour of their content:

> My darling Amal … I hope that you are happy and looking forward to the day when I shall return to Cairo or you come to England, but I know we must be together again … you are my wife and no one can do anything about it, only yourself can do anything about it if you wish. I shall try everyway to live up to being your husband. I know I can do it because in England sex never troubles me, it's because of the climate and more so because it would not be you. I wish you were here now … Your loving husband Bill.[92]

Interspersed with such professions of love, however, were hints that his time in Cairo had not been smooth sailing. There were references to other people being 'jealous'. Another letter spoke of the 'injustice' that had been done by others, and how he had been 'in a lot of trouble at Head Office'.[93] There were also references to his family in England – his three young sons, and their mother Mary.

[87] 'That was no lady – that was my other wife', *Manchester Evening News*, 21 July 1986. A final 'tell' was whether his clothes had any minor repairs such as buttons being sewn back on, the implication being that it would only be another woman who would do this.

[88] All the archival material referred to in this case study is contained in TNA, DPP 2/4027. The title of this section is taken from the scribbled note that prefaced the discussion between officials as to whether Flounders should be prosecuted.

[89] TNA, DPP 2/4027, Durham County Constabulary, File No HQ 605/65, 15 August 1965.

[90] ibid, statement by William Flounders, 9 January 1965; statement by Amal Abdel Halim El Said, 22 May 1965. They gave slightly different accounts of when they met: he said January, she said it was April or March.

[91] ibid, Durham County Constabulary, Statement by William Flounders, 9 January 1965.

[92] ibid, exhibit No 10, letter dated 18 September 1964.

[93] ibid, exhibit No 10, letter dated 17 September 1964.

While we do not have Amal's letters to William, it seems that she did – understandably – ask questions about Mary. William was quick to reassure her that there was no ongoing relationship between them:

> You said I was living with Mary, well I am not, my sister is looking after the three boys for me while I am away. My own house is closed up now until I am away. Mary left when she came out of hospital. Never forget that I love you and always will, do not let anyone say anything else. You are my wife and always will be, that's the way I want it.[94]

At this point we should turn to Mary. She and William had met in Salford back in 1953, where Mary was lodging with William's aunt, and they started going out together. This caused some friction with William's aunt, and Mary was told to leave the house. She and William moved to Bolton, where they took separate lodgings. A year later they began living together as 'man and wife'. Mary then formally changed her surname by deed poll to Flounders, and their first child was born in 1957. When William's firm sent him out to India in 1958, she went out too, and their second child was born there. Back in England, they settled in West Hartlepool, and bought a house. Their third child was born in 1961. When William was sent to Cairo in 1963, she was unable to accompany him, but she received an allowance via his employers. Until July 1964, William wrote to her 'every day'.[95]

In August 1964, Mary fell ill and had to have an operation. Her brother thought that William should come home, and contacted his firm.[96] While William was on his way back, however, Mary received an unexpected letter:

> Madam Mary, this is to say that Mr William Flounders turned Moslem and married me, Amal, an Egyptian woman three weeks ago. I am three months having a baby to Bill and if I went to Cairo to cause trouble for Bill it would only make matters worse because he had said that he wasn't married.

Upon Mary showing this letter to William, he flatly denied knowing Amal and claimed to be baffled by the letter. When another letter from Amal arrived, he admitted that he had known her in Egypt and had been out with her. As Mary later stated, she had simply not believed Amal's claim that he had married her, adding 'I didn't think how he could have when he thought so much of me'.[97]

Even so, the correspondence seems to have prompted Mary to act. She told William that she was 'fed up' with the way that they were living and asked if they could get married. The reason why they had not done so previously was that William was already married when she first met him. Back in 1941, he had married a woman named Doreen. This marriage had broken down in around 1946, but Doreen was still alive and living in London. William reassured Mary that he was sure that Doreen had divorced him, but that he would write to her to make sure. In his letter he told Doreen that she need only reply if she had not divorced him. No reply was received from Doreen, and on Boxing Day 1964 Mary and William married at the West Hartlepool register office.[98]

[94] ibid, exhibit No 10, letter dated 3 October 1964.
[95] ibid, statement of Mary Flounders, 22 May 1965.
[96] ibid, statement of Benjamin Arthur Harker, 24 May 1965.
[97] ibid, statement of Mary Flounders, 22 May 1965.
[98] ibid, Durham County Constabulary, File No HQ 605/65, 15 August 1965.

Two weeks later, as we have seen, Amal arrived in England, and William was questioned by the police. At this point he had to admit to Mary that he had in fact gone through a ceremony of marriage with Amal in Cairo. But in his statement to the police, he claimed to have been told that this marriage would not be legally recognised and that he had believed himself free to marry Mary.[99]

On the face of it, that was not an unreasonable claim – William having conveniently omitted to mention his earlier marriage to Doreen when questioned by the police. The ceremony at the register office in Cairo had complied with all the formalities required by Egyptian law. The complicating factor was that Egyptian law permitted men to take more than one wife, and English law did not recognise any such potentially polygamous marriage as valid.[100] It had also been held that a man who had married in a jurisdiction that permitted polygamy would not be guilty of bigamy if he subsequently married someone else in England or Wales.[101]

No further action was taken at this stage. But on 20 May 1965, Amal finally arrived in West Hartlepool.[102] Two days later, William came to the West Hartlepool police office to complain that Amal was 'persistently bothering' him and Mary.[103] At this stage he acknowledged his earlier marriage to Doreen – which the police had just discovered for themselves, Amal's arrival having prompted them to make further inquiries into William's past.[104] This changed everything. As long as the marriage to Doreen was still subsisting, William had committed bigamy at least once, when he married Mary. And the revelation that his marriage to Amal was his second, rather than his first, raised the possibility that he was also guilty of bigamy in marrying her. After all, for these purposes, only the first marriage had to be unquestionably valid.[105]

The next few days saw a flurry of activity as the police tracked down and took statements from the various individuals involved. William's first wife, Doreen, confirmed that she had never taken any steps to obtain a legal separation or divorce. The reason why she had not replied to William's letter to tell him this was that she had never opened it. As she told the police, 'I have no wish to know anything about him'.[106] Statements were also taken from Amal and Mary, from the vicar who had conducted the 1941 wedding, and from the superintendent registrar to whom William and Mary had given notice of their intention to marry.

The Chief Constable then sought the advice of the Director of Public Prosecutions, Norman Skelhorn, as to whether William should be prosecuted for bigamy.[107] The reason why this was even a question reflected a change in practice since the end of the Second World War. In 1945, 75 per cent of cases known to the police resulted in a

[99] ibid, statement by William Flounders, 9 January 1965.

[100] A marriage was 'potentially' polygamous if it was contracted under a system that permitted polygamy, even if it was monogamous in practice.

[101] *R v Sarwan Singh* [1962] 3 All ER 612; see further *Double Trouble*, ch 10.

[102] The delay was due to the fact that she was originally refused entry. She had been granted a visa permitting her to stay for three months: TNA, DPP 2/4027, Durham County Constabulary, File No HQ 605/15, 13 August 1965.

[103] ibid, statement of Detective Constable Uden, 13 August 1965.

[104] ibid, Durham County Constabulary, File No HQ 605/15, 13 August 1965.

[105] On the significance of the status of the second marriage, see the case study of Henry Allen in chapter 3.

[106] ibid, statement by Doreen Flounders, 24 May 1965.

[107] ibid, letter from the Chief Constable to the DPP, 14 August 1965.

prosecution.[108] By 1965, it was just 35 per cent.[109] As the previous DPP had explained in 1963, he would often advise against a prosecution. In his view, the purpose of the law of bigamy was 'not … to punish errant husbands or keep the Registrar-general's records straight, but to prevent the seduction of a woman by a fraudulent marriage ceremony'.[110]

The file in the National Archives contains several pages of scribbled notes in different handwriting as officials debated whether a prosecution was merited. The first took the view that William should not be prosecuted, given that Mary had been aware of his marriage to Doreen, and Amal had been aware that he had had children with Mary, not to mention the 'difficulty and expense' involved in proving the Cairo ceremony.[111] The second writer, however, felt that a prosecution was justified, noting 'I feel that he is making a habit of this', and the third agreed.

There remained the legal question of whether William could be prosecuted for the ceremony in Cairo. The Privy Council had just considered a case referred from Ceylon, in which a man who had married in a Christian ceremony had subsequently converted to Islam and married again.[112] Their view had been that the man had been entitled to change his religion and that he had not committed bigamy in marrying for a second time, since the law of Ceylon recognised Muslim polygamous marriages. However, counsel thought that William's case was 'quite different', given that the first marriage was celebrated in England and the status of the second was being decided by an English court. As he noted, '[i]t would be a very remarkable state of affairs if any married Englishman could go to the East and contract a number of polygamous marriages and return to this country, with or without his wives but with impunity'.[113]

William was duly committed to the Durham quarter sessions, to be tried on two counts of bigamy.[114] The trial, appropriately enough, was held on 14 February. Both Mary and Amal were in court, but neither of them was called upon to say anything.[115] As William pleaded guilty, the only issue to be decided was the appropriate sentence.

The report prepared by the probation officer painted a picture of William as a good worker and family man who had been 'wronged' by his first wife and who had a strong and stable relationship with Mary:

> The couple have no secrets from each other and are obviously very much in love. Mary appears as a responsible person who has cooperated with Flounders to build a happy home. They seem to have been drawn closer together by this present trouble. In the role of husband and father

108 Calculated from Home Office, *Criminal Statistics: England and Wales 1939-1945: Summary of statistics relating to crime and criminal proceedings for the years 1939-1945* (Cmd 7227, 1947).

109 Calculated from Home Office, *Criminal Statistics: England and Wales, 1965* (Cmnd 3037, 1966).

110 'Who is the DPP?', *Daily Mail*, 7 September 1963. The then DPP was Theobald Matthew, who had held the post since 1944.

111 TNA, DPP 2/4027, Note, 23 August 1965, 3770/65.

112 *Attorney-General of Ceylon v Reid* [1965] AC 720.

113 TNA, DPP 2/4027, Advice, 7 January 1966.

114 The fact that he could be tried at the quarter sessions, rather than at the assizes, was the result of the Criminal Justice Administration Act 1962: see further *Double Trouble*, ch 10. He was also charged with signing a false notice contrary to s 3(1)(a) of the Perjury Act 1911.

115 '"Wives" in court for bigamist's trial', *The Guardian Journal*, 15 February 1966. Both had given their evidence previously, before the magistrates: Depositions of witnesses, 7 January 1966. Doreen had indicated that she had no wish to take any part in the proceedings, and evidence of the first marriage was accordingly given by one of the witnesses.

> Flounders has proved to be kind and considerate. Mary adopted a broad-minded attitude to his extramarital activities abroad … His personal future lies with Mary and their three children in a comfortable happy home where he has full support and security with the incentive for proper living. He hopes that by the end of the year they will in fact be able to marry.[116]

William was given a conditional discharge, and left the court arm-in-arm with Mary.[117] Amal, meanwhile, indicated that she planned to return to Egypt.[118]

William's case was very much of its time in several respects – the subterfuges that he and Mary adopted at the start of their relationship, the legal questions around polygamous marriages, and the debate as to whether he should be prosecuted. The Probation Officer's emphasis on the stability of his relationship with Mary also resonated with the report put out by the Law Commission that same year, which advocated reforming the law of divorce to allow long-separated couples to divorce and formalise their stable but 'illicit' unions.[119] Its focus was on cohabiting unions rather than bigamous ones, but the policy was the same in both cases: to allow individuals to move on from a first failed marriage in order to be able to regularise a new relationship.

[116] TNA, DPP 2/4027, Probation Officer's report, 7 February 1966.
[117] 'Bigamist chooses "wife" No. 3', *The Journal*, 15 February 1966.
[118] 'West H'pool Man was "Married" Three Times', *Hartlepool Northern Daily Mail*, 15 February 1966.
[119] Law Commission, *Reform of the Grounds of Divorce: The Field of Choice* (Cmnd 3123, 1966) 37.

12

Fraudsters, Fortune Hunters, and the Super-Bigamists

There is stiff competition for the title of 'most-married bigamist'. In the early decades of the eighteenth century, one multi-aliased bigamist was alleged to have had '17 or 18 Wives now living',[1] while another boasted at his trial that 'he had had an Hundred Wives' and, if set at liberty, 'would have an Hundred more'.[2] The mid-nineteenth century saw a bigamist whose list of aliases would, according to the *Morning Chronicle*, 'exhaust the nomenclature of the very thickest of London directories',[3] and who was rumoured to have married nearly 50 women. In the event this was never tested, as he was sentenced to death for a different offence.[4] One suspects there may well have been a degree of exaggeration in some such accounts. In any case, without at least the names of the wives, they are impossible to verify, given these men's propensity for using aliases. So, for my case studies of 'super-bigamists', I have selected ones where there were multiple convictions for bigamy rather than simply claims of multiple marriages: Gloucester Gale (convicted in 1859 and 1873) and John Woodgate Kinsella (convicted in 1900, 1908 and 1918).

In the case of the latter, bigamy seems to have been simply a straightforward scam to get money. This also seems to have been the motivation for Mary Stokes in the late seventeenth century. Although her case is less well documented than others, it is included here for gender balance – female bigamists being generally less likely to engage in scams – and as a graphic example of the risks that multiple bigamists were running at that time. Both she and Woodgate Kinsella seem to have relied on obtaining small sums of money from multiple spouses and moving on swiftly. By contrast, Thomas Connor and Philip Moss Walmsley both married exceptionally wealthy second wives. For these two fortune hunters, there were greater financial benefits, and less risk, in maintaining the relationship with their second spouse. More recently, William Allen Jordan, described as '[a]n inveterate exploiter of vulnerable women', maintained relationships with different spouses and partners simultaneously while conning them out of substantial sums of money.

[1] *OBP*, 19 April 1721 (Robert Booth – alias Browne, alias Buckley, alias Bowyer, alias Bromley, alias Bartue, alias Brooks, alias Bruce, alias Butler, alias Bartey, alias Thomas Bartlet).

[2] *OBP*, 27 February 1718 (Hugh Coleman).

[3] 'A Modern Bluebeard', *Morning Chronicle*, 8 March 1858.

[4] Subsequently commuted to life imprisonment: TNA, *Prison Registers and Statistical Returns*, HO24/17. For the details of his case, see 'The Man With Twelve Wives', *The Standard*, 13 March 1858; *OBP*, 5 April 1858.

All these cases, unsurprisingly, involved a degree of deception. But for my final group of 'fraudsters', I have chosen three where the deception practised was linked to the bigamy but went beyond the lies designed to inveigle the other party into the marriage. For Hugh Titus Crawford, it was a complex deception to obtain money from the family of the woman he was planning to marry. For Barbara Wilson, it was an attempt to secure her position after her bigamous husband's death. And for Alexander Borromeo, it was an entirely separate scam that led to his previous bigamy being discovered – showing how any publicity was bad for bigamists.

'An Idle Kind of a Slut': Mary Stokes, 1692 and 1693

At the Old Bailey in December 1693, Mary Stokes stood accused of bigamy. It was not her first time. Only the previous year she had been tried and convicted of marrying William Carter while her first husband Thomas Adams was still alive. Both husbands had been in court, and the proof against her had been very clear. It was also noted that she had changed her surname to Elliot, and 'gave out that she was a maid, and had an estate; all which was look'd upon to be a cheat'.[5]

At her second trial, Mary claimed she had been told that her previous bigamy conviction meant 'she might safely marry another husband'.[6] But her behaviour was hardly consistent with that of someone who had genuinely believed they had a right to remarry. The only possible point in her favour was that her latest wedding had taken place in the same church as her first. But the church in question was St James', Duke's Place, which was notorious for the number of marriages that it conducted. The chances of the incumbent recognising her from five years earlier were very slim. More damningly, she had stayed with her latest husband just one night, and had 'run away in the morning'. That, it seemed, was part of a pattern: it now emerged that she had remained with her first husband Thomas for only eight days after their wedding. And there had also, it transpired, been yet another husband, making four in five years. As the report in the *Proceedings* concluded, 'it appeared, that she was an idle kind of a slut, for she would get what money she could of them, and then run away from them'. The jury found her guilty.

After her first conviction, Mary had been able to plead 'benefit of clergy' – an archaic privilege that allowed those who were literate to escape the death penalty. She had been lucky that this had been available to her: it was only two years since the law had been changed to allow women to plead this on the same terms as men.[7] But it was a privilege that was available only once. Her second conviction meant that she was sentenced to hang – the last bigamist upon whom such a sentence was recorded in the *Proceedings*.

'The Whole of the Money was Lost': Thomas Connor, 1846

In the summer of 1846, Thomas Connor and his wife Mary were walking arm-in-arm through Holborn when they suddenly encountered Thomas' first wife Maria – who

[5] *OBP*, 31 August 1692.
[6] *OBP*, 6 December 1692.
[7] Benefit of Clergy Act 1691, s 6; see further *Double Trouble*, ch 2

immediately claimed Thomas as her husband. Thomas attempted to laugh it off as a joke, but a friend of Mary's happened to come by and thought fit to communicate these details to her father, William Carr Burt. He took the matter extremely seriously and, having ascertained the details of Thomas' two marriages, instigated a prosecution for bigamy.[8]

At the Clerkenwell police station, it was established that Thomas had married Maria in 1839.[9] Maria was the daughter of a respectable tradesman, but the couple had run into financial difficulties and had been obliged to separate to enable Thomas to resume his former role as a tutor.[10] At the start of 1843, while he was working at an establishment in Twickenham, he met Miss Mary Carr Burt, then in London on a visit to her uncle.[11] Thomas paid his addresses to her, representing himself as a bachelor, and the pair agreed to marry when Mary turned 21 and would inherit certain property.

As Mary later admitted, they had 'lived together' before the marriage. It is easy to see why Thomas would have wanted to persuade her to do this, since it would have made it far harder for her to back out of their engagement. During that time, her sister heard a rumour that Thomas had been married before, but he denied it. He went so far as to take Mary and her sister to meet the woman who was supposed to be his wife. Who this woman was is unclear,[12] but she came to their wedding at Marylebone church on 27 June 1843.[13]

Mary brought to the marriage £2,600 in cash and £400-worth of silver plate and furniture, which Thomas invested in a fur business. They lived together for three years, having a house in the country and two servants. This standard of living, it seems, was not quite as stylish as Mary would have liked: when allusion was later made to Thomas sharing her money with her, her tart response was, 'I do not know that; I think he shared the better half.'[14] In the meantime, Thomas continued to visit Maria, but omitted to tell her that he had remarried.[15]

At the Central Criminal Court in July 1846, counsel for the prosecution described the case as 'one of the most heartless' that he had ever come across. Thomas' counsel protested that it was not *quite* that bad, but the best he could say by way of mitigating Thomas' offence was that he had continued to live with 'the unfortunate young lady' and that the money had been 'expended for their joint support' rather than being simply squandered. Upon being recalled for further questions, Mary confirmed that the fur business had proved unsuccessful and that 'the whole of the money was lost', with not

[8] According to various newspaper reports, Maria herself assisted the process by sending her marriage certificate to Mr Burt: see eg 'Clerkenwell: Bigamy', *Globe*, 27 June 1846.

[9] Ancestry, *London Church of England Parish Registers*, P69/AND2/A/01/MS 6672/9 (marriage at St Andrew's, Holborn).

[10] 'Clerkenwell: Bigamy', *Globe*, 27 June 1846; 'Clerkenwell: Bigamy', *Sun*, 27 June 1846.

[11] 'Clerkenwell: Bigamy', *Morning Herald*, 27 June 1846.

[12] On first reading the account of Thomas' trial in the *Proceedings*, I had assumed that the woman in question was in fact Maria, and that she had deliberately denied her marriage to Thomas as part of a joint scam, but the newspaper coverage of the proceedings before the magistrates make it clear that she was not aware of his remarriage.

[13] Ancestry, *London Church of England Parish Registers*, P89/MRY1/214.

[14] *OBP*, 6 July 1846.

[15] 'Clerkenwell: Bigamy', *London Evening Standard*, 27 June 1846.

a single shilling remaining, and that her other goods had been seized to pay Thomas' debts.[16]

The jury having found Thomas guilty, the Common Serjeant had to decide on the appropriate punishment. He told Thomas that 'it had long been his opinion that the offence of bigamy had been too leniently dealt with' and that, in his view, there was 'no crime that was the means of inflicting more misery upon its victim, and also upon society at large'.[17] Taking into account Mary's age, innocence and wealth, he sentenced him to the maximum possible – seven years' transportation.[18]

Thomas was neither the first nor the last financially exploitative bigamist to be sentenced to transportation.[19] That said, such sentences were becoming rarer, at least when viewed as a percentage of those convicted. Between 1805 and 1836, 26 per cent of convicted bigamists were sentenced to be transported, but between 1837 and the cessation of the practice in 1853 that figure was just 7 per cent.[20] Those cases deemed serious enough to justify a sentence of transportation tended to have multiple aggravating factors: the ill-treatment of one or both spouses, the abandonment of the second spouse, and sometimes a whole sequence of bigamous marriages. Thomas' defence counsel was correct in noting that his case was not as heartless as some.[21]

'That Villainous Man': Philip Moss Walmsley, 1854

So often when reading a bigamy trial, I start to wonder what the people involved looked like. Early newspaper accounts tended to be sparing with such details, illustrations were rare, and photographs only included from the 1880s. Reports of the assizes focused on the key details of the case rather than on such flummeries as dress or appearance. But news stories were often more illuminating. And in the case of Philip Moss Walmsley, the press seem to have been obsessed with his luxuriant black beard and curling (if not positively twirling) moustache.[22] He was essentially a pantomime Victorian villain – and not just in his looks.

Philip's first marriage, to Margaret Hulme Munns, had taken place in 1840, when he was just 19 and she a year or so younger. Their daughter, Margaret Ann, was baptised in September 1841, and a son, Philip, followed in 1843. Their nurse described them as

[16] 'Central Criminal Court', *Globe*, 7 July 1846; 'Bigamy', *Daily News*, 7 July 1846; 'Central Criminal Court', *Sun*, 7 July 1846.

[17] 'Bigamy', *Daily News*, 7 July 1846.

[18] *OBP*, 6 July 1846.

[19] He remained in prison in England until 1849, when he was finally sent to Australia on the *Randolph* convict ship, arriving in Sydney four months later: TNA, *Convicts transported*, HO11/16.

[20] The fall in the number of bigamists being sentenced to transportation is explored further in *Double Trouble*, ch 7, and in R Probert and L D'Arcy-Brown, 'The transportation of bigamists in early nineteenth century England and Wales' (2019) 40 *Journal of Legal History* 223.

[21] Mary, it should be noted, did not wait long to remarry. On 13 September 1846, at St George's church in Bloomsbury, she tied the knot with one John O'Connor – who, in an intriguing twist, just so happened to be Thomas' brother: Ancestry, *London Church of England Parish Registers*, P82/GEO1/031. As her previous marriage to Thomas was void, her marriage to his brother was not within the prohibited degrees (on which see further chapter 10).

[22] 'Central Criminal Court', *London Evening Standard*, 4 December 1854; 'Central Criminal Court', *Daily News*, 5 December 1854; 'Bigamy' *Bristol Mirror*, 9 December 1854.

'two beautiful children', the son being 'the image' of his father, or, as one newspaper less flatteringly reported, 'the image of that villainous man'.[23]

Not that Philip would have known what his son looked like, as an unspecified 'act of dishonesty' had led to his own father sending him out to India.[24] The *East-India Register and Army List* for 1844 records Philip Moss Walmsley as an Ensign in the Sixteenth Regiment of Bengal Native Infantry, stationed in Etawah in present-day Uttar Pradesh. Later editions of the *Register* record him as having been promoted to Lieutenant in 1845, serving in Barrackpore and then Benares. On 13 November 1849, however, he was tried by a General Court Martial at Fort William in Calcutta, charged with 'highly unbecoming conduct, and abuse of his authority'. The charge concerned events that had taken place in the town of Patna earlier that year. On the evening of 15 May, he had been involved in what was referred to as a 'disturbance' – reading between the lines, some kind of drunken punch-up – during which two of his friends had been arrested and locked up in the police station. Philip had then commanded a 'large portion' of his regiment to march into the town, bayonets at the ready, with the view of liberating them. He had compounded his culpability by breaking his subsequent arrest in travelling from Barrackpore to Calcutta without leave 'in direct disobedience of Station Orders, and of the orders of the Officer commanding the Regiment'. He was found guilty, and cashiered.[25]

His Army career having come to an ignominious end, he returned to England – but not to Margaret, whom he had neglected for some time. The 1851 census records her and their two children living with her mother, who subsequently gave evidence that Philip had not provided any support 'for many years', other than a one-off payment of £25.[26] Philip was also in financial difficulties at this time – as is evident from his appearance at the Central Criminal Court in July 1851, charged with stealing 23 spoons and seven forks from the home of Joseph Lavies.[27] Joseph was in fact an old friend whom Philip had been visiting, and, as his counsel explained, he had taken the flatware in a 'moment of excitement' in order to help him out of some temporary difficulties.[28] Joseph had no wish to press the charges, and Philip was acquitted.

A more lucrative – and potentially less risky – opportunity then presented itself. Philip became acquainted with a wealthy young woman, 23-year-old Augusta Annie Lewis, who was entitled to around £10,000 from her father's estate and a further £1,200 from her mother. With 'the help of the beard and moustache', as one newspaper commented, he soon captured her heart.[29] Before the wedding took place, he took the precaution of entering into an agreement with Margaret to allow her a small annuity in return for her promising not to molest or make any inquiries concerning him.[30] Philip and Augusta were then 'married' at St George's, Ramsgate,

[23] *OBP*, 27 November 1854; 'Gross Case of Bigamy', *Blackburn Standard*, 13 December 1854.

[24] 'Central Criminal Court', *Daily News*, 4 December 1854; *OBP*, 27 November 1854.

[25] *East-India Register and Army Lists for 1844, 1849, 1850*; *Records of the Indian command of General Sir Charles James Napier, G.C.B.* (Calcutta, RC Lepage & Co, 1851) 69.

[26] TNA, 1851 census, HO107/1479, folio 236, p 6.

[27] *OBP*, 7 July 1851.

[28] He had pawned them for 25 shillings: *Reynolds's*, 22 June 1851.

[29] *Daily News*, 5 December 1854.

[30] 'Central Criminal Court', *Morning Herald*, 4 December 1854.

on 11 May 1853.[31] It seems, however, that he was rather too keen to get his hands on the money. Suspicions were raised, enquiries were set in train, and the existence of the first Mrs Walmsley and her two children was discovered (although not before Philip had managed to squander around £3,000 of his bride's fortune).[32]

At the Central Criminal Court, Philip apparently cut an elegant figure in the dock, where he stood 'gracefully, easily, as though his polished boots glistened on the softest velvet rugs of Belgravia'.[33] But there was no doubt as to the outcome. Even his counsel admitted that there was no point in struggling against the evidence, although he did try to make the most out of the fact that neither Margaret nor Augusta had been responsible for bringing the prosecution.[34] Philip was convicted and sentenced to two years' imprisonment, with the Recorder expressing some doubts as to whether he was 'performing his duty to the public in not inflicting a more severe sentence'.[35]

Various commentators thought the sentence should definitely have been more severe – especially given that the thief whose case followed Philip's was sentenced to four years' penal servitude for stealing some boots.[36] Indeed, Philip might well have got more than two years if he had been found guilty of stealing the spoons. As *Lloyd's Weekly Newspaper* put it:

> How small is the property value of a woman's maiden honour and peace of mind! To steal forty shillings from a woman's person is to have seven years' imprisonment; to steal a woman's person itself, is to get quit with less than a third of the punishment, The moral of this to scoundrels is, – you may steal and break a woman's heart, but keep your hands out of a woman's pocket.[37]

The Italian Conference Imposter: Alexander Borromeo, 1858

In March 1858, newspapers around the country reported on a Conference of Italian delegates meeting in London to discuss the possibility of the country's various constitutional states coming together in some form of union.[38] It was a particularly hot topic in light of the recent attempt on the life of Napoleon III in Paris by Italian nationalists, which the Conference roundly condemned. Chaired by a man named Borromeo, virtually every day there was something new to report from the Italian

[31] *OBP*, 27 November 1854.
[32] 'Serious Charge of Bigamy', *The Era*, 12 November 1854.
[33] 'Woman and Her Robber', *Lloyd's Weekly Newspaper*, 10 December 1854.
[34] 'Central Criminal Court', *London Evening Standard*, 4 December 1854.
[35] 'Central Criminal Court', *Morning Herald*, 4 December 1854.
[36] *Daily News*, 5 December 1854.
[37] 'Woman and Her Robber', *Lloyd's Weekly Newspaper*, 10 December 1854.
[38] The following is just a small selection to show the geographical reach of the story and the range of newspapers that reported it: 'Conference of Delegates from Italy', *Suffolk Chronicle*, 6 March 1858; 'Meeting of the Italian Constitutional Party in London', *Caernarvon & Denbigh Herald*, 6 March 1858; 'Freedom of Italy', *Dundee, Perth and Cupar Advertiser*, 9 March 1858; 'An Italian Conference in London', *Scarborough Mercury*, 13 March 1838; 'The Italian Constitutional League', *Dorset County Express and Agricultural Gazette*, 16 March 1858.

Conference – letters from supporters, an address to monarchs and statesmen across Europe, discussions between delegates, and criticism of the silence of other Italian refugees as regards the attempted assassination.[39]

But it soon emerged that the Italian Conference was a complete invention.[40] The *British Standard*, preening itself on not having been taken in, noted that if all the papers that published reports of the supposed Conference had paid for the copy supplied to them, the writer would have received a sum of around £60 to £70.[41] The proprietors of the duped *Morning Star* immediately applied for a summons against their correspondent, who just so happened to be Borromeo himself, and a warrant was issued for his arrest.[42] Over the next few weeks the press speculated as to Borromeo's whereabouts, but in May he was eventually discovered lecturing in Reading on the pseudoscientific field of 'electro-biology', of all things.[43] He was taken before the magistrates at Bow Street, charged with obtaining money by false pretences, and committed for trial at the Middlesex quarter sessions.

At his trial a few days later, among the witnesses giving evidence of his authorship of the fake news reports was a young woman named Henrietta Shelley. There was some question as to whether she was his wife, but counsel for the prosecution told the court that although Henrietta had been under the impression that she was Alexander's legal wife, no legal ceremony of marriage had taken place between them. As Henrietta herself explained:

> It was in my mother's drawing room and there was no one present except ourselves. He said he was a count of the Holy Roman Empire and as such could not enter a Protestant church but that his word made me his wife.[44]

Since she was not his wife, there was no bar to her giving evidence against him. Borromeo was duly convicted, and sentenced to a year's hard labour in the House of Correction.

Counsel for the prosecution then revealed Borromeo's true identity. He was the son of Irish parents – which explained the 'heavy Irish brogue' noted by many journalists when he was first brought before the magistrates.[45] His real name, as he had previously admitted before the magistrates, was Tucker, but he had become acquainted with the Borromeo family in Milan and assumed their name. And in addition to his 'cruel and heartless' conduct to the deceived Henrietta, there was now a charge of triple bigamy against him.[46]

As this well illustrates, any light of publicity could be bad news for bigamists. Borromeo's first wife, Mary Ann, had spotted the name Tucker in the newspaper reports

[39] 'The Italian Constitutionalists', *The Globe*, 3 March 1858; 'The Adjourned Meeting of Italian Delegates', *London Evening Standard*, 4 March 1858; 'Conference of Italian Delegates', *Sun*, 6 March 1858; 'Conference of Italian Delegates', *London Evening Standard*, 9 March 1858; 'Conference of Italian Delegates', *Morning Advertiser*, 10 March 1858; 'Conference of Italian Delegates', *Morning Advertiser*, 12 March 1858.

[40] 'The Pretended Italian Conferences', *Daily News*, 16 March 1858.

[41] 'The Italian Conferences', *British Standard*, 19 March 1858.

[42] 'Bow Street', *The Globe*, 25 March 1858.

[43] 'The Italian Conference Hoax', *The Globe*, 13 May 1858.

[44] 'Middlesex Sessions: The Italian Conference Imposter', *Daily News*, 21 May 1858.

[45] 'The "Italian Conference" Hoax', *The Globe*, 13 May 1858.

[46] 'The Pretended Italian Conferences', *The Examiner*, 22 May 1858.

of the committal proceedings. She had then identified Borromeo as the man she had married in 1842 under the name Charles Tucker de St Hilaire, and who had deserted her in around 1846. Upon further investigation, it transpired that in 1847 he had gone through a second ceremony with an Anna Maria Froggatt at Gretna Green. She had been visiting friends in Preston when she became acquainted with him, this time passing as a Frenchman named Marco Emile de St Hilaire. Their daughter Madeleine was born in March 1849,[47] but in 1851 he had moved on again, leaving Anna and Madeleine behind.[48] In 1853 he was in Sligo, where he met and married Margaret Murray, this time under the name of Alessandro Borromeo. He stayed with her for almost three years, during which time she bore him a child. But then he had left her too, this time on the pretext that he would be better able to earn money elsewhere.[49]

Given the necessity of proving marriages in different parts of the United Kingdom, bringing a prosecution was likely to be expensive and time-consuming. At this point, the Associate Institution for Improving and Enforcing the Laws for the Protection of Women stepped in. Its prosecuting officer, Henry Allen, personally travelled to Gretna Green and Sligo to gather the necessary evidence.

At his trial at the Central Criminal Court, Alexander embarked on a very lengthy defence. He denied having married Mary Ann, claiming that he was in Paris at the time. He also denied ever having seen Anna Maria prior to the hearing in front of the magistrates. He claimed that the case against him, like the previous charge for false pretences, was the result of a conspiracy. Despite these vehement denials, the jury had no hesitation in finding him guilty. The Common Serjeant, having sentenced him to four years' penal servitude and reproved his conduct in no uncertain terms, was willing to order all the usual costs to be paid, and commended this as 'a very proper prosecution'.[50]

Alexander's conviction meant that his various wives could finally move on with their lives. Mary Ann was able to divorce him,[51] and Anna Maria and Margaret were free, no longer left wondering what had happened to the man they had married. But perhaps the most astonishing aspect of his case is how quickly his various marriages were discovered once his original name was made public. Given the distance between his bigamous marriages, and the different aliases he had adopted, he might otherwise never have been caught.

The Captain, the Actress, and the Suppositious Heir: Mrs Wilson, 1862

Around midnight on 12 July 1860, a man might have been observed entering a house in Charlwood Street in Pimlico, carrying a bundle. The following morning, the household woke to the news that the lady lodging there, a Mrs Wilson, had been confined during

[47] Ancestry, *Yorkshire Church of England Baptisms, 1813–1923*, PR138/2/32.
[48] *OBP*, 16 August 1858.
[49] ibid.
[50] 'Central Criminal Court', *Morning Chronicle*, 17 August 1858.
[51] *Daily News*, 20 July 1861.

the night and had given birth to a son.[52] The gender of the baby was of considerable significance. Mrs Wilson's husband, Captain Wilson – or, to give him his full name, William Rokeby Langham Hazelriggs Le Hunte Wilson – was a wealthy man, his family estate in Gloucestershire worth around £5,000 per year.[53] The estate was, however, 'entailed', which meant that William had only a life interest. Upon his death, it would pass to the next male heir – who, in the absence of a legitimate son, would be William's younger brother John. But the baby who had made such a fortuitous appearance was not the son of Captain Wilson. He was not even the son of Mrs Wilson. And there was also, as it later transpired, a question mark over the marital status of 'Mrs' Wilson.

She had been born Barbara Catherine Ann Morris in 1826. In 1857 she was employed as an actress in a small theatre in Northampton. It was here that she met William, then a captain in the Northamptonshire militia, who happened to be quartered there with his regiment. He was immediately smitten with her, and she 'confessed' to him that she was the widow of a Captain Gordon, whose death had left her in straitened circumstances, compelling her to take to the stage to support herself.[54]

Whether there had ever been a Captain Gordon in Barbara's life is unclear, but she does not appear to have married anyone of that name. Nor did she believe herself to be a widow. When she visited her younger sister Rhoda to announce that she was going to be married to William, Rhoda's first question was, 'What will you do with Jonathan?' – to which Barbara had responded, 'He is all right; he is in America.'[55] The Jonathan in question was Jonathan Gotobed, whom Barbara had married some 10 years earlier.[56]

Regardless of this impediment, her wedding to William went ahead at St Pancras parish church in January 1858, with Barbara signing the register as Barbara Catherine Howard Morris Gotobed Gordon.[57] Our knowledge of their early married life comes from a young woman named Frances Earle, who went to live with Barbara as a paid companion in March of the same year. There came one day a nasty moment for Barbara when she was out in the carriage with William and Frances and suddenly spotted Jonathan. William, observing his wife's changing countenance, asked her who he was. Barbara told him that it was 'an old admirer'. When William turned away, Barbara confided in a whisper to Frances that it was in fact her husband.[58]

In January 1860, William's mental health deteriorated and he was admitted to the brand-new Barnwood House asylum near Gloucester, where he was to remain for some months.[59] During his absence, Barbara hatched an audacious plan. Her older sister Amelia – whom she was employing as a cook – was several months pregnant. If the child proved to be a boy, Barbara would pass it off as her own. As mother of the supposed heir,

[52] 'Extraordinary Charge of Conspiracy', *Western Daily Press*, 15 April 1861.

[53] 'Extraordinary Charge of Conspiracy', *Hereford Journal*, 17 April 1861.

[54] 'An Actress in the Divorce Court', *Birmingham Daily Post*, 8 June 1874.

[55] *OBP*, 16 June 1862.

[56] The wedding of Jonathan Gotobed and Barbara had taken place on 22 August 1848, at St Helen's Chapel, Billericay, Essex, according to the rites and ceremonies of the Roman Catholic Church: *OBP*, 16 June 1862.

[57] Ancestry, *London Church of England Parish Registers*, P90/PAN1/119 (marriage at St Pancras parish church, 12 January 1858).

[58] *OBP*, 16 June 1862.

[59] TNA, *Commissioners in Lunacy, 1845–1913. Lunacy Patients Admission Registers*, MH 94/17. William was admitted on 14 January and discharged on 21 August 1860.

she would be in a far better position in the event of her husband's death, especially given that William's family were not particularly happy about his marriage to her.

Upon Amelia giving birth to a son on 1 April, the plan was put into action. Barbara and Frances immediately left Gloucestershire for Ireland, and a couple of months later took lodgings in Charlwood Street in London. There Barbara told the landlady that she was pregnant and expected to be confined very soon. On 12 July she declared herself to be unwell and remained in her room. At this point a telegram was dispatched to Gloucestershire asking Amelia and her husband Charles to bring some baby linen and a bassinet. They duly did so – but they also brought the son to whom Amelia had given birth some months earlier.

Upon their arrival, Frances met them at the station and took them to a coffee house. There Charles waited with the baby until almost midnight, so that he could be smuggled upstairs to Barbara's room after the rest of the household had gone to bed. The 'doctor' in attendance then announced in the morning that Barbara had given birth to 'a fine boy'.[60] After a suitable period for Barbara to recover, she and Frances returned to Gloucestershire, to general rejoicing at the birth of the heir.

The obvious flaw in the plan was that the already four-month-old baby was far too large to pass as newly born, as various astute observers noted.[61] The other weak link was Frances. Before long she had left Barbara's employment and told the rest of William's family everything that had happened. Barbara was duly arrested and charged with unlawfully conspiring with Charles and Amelia to 'falsely and fraudulently' pass off their son as that of her and William in order to defraud William's brother.[62] After some discussion, the magistrates resolved that she should be sent for trial at the Central Criminal Court.[63] In the event, she was never tried on the charge of conspiracy. The case was first postponed (on account of the absence of Charles and Amelia, who had strategically absconded) and then seems not to have been pursued.[64]

In the meantime, William's family also instigated proceedings against Barbara for bigamy.[65] Evidence of her marriage to Jonathan Gotobed was provided, and the case against her seemed clear. But when she was re-examined in November, her defence counsel dropped a bombshell, claiming that Jonathan was himself already married at the time of his marriage to Barbara.[66] If so, that would have made their marriage void and left her free to marry William. At her subsequent trial, a witness spoke of seeing Jonathan in Canada in the 1840s, with a woman whom he had introduced as his wife, and who was still alive when Jonathan had married Barbara in 1848. At this point, the judge, Mr Justice Crompton, intervened to ask whether counsel for the prosecution still wanted to press the case, noting that, even if there might be some 'technical difficulty' in proving that Jonathan had married in Canada, 'if there was reasonable doubt of the

[60] 'Extraordinary Investigation: The False Heir', *Morning Chronicle*, 15 April 1851; 'Extraordinary Charge of Conspiracy', *Hereford Journal*, 17 April 1861; 'Serious Charge of Conspiracy', *Potter's Electric News*, 17 April 1861.

[61] 'Extraordinary Charge of Conspiracy', *Hereford Journal*, 17 April 1861.

[62] 'Extraordinary Charge of Conspiracy', *Western Daily Press*, 15 April 1861.

[63] This was a possibility following the Central Criminal Court Act 1856.

[64] 'Law and Police', *John Bull*, 15 June 1861.

[65] 'The Police Courts', *Daily News*, 30 October 1861.

[66] 'The Late Charge of Bigamy', *Standard*, 18 November 1861.

fact, the defendant ought to be absolved from a charge like the present'.[67] The jury, upon being asked their view of the case, concurred that it was unnecessary to hear any further evidence, and returned a verdict of not guilty.

William had stood by Barbara when she had first been arrested, even being willing to put up the money so that she could be bailed. But at some point they separated. In 1873, William, now living in Paris, sought a decree of nullity. His petition gave no hint of the turbulent history of their marriage, simply reciting the date of their wedding and that of Barbara's earlier wedding to Jonathan. The court declared William 'to have been and to be free from all Bond of Marriage' with Barbara on the ground that she was the lawful wife of Jonathan Gotobed.[68] The question of whether or not Jonathan already had a wife living when he married Barbara was not raised. As can often be the case, two courts with differing standards of proof and different evidence before them had come to different conclusions.

The Enigma of Gloucester Gale, 1859 and 1873

Of all the bigamists I have studied, Gloucester Gale remains the most enigmatic. At no point did he offer any explanation for his extraordinary conduct, simply pleading guilty at both of his trials. His motivation does not appear to have been financial – indeed, he insisted that any money his latest bride-to-be might have should be settled on her. It may have been sexual, but the sheer amount of effort – and admin – involved in his swift succession of bigamous marriages suggests that there was something more than this.

Gloucester's first marriage was in 1849, to his cousin Eliza Cecilia Gee.[69] The 1851 census found them living together in Westminster,[70] but they moved around quite a lot over the next few years.[71] In November 1857, he went through a bigamous ceremony of marriage with Celia Maria Wye, who was apparently possessed of around £1,600, adopting the alias George Garden.[72] After this the weddings came thick and fast: Lydia Murch in January 1858,[73] Sarah Ann Drewett in May,[74] Martha Gover in July[75] and Fanny Terrall in August,[76] each in a different London church and with a different alias.

[67] *R v Wilson* (1862) 3 F & F 119; 176 ER 53.

[68] TNA, *Divorce and Matrimonial Causes Files*, J77/139/2993.

[69] Ancestry, *London Church of England Parish Registers*, DRO/079/008 (marriage at Christ Church, Turnham Green, 11 January 1849). In the marriage register he was described as a 'gentleman', as was his father Charles.

[70] TNA, 1851 census, HO 107/1510, folio 528, p 12. Gloucester was recorded as 'Annuitant (Gentleman)'.

[71] Eliza's subsequent divorce petition gives details of their living in Brentford and Acton and at several different addresses within Middlesex: TNA, *Divorce and Matrimonial Causes Files*, J77/20/G55.

[72] Ancestry, *London Church of England Parish Registers*, P83/MRY1/1223 (marriage at St Mary, Islington, 30 November 1857).

[73] Ancestry, *London Church of England Parish Registers*, P74/TRI/013 (marriage at Holy Trinity, Chelsea, 3 January 1858, as George Thomas, first mate in the merchant services).

[74] Ancestry, *Westminster Church of England Parish Registers*, STG/PR/7/47 (marriage at St George, Hanover Square, 3 May 1858, as George Geer, mariner).

[75] Ancestry, *London Church of England Parish Registers*, P89/ALS/065 (marriage at All Souls, Langham Place, 13 July 1858, as Edward Swain, mariner).

[76] Ancestry, *London Church of England Parish Registers*, P92/SAV/3059 (marriage at St Saviour, Southwark, 17 August 1858, as Edward Gordon, sailor).

Gloucester might have thought he was being clever in pretending to be a seafarer – as he did for his marriages to Lydia, Sarah Ann, Martha and Fanny. It gave him the perfect excuse for his absences. It was, however, to prove his undoing. The suspicions of Mr Coleman, the clerk to the Registrar General of Seamen, were raised when several women, including Sarah Ann, came to his office in Adelaide Row making inquiries after their husband or fiancé, whose initials were almost always 'GG'.

Mr Coleman, together with Sarah Ann, went to the Lord Mayor. At this point, Sarah Ann did not know whether she was Gloucester's legal wife or not, but given the evidence of his activities in marrying or proposing to other women, she certainly wanted to expose him, not least in order to put other women on their guard. The Lord Mayor promised to do everything he could 'to bring such a vile wretch to justice',[77] and the matter was placed in the hands of the City police. Several more women came forward upon learning of the investigation. It took Inspector Leonard and Detective Constable Green two months to track Gloucester down. But eventually, on Sunday 19 December 1858, he was arrested in Egham, at the home of his second wife. She was at church when the police arrived, but he left her a letter saying, 'My sins have overtaken me at last, speak a good word for me.'[78]

There is no evidence that she, or any of Gloucester's other wives, said anything in his favour. At the Clerkenwell Police Court the following day, each simply gave the bare facts of the date of the ceremony, the alias he had used, and the time he had spent with them.[79] Here it emerged that he had managed to maintain relationships with several of his wives simultaneously. He had never actually left his first wife – who, believing him to be a traveller, had taken his lengthy absences from home for granted and had 'never had the most remote suspicion of his marrying anyone else'.[80] His second wife, Celia, thought him to be a collector for a large mercantile house and was similarly unsurprised by his absences. Lydia reported that he had left her on the pretence of going on a voyage in February 1858, but that they had spent another week or 10 days together in April. The final three wives, by contrast, all reported that he had left them shortly after the wedding – spending a week with Martha, five days with Sarah Ann, and just one day with Fanny. It was also reported that he had recorded all his matrimonial transactions in a pocket memorandum book that was found on his person. He might otherwise have found it difficult to keep track: as the book recorded,

[77] 'Mansion House: Caution to Unmarried Ladies', *Morning Herald*, 28 October 1858. The proceedings, which included a detailed physical description of Gale, were widely reported around the country with headlines including 'Systematic Bigamy', *Liverpool Mercury*, 29 October 1858; 'A Wholesale Bigamist', 30 October 1858; 'An Extraordinary Villain', *Derby Mercury*, 3 November 1858; 'Simple-minded ladies and an accomplished villain', *Belfast Morning News*, 3 November 1858; 'A Matrimonial Miscreant', *Elgin Courier*, 5 November 1858; and 'Ladies Beware!', *Derbyshire Advertiser and Journal*, 5 November 1858.

[78] 'Assize intelligence', *The Sun*, 24 December 1858.

[79] More or less identical reports appeared in a number of London newspapers under the alternative headings of 'The Husband of Many Wives' and 'Apprehension of a Notorious Polygamist': *Morning Post*, 21 December 1858; *Morning Herald*, 21 December 1858; *London Evening Standard*, 21 December 1858; *The Sun*, 21 December 1858; *St James' Chronicle*, 21 December 1858; *The Globe*, 21 December 1858. The story was quickly taken up around the country: 'A Heartless Polygamist', *Northern Daily Times*, 22 December 1858; 'The Bloodless Blue Beard', *Newcastle Daily Chronicle*, 23 December 1858; 'A Frequent Visitor to the Hymeneal Altar', *Suffolk Chronicle*, 24 December 1858; 'A Marrying Scoundrel', *Belfast Morning News*, 24 December 1858; 'A Husband with Six Living Wives', *Dundee, Perth and Cupar Advertiser*, 24 December 1858.

[80] 'The Husband of Many Wives', *Morning Chronicle*, 21 December 1858.

on one single Sunday banns were proclaimed in three different churches for three different marriages.[81]

At his subsequent trial at the Central Criminal Court in January 1859, Gloucester pleaded guilty to all five counts of bigamy and, in a faint voice, 'begged for mercy on account of his illness and the trouble he had undergone'.[82] Counsel for the prosecution, who had been instructed by the same organisation that had established the case against Borromeo, then set out the facts in aggravation of punishment – which really spoke for themselves. All that counsel for the defence could plead in mitigation was that Gloucester had not appropriated the £1,600 belonging to his second wife but had made it over to her so that she would have the benefit of it.[83] The Recorder told Gloucester that it would be 'useless' to talk to him, given his conduct, and sentenced him to four years' penal servitude.[84] As one newspaper rejoiced, this would 'prevent the possibility of his "rewiving" – at least for some years to come'.[85]

In the event, it was less than four years before Gloucester married again. Having been released early from prison,[86] within six months he had gone through a ceremony of marriage with one Lavinia Bannister, using the name of William Briant.[87] Their daughter, Honour – named after Gale's mother – was born a year or so later.

It is possible that this was a legal marriage. While Gloucester was in prison, Eliza, his first wife, had petitioned for divorce, with the decree *nisi* having been granted in February 1862.[88] There would have been plenty of time for the divorce to have been finalised before Gloucester's September wedding to Lavinia, the waiting period being then only three months.[89] But a divorce was not automatic after that period had passed: application had to be made for the decree to be made absolute. The cover of Eliza's divorce petition does not state exactly when the decree absolute was granted, but the final year mentioned is 1863.[90] If that was when the divorce was finalised, Gloucester had committed bigamy yet again.

[81] 'Gale, the Wholesale Bigamist', *Weekly Mail*, 2 January 1859.

[82] *The Sun*, 5 January 1859. *The North British Daily Mail*, 12 January 1859, contemptuously described him as 'whimpering'.

[83] He had also, when before the magistrate, acknowledged that he had 'several little articles belonging to the young ladies which he should like to be given up to them' ('Committal of the man with seven wives', *St James's Chronicle*, 1 January 1859). His offer to return these items was presumably intended to curry favour, but the fact he had collected them in the first place has unfortunate overtones of the trophies retained by stalkers and serial killers.

[84] 'Central Criminal Court This Day', *The Globe*, 5 January 1859; *OBP*, 3 January 1859. Gale was sent first to Millbank, then Lewes, then Woking: TNA, *Metropolitan Police: Criminal Record Office: Habitual Criminals Registers and Miscellaneous Papers*, PCOM 2.

[85] 'Notes of the Week', *Francis's Metropolitan News*, 15 January 1859.

[86] He was released on licence on 31 March 1862.

[87] Ancestry, *Church of England Marriages and Banns, 1754-1936*, P69/ALH6/A/A/01/MS 17827/3 (marriage at All Hallows Staining, City of London, 14 September 1862).

[88] 'Bigamy Extraordinary', *The Era*, 16 February 1862. Perhaps surprisingly, Eliza's petition only mentioned one of Gale's bigamous marriages, that to Sarah Ann, and omitted any mention of his conviction altogether: TNA, *Divorce and Matrimonial Causes Files*, J77/20/G55. It might have been that she felt it unnecessary to add the others, or that this was the only one that she was able to show was followed by adultery. The case provides a warning against assuming that there was no prosecution simply because the petition did not mention it – on which see further *Double Trouble*, ch 8.

[89] Matrimonial Causes Act 1860, s 7.

[90] TNA, *Divorce and Matrimonial Causes Files*, J77/20/G55.

In the event, the status of that 1862 marriage was never called into question, as Lavinia's family discovered his true identity, including his past marriages and prison sentence.[91] One might have imagined that this would have been a red flag that would have impelled Lavinia to leave him. Instead, the pair went through a second ceremony, in 1864, with Gloucester using his real name for the first time since his first marriage.[92] The wedding took place at St Anne's, Soho, on 14 September 1864 – the second anniversary of their first ceremony, which at least avoided any confusion about when to celebrate their wedding anniversary. Two more children followed, Lavinia in 1865 and Charles Herbert in 1867, and the family was still intact at the time of the 1871 census.[93]

But in May 1871, less than a month after that census was taken, Gloucester, now calling himself William Morgan, went through what was at least his tenth wedding ceremony, with Mary Ann Furtado.[94] She had no idea of his past, only discovering that he was a married man when Lavinia, accompanied by her two daughters, came to the house and claimed Gloucester as her husband.[95] He was duly arrested and once again committed for trial at the Central Criminal Court.[96] There he again pleaded guilty.[97] This time he was sentenced to 10 years' penal servitude.

Given Gloucester's success rate in persuading so many women to marry him so quickly, the reader may have been picturing him as some kind of mid-Victorian sex god. But he was, according to the press, a slightly built man, of 'a somewhat sinister cast of countenance', with large sandy whiskers and a small moustache.[98] At the time of his initial committal hearing, he also had his arm in a sling and was walking with a limp. One journalist who had been present disparaged him as an 'insignificant-looking scamp' and wondered how 'so many women in such good stations of life could be thus deluded by an adventurer so destitute of all the attributes ordinarily looked upon as essential to success with womankind!'.[99]

The Scottish *North British Daily Mail* took the opportunity to muse at length on what it saw as the greater gullibility of the English, suggesting that Gloucester's apparent generosity with money had been an incentive. Here Gloucester's technique differed from that of more obviously mercenary bigamists. He never made the mistake of seeming too keen to get his hands on the women's money. Instead, he disarmed them by

[91] 'An Inveterate Bigamist', *London Evening Standard*, 6 February 1873.

[92] Ancestry, *Westminster Church of England Parish Registers*, STA/PR/4/21. Given that Gale had lived in this parish with his first wife, his remarriage is also a good example of how easy it was for those who had been divorced to get remarried in church as long as they did not acknowledge the prior marriage.

[93] Minus Charles, who had died in 1869, and with Gloucester recorded as William G Gale: TNA, 1871 census, RG10/123, folio 95, p 7.

[94] Ancestry, *London Church of England Parish Registers*, P84/BAN/005 (marriage at St Barnabas, Kensington, 1 May 1871).

[95] 'Extraordinary charge of bigamy', *The Globe*, 4 March 1873.

[96] Various newspapers produced a slightly garbled version of the story in which Gale had married his second wife before being freed from his first, and had been sent to prison for this offence before marrying a third time. Even this was enough for them to opine that he must have 'a decided penchant for that peculiar offence': 'Law and Police', *Illustrated London News*, 15 February 1873.

[97] *OBP*, 3 March 1873.

[98] 'The Husband of Many Wives', *Morning Post*, 21 December 1858.

[99] 'From Our London Correspondent', *Inverness Advertiser*, 11 January 1859. 'A Man After Brigham Young's Heart', *Leeds Times*, 24 December 1858.

insisting that it should be settled on them. As one young lady who had been due to marry him explained, Gloucester had appeared 'so honourable a man that nobody could doubt his word', telling her that he was very anxious for her property to be settled on her 'in case he should prove a bad husband'.[100] Above the resulting laughter, the Lord Mayor had commented cynically that it was 'only men of bad heart who commence in that strain'. And, of course, insisting that his wives should retain their own property did not preclude him from sharing the benefit of it. It was subsequently alleged by the detective who arrested him the second time around that Gloucester, aka 'Mr Morgan', had never done a day's work in his life but had lived on the resources of the women he had married.[101] The *Pall Mall Gazette* used this to have a dig at the women's movement:

> Woman asks nothing more than that she should be permitted to be the bread-winner of the household, and so far as Mr Morgan is concerned she evidently met with no opposition. Many advanced women also hold that marriage is simply a contract to be determined by either party at will. This, again, is entirely Mr Morgan's view; and yet for carrying it into practice, notwithstanding all he has probably suffered, he is shut up for ten years.[102]

As that illustrates, some commentators used Gloucester's case as a pretext to push their own agendas, whether anti-English or anti-feminist. It was, after all, something of a blank canvas, in the absence of any indication as to his motives. And the conclusion of Gloucester's story is also a tantalising blank. After his second trial, this master of aliases disappears from the records entirely.[103]

'A Credulous Widow and a Sham Detective': Hugh Titus Crawford, 1891

At the Central Criminal Court on 14 September 1891, a man going by the name of Hugh Titus Crawford pleaded guilty to two counts of bigamy. His sentence – five years' penal servitude – indicated that this was an exceptionally serious case, and the *Proceedings* noted that there was another indictment against him for unlawfully obtaining money from another woman by false pretences.[104] The fact that this woman had the same surname as one of his bigamous brides hinted that this case might have a complex backstory. Even so, the career of fraud and deception that was uncovered was truly astonishing.[105]

To start with, Hugh Titus Crawford was not his real name. Under the name of Thomas Henry Dillon, he had married a young woman named Sarah Elizabeth Saxby at

[100] 'Mansion House: Caution to Unmarried Ladies', *Morning Herald*, 28 October 1858.
[101] 'Extraordinary charge of bigamy', *The Globe*, 4 March 1873. He may have felt impelled to make this point because Gale had somewhat incongruously described himself as a labourer.
[102] *Pall Mall Gazette*, 5 March 1873.
[103] By the time of the 1881 census, his (second) legal wife Lavinia was describing herself as a widow (TNA, 1881 census, RG11/542, folio 59, p 28) but this may have been simply to avoid awkward questions about what had happened to her husband.
[104] *OBP*, 14 September 1891.
[105] The title of this case study is taken from a piece that appeared in one of the local newspapers: 'A Credulous Widow and a Sham Detective', *Norwood News*, 22 August 1891.

Scarborough in December 1879.[106] The pair were still together at the time of the 1881 census, lodging with Sarah's mother.[107] Two daughters were born to them, Alisa in October 1881 and Amy in January 1885. But in July 1885 he deserted them and came to London.[108] On 25 October 1886, he appeared at the Clerkenwell quarter sessions, under the name of James Arthur Dillon, and was sentenced to 18 months' imprisonment for attempted fraud.[109] After his release, in August 1888 he went through a ceremony of marriage at Hackney parish church with a domestic servant named Alice Mary Ann Adams, this time under the name of Hugh Thomas Douglas.[110] She subsequently gave evidence that she had left him in January 1890 on account of how badly he had treated her.[111] It was also alleged that there had been other robberies for which he had not been prosecuted.[112]

Most outlandish of all, however, was the scheme that he concocted as regards the Grosutt family. Jane Grosutt, a 57-year-old widow, had just taken over as the landlady of the Wheatsheaf public house, Portman Square, where Hugh used to drink occasionally.[113] Her oldest son William was in prison, having been sentenced to four months for embezzling from his employers. Upon learning of this, Hugh represented himself to Jane as Detective Inspector Arthur Hare.[114] He told her that the police had another warrant for William's arrest, for a more serious offence that would see him sent down for five or even 10 years' penal servitude. After thoroughly frightening the already worried Jane, he reassured her that he would be able to get William released, but that it would cost a lot of money.[115]

Two weeks later, he told Jane that he had 'formed a strong affection' for her daughter Florence and asked her if she would consent to their marriage. He represented himself as being a man of means, shortly due to inherit £49,000 in addition to his annual salary of £1,000. At the same time, he claimed that he was short of ready cash on account of the money he had expended on William's behalf, and asked Jane to lend him £25. Over the next couple of months, he showed her various telegrams purporting to come from various well-known figures, including the Home Secretary. The trusting Jane lent him further sums, amounting in total to £210. At one point he even pretended that he would be bringing William home that night, taking some of William's clothes with him, and Jane sat up until the early hours of the morning waiting – in vain – to see her son.[116]

[106] The marriage register described him as a butler: TNA, *Divorce and Matrimonial Causes Files*, J77/600/18343.

[107] TNA, 1881 census, RG11/4803, folio 33, p 19.

[108] TNA, *Divorce and Matrimonial Causes Files*, J77/600/18343.

[109] TNA, *Criminal Registers*, HO27204, p 250.

[110] Ancestry, *London Church of England Parish Registers*, P79/PET/015 (marriage at St Peter, Hackney, 5 August 1888).

[111] 'An Alleged Sham Detective Charged With Bigamy', *London Evening Standard*, 2 September 1891.

[112] These included robbing the parents of a friend with whom he was staying, as well as his employer – with whom he had obtained his post by means of a sham reference: 'Frauds by a Sham Detective', *London Evening Standard*, 27 August 1891.

[113] 'A Credulous Widow and a Sham Detective', *Norwood News*, 22 August 1891.

[114] There was in fact a real Inspector Hare, but he was on his 'annual leave' in the West of England at the time: *The People*, 23 August 1891.

[115] 'A Sham Detective: Alleged Heartless Frauds', *London Daily Chronicle*, 20 August 1891.

[116] 'Alleged Heartless Frauds', *London Daily Chronicle*, 27 August 1891.

As the date of William's actual release grew closer, 'Inspector Hare' had to hatch another plan. He told Jane that he had lost his job on account of his efforts on William's behalf, and that unless Florence married him at once he would 'blow his brains out'. The wedding went ahead at the Marylebone register office on 2 July 1891,[117] and he made his escape with Florence to Taplow in Buckinghamshire – with the intention, he claimed, of letting matters blow over. Even then he could not resist one final attempt to extract money from Jane. The letter she received from him pleaded, 'For God's sake send me £30 to save Flo, your son and myself, as they are on [to] me.'[118]

On 15 August, William was finally released from prison. In a last-ditch attempt to avoid discovery, Hugh went to meet him and tried to get him to go abroad immediately.[119] But William refused, and returned home to his family – upon which the deception was revealed. A few days later, Hugh was charged with obtaining money by false pretences at the Marylebone Police Court.[120] And a week later his full history – including his two prior marriages – was revealed.[121]

Reporters' descriptions of him as he stood in the dock go some way towards explaining his success with women – a good-looking man with a splendid physique, gentlemanly attire, a general air of authority, and a plausible manner. The only negative that observers could find in his appearance was that his eyes were shifty, though one suspects that they were being wise after the fact.[122] Even after pleading guilty, he was still trying to sweet-talk his way out of trouble: upon a previous conviction being proved against him, he tried to argue that the man convicted was his twin brother.[123] As the *Pall Mall Gazette* observed upon hearing of his five-year penal sentence, 'many a man has got more who less deserved it'.[124]

There was at least a happy-ever-after for the women that he had treated so badly. Florence and Alice both remarried the following year, perhaps relieved to find that they were not legally tied to him.[125] His legal wife Sarah was able to obtain a divorce on the basis of his adultery, bigamy and desertion, and she too then remarried at the age of 45.[126] Hugh's subsequent career was less happy. He was released early from prison in July 1895.[127] Within a year he was back inside, this time for a seven-year stretch.[128]

[117] TNA, *Divorce and Matrimonial Causes Files*, J77/600/18343.

[118] 'Wheedling a Widow: A Sham Detective Accused of Getting a Wife and Money by Lying Tales', *Weekly Dispatch*, 23 August 1891.

[119] 'Extraordinary Charge of Fraud', *Morning Post*, 27 August 1891.

[120] 'Police Intelligence', *London Evening Standard*, 20 August 1891.

[121] 'Extraordinary Charge of Fraud', *Morning Post*, 27 August 1891.

[122] 'A Wheedler of Women', *Weekly Dispatch*, 30 August 1891.

[123] *Daily News*, 17 September 1891.

[124] *Pall Mall Gazette*, 17 September 1891.

[125] Ancestry, *London Church of England Parish Registers*, DRO/052/022 (marriage of Florence at St Mary, Acton, 7 September 1892); *Surrey Church of England Parish Registers*, P49/100/1/12 (marriage of Alice Mary Ann Adam to Binyoun George Everett at St John's, Reigate, 3 April 1892).

[126] TNA, *Divorce and Matrimonial Causes Files*, J77/600/18343. She was able to use what was known as the *in forma pauperis* procedure, under which poor persons were exempted from paying court fees.

[127] TNA, *Metropolitan Police: Criminal Record Office: Habitual Criminals Registers and Miscellaneous Papers*, MEPO 6/7.

[128] 'A Career of Crime', *Illustrated Police News*, 6 June 1896; TNA, *Metropolitan Police: Criminal Record Office: Habitual Criminals Registers and Miscellaneous Papers*, MEPO 6/15. Each time he was convicted, the list of aliases noted in the file grew a little longer: this time the crime was committed under the name of George Courtney. See also 'Ex-Convict's Action Against A Baroness', *The Times*, 4 March 1914.

Advertising for a Spouse: John Woodgate Kinsella, 1900, 1908, 1918

In September 1900, Mary Ann Dormer, a 37-year-old laundress, was reading the *People* newspaper when an advertisement caught her eye:

> *'Superior working man, 29, with £30, wishes to correspond with superior domestic or others with about same capital, with a view to speedy matrimony.'*

Such advertisements were a commonplace of the period. Matrimonial advertisements had a long history, but the closing decades of the nineteenth century saw an upsurge in their popularity. New publications dedicated exclusively to such advertising were launched, with titles ranging from the practical (the *Matrimonial Intelligencer*) and the arch (*Cupid's Cosmopolitan Carrier*) to the blatantly aspirational (*Aristocratic Matrimonial & Marriage Envoy*). Historian Francesca Beauman notes that between 1870 and 1900 there were at least 20 such publications, making matrimonial advertisements 'more widespread and more popular than at any time up until Internet dating went mainstream in the 2000s'.[129]

Nor was there anything about this specific advert that would have rung any alarm bells. The advertiser's focus on his financial status rather than his personal characteristics was entirely in accordance with expectations.[130] Indeed, when trying to find the original advert, it was hard to distinguish it from several very similar ones. The desire for a speedy marriage was similarly nothing out of the ordinary. A couple of weeks later, the 'Matrimonial' column was headed by an advertisement that simply stated, 'Gentleman is anxious to hear from suitable Lady wishing early marriage.'[131]

For Mary Ann, one attraction of this particular advertisement might well have been that the advertiser was more specific about himself than about his ideal mate. Most of the other advertisements that week asked for a 'lady', generally one who was young, and either referred vaguely to 'means' or named much larger sums.[132] Mary Ann met none of these criteria. But she did have a nest-egg saved up from her years of toil.

Having written to the address indicated, she received the following letter:

> Dear Miss Dormer, Thanks very much for your letter. I should be very pleased to meet you. I must tell you I wish to get married at once. The reason is that I am a cabinetmaker, and my firm are going to make me a foreman on condition I get married directly. If I came to Reading and you thought we should suit each other, would you risk the marriage? Particulars of myself

[129] F Beauman, *Shapely Ankle Preferr'd: A History of the Lonely Hearts Ad, 1695-2010* (London, Chatto & Windus, 2011) 128.

[130] J Phegley, *Courtship and Marriage in Victorian England* (Santa Barbara, Praeger, 2012) 85–86; H Cocks, 'The cost of marriage and the matrimonial agency in late Victorian Britain' (2013) 38 *Social History* 66.

[131] *People*, 30 September 1900.

[132] *People*, 9 September 1900. According to Cocks (n 130) 83, the average income stated by advertisers 'was a very genteel £1182 for men and £1491 for women' (based on a survey of just under 500 ads from two matrimonial newspapers in 1894).

> are: Age 27, dark, medium height, total abstainer, wages £2 10s. weekly. I can assure you if we agreed to each other I would do my utmost to make your life happy, for my sole aim in life is to be happy. – Yours truly, Reg. Wilson.

They duly met, and were married in the register office in Reading on 18 October 1900. After the wedding they went to London, with Mary Ann paying their travelling expenses. On 5 November, as they were travelling down Pentonville Road, 'Reginald' stopped their cab and asked her if she would buy him some cigarettes. She got out of the cab, then turned back to ask him to make the purchase himself. But he had disappeared. She waited an hour to see if he would come back. When he did not, she went to the police for help.

A fortnight later, her supposed husband was arrested for bigamy. His somewhat blasé response was to acknowledge that he had had 'a pretty good innings' and must now 'put up with it'.[133] Exactly *how* good an 'innings' he had had gradually emerged over the following days.

His real name was John Woodgate Kinsella, and he had been born in Leeds in around 1871.[134] At the time of his first marriage, in 1894, he added a few years to his age so that he would appear older than his bride, 26-year-old Selina Winifred Woodgate Clisby.[135] Their son, Herbert, was born in October 1895, and the family lived together until February 1899.

Later that year he started his career of fraud. On 6 January 1900, he married a widow named Mary Beale at Cheltenham register office, using the name John King. He proceeded to sell up Mary's property, told her a story about needing to go to Birmingham as an engine fitter, and deserted her at Liverpool Street Station. Four days later he went through another ceremony of marriage with Marion Jennings, a housemaid who had spotted his advertisement in the *Gloucestershire Echo*, with John now assuming the alias Frederick Hall. Over the next few months they lived together somewhat sporadically. On 27 September, he married yet another domestic servant, Agnes Lane, this time in the register office at Kingston-upon-Thames, leaving her just five days later.[136]

With Mary Ann Dormer, that made five marriages in total, four of them bigamous. But it was speculated that there might be others. It was reported that the police had seized 42 letters, photos, and pawn tickets relating to jewellery – including a ring and watch belonging to Mary Ann.[137] Whatever the truth of the matter, the evidence was more than sufficient to charge John with bigamy. At the Clerkenwell Police Court, Marion, Agnes and Mary Ann all came forward to explain how they had been duped and swindled by him.[138]

[133] '"A Pretty Good Innings": Alleged Bigamy and Robbery', *Echo*, 19 November 1900; 'Police Intelligence: Clerkenwell', *The Standard*, 20 November 1900; 'Servant Girls Betrayed', *Weekly Times & Echo*, 25 November 1900.

[134] TNA, 1881 census, RG11/4520, folio 71, p 19.

[135] Ancestry, *Anglican Parish Registers*, M320/7/2/4 (marriage at St Michael, Hulme, 14 April 1894).

[136] 'Alleged Betrayal of Servant Girls: Reported Wholesale Bigamy and Desertion', *Westminster Gazette*, 27 November 1900; 'Bigamy in Cheltenham: Marriage by Advertisement: Wedded Twice in a Week: An Extraordinary Career', *Cheltenham Chronicle*, 1 December 1900.

[137] 'Police Intelligence: Clerkenwell', *The Standard*, 20 November 1900; 'Living By Bigamy: The Meaning of Matrimonial Advertisements', *Lloyd's*, 2 December 1900.

[138] 'Very Much Married: Astounding Allegations in a Bigamy Case', *Morning Leader*, 28 November 1900; 'Extraordinary Charge of Bigamy', *London Evening Standard*, 28 November 1900.

At the Central Criminal Court on 10 December 1900, John pleaded guilty to feloniously marrying Mary Beal, Mary Ann Dormer and Mary Ann Jennings.[139] In passing sentence on him, the Recorder commented that it was hard to think of a worse case of bigamy. As he put it:

> The prisoner had made it a regular business to get hold of these foolish women, to take all they had in the world and then to decamp. He had, apart from robbing them, done great injury to these women by jeopardising their characters, and inducing them to believe he was in a position to make honest wives of them when he was not. He must go to penal servitude for five years.[140]

Selina, his first wife, clearly had no desire to take him back. Upon John being released from prison, she promptly petitioned for a divorce. Given her limited income and the unlikelihood of John being able to pay her costs, she was able to use the pauper's procedure.[141] She explained that she had not petitioned before on account of her husband being in prison, as well as her lack of means. In the circumstances, her delay was hardly unreasonable, and the divorce was granted in 1905.[142]

John, meanwhile, was barely out of prison before he went through another bigamous marriage ceremony, in December 1904. Since this was before his first wife had divorced him, this marriage was void and bigamous.[143] After that, his next marriage was to Marion Aspinall in November 1907, the surprisingly long gap between the two ceremonies being accounted for by the fact that he had spent six months in prison for theft of jewellery in between them.[144] With John now being divorced, this marriage was actually legal. But then two more weddings had followed in January 1908 alone. The prosecutrix was one of the latter: 24-year-old Beatrice Heath, another servant, from whom he had obtained £15.[145]

This time John was sentenced to seven years' penal servitude.[146] The month after his release, the *Police Gazette* included him in a confidential list of 'expert and travelling criminals', with a description of his appearance and a concise summary of his 'method':

> Advertises in the matrimonial columns of newspapers to the effect that he is desirous of corresponding with a lady possessed of means with a view to early marriage, replies to be sent to a certain number at the box-office of the journal. On receipt of communications he arranges interviews with his correspondents, usually at an accommodation address, represents he is about to commence business at a neighbouring town, arranges for the marriage ceremony and, before leaving, affects to have mislaid his purse and obtains a small loan. In due course becoming married at a registrar's, he stays in furnished apartments with his victim for a few

139 *OBP*, 10 December 1900.

140 'Alleged Bigamy at Cheltenham', *Gloucester Citizen*, 12 December 1900.

141 Her application explained that she was employed as a machine hand at the weekly wage of 16 shillings and 7 pence: TNA, *Divorce and Matrimonial Causes Files*, J77/830/5254.

142 ibid.

143 Ancestry, *West Yorkshire, Church of England Marriages and Banns*, WDP92/1/3/1 (marriage to Annie Kaye at Holy Trinity Hepworth, 27 December 1904).

144 TNA, *Calendar of Prisoners*, HO140/269; Free BMD, Q4 1907.

145 'Man With Nine Wives: Women Duped By Advertisements', *Nottingham Evening Post*, 13 March 1908; 'Another Alleged Bigamist', *Manchester Courier*, 17 February 1908; 'Penal Servitude: Man Pleads Guilty to Marrying Many Wives', *Western Times*, 14 March 1908.

146 TNA, *Calendar of Prisoners*, HO140/269.

> days, obtains from her all her money and jewellery, deserts her and proceeds to practice his deception on another, in some instances negotiating with a second party before he has left the first.[147]

The police were clearly suspicious that John might reoffend. And justifiably so. Three years after his release he was convicted of 'double bigamy' and larceny at Manchester and sentenced to yet another term of seven years' penal servitude.[148] He had spent far longer in prison than he had with any of his wives, individually or collectively.

'An Inveterate Exploiter of Vulnerable Women': Wiliam Allen Jordan, 2006

In the summer of 2024, a powerful documentary appeared on British TV screens. 'The Other Mrs Jordan – Catching the Ultimate Conman' focused on the deceptions perpetrated by William Jordan, a 'convicted sex offender, conman and career criminal'.[149] The programme took its title from a telephone call that Mary Turner Thomson had received in April 2006. The caller had asked if Mary was Mrs Jordan, before going on to tell her, 'I'm the other Mrs Jordan.'[150]

This was the point at which Mary had realised that the man she had loved, married and had children with simply 'didn't exist'. Nor was the other Mrs Jordan the only other woman in William's life. Piecing together the facts, Mary ascertained that he had at one point had seven different relationships on the go at once and had fathered multiple children.[151] After she called the police, William was arrested. He pleaded guilty to fraud, bigamy and various other offences at Oxford Crown Court – for which he was sentenced to five years in prison.[152]

The following year, Mary published a book about her experience of being married to a bigamist – which should be compulsory reading for anyone who still thinks that bigamy is a comical or victimless crime. As she wrote:

> In the past, when I have read about bigamists' wives I have wondered at their stupidity. I thought that they must be really gullible to not have known – but I was wrong. Will was, and is, very, very good at what he does. He finds a victim, then finds a weakness and uses it. He

[147] TNA, *Metropolitan Police: Criminal Record Office: Habitual Criminals Registers and Miscellaneous Papers*, MEPO 6/18.

[148] 'Man Who Married Thirteen Wives: Seven Years for a Super-Bigamist', *Western Gazette*, 22 February 1918; TNA, *Metropolitan Police: Criminal Record Office: Habitual Criminals Registers and Miscellaneous Papers*, MEPO 6/35.

[149] J Grant, 'SERIAL BIGAMIST: The Other Mrs Jordan: Who is William Jordan and where is he now?', thescottishsun.co.uk, 11 August 2024.

[150] 'The day I learned about my husband's double life', *Daily Express*, 9 June 2007.

[151] 'The amazing day when I met my husband's wife', *Evening News*, 31 March 2008; 'My Husband: The bigamist with 11 kids', *Evening News*, 31 March 2008; 'Hubby I met online had 5 fiancées, 2 wives and 12 kids', *Scottish Daily Record*, 26 February 2013.

[152] 'Five Years For Bigamist Who Robbed His Wife of £200,000', *The Herald*, 22 December 2006; 'Jailed: The bigamist who posed as CIA spy', *Daily Express*, 22 December 2006.

> has been doing it all his life … the best comparison I can draw is that of a cat playing with a mouse: the cat has no emotion or compassion for the mouse; it is just a game and about control. Will is the predator; we are the prey.[153]

In the meantime, William Jordan appealed against his sentence. The five years was the aggregate of several sentences for different offences that were to run consecutively – including 21 months for the bigamy and another 21 months for various counts of obtaining property by deception. The latter involved another woman with whom William was in a relationship, from whom he had 'borrowed' money that was never repaid and whose credit card details he had used.

The Court of Appeal, having reviewed William's offences and read the letters and victim impact statements of the women involved, took the view that the trial judge's approach had been absolutely correct:

> He was and is an inveterate exploiter of vulnerable women, not just financially but emotionally. We take the view that these offences are very serious indeed. In our judgment, a total sentence in this case of five years was not a day too long.[154]

[153] 'The Other Mrs Jordan', *The Guardian*, 26 May 2007.
[154] *R v William Allen Jordan* [2007] EWCA Crim 1729, [14].

13

After the Trial

What happened after the trial was just as varied as what had gone before. We have already seen hints of this in earlier chapters. Some bigamists were reunited with their legal spouse. Others stayed with their second spouse, or moved on to a new partner. On occasion they were able to remarry legally, where the first marriage had been ended by death or divorce. Others, as far as we can tell, refrained from embarking on any further matrimonial adventures.

The case studies in this chapter allow us to go beyond the bare fact of the bigamist's post-trial living arrangements, as each involved a subsequent legal dispute or criminal proceedings.[1] Indeed, for Dorothy Poppleton and Philip Blake, it is only because there was a subsequent legal dispute that we know what happened after their bigamy trial. In Dorothy's case the information is indirect, refracted through the lens of claims made by her second husband, but it nonetheless provides an important insight into the uncertainty (and hostility) that individuals might face once they had left court or been released from gaol.

Here it is worth reiterating that a trial for bigamy was only about one question: was this person guilty of the criminal offence of bigamy? It was not the role of the criminal courts to give a conclusive answer to the question of the bigamist's marital status. The case of Thomas Gordon illustrates how a conviction for bigamy was not conclusive evidence that the accused's second marriage was void, and how it was open to a different court to come to a different conclusion on this point after reviewing the evidence afresh. Nor did a conviction for bigamy determine the outcome of other disputes, as we will see in the case of Dorothy Josephine Wagstaffe, who was convicted of bigamy after the death of her second husband and subsequently embroiled in a legal dispute as to whether she was entitled to the very considerable sum of money that he had left to her as his 'wife'.

Looking at what happened after the trial also provides a warning against romanticising either a reunion with the first spouse or the bigamist remaining with their second spouse. Two examples are featured here: William Bond, accused of an assault on his first wife in 1860, and Caroline Pantland Morant, complaining of the actions of her second husband in 1874. Nor, after 1858, did the new availability of divorce necessarily result in the bigamist being freed to remarry the second spouse legally. Three cases are featured here: the unsuccessful petition of the first wife of Richard Clement Gray; the successful petition of the legal (but chronologically third) wife of

[1] In each case, the date given is the date of the subsequent proceedings rather than the original trial.

Leonard George Crowle (which, in a further twist, cited his adultery with his second wife); and the petitions by the first *and* second husbands of Emma Georges Horridge for divorce and nullity respectively.

An 'Unfortunate Marriage': Dorothy Poppleton, 1716

In 1716, Michael Malard appeared in the settlement examinations for the London parish of St Martin in the Fields, in which he referred in passing to his wife Dorothy.[2] Whether she was actually his wife was something of a moot point. Two years earlier, Dorothy had been tried for bigamy at the Old Bailey for having married Michael during the lifetime of her first husband Peter, but had been acquitted on the basis of the seven-year defence.[3]

That Michael was being questioned as to his settlement suggests that he was in financial need, and that the parish responsible for his support needed to be determined. He had been in receipt of an allowance, but this, as he stated in a petition for funds the following year, had been stopped as a result of his 'unfortunate marriage' to Dorothy.[4] At this point it is necessary to provide some background on who Michael was and why he was receiving an allowance in the first place, to put his petition in context. Michael had been born in France, to Roman Catholic parents, and had become a pastor in Belleville-en-Beaujolais. After coming to England in 1700, he had converted to Protestantism and joined the French Church in the Savoy, a popular place of worship for French Huguenots. There had been considerable sympathy for those who had fled religious persecution in France in the late seventeenth century,[5] with various charitable appeals raising sizeable sums of money for their support. Substantial sums were also provided by the King and Queen, William and Mary, with an annual Royal Bounty of £15,000 being formally established in 1696.[6] The distribution of this sum was in the hands of the French Committee, a group of respected members of the Huguenot community, and it was through them that Michael had been receiving his allowance.

In his 1717 petition to the Committee, he alleged that he had been manipulated into marrying Dorothy to 'ruin' him.[7] He also claimed that he had suggested to her that they should separate, in order 'to take away the scandal', but she had refused. He accordingly

[2] Ancestry, *Westminster Poor Law Records*, STM/F/1/5011.

[3] See further chapter 6.

[4] M Malard, *The case, and humble petition of Michael Malard, never a monk, but pastor of the church of Belleville, in Beaujolois in France, To the Honourable Committee, newly Established for the Relief of the Proselytes* (London, 1717) 25.

[5] It has been estimated that between 80–100,000 French Protestants came to England after the revocation of the Edict of Nantes in 1685, although many went on to settle elsewhere: R Gwynn, *Huguenot Heritage: The history and contribution of the Huguenots in Britain* (London, Routledge & Kegan Paul, 1985) 35. By the start of the eighteenth century, the number of refugees had fallen to an 'insignificant trickle': D Desert, 'The Strangers and the Established Church' (2003) 27 *Proceedings of the Huguenot Society of Great Britain and Ireland* 1, 8–9.

[6] J Hoppit, *A Land of Liberty? England 1689-1727* (Oxford, Oxford University Press, 2002) 215.

[7] Malard (n 4) 6.

asked the Committee for funds to pay his lawyer to 'manage my business at Doctors' Commons, either to part or to break the marriage'.[8]

But if Dorothy's first husband was still alive, and her marriage to Michael therefore void, why would Michael need a lawyer to ask the church court sitting at Doctors' Commons to end that marriage? The short answer is that he could not be absolutely sure that his marriage to Dorothy *was* void. For one thing, being told by an Old Bailey judge that he was free to remarry was not the same as having a formal decree confirming that his marriage was void. Only the church courts had the power to conclusively determine that point. For another, the evidence of Dorothy's first marriage was in fact quite flimsy. It appears from Michael's petition that he had been expecting some witnesses to come forward with more specific evidence, but the individuals in question had since denied knowing anything of the ceremony and failed to appear.[9] So Michael might well have been concerned that the same would happen if he was called upon to maintain Dorothy or pay her debts. Without proof of her first marriage before them, a different court might find that he was liable for her.

It seems, however, that Michael's request for funds was unsuccessful. In a subsequent publication, one of the ministers of the French Church, Jean-Armand Dubourdieu, spent several pages castigating Michael's 'frivolous excuses' for not separating from Dorothy.[10] He dismissed Michael's desire to have the invalidity of his marriage confirmed by a church court, arguing that he was running the risk of eternal damnation for adultery if Dorothy was genuinely married to Peter.

There was, it should be noted, a much bigger issue behind all this, which is that Michael was also mounting a full-scale attack on the French Committee for the way in which it distributed funds between different sections of the French community. Were it not for this, it is unlikely that the dispute over the withdrawal of his allowance would have been published. That background controversy also means that we have to bear in mind the possibility that Michael's 'unfortunate marriage' was just a pretext for the removal of his allowance. Even so, the exchanges cast light on the dilemma facing the second spouse after a trial for bigamy had resulted in an acquittal, and the criticism that they might face for having married without due caution.

Attempted Murder: Philip Blake, 1768

In February 1768, Phillis Ewen prosecuted Philip Blake for bigamy. They had been together for five years, but she had been unaware of his prior marriage until she was informed of it by a woman who had been aware of how badly Philip treated her and wanted to let her know that she was not legally bound to him. Phillis investigated

[8] ibid.

[9] Had it not been so clear that Dorothy would be acquitted because more than seven years had passed since she last saw Peter, there would have been close scrutiny of whether her first marriage could be proved. There are no cases where an individual was convicted of bigamy on such circumstantial evidence: see further chapter 2.

[10] *An appeal to the English nation; or the body of the French Protestants, and the honest proselytes, vindicated from the calumnies cast on them by one Malard and his associates* (London, 1718) 17.

and was able to obtain proof of Philip's first marriage to Sarah, which had taken place almost 30 years earlier.[11] Sarah's continued existence was proved by her former apprentice, who commented that Philip had also behaved badly to Sarah, and that they had parted after two or three years. Philip sought to deny knowing Sarah, but the jury did not believe him, and he was convicted and branded.[12]

After his trial, Philip had an accident in which he hurt his leg, and he begged Phillis to visit him, describing himself as a 'dead man'. According to her later testimony, 'all his discourse was, that he repented of his past life, and begged I would let him come and live with me again'. She, however, steadfastly refused: 'I told him I could not answer [for] it before God nor man.' Philip then began to resort to veiled threats, telling Phillis that if she did not let him return to her, it would be 'the utter ruin' of them both.[13]

On the night of 2 May he came to her house. Each of them provided very different accounts of what happened next. Philip's version was that he had asked her for some beer, and, on being refused, for a 'little water'; that Phillis had agreed to be 'friends' with him, and that his pistol had gone off accidentally when he went to kiss her. That of course begged the question as to why he was brandishing a pistol in the first place – something he sought to explain by saying that he planned to do away with himself if she would not have him back. Phillis, by contrast, gave an account of a violent struggle that culminated when Philip clapped his left arm around her head, held it to his chest, and fired a pistol, shooting her in the neck – a story that was corroborated by her scars.

Whatever Philip's intentions had been, his immediate reaction was to run away He was found with his throat cut the following morning. He survived, but was taken before the magistrate Sir John Fielding at Bow Street. On 6 July 1768, he was convicted of 'unlawfully, knowingly, and feloniously shooting off a pistol loaded with gunpowder and a leaden ball' at Phillis, and was sentenced to hang.[14] He was executed at Tyburn before the end of the month.[15]

A Pardon and a Disputed Inheritance: Thomas Gordon, 1824

On 13 September 1818, Thomas Gordon and Frances Eliza Lawes were married at St Marylebone church in London.[16] They had known each other a month, having met at the house of Thomas' brother William, where Frances was lodging. It was a brief courtship, especially for a woman possessed of some wealth – according to her sister Susan, she had around £2,000 in the bank and other money besides, giving her an income of

[11] London Archives, *Gaol Delivery Sessions at The Old Bailey Post-1754*, OB/SP/1768/02/017, 20 February 1768, Philis Eivens of Kensington and Nicholas Osborne of Knightsbridge make statements in the case against Phillip Blake, who is charged with bigamy.

[12] *OBP*, 24 February 1768.

[13] *OBP*, 6 July 1768.

[14] ibid.

[15] *Oxford Journal*, 30 July 1768.

[16] Ancestry, *London Church of England Parish Registers*, P89/MRY1/188.

around £180 per year. But Frances was already in her forties, considerably older than most first-time brides. And even though she had not known Thomas for long, she did have a long-standing connection with his family: she had lodged with William and his wife before, and had known the latter for 30 years.[17]

According to Thomas, he and Frances lived together happily. The only fly in the ointment was Frances' sister Susan, who 'taunted' Frances with not being validly married to Thomas and claimed that his former wife Harriet was still alive.[18] Susan even had handbills printed and sent to all ports, offering a reward of 30 guineas for anyone who could provide proof of Harriet having been alive when Thomas married Frances. After Frances' death in March 1820, Susan challenged Thomas' right to administer her estate, claiming that Frances' money should come to her as next of kin. She also had Thomas arrested for bigamy.

At Thomas' trial at the Old Bailey the following October, wildly different accounts were given as to the fate of his first wife Harriet. The only undisputed facts were that they had married at Woolwich in 1809, that Thomas had then gone to sea,[19] and that Harriet, in his absence, had resorted to prostitution. Two witnesses for the prosecution, Ellen Barker and John Johnston, claimed to have seen Harriet alive since Thomas' marriage to Frances in 1818. Against this, one of the witnesses for the defence, Eliza Millington, claimed not only that Harriet had died in 1815 but that she had seen the body herself, 'in Magdalen ward … dead upon the bed'. That, however, was difficult to verify, as Harriet had apparently been passing under the name of Mary White at the time. While the register of deaths confirmed that a Mary White had died in the Magdalen Ward of the 'foul disease' (probably syphilis), it was hardly an uncommon name. And Eliza's credibility was undermined by the fact that she had been living with Thomas, as well as by her having previously told Susan that Harriet was alive and well and living in Plymouth.[20]

To make matters even more complicated, there were also allegations and counter-allegations of bribery and of who could or could not be believed. Sarah Short, the wife of a Woolwich innkeeper, claimed that Thomas had tried to bribe her to swear that he was not the same man who had married Harriet. But it was argued in return that Sarah had been bribed to say that Thomas had tried to bribe her, with another witness claiming to have overheard her saying, 'What does it signify whether the first wife is alive or not, what odds is it, so as we can get the reward?' One witness said that he would not believe Sarah 'because he had regularly seen her drunk', while the parish clerk said that she was a 'most respectable' woman, whose version of events should be credited.[21]

It is not my intention here to detail all the twists and turns of the various claims and counter-claims as to who was where at what time, and under what name, who had said what to whom, and who had been offered money to say it. Suffice it to note that all this occupied the court for almost five hours, following which the judge, Mr Justice Park,

[17] *OBP*, 28 October 1820.
[18] *Wilkinson (formerly Lawes) v Gordon* (1824) 2 Add 152; 162 ER 250.
[19] He had served as a gunner on HMS *Venus*.
[20] *OBP*, 28 October 1820.
[21] ibid.

summed up the evidence 'at considerable length'. The jury, however, had no doubt and immediately found Thomas guilty.[22] Park accordingly sentenced him to transportation for seven years, perhaps reflecting the suspicion that he had married Frances for financial gain.[23]

Like others before him, Thomas sought a pardon.[24] While his petition contained no new evidence or claims, it did present all the facts in a way that emphasised his own good character and that he had acted in good faith. He explained that he had been overseas, serving in his Majesty's navy, and that upon returning to England he had been informed that Harriet had died. His enquiries had led him to conclude that this was true, and he had heard nothing to the contrary before his marriage to Frances – who, he emphasised, had been fully aware of his prior marriage. As for the evidence against him, he alluded to Susan's handbills and noted his belief that some of the witnesses had been induced to give evidence by the promise of financial reward. He also acknowledged that the evidence given by some of his own witnesses had not exactly helped his case, noting his concern that the 'misrepresentations' in the evidence given by Eliza Millington 'caused an unfavourable impression against your Petitioner' and had contributed to the severity of his sentence. Finally, he argued that given Frances' death, there was no one who was materially affected 'even if the facts stated against him had been unquestionably true'.[25]

By itself, Thomas' petition would probably not have secured him a pardon. But it was supported by a whole host of sworn statements from others casting doubt on the evidence that had been given at his trial. Several said that Ellen Barker and John Johnston, the witnesses who had claimed to have seen Harriet after Thomas' marriage to Frances, had been paid for their evidence and had since admitted it was not true.[26] The woman that they had seen was a different person entirely, it transpired, who confirmed that she had never been married to Thomas, or lived with him.[27] And others came forward to confirm Harriet's death, swearing that they had met her in 1815, when she was 'dangerously ill', and that on subsequently inquiring for her at the hospital they had been shown her dead body.[28]

The case against Thomas was then reviewed by the Recorder, Sir John Silvester. He noted that the witnesses for the prosecution had not been cross-examined as to whether they had received any part of the offered reward. He thought that there was 'reasonable' evidence of Harriet's death, given 'the situation in life and character of the parties', and that, had all the facts set out in the affidavits been presented to the jury at the Old Bailey, Thomas might well have been acquitted. Taking into account Thomas' reputation as 'an

[22] 'Old Bailey Sessions: Extraordinary Case of Bigamy', *Morning Herald*, 2 November 1820.

[23] *OBP*, 28 October 1820 (see in particular the evidence of Alexander Grant). On financial exploitation as an aggravating factor in bigamy cases, see *Double Trouble*, ch 5.

[24] For an earlier example, see the case of William Martin Lolley (chapter 5).

[25] TNA, *Judges' Reports on Criminals 1784-130: Correspondence*, HO47/60/2, folio 79.

[26] ibid, affidavits of Gideon John Matthews, folio 56 and folio 72; George Rawlins, folio 57; John Campling, folio 70; John Davies, folio 74.

[27] ibid, affidavit of Caroline Lindsell, folio 59.

[28] ibid, affidavits of Mary Litster and Sarah Campell, folio 66. Ann Cowan's affidavit was in similar terms. William Jones and Rachel Brooks, who had known Harriet well, also confirmed that they had not heard from her for more than 10 years and believed she had died in 1815: folio 65. They also confirmed that she was passing by the name of White.

honest man and a brave intrepid faithful sober and diligent officer', he thought that the case was one that deserved 'the Royal mercy'.[29] The Home Secretary, Lord Sidmouth, agreed,[30] and Thomas was set free.

But a pardon was not the same as an acquittal. Nor was it confirmation that his second marriage was valid. And there was still the question of who was entitled to Frances' money. At this time, wills and the administration of estates were still dealt with by the church courts, and the case duly came before the Prerogative Court in the spring of 1824. As the judge, Sir John Nicholl, noted, the key question was whether Frances was married to Thomas or not. He pointed out that the burden was on Frances' sister Susan, as the person questioning the validity of the marriage, to prove its invalidity. And he firmly rejected the idea that Thomas' conviction for bigamy precluded the church court from re-examining his marriage's status. It was, after all, still the church courts that had exclusive jurisdiction to determine whether a marriage was valid or not. Although their role was increasingly being questioned, this was all the more reason to fiercely defend it.

There were also, in Nicholl's view, several good reasons why the guilty verdict should not be regarded as conclusive in this particular case. For one thing, there was Thomas' subsequent pardon – which, he suggested, would only have been granted 'upon just grounds after all due attention to the merits and circumstances of the case'.[31] The fact that Thomas had attempted to bribe witnesses ahead of the original trial was, he admitted, 'highly improper' but did not necessarily imply 'any consciousness of guilt on his part'.[32] He was far more critical of Susan's attempts to find out whether Thomas was already married.

In the event, though, it was unnecessary for him to decide whether Thomas' marriage to Frances had been valid. Frances had in fact executed two identical wills, one on the assumption that she was Thomas' wife, the other in her maiden name.[33] Both made Thomas her sole executor and universal legatee. Having dismissed Susan's argument that Frances had been of 'unsound mind' when she made these wills, Nicholl granted probate to Thomas as executor and made Susan liable for the costs.

So Thomas got Frances' money without the question of whether their marriage was valid ever being resolved. He might have been a loving husband hounded by a sister-in-law who wanted Frances' money for herself. Equally, he might have been a cynical chancer who bribed witnesses to say that his first wife was dead. Obviously one set of witnesses were lying, but a judge reading affidavits was not necessarily better equipped to determine who was telling the truth than the jury seeing the witnesses in court and hearing them being cross-examined. Sequels can raise more questions than they answer.

[29] ibid, letter from Silvester to Sidmouth, 14 May 1821.

[30] Sidmouth had also approved the pardon in Lolley's case in 1814 (see chapter 5), reflecting his lengthy tenure as Home Secretary – almost 10 years, a record now unlikely to be beaten.

[31] *Wilkinson v Gordon* (n 18) 163.

[32] ibid 164.

[33] It should be noted that married women generally had no power to make a will, given the rules restricting their ownership of property, but that a wife could make a will in relation to her separate estate: AA Tait, 'The Beginning of the End of Coverture: A Reappraisal of the Married Woman's Separate Estate' (2014) 26 *Yale Journal of Law and Feminism* 165.

A Reunion and its Ugly Sequel: William Bond, 1860

In January 1858, the *Western Times* reported that a warrant had been issued for the arrest of William Bond on a charge of bigamy. He was being pursued by Harriet, his second wife, whom he had married in Bristol but quickly deserted. It was rumoured that he had returned to Exeter, where his first wife Catherine kept a lodging house.[34] Within a matter of days, William was in custody and Catherine was seeking an order to protect her property against him.[35]

Catherine was just one of the many women up and down the country applying for such an order under section 21 of the new Matrimonial Causes Act 1857.[36] Given that William had deserted her as long ago as 1853, and had committed bigamy into the bargain, it should have been a straightforward enough case. The problem was that he had come back to her the previous year – not, it appears, to resume their relationship, but simply because he had nowhere else to go, and was being pursued by his creditors. Catherine had allowed him to sleep under her roof, and to take his meals in the kitchen. As *Trewman's Exeter Flying Post* acerbically observed, if Catherine had been 'less humane, and closed her doors against the scamp (as he richly deserved), the law would have afforded her relief'; as it was, she would have to wait until after William's trial for bigamy to seek the protection of section 21.[37]

In the event, there is no evidence that she did so. At the Devon assizes in March that year, William was duly convicted and sentenced to six months in prison. (It would have been more, but the judge took the view that Harriet had been incautiously hasty in marrying William.)[38] After William had served his sentence, he returned to Catherine once again.

In 1860, William was back before the magistrates, this time for assaulting Catherine. It took several weeks for her complaint to be heard, as for some time she had been too ill to come to the court.[39] When she finally appeared, she told the magistrates that although William had threatened her on several occasions, they had not had 'any words' that day, but had conversed pleasantly. After taking tea up to one of her lodgers, she had sat down to supper in the kitchen. William had stood behind her, and, without any warning, struck her on the back of her head. She had staggered upstairs, bleeding profusely. The maidservant subsequently discovered a poker on the table, and the surgeon confirmed that Catherine's injuries were consistent with that being the weapon William had used.

William's story was that Catherine had been drunk, prompting him to give her 'a flip with a little stick', following which she had banged her head against the wall. His lawyer suggested that this was a far more likely story than that William should switch so suddenly from apparent affection to a violent attack. The Bench, however, took the view that it was 'a most unmanly assault', and sentenced William to another six months'

[34] 'Bigamy', *Western Times*, 16 January 1858.
[35] 'First Application Under The New Divorce Act', *Trewman's Exeter Flying Post*, 28 January 1858.
[36] For an explanation of such orders, see the case study of William Tompkins in chapter 8.
[37] 'The Application Under the Divorce Act', *Trewman's Exeter Flying Post*, 4 February 1858.
[38] 'Bigamy – An "Active Partner Wanted"', *Trewman's Exeter Flying Post*, 18 March 1858.
[39] 'Exeter Guildhall', *Western Times*, 30 June 1860.

imprisonment with hard labour.[40] In the census the following year, Catherine was living with her sister in Exeter.[41] Happily, so far as can be ascertained, there were to be no further reunions with William.[42]

A (Largely) Stable Bigamous Marriage: Caroline Pantland Morant, 1874

In 1872, the *Law Journal* reported the case of an 'Enoch Arden' who had 'turned up after thirteen years and prosecuted the wife whom he had deserted'.[43] By itself, this would not have been particularly worthy of note. There were plenty of first husbands who were sufficiently aggrieved by their wife's remarriage during their absence to instigate a prosecution for bigamy. As we shall see, the case attracted attention largely on account of an exchange between the judge and the first husband after the trial had concluded. It also provides a good example of a (largely) stable bigamous marriage.

The 'Enoch' in this case was a Joseph Thomas Morant, who in 1853 had married Caroline Pantland Hughes at the church of St Mary Haggerston in Hackney.[44] Joseph was just 19 at the time of their wedding, and Caroline two years younger. According to Caroline, Joseph turned out to be a most unreliable husband, deserting her on six occasions in the first six years of their marriage. In 1859, he enlisted in the army and was sent out to India, leaving Caroline with three children to look after and a fourth on the way. Deprived of his support, Caroline and her children returned to live with her parents.[45]

Over the years, Caroline made numerous attempts to find out what had happened to Joseph. She made enquiries for him at the East India House, where she was told that he had enlisted as a single man. Despite repeated attempts, she could gain no news of him. In 1864, she consulted Joseph's brother, who similarly confirmed that he had heard nothing of Joseph.[46] In November of that year, she went through a ceremony of marriage with John Thorne at Hoxton church, describing herself as a widow.[47]

It was another eight years before Joseph turned up. Caroline may well have been expecting this: she had, it turned out, received a letter confirming that he was alive the year after she had married John.[48] Accompanied by John and her mother, she went to the local police station to give herself up and was committed for trial.[49] At the Central

[40] 'Brutal Assault on a Wife', *Exeter and Plymouth Gazette*, 7 July 1860.

[41] TNA, 1861 census, RG9/1393, folio 11, p 16.

[42] The 1871 census recorded her as a lodger in another house in Exeter: TNA, RG10/2061, folio 24, p 41.

[43] 'Bigamy' (1872) 7 *Law Journal* 591. For Tennyson's poem 'Enoch Arden', see chapter 6.

[44] As so often in these cases, there are different spellings of Caroline's name, her middle name appearing variously as Portland, Pentland and Pantland. The latter is the name by which she was indicted at the CCC: *OBP*, 19 August 1872.

[45] TNA, 1861 census, RG9/138, folio 141, p 57.

[46] 'The Bigamy Case', *North Londoner*, 20 July 1872.

[47] Ancestry, *London Church of England Parish Registers*, P91/JNB/045 (marriage at St John the Baptist, Hoxton, 7 November 1872).

[48] 'The Bigamy Case', *North Londoner*, 20 July 1872.

[49] 'Law and Police Intelligence', *Islington Gazette*, 2 July 1872; 'The Charge of Bigamy', *Hampstead and Highgate Express*, 6 July 1872.

Criminal Court, her mother gave evidence of Caroline's efforts to obtain news of Joseph and said they had both thought that Joseph was dead before Caroline married John. Caroline was duly acquitted.[50]

Joseph then stepped forward and asked if he 'was to have his wife back'. The response of the judge, Mr Commissioner Kerr, showed that he clearly had very little sympathy for Joseph:

> Certainly not. How can a fellow like you have the face to complain, seeing that you suddenly leave your wife and remain from her for 13 years without ever once communicating with her? It is preposterous to make such a request.[51]

As the *Law Journal* dryly commented, Kerr was 'somewhat usurping the office of the Judge-Ordinary': the power to make (or deny) an order for restitution of conjugal rights lay solely with the Divorce Court.[52]

Caroline's case was relatively unusual in terms of the time that had elapsed between her second wedding and her trial. Across all bigamy trials at the Central Criminal Court in the preceding decade, only another five, just 4 per cent, involved a prosecution being brought more than eight years after a potentially bigamous marriage.[53] And in two of those five cases, the bigamist had already parted from their second spouse some time before the trial.[54] So Caroline's case was even more unusual as an example of a long-lasting bigamous marriage still subsisting at the time of the trial.

Her second husband, John, loyally affirmed that Caroline had been 'a good wife' to him, and they remained together.[55] That said, their subsequent relationship was marred by occasional violence. In 1874, they made an appearance at the Clerkenwell Police Court when Caroline complained that John had assaulted her. She explained to the magistrate that she had been living with John since her trial, up until a couple of weeks earlier, but his temper had become so bad 'that she did not and would not do so any more'.[56] She did not wish him to be punished, but simply bound over to keep the peace – 'to keep away from her, and not to annoy her any more'. John denied assaulting her, but agreed to be bound over, promising that he had no intention of harming Caroline as he 'loved her too dearly'.[57]

Despite this, there was clearly a subsequent reconciliation between Caroline and John. Joseph died in the first quarter of 1876, and within a few months Caroline and John had gone through a valid ceremony of marriage.[58] Still together at the time of

[50] *OBP*, 19 August 1872; 'Trials for Bigamy', *The Globe*, 26 August 1872. While the judge's direction to the jury was not reported, we can infer that he must have told them that a belief in the death of the first spouse was a defence. For the varied judicial views on this, see chapter 7.

[51] 'Central Criminal Court', *The Times*, 26 August 1872.

[52] 'Bigamy' (1872) 7 *Law Journal* 591.

[53] Based on 125 cases tried at the CCC between 1 January 1863 and 31 December 1872 for which the date of the second marriage could be ascertained.

[54] The second wife of Francis George Fisk had left him a year prior to the trial, upon learning of his prior marriage (*OBP*, 13 July 1863), and Eliza Lumley's first husband had separated from her some years earlier (see chapter 4).

[55] *OBP*, 19 August 1872.

[56] 'Clerkenwell: A Strange Case of Assault – A Real "Enoch Arden"', *The Standard*, 12 August 1874.

[57] ibid.

[58] Free BMD, Islington Q2 1876, marriage between John Thorne and Caroline Pantland Morrant.

the 1911 census, they recorded the duration of their marriage as being 44 years – dating it from their first bigamous marriage rather than their second legal one.[59]

Barred from Divorce: Richard Thomas Clement Gray, 1861

In 1853, Richard Thomas Clement Gray was convicted of bigamy at the Central Criminal Court.[60] His was one of the cases used to highlight the need to reform divorce law. Upon being arrested and charged with bigamy, he had not attempted to deny the charge but told the police sergeant that he considered himself to be the injured party, on the basis that his wife Mary Louisa had for the previous five years been living 'in a state of adultery with an omnibus proprietor'.[61] In passing sentence, Mr Russell Gurney had commented that this was 'one of those unfortunate cases' in which 'if a man was not possessed of wealth he had no power to remedy his situation'.[62] Given that Richard had not deceived his second wife, and obtained no money by his second marriage, Gurney deemed a month's imprisonment in Newgate to be sufficient punishment.[63] In the view of *The Globe*, this was a 'nominal' sentence, 'virtually repealing the law'. As it noted:

> Legal authority, of course, must assert itself against individual rebellion; nevertheless, it may be said that the law was broken in the desire to observe it. There can have been scarcely any motive for the second marriage, except the desire to be as regular as possible, in outward form as well as conduct. It is manifest that if Gray had possessed the means, he would have complied with all necessary regularities. To that end, it would have been requisite to obtain a separation and divorce from his former wife; and the judge evidently thought that the facts were such as would have enabled him to do so.

Whether Richard would have been able to obtain a divorce even if he had been possessed of sufficient funds was, however, open to question. Mary Louisa's solicitor told the court that he had been instructed to say that what had been stated about her was untrue, and that she had in fact been compelled to leave Richard 'in consequence of his ill-treatment and infidelity'.[64] If true, this would have prevented Richard from obtaining a divorce *a mensa et thoro*, the necessary precursor to a private Act of Parliament.

Once he had been convicted of bigamy, his chances of obtaining a divorce from Mary Louisa were basically zero, even after the law was reformed. Under the Matrimonial Causes Act 1857, the new Divorce Court could refuse to grant a decree to a petitioner who had committed adultery – as Richard clearly had.[65] And right from the start it

[59] TNA, *Census Returns of England and Wales, 1911*, RG14.
[60] *OBP*, 28 November 1853.
[61] 'Singular Charge of Bigamy', *Morning Post*, 22 November 1853.
[62] 'Bigamy', *Lloyd's Weekly Newspaper*, 4 December 1853.
[63] Contrast the even lower sentences handed down at the assizes in similar cases, such as that of Benjamin Griffiths, discussed in chapter 9. For sentencing trends in this period, see generally *Double Trouble*, ch 7.
[64] 'Bigamy', *Lloyd's Weekly Newspaper*, 4 December 1853. The lawyer's careful phrasing is significant.
[65] His second wife, Mary Ann, had in any case left him in around 1859, as she subsequently told the Divorce Court: *Gray v Gray (the Queen's Proctor intervening)* (1862) 2 Sw & Tr 554; 164 ER 1112.

was clear that divorces would only be granted to adulterous petitioners in the most exceptional circumstances.

As a result, it was Mary Louisa who petitioned for a divorce under the new law, on the basis of Richard's bigamy and adultery with Mary Bagnall Adams.[66] At the Divorce Court, her lawyer claimed that Richard had deserted Mary Louisa in 1849. In addition to the details of Richard's bigamous marriage and subsequent trial, he also stated that Richard had been in prison even *before* his bigamy trial, where he had 'formed an improper connexion with two females', and that he had subsequently been sentenced to another spell in prison for counterfeiting Bass beer labels.[67] Richard did not appear to contest any of these allegations, and the Judge Ordinary made a decree *nisi* for the dissolution of their marriage.[68] All that was needed was for three months to pass, and then Mary Louisa could apply for the decree to be made absolute.

This two-stage process for obtaining a divorce was very new. It had not been part of the practice of the ecclesiastical courts. It was not even part of the 1857 Act. But the increase in the number of divorces – from 36 in the preceding decade to 24 in 1858 alone and 117 in 1859 – had both surprised and alarmed the establishment. The reaction was to set up extra-judicial processes to ensure that divorces were being properly granted. Further legislation in 1860 accordingly provided that every decree of divorce was to be a decree *nisi* (that is to say, 'unless' it was set aside). During the three-month period that had to elapse before it could be made absolute, any person could show that it should not be, on account of either collusion or 'material Facts not brought before the Court'.[69] Individuals could also give evidence to the Queen's Proctor, who could intervene in the suit to establish that the parties had colluded.

This is exactly what happened in Mary Louisa's case. On 20 March 1861, the Queen's Proctor applied for leave to intervene. His reason for doing so was the information that had come to his attention about Mary Louisa's relationship with the omnibus proprietor, now named as Thomas Kendall. He also alleged that Mary Louisa 'has been acting in collusion with the respondent Richard Thomas Clement Gray, for the purpose of obtaining a divorce contrary to the justice of the case'.[70]

At this point, Mary Louisa tried to withdraw her petition. This being the first case in which this had occurred, no less a person than the Attorney General attended to contest her right to do so. The Judge Ordinary, Sir Cresswell Cresswell, agreed that Mary Louisa's petition could not now be withdrawn. As he explained:

> it is important, in the interest of the public and in the interest of morality, if a woman comes forward presenting shamelessly her sham case – a case not founded on truth, but on collusion with her husband – that her conduct should be fully exposed, and that the disgrace which belongs to such a transaction should be thoroughly understood.[71]

There was also a more practical reason, in terms of the implications for who would be liable to pay the costs. If the Queen's Proctor succeeded in establishing collusion, then

[66] TNA, *Divorce and Matrimonial Causes Files*, J77/20/G36.
[67] '*Gray v Gray*', *Morning Advertiser*, 19 January 1861.
[68] TNA, *Divorce and Matrimonial Causes Files*, J77/20/G36.
[69] Matrimonial Causes Act 1860, s 7.
[70] *Gray v Gray* (1861) 2 Sw & Tr 263; 164 ER 996, 996–97.
[71] 'Law Intelligence: Court of Probate and Divorce: *Gray v Gray*', *Sun*, 18 April 1861.

either Richard or Mary Louisa could be made responsible for paying his costs as well as their own. Mary Louisa appealed against Cresswell's decision, but her appeal was dismissed by the court.[72]

The case ground on, with Mary Louisa and Richard both knowing that there was now no chance of them being able to obtain their freedom to remarry. The Queen's Proctor's information as to Mary Louisa's relationship with Thomas was, after all, very specific and detailed. The issue of whether they had colluded came back before the Divorce Court – this time with a jury in attendance – in March 1862. At least on this point the decision went in her favour, with Cresswell instructing the jury that the Queen's Proctor had not produced any evidence of an agreement between Richard and Mary Louisa as to how she would present the divorce they both desired.[73] So at least neither of them were asked to pay the costs incurred by the Queen's Proctor. It was a minor consolation: she and Richard remained legally bound to each other for the rest of their mutual lives.

Acquitted, Divorced, Annulled: Emma Georges Horridge, 1871

On 31 May 1871, two linked cases came before Lord Penzance in the Divorce Court. One was a petition by Charles Pooley Georges for a divorce from his wife Emma on the ground of her adultery with Frank Horridge. The second was a petition for nullity by Frank himself in relation to his marriage with Emma.

Emma Dixon Johnson was born in Yorkshire in 1844 – meaning that she had just turned 17 when she married Charles in March 1861, rather than the 18 she claimed to be in the marriage register.[74] Charles was 10 years older, a lieutenant in the Royal Navy. Over the next couple of years they moved around the country, living first at Thorpe in Yorkshire, then at other times at Leeds, Harrogate, Scarborough, Chester, Liverpool, Rugby, and finally London. But in August 1863, Emma – at least according to Charles' subsequent petition – left him 'without reasonable cause'.[75]

Three years later, on 25 June 1866, Emma went through a ceremony of marriage with Frank in Scarborough parish church, describing herself as a widow.[76] Frank was a captain in the Cornwall Light Infantry Regiment, and Emma travelled with him to Gibraltar and Mauritius.[77] How and when her earlier marriage came to light does not appear from any of the reports, but it appears to have been Frank's father who was responsible for bringing the prosecution.[78] In June 1870, Emma was arrested in Worthing and was brought before the Scarborough police court.[79]

[72] '*Gray v Gray*', *Morning Herald*, 4 June 1861 (the judges in question being Cresswell, Wightman and Williams JJ).

[73] *Gray v Gray (the Queen's Proctor intervening)* (1862) 2 Sw & Tr 554; 164 ER 1112.

[74] Ancestry, *Cheshire Parish Registers*, P77/3/3 (marriage at Over Peover parish church, 21 March 1861).

[75] TNA, *Divorce and Matrimonial Causes Files, Georges v Georges and Horridge*, J77/104/1592.

[76] She also knocked a year off her age this time.

[77] 'The Scarbro' Bigamy Case', *Leeds Mercury*, 8 August 1870.

[78] ibid.

[79] 'Scandal in High Life at Scarborough', *Newcastle Journal*, 29 June 1870.

At the York assizes, evidence was given of the two ceremonies, with one of the witnesses adding that Charles had treated Emma with great cruelty, including physical violence, and then deserted her.[80] It was also stated that Emma had claimed to have received a letter from Charles in 1865 to say that he was dying and asking her to go to him. Her friends had advised her not to go, in case it was a 'ruse' by him to get her back. A few days later she had received another letter, from a Dr Robinson, to say that Charles was dead. The judge thought it was 'clear that this lady believed her husband to be dead', but that an offence had still been committed.[81] Counsel for the defence then reminded him of the case of *R v Turner*,[82] and argued that Emma should be acquitted. Emma's uncle confirmed that he had read the letter, and that it explicitly stated that Charles had died, although he had not been able to find it again. The judge instructed the jury that if they believed Emma had received a letter saying that Charles was dead, it would be their 'very pleasing and satisfactory duty to say she is not guilty'. With this very unsubtle steer as to what their decision should be, the jury unsurprisingly acquitted Emma.[83] She was lucky, however, that her case came to trial when it did. The following year saw a narrowing of the defence accepted in *Turner* and then an outright rejection.[84]

By this time, however, both Charles and Frank had already filed their respective petitions for divorce and nullity.[85] Emma's acquittal for bigamy made no difference to the likelihood that they would be granted the orders they sought: all Charles needed to show was that Emma had committed adultery with Frank, and all Frank needed to show was that Charles was still alive.

Even so, Charles was lucky that Emma chose not to defend the divorce, if the allegations made about him at her trial were true: his cruelty, desertion, and wilful separation were all factors that would have justified the Divorce Court refusing to grant a decree.[86] But there was no hint of any bad behaviour by Charles in the evidence he put before it. Instead, the story that was told was that Charles had wanted them both to go out to Australia with some of his friends, Emma had refused, and they had quarrelled. Charles had gone to Brighton for a few days to allow things to cool over, but when he returned, Emma was gone. He had written to ask her to come back, but she had refused.[87] All this was carefully crafted to negate any idea that it was Charles who had deserted Emma, and the divorce was granted.

Frank was also lucky, in that he escaped being saddled with the costs of the divorce case.[88] The common practice was for the co-respondent to be required to pay. But Frank denied having committed adultery with Emma, on the basis that he had believed he

[80] 'The Scarbro' Bigamy Case', *Leeds Evening Express*, 9 August 1870; 'Summer Assizes: Crown Court', *Evening Mail*, 9 August 1870.
[81] 'Summer Assizes: Crown Court', *Evening Mail*, 9 August 1870.
[82] *R v Turner* (1862) 9 Cox CC 145.
[83] 'Summer Assizes: Crown Court', *Evening Mail*, 9 August 1870.
[84] See further chapter 7.
[85] TNA, *Divorce and Matrimonial Causes Files, Georges v Georges and Horridge*, J77/104/1592 (petition filed 1 July 1870); *Horridge v Georges (falsely called Horridge)*, J77/104/1598 (petition filed 4 July 1870).
[86] Matrimonial Causes Act 1857, s 31.
[87] '*Georges v Georges and Horridge*: A Wife's Bigamous Adultery', *Illustrated Police News*, 10 June 1871.
[88] TNA, *Divorce and Matrimonial Causes Files, Georges v Georges and Horridge*, J77/104/1592.

was validly married to her. Having been granted a decree of nullity confirming that his marriage to Emma was void, Frank went on to remarry.[89]

Of course, Frank did not actually need a decree of nullity. His marriage to Emma was automatically void, without the need for any decree. Even so, it was a prudent step to take, since it avoided him having to prove the invalidity of his marriage to Emma should questions arise at a later date. As our next case study shows, those who did not do so might find themselves on trial for bigamy.

Two Acquittals and a Divorce: Leonard George Crowle, 1880

In June 1880, Emma Crowle sought a divorce from her husband Leonard on the basis of his adultery and cruelty.[90] As she explained in her petition, she had previously prosecuted Leonard for bigamy, but he had been acquitted because his first wife was herself married to someone else. In an additional twist, it was this first wife with whom Leonard was alleged to have committed adultery. To unpick this matrimonial tangle, we have to look back at not one but two bigamy trials.

The wedding of Leonard George Crowle and Emma Wheeler had taken place in February 1879.[91] It had appeared to be an entirely suitable match. He was a widower with two children in their early teens, his first wife Martha having died in 1873.[92] Emma was a 34-year-old spinster, the daughter of a builder from Uxbridge. Leonard had met the Wheeler family the previous October and had courted Emma with the full knowledge and approval of her parents.[93]

Unfortunately, the marriage quickly foundered on account of Leonard's appalling behaviour. As Emma later explained, she immediately discovered that Leonard was a man 'of drunken and dissolute habits'.[94] Within a month of their wedding, he forced her to go to the bank and draw out the money in her account, amounting to some £300. He also disposed of the furniture that she had brought to the marriage, worth around £100.[95] Throughout the months that followed, he subjected her to violent assaults. After a particularly severe beating on 12 July, she finally escaped to her father's house.[96]

While Leonard's cruelty would have given Emma grounds for a judicial separation, there was little need for her to seek such redress while she was sheltered under her father's roof. By itself, however, it did not entitle her to a divorce. For that she would also need to show that Leonard had committed adultery.[97] But it was not long before she was

[89] In fact, he went on to marry *three* times – in 1873, 1875 and 1889 – but entirely legally, as his second and third wives both died.

[90] TNA, *Divorce and Matrimonial Causes Files*, J77/245/6980.

[91] Ancestry, *Westminster Church of England Parish Registers*, SPES/PR/2/13 (wedding at St Peter's church, Pimlico, 13 February 1879).

[92] Ancestry, P70/Mry2/073 (burial at St Mary's Battersea); TNA, 1871 England Census, RG10/60, folio 100, p 29.

[93] 'Police', *The Times*, 29 March 1880.

[94] TNA, *Divorce and Matrimonial Causes Files*, J77/245/6980.

[95] 'Police', *The Times*, 29 March 1880.

[96] TNA, *Divorce and Matrimonial Causes Files*, J77/245/6980.

[97] Matrimonial Causes Act 1857, s 27.

able to procure evidence of this. The following year, one March evening, she happened to be in Peckham, where she encountered Leonard walking arm-in-arm with another woman.[98] The woman in question was Eliza Emily Hardcastle, and it transpired that Leonard had been sleeping with her since Emma had left him. As Emma also discovered, Leonard had also married Eliza – in 1876, three years prior to her own wedding with him. If this marriage was valid, then Emma's marriage to Leonard was void, and she would be free of him.

Emma immediately had Leonard charged with bigamy at the Westminster police court. The evidence against him seemed clear enough. But in his defence, he pleaded that Eliza had herself been married before. He explained that he had prosecuted her for bigamy, and that although she had been acquitted 'through some flaw', he had been a 'free agent' when he married Emma.[99]

Had Eliza been *convicted* of bigamy, then that would have been the end of the matter. But her acquittal raised the possibility that her first marriage had been void, which would have made her marriage to Leonard valid and his marriage to Emma bigamous. The magistrate, perhaps grateful that it was not his job to try to sort out the tangle, committed Leonard for trial at the Central Criminal Court.

At this point we need to backtrack a couple of years to Eliza's own trial for bigamy at the Central Criminal Court in 1878. Her first marriage, to William Alfred Hardcastle, had taken place back in 1855.[100] They were together in both the 1861 and 1871 censuses, and were doing well enough to keep two servants.[101] Exactly when they had separated is not clear. According to Leonard, he had first met Eliza around 1873 when making a purchase from her shop in Kennington.[102] William was clearly still on the scene, as Leonard had seen him and asked Eliza who he was. Eliza acknowledged that she had lived with William, but omitted to mention their marriage. She also claimed that her children had been fathered by the family doctor, rather than by William. Despite this, it appears that they were still together in January 1876 when the business ran into financial difficulties.[103] Less than six months later, Eliza went through a ceremony of marriage with Leonard at Clapham parish church, describing herself as a spinster, and changing her father's surname from Harris to Hardcastle.[104]

Leonard discovered Eliza's former marriage in February 1877, but it was not until December that he prosecuted her for bigamy. The magistrate at the Wandsworth police court was distinctly unsympathetic, commenting that there was 'an enormous difference' between men and women when it came to the crime of bigamy and implying that Leonard was simply seeking a means of getting rid of Eliza.[105] Nonetheless,

[98] 'Police', *The Times*, 29 March 1880.

[99] ibid.

[100] Ancestry, *Bexley Parish Registers*, PA290B/1/D/4 (wedding at St Michael, East Wickham, 5 July 1855).

[101] TNA, 1871 census, RG10/614, folio 52, p 26.

[102] 'The Extraordinary Charge of Bigamy', *East London Observer*, 29 December 1877.

[103] *London Gazette*, 28 January 1876, noting the proceedings in the London Bankruptcy Court.

[104] Ancestry, *London Church of England Parish Registers*, P95/TR/1/116 (marriage at Clapham Parish church, 20 June 1876).

[105] 'Wandsworth', *Daily News*, 17 December 1877. There was some reason for the magistrate's comments, since Leonard had explained that he had only prosecuted Eliza after she had taken to drink (and, later, that they had separated after she brought another man home).

after proof of the first marriage had been provided, he had no option but to commit Eliza for trial.[106] It is possible that the jury at the Central Criminal Court took the same jaundiced view of Leonard's actions. That would explain why they acquitted Eliza, despite the clear evidence of the two ceremonies and the absence of any legal defence.[107]

Nonetheless, no doubts had been raised about the validity of Eliza's first marriage. As a result, Leonard's marriage to Eliza was void, and he had been entirely justified to regard himself as free to remarry Emma in 1879. He was vindicated when he was acquitted at the Central Criminal Court in April 1880.[108]

This brings us back to Emma's petition for divorce. Given the sequence of events, petitioning on the basis of bigamy with adultery was not an option: while the divorce courts had a broader definition of bigamy than the criminal courts, it obviously did not stretch to a void marriage that had taken place *before* the legal marriage. On the other hand, the fact that Leonard was not legally married to Eliza meant that resuming his relationship with her after he had married Emma clearly constituted adultery. And Emma already had ample evidence of Leonard's cruelty. Together, this was enough to give her grounds for divorce, and the Divorce Court had no hesitation in granting the decree *nisi*.

It was Leonard who was the main beneficiary of this. At the time that the next census was taken in April 1881, he was living with a 19-year-old girl named Nellie, who was described as his wife, together with his daughter from his first marriage, who was only three years younger. The description of Nellie as his wife was a trifle premature, given that his divorce from Emma had not been finalised. But on 21 June 1881 the decree was made absolute,[109] and on 14 November 1881 Leonard was able to marry Nellie legally at St Giles' church in Camberwell, describing himself as a widower.[110] Emma, by contrast, never remarried.[111]

A Disputed Will: Dorothy Josephine Wagstaff, 1908

In 1906, Berners Shelley Wagstaff brought a claim against the estate of James Poole Wagstaff, his father's cousin. James had died three years earlier, having made a will that primarily benefited the woman he described as 'his dear wife Dorothy Josephine Wagstaff', with Berners being entitled to the residuary estate on her death or remarriage. But Berners' claim was that Josephine[112] was not entitled to anything from James – on the basis that their marriage had been bigamous.

[106] 'Wandsworth: The Charge of Bigamy', *Daily Telegraph*, 24 December 1877.
[107] *OBP*, 14 January 1878.
[108] *OBP*, 26 April 1880.
[109] *Divorce and Matrimonial Causes Files*, J77/245/6980.
[110] Ancestry, *London Church of England Parish Registers*, P73/GIS/039 .
[111] She was living with her father in the 1881 census (RG11/1332, folio 12, p 17) and her sister in 1891 (RG12/53, folio 26, p 6). She died in 1899: BMD Q2.
[112] For consistency, I have used the name by which she was generally known, rather than the name under which she was tried.

The wedding of James Wagstaff and Josephine Jallard had taken place at St George's Hanover Square on 21 December 1893, with the bride being described as a widow.[113] It had been a quiet affair, with just one guest – Charles Noble, an old friend of James' – in attendance.[114] Charles had given Josephine away and signed the register as a witness. The other witness was the verger, the only other person present apart from the vicar. There was no formal wedding breakfast, just lunch at the Langham Hotel, where the couple spent a week before returning to James' home of Manor Park in the small town of Potton in Bedfordshire.[115]

None of this would necessarily have raised any suspicions about the status of the wedding. Although St George's was not their local church, it was popular with the elite. Moreover, James' club was also located in Hanover Square, and it was there that he was (apparently) residing at the time of the wedding. Nor was it surprising that the marriage of a 51-year-old bachelor and a 30-something widow should be celebrated without much fuss. Even the bride's black wedding dress would not have raised eyebrows. And since James sent an announcement of the wedding to the newspapers, the couple were clearly not trying to keep it a secret.[116]

After returning to Potton, James and Josephine lived together for almost a decade. A daughter was born to them in 1895, but sadly died at the age of nine months. When James died in 1903, the family monument in Potton graveyard recorded an impressive CV: a captain of the 7th Middlesex Rifle Volunteers, Fellow of the Royal Geographical Society, Justice of the Peace, Deputy Lieutenant, and High Sheriff of Bedfordshire. All this was prefaced by a description of James – carved in stone in large capitals – as 'MY DEAR HUSBAND'.

But Berners' claim that the marriage was bigamous was entirely justified. On 19 November 1906, 'Mrs Wagstaff' made a dramatic entrance at the Kensington police station and stated that she wished to give herself up. She acknowledged that her legal husband was Alfred Gibson Jalland, whom she – then known as Jeanie Josephine D'Eyncourt Burns – had married in Lancashire in 1884.[117] She added, however, that James had known that her first husband was still alive at the time of their marriage ceremony in 1893, and, moreover, that it was James who had persuaded her into the bigamous marriage.[118]

The story that emerged was that Josephine had met her first husband, Alfred, the son of a Nottingham architect, when she was a nurse and he was a medical student.[119]

[113] Ancestry, *Westminster Church of England Parish Registers*, STG/PR/7/77.
[114] 'The Police Courts: A Confession of Bigamy', *The Times*, 12 December 1906.
[115] 'Tale of Two Husbands: Lady Confesses Bigamy And Is Sent For Trial', *Evening Star*, 11 December 1906; 'Bigamous Marriage: Wagstaff Estate: Chancery Suit Resumed', *Evening Echo*, 21 March 1907.
[116] The announcement appeared in the *London Evening Standard*, 25 December 1893.
[117] Lancashire OnLine Parish Clerk Project, marriage at All Saints' Church, Chorlton upon Medlock, 18 March 1884.
[118] 'The West London Bigamy Confession', *Pall Mall Gazette*, 27 November 1906.
[119] 'Lady's Strange Bigamy Confession: Romantic Story of Two Husbands', *Lloyd's Weekly Newspaper*, 25 November 1906. The details given about Alfred can be verified from other sources. He had been born in Nottingham in 1860, where he had spent his childhood. His father, Robert, was described as an architect and surveyor and, at least in 1861, the family was sufficiently well-off to have a live-in servant (TNA, 1861 census, RG9/2468, folio 59, p 11; 1871 census, RG10/3508, folio 62, p 6). In 1879 Alfred went up to Cambridge to study at Sidney Sussex College, and by 1882 he had embarked on medicine as his career, with the Medical Students Register recording him as commencing his studies on 9 February 1882.

They had agreed to marry on the understanding that they were not to live together until he had qualified. Alfred then went to Edinburgh to continue his studies, and Josephine took up a post as a nurse at the Manchester Infirmary, before going on to be employed as a matron at the county lunatic asylum at Canterbury.[120] It was while she was visiting London to engage some new servants that she had first encountered James. After corresponding for some time, James had suggested that Josephine should become his housekeeper. Although he was aware that she was a married woman, having been introduced to Alfred when he was in London, he suggested that she should pass as a widow. He then sought to persuade her that she and Alfred were 'not married in the ordinary sense of the word' and that she was not bound by the ceremony that had taken place.[121] After some time she consented to marry him, James obtained the licence, and it was only when she came to sign the register that she discovered that her name had been given as *Dorothy* Josephine.[122] This last point made no difference to whether she was guilty of bigamy, but she clearly wanted to emphasise that it was James who had supplied the wrong name, to deflect any suspicion that she had deceived him.

With the facts of both marriages established, Josephine was committed for trial at the Central Criminal Court.[123] It was, according to one report, the 'first great sensational scene' to occur in the new building.[124] Visually this was true: Josephine, clad in her rich furs, made a striking figure in the dock.[125] But as a courtroom drama it was sadly lacking in excitement. With Josephine having pleaded guilty, the focus was solely on the factors that might affect her punishment. And even here there wasn't much disagreement. Counsel for the prosecution made no attempt to cast Josephine's actions in a negative light, even acknowledging that the inquiries made by the police had corroborated her statement that James had known of her prior marriage.[126]

Nonetheless, there were some new revelations from Josephine's counsel, Mr Horace Avory KC, about her relationships with both Alfred and James. New details were provided to explain why Josephine and Alfred had never lived together. In this version they had travelled together to Edinburgh on the day of their wedding – but this was followed by Alfred getting 'horribly drunk' with some fellow medical students, ending up in the arms of a prostitute, and failing to return to his waiting bride for two or three days.[127] Josephine had then – understandably – refused to live with him, instead supporting herself through her various nursing posts. Nonetheless,

[120] 'Self-Accused: Lady's Confession of Bigamy: Sensational Story', *The People*, 25 November 1906. By 1891 Alfred was living in Clerkenwell, in the home of one Edwin Gill, described as a medical assistant: TNA, 1891 census, RG12/228, folio 71, p 27.

[121] 'Lady's Strange Bigamy Confession: Romantic Story of Two Husbands', *Lloyd's Weekly Newspaper*, 25 November 1906.

[122] 'Beauty and Wealth Without Happiness', *The Penny Illustrated Paper*, 1 December 1906.

[123] 'The Police Courts: A Confession of Bigamy', *The Times*, 12 December 1906; 'Bigamy Romance', *London Daily Chronicle*, 12 December 1906.

[124] 'Nurse's Romance: Sequel to confession of bigamy', *Daily Record*, 11 January 1907. Newgate Prison and the old Central Criminal Court had been demolished in 1904 and the present-day Court built on the site. Josephine's trial took place before it had even been formally opened by Edward VII in February 1907.

[125] 'Trial and Release of Mrs Wagstaff: Special Interview: Story of J.P.'s Wedding Plot', *London Daily Chronicle*, 11 January 1907.

[126] 'Central Criminal Court', *The Times*, 11 January 1907.

[127] 'Romance of a Lady Bigamist', *Daily Express*, 11 January 1907.

she had remained in communication with Alfred and even nursed him when he had been ill.[128] Mr Avory somewhat glossed over the precise circumstances under which Josephine had met James, placing more emphasis on James' meetings with Alfred and his awareness of Alfred being Josephine's husband. There was, he noted, a witness who had overheard a conversation between the two in which James had said to Alfred, 'What a pity a splendid woman like your wife should have to go out in life as a single woman and take up these posts.' Mr Avory was also keen to emphasise that James was no unworldly bachelor. In his possession, he told the court, were letters showing that James had been leading a 'profligate life' both before and after his marriage to Josephine. In essence, this portrayed Josephine as an innocent, bamboozled by an older man into committing bigamy without realising that she was committing a criminal offence. He concluded by declaring that Josephine was 'the only person who had suffered any injury at all by either of the ceremonies of marriage she had gone through'.

Given that there was no dispute as to whether James had known of Josephine's earlier marriage – and also that there were proceedings pending in Chancery in which this specific issue would have to be determined – the Recorder declined to hear any further evidence. Addressing Josephine, he told her that he accepted the statements made by Mr Avory, and that justice would be served by a nominal three-day sentence – which meant that she could be immediately discharged.[129]

There was, therefore, no doubt that the marriage of James and Josephine was void. And there was a lot of money at stake. James had left an estate of around £180,000. When invested as he had directed, this would produce an annual income of between £11,000 and £12,000 – getting on for £2 million today.[130]

The case came before Mr Justice Kekewich in the Chancery Division of the High Court in March 1907. The first question was one of fact: could it be shown that James had known that Josephine was already married at the time they went through the ceremony? Various statements had, of course, already been made to the effect that he did know. But that was not the same as proving it in court.

If James had not known, then that would be the end of the case. It had been established in the late eighteenth century that where a legacy had been left to an individual 'under a particular character, which he has falsely assumed, and which alone can be supposed the motive of the bounty, the Law will not permit him to avail himself of it'.[131] In that case, *Kennell v Abbott*, the testatrix had died believing herself to be lawfully married, and the man who had 'grossly abused her' by deceiving her into a bigamous union was denied the legacy. Similarly, in *Wilkinson v Joughin*, where it was the wife who had committed bigamy and who stood to receive a legacy, it was held that she had 'imposed in a gross manner upon the testator' by representing herself to

[128] According to the evidence given by his landlady in the subsequent Chancery proceedings, Alfred 'seemed to have a kind of helplessness in his limbs, which induced him to stay late in bed' – a symptom which provoked unsympathetic laughter in the court: 'The Wagstaff Will Suit: More Remarkable Evidence', *Belfast Newsletter*, 21 March 1907. Josephine herself described Alfred as suffering from paralysis: 'Bigamous Marriage: Wagstaff Estate: Chancery Suit Resumed', *Evening Echo*, 21 March 1907.

[129] *OBP*, 8 January 1907.

[130] 'Mrs Wagstaff's Romance: Sequel to Bigamy Sensation', *Evening Express* (Liverpool), 24 December 1906.

[131] *Kennell v Abbott* (1799) 4 Ves Jun 802, 809; 31 ER 416, 419.

be a widow, and the gift to her in his will was invalidated.[132] By contrast, in *Giles v Giles*,[133] where the testator had known that his wife's first husband was still living, the court had held that she was entitled to what he had left her in his will. The Master of the Rolls, Lord Langdale, had observed that if both spouses had had a 'guilty knowledge', then 'no fraud was committed upon the testator', and that it was not the role of the Courts of Equity 'to punish parties for immoral conduct by depriving them of their civil rights'.[134]

So everything hinged on whether James had known of Josephine's previous marriage at the time he made the will in her favour. After hearing the evidence of the various witnesses, Kekewich held that James had known that he was not legally married to her. The judgment that he delivered was nonetheless remarkable for his ability to enter imaginatively into what James must have been thinking. While emphasising that he was only presuming what must have been in James' mind from the evidence before him, he expanded on the life of 'constant deceit' that James had been living, his 'constant fear' lest it be discovered that he was living with another man's wife. This enabled him to come up with a reason why James had described Josephine as his wife despite knowing she was not:

> It seems to me that I must conclude a determination on his part to brave it out to the end, to be determined that even in his last will, which was not to be looked at except by his solicitor until after his death, he should assume the role of the married man, taking care of his dear wife. He employed a solicitor, but he determined to tell his solicitor no secrets; it was foolish, and more than foolish – extremely cruel to the lady whom he desired to benefit, to whom he owed so much – but he determined to die as the husband of the lady with whom he was living.[135]

The second question was one of law. It was well established that the word 'wife' could, in appropriate circumstances, be construed as including a woman who was not validly married to the testator, whether because their marriage was void or even where there had been no ceremony at all. So it was clear that Josephine would, at the very least, be entitled to the contents of James' two houses, which he had left to her as his 'dear wife' with no conditions attached. More difficult was the clause setting out how the residue of James' estate was to be dealt with. He had left the income from it to 'my said wife during her life, if she shall so long continue my widow, for her own use and benefit'. But could Josephine continue to be James' widow if she had never been his legal wife?

A couple of decades earlier, the Court of Appeal had addressed this scenario in *In re Boddington*.[136] In that case, a husband had made a will leaving a legacy of £200 to his wife, together with a further £300 'so long as she shall continue my widow and unmarried'. The marriage was subsequently annulled on the ground of the husband's impotence, and he died a few months later without making a new will. In this case, the court had held that although the wife was entitled to the £200 on the basis that his

[132] *Wilkinson v Joughin* (1866) LR 2 Eq 319, 322.
[133] *Giles v Giles; Penfold v Penfold* (1836) 1 Keen 685; 48 ER 471.
[134] ibid 693. In a similar vein, see *In re Pitts' Will; ex parte Nicholson* (1859) 8 WR 157; *Peter v Nicholls* (1871) LR 11 Eq 391.
[135] *In Re Wagstaff; Wagstaff v Jalland* [1907] 2 Ch 35, 42.
[136] *In re Boddington* (1883) 22 Ch D 597.

intention to benefit her was clear, she was not entitled to the £300 as she could not be his 'widow' once their marriage had been annulled. As well as relying on *Boddington*, counsel for Berners Wagstaff had a further argument. This was that even if the word 'widow' could be construed as including the relict of a void marriage, Josephine had ceased to be James' widow, 'even in a secondary sense', when she had admitted her bigamy.

Kekewich, however, took a different view. In his opinion, the term 'widow' did not have to be interpreted so strictly as to exclude a woman who was not the legal wife of the testator. As he added, it 'would have been a cruel mockery' for James to have made a will with the intention that Josephine would have been deprived of the income of the estate if it was discovered that she was not in fact his widow:

> I think I am not bound to attribute any such intention to the testator. It seems to me to be contrary to all rules, and to all that I know about the testator. He intended to provide for her, and he cannot have intended in providing for her to take away the income in the very words in which he professed to give it.[137]

The final question was whether there were any circumstances upon which Josephine would cease to be entitled to the income from the estate during her lifetime. What, for example, should happen if she were to return to her lawful husband, Alfred Jalland? James had specified that the residuary estate would pass to Berners 'after her decease or second marriage'. Kekewich took the view that the reference to 'after her second marriage' meant 'unless and until she contracts a marriage subsequent to my death'. This did not, in his view, include Josephine either 'proclaiming herself as the wife of Mr. Jalland or by re-uniting herself to him'.[138]

Even then Berners did not give up. He appealed to the Court of Appeal, challenging both the judge's findings of fact and his interpretation of the law. Reading the official law report of the judgment that was handed down in November 1907, one might get the impression that the key issue was almost exclusively one of law, and whether Kekewich's interpretation of the terms 'wife' and 'widow' was correct.[139] Although this did form part of Berners' challenge, most of the time before the appellate court was spent on the question of whether James had really known of Josephine's earlier marriage, with Berners' counsel pointing out the inconsistencies in the stories that she and Alfred had told at different times.

But it was, in the words of the Master of the Rolls, Sir Herbert Cozens-Hardy, 'so difficult as to be almost hopeless' to try to challenge the findings of the court below.[140] As he pointed out, an appellate court always had to be very careful before coming to a different view of the facts, given that it did not have the advantage of seeing the witnesses and judging whether they were telling the truth. While he acknowledged that the story was a strange one, he thought it was 'more probable as a true story than as a false one'. He also noted that Josephine had been 'severely cross-examined by one of the ablest counsel at the Bar' without her testimony being substantially shaken, and that key points of the story were corroborated by witnesses 'whose integrity could not be impugned'. The

[137] *In Re Wagstaff* (n 135) 43.
[138] ibid 45.
[139] *In Re Wagstaff; Wagstaff v Jalland* [1908] 1 Ch 162.
[140] '*In Re Wagstaff-Wagstaff v Jalland*: Remarkable Will Case', *The Times*, 26 November 1907.

Court of Appeal therefore upheld Kekewich's finding that James knew, and confirmed his interpretation of James' will.

The upshot was that Josephine got the money – and would only lose it if she went through a further ceremony of marriage. This she was unlikely to do. When Kekewich had referred in his judgment to the possibility of Josephine reuniting with her first husband, this was no idle speculation – because this is precisely what happened. The 1911 census recorded her living in some comfort in Bedford, with a housemaid, cook and nurse in attendance.[141] Also in the household was Alfred, and an 11-year-old child named Dorothy Josephine Wagstaff, described as her adopted daughter. Under the column 'Completed years the present marriage has lasted', she wrote '27', referring back to their 1884 wedding. She and Alfred then remained together until her death in 1935, when she was recorded as 'wife of Alfred Gibson Jalland' – which was true, if not the whole truth. A modest Celtic Cross in the corner of a cemetery in Eastbourne invites passers-by to 'pray for the repose of the soul of Josephine Jalland'. There is no hint that she had once been at the centre of a sensational bigamy case that made headlines around the world.

[141] TNA, RG14, *Census Returns of England and Wales, 1911*. Josephine, unusually, was described as 'head' and Alfred as 'husband'.

14

The Unprosecuted

One of the most common questions asked about bigamy, but also one of the hardest to answer, is how many bigamists were never prosecuted. Given some of the wildly speculative claims that have been made about this, it is necessary to spend a little time looking at the evidence in order to put the case studies that follow in context.[1]

Judging from the official statistics that are available from 1857, a high percentage of cases of bigamy known to the police resulted in a prosecution. Only after the Second World War did this begin to change.[2] But, of course, official statistics only cover those cases that came to the attention of the authorities in the first place. Social historian Ginger Frost, writing about bigamy in the nineteenth century, has claimed that only one-fifth of bigamy cases were ever prosecuted.[3] She has also suggested that 'communities accepted bigamous families under certain conditions' – in essence, if the bigamist had a good reason for leaving the first spouse, was honest with the second, and, in the case of male bigamists, was able to support both families.[4] But the one-fifth estimate derived from a mistaken premise,[5] and her claims about the supposed acceptability of bigamy are based solely on cases that came to trial. She does not provide any actual examples of bigamous families being accepted by the community. That the occasional honest or hard-done-by bigamist got a lower sentence can only tell us what factors a judge regarded as mitigating the offence; it tells us nothing about how the community

[1] L Stone, *The Family, Sex and Marriage in England 1500-1800* (New York, Harper & Row, 1977) 40, claiming that bigamy was 'easy and common' and *Uncertain Unions and Broken Lives: Marriage and Divorce in England, 1660-1857* (Oxford, Oxford University Press, 1995) 254, speculating, without any evidence that it was 'at least likely that thousands, probably tens of thousands, of English men and women committed bigamy in the seventeenth and eighteenth centuries and went unpunished'.

[2] See further *Double Trouble*, ch 10.

[3] G Frost, *Living in Sin: Cohabiting as Husband and Wife in Nineteenth-Century England* (Manchester, Manchester University Press, 2008) 72.

[4] ibid 78, 82.

[5] *Double Trouble*, ch 8. In summary, Frost's one-in-five estimate was based on a study of late-nineteenth-century divorce petitions citing 'bigamy with adultery' as the ground for divorce. That analysis, by historian Gail Savage, had shown that only one in eight of the petitions made any reference to the respondent having been prosecuted for bigamy, and it was inferred from this that most of the rest had not been prosecuted. However, when I cross-checked such petitions against other sources, it quickly transpired that they were a very bad guide to whether the respondent was ever prosecuted: some respondents were not guilty of bigamy in the criminal sense and so could not be prosecuted, others had yet to be tried, and others had simply left the country and were beyond the reach of the law. Once we exclude those cases of 'bigamy' where we would not expect there to be a prosecution, and add in all those cases that *were* prosecuted, then over half of the bigamous marriages cited in these divorce petitions did in fact result in a prosecution.

regarded it.[6] In any case, given that deception was endemic and most of the population subsisted on wages that were barely sufficient to support one family, let alone two, few bigamists would have been able to meet the conditions identified by Frost.

Equally, we need to be wary of relying on newspaper reports of community reactions to bigamy, if only because they are almost always skewed towards cases of *disapproval*. In one case from Gloucester, the public sympathy and support initially reported to have been extended to the deceived second wife rapidly vanished when it transpired that she had taken her bigamist husband back; their customers dropped away, the neighbours 'having refused to hold intercourse with persons so conducting themselves', and their business had to be put up for sale.[7] Even more dramatically, the light sentence handed down to one bigamist at the Devon assizes in 1858 allegedly resulted in a riot when he returned to his home town with his second wife.[8] And the 1873 bigamous marriage of a miner's wife led to reports of effigies of her and her new husband being burnt in their village.[9] Such extreme reactions were clearly untypical.

But with a large enough sample, it is possible to identify some shared characteristics that explain why certain individuals were not prosecuted. Having put out a call for information on the topic, hundreds of helpful family historians replied with details.[10] My analysis of this material yielded two key findings. The first was that most of the unprosecuted might not have been guilty of bigamy at all: as many as 64 per cent might have had a good defence on the basis of seven years' separation or, after 1889, a genuine belief in the death of the first spouse.[11] The second related to the distance that the remainder had put between their first and second marriages: over half (53 per cent) of those who had not waited seven years to remarry had put 50 miles or more between the two ceremonies, with the mean average being a staggering 1,746 miles.[12]

From this, we can draw two broader conclusions. First, the fact that so many waited so long to remarry indicates a desire to avoid committing bigamy in its criminal sense. Given what we know about misunderstandings of the seven-year defence,[13] it is entirely possible that many of those who waited even believed that their second marriage was valid. Second, the fact that others moved so far tells us that they knew they were doing wrong and hoped to escape detection. This, it should be noted, applies to the prosecuted sample as well as the unprosecuted: virtually no one committed bigamy in the same place as they had married legally. In short, although some bigamists did manage

[6] On the factors that would be seen as either aggravating or mitigating the offence, see *Double Trouble*, chs 5 and 7. For the dangers in assuming that a light sentence reflected approval of the relationship, see the case of John Taylor in chapter 9.

[7] 'Apprehension for Bigamy', *Gloucestershire Chronicle*, 28 October 1843.

[8] 'Riot at Brixham', *Morning Post*, 16 December 1858.

[9] 'Remarkable Case of Bigamy Near Castle Eden', *Shields Daily News*, 16 January 1874.

[10] For the details of the call for information, and the full findings, see R Probert, 'Escaping detection: illegal second marriages and the crime of bigamy' (2022) 6 *Journal of Genealogy and Family History* 27.

[11] N = 264. On average 16 years had elapsed between the first and second marriages – almost seven years longer than the equivalent figure for a comparator sample of 134 bigamists prosecuted at the assizes in the 1850s. The unknown factor, of course, is whether the remarrying spouse knew that their first spouse was still alive.

[12] Again, this was considerably longer than for those prosecuted: within my comparator sample the mean distance was 97 miles and the median just 18 (n = 137). Where one of the locations was outside England and Wales, the estimated distance is almost certainly an underestimate: distances were calculated as the crow flies, and the actual mileage covered in crossing the oceans would have been considerably higher.

[13] See chapter 8.

to escape prosecution, there is no evidence to support the idea that this was because bigamy was acceptable within their communities.

The case studies in this chapter focus on those who were not just unprosecuted but effectively unprosecutable. In the case of Henry Cecil, it seems likely that he managed to conceal his bigamy from everyone except (perhaps) his second wife. Thomas Estcourt Cresswell's alleged bigamy, by contrast, attracted considerable publicity, but the case against him was at best unprovable, while the 'Gentleman of great Property' who was allegedly due to be tried at the Surrey assizes in 1766 seems to have been a complete invention. Sir Harcourt James Lees strategically left the country to ensure that he would not end up in the dock. Conversely, Ann Stimson's first husband was on the other side of the world; had she ever been accused of bigamy, the prosecution would have faced the challenge of proving he was still alive. Finally, in the later part of the twentieth century, Roggee Goodfellow Sammy-Joe was not prosecuted on account of doubts as to whether a man could be convicted of bigamy if his first marriage was potentially polygamous.

The Unprovable: Thomas Estcourt Cresswell, 1742 and 1744

In 1750, the clergyman Henry Gally published a pamphlet railing against the evils of clandestine weddings. One particular problem, he noted, was the risk that someone who had married in good faith might suddenly find that their marriage was void on account of their supposed spouse's previous clandestine wedding. That, he claimed, had been the case for Mr Cresswell and Miss Warneford. The couple had been publicly married:

> yet, as a clandestine marriage between Mr Cresswell and Miss Scrope, is alleged to have been then subsisting, the marriage between Mr Cresswell and Miss Warneford thereby became illegal and null; and their issue was illegitimate. Now as Miss Warneford proceeded in this affair *bona fide*, what amends can be made to her and her children, for so great an injury? And it appears farther, that the case of Miss Scrope was the same with that as Miss Warneford. For upon her searching the register of the Fleet, where they were married, for her marriage with Mr Cresswell, a prior marriage was found entered there between Mr Cresswell and another woman, who was then, and is still living. So that Miss Scrope received from Mr Cresswell the very same injury, which he afterwards practised towards Miss Warneford: and if they had had any children by this marriage they would all have been illegitimate.[14]

The Reverend Gally's readers may well have felt considerable sympathy for both Miss Warneford and Miss Scrope as well as for the unknown but presumably abandoned first wife. They may also have wondered why the duplicitous Mr Cresswell was not being prosecuted for bigamy.[15] But there is a hint in Gally's prudent use of 'alleged'. As the

[14] H Gally, *Some Considerations upon Clandestine Marriages* (London, 1750) 17–18 (spelling modernised and Warnsford corrected to Warneford). See also L Stone, *Road to Divorce: England 1530-1987* (Oxford, Oxford University Press, 1990) 119, who relied on this to claim (erroneously) that the Cresswell-Warneford marriage was declared to be void.

[15] cf E Wilputte, 'Haywood's Tabloid Journalism: *Dalinda: or, The Double Marriage* and the Cresswell Bigamy Case' (2014) 4 *Journal for Early Modern Cultural Studies* 122, 126, 134, who claims, without any evidence, that Thomas was prosecuted.

lengthy accounts left by Thomas Estcourt Cresswell and Elizabeth Scrope reveal, much more was alleged than was ever actually proved.

The story first came to public attention in October 1747, when an anonymous letter appeared in the *General Evening Post* alleging that a 'Mr C' had secretly married 'Miss S' and then gone on, with her acquiescence, to marry a 'Lady of a large Fortune', by whom he had two children. The first marriage, it claimed, had only been discovered when 'Mr L', 'a Gentleman of a considerable Estate', paid his addresses to 'Miss S', prompting the jealous 'Mr C' to boast of having already slept with her. Upon 'Mr L' reproaching her, she revealed that she and 'Mr C' were married.[16] By the end of the month, 'C' was revealed as Thomas Cresswell and 'S' as Elizabeth Scrope, when 'Mr L' – Lancelot Lee – wrote a follow-up letter seeking to exonerate Elizabeth and paint Thomas as the villain of the piece. A third letter then appeared, this time from Thomas, questioning many of Lancelot's claims and flatly denying others,[17] on which he subsequently expanded in a 78-page pamphlet.[18] Finally, Elizabeth weighed in with her own answer to all the claims and counter-claims – which ran to a whopping 232 pages.[19]

This is a case where it makes sense to work backwards from the known facts and then consider the likelihood of other claims being true. Of the three alleged weddings mentioned in Gally's pamphlet, the only one that can be verified is that of Thomas Cresswell and Ann Warneford. This took place on 6 February 1744, in Ann's home parish of Bibury in Gloucestershire.[20] Nor does Thomas appear to have made any attempt to conceal his courtship of Ann – if his investigation into her financial standing deserves such a term. Her main attraction to him appears to have been the fact that she possessed sufficient money to enable him to pay off a mortgage of £8,000 on his estate.

Thomas was very frank in his *Narrative* about the failure of his marriage to Ann, reporting that he had 'heartily repented' of having married her.[21] She may well have felt the same way, given that Thomas had resumed having sex with Elizabeth. Here we are of course dependent on the accounts given by the parties themselves, but both Thomas and Elizabeth acknowledged that they had been sleeping together. Their only real point of difference was when they had first begun to do so. Thomas said that it was after they had sat down and read the marriage service in the *Book of Common Prayer* together one Sunday afternoon. But Elizabeth, while acknowledging their having read the service, claimed that they did not have sex until after they were married by a clergyman.

[16] *General Evening Post*, 3 October 1747.

[17] An enterprising publisher then gathered the three letters together and published them under the moralising title, *The miserable effects of grasping at riches By any Unlawful or Unseemly Methods; exemplified In the melancholy and remarkable Instance of Anxiety and Distress, at this Time laboured under by some Persons who once seemed by Nature formed for, and might have otherwise enjoyed, every Delight this Earth affords. With A Word of Advice to the interesting Parties, in Relation to their future Conduct* (London, 1748). The authorship of this pamphlet has been attributed to Lancelot Lee, but it seems implausible that he would choose such a title.

[18] TE Cresswell, *A Narrative of the Affair Between Mr Cresswell and Miss Scrope … By which may be discovered the Falsities, Misrepresentations etc in a Letter in the General Evening Post, October 31, signed Lancelot Lee* (London, 1748). It was clear from the title that Thomas did not think that Lancelot had written the first letter.

[19] E Scrope, *Miss Scrope's Answer to Mr Cresswell's Narrative* (London, 1749).

[20] Ancestry, *Gloucestershire Church of England Parish Registers*, Gdr/V1/33.

[21] Cresswell (n 18) 37–39.

This brings us on to that supposed marriage, which Elizabeth claimed took place in a house in the vicinity of the Fleet Prison on 23 April 1742. To explain the absence of any record, she also claimed that Thomas had refused to pay the fee for registering it.[22] She said that she had subsequently returned to see if she could obtain any evidence of the ceremony, but the clergyman had apparently died and she had no clue as to the identity of the woman who had witnessed it. It is possible that it all took place as Elizabeth said. Nevertheless, there are reasons to be sceptical. For one thing, it seems surprising that neither the clergyman nor the witness (as far as we know) made any record of the ceremony subsequently. Any wedding of a lady and gentleman, where the gentleman refused to pay for the ceremony to be registered, might be expected to alert those in attendance to the possibility of future disputes, and of money to be made by those in possession of the relevant evidence. Moreover, it needs to be borne in mind that by the time Elizabeth made these claims she was hoping to marry Lancelot. Claiming that she was married to Thomas might seem an odd strategy to adopt, but the alternative was to admit to having sex with him *without* being married – in which case there was a high chance that Lancelot might no longer want to marry her. Claiming an actual but unprovable marriage was therefore her best hope – especially when combined with the allegation that she had later discovered her marriage to Thomas to be void, which we will come onto in a moment.

Thomas, meanwhile, made no mention of any ceremony in the Fleet and consistently denied being married to Elizabeth – save in a conversation with Mrs Warneford, Ann's mother. When questioned by her following the revelations in the *General Evening Post*, he told her that he was married to Elizabeth 'but they could not prove it', and that he and Ann might still live happily together. Her response was that his prior marriage made it impossible for Ann to live with him 'in point of conscience'. When read against his litany of complaints about Ann and his clear desire to be free from her, it seems entirely possible that Thomas was playing fast and loose with the truth. After all, he had no interest in his marriage to Ann being annulled, since he would lose his entitlement to her money. But telling Ann's mother that he was already married and then offering to continue to live with Ann was almost guaranteed to elicit this kind of indignant response. A separation agreement was duly drawn up between Thomas and Ann.

What, then, of the allegations that Thomas went through a ceremony in the Fleet with another woman *before* he married Elizabeth? Here the evidence is even more oblique, fragmentary and frustrating. Lancelot dropped hints but his claims tailed off into lines of asterisks.[23] Thomas in turn claimed that his comments on the matter had been erased by the friend who took his pamphlet to the printers as being 'of no consequence' to the Scrope family.[24] The most specific claim came from Elizabeth, who said that Lancelot had discovered this earlier wedding when searching for evidence of her marriage to Thomas.[25] But she added that she had refrained from naming the woman in question out of consideration for her and her family.

[22] ibid 39.
[23] *The miserable effects* (n 17) 24.
[24] Cresswell (n 18) 74.
[25] Scrope (n 19) 121.

It had always seemed somewhat implausible to me that Lancelot would have just stumbled across an entry of Thomas' prior marriage. There was, after all, no central register of Fleet weddings but rather hundreds of private notebooks kept by different people. Of course, if he *had* found a record referring to a Thomas Estcourt Cresswell, there would have been every reason for him to regard this as conclusive proof of Thomas' bigamy. But according to Elizabeth, the register that she claimed Lancelot had discovered had only referred to 'this lady's and Mr Cresswell's Christian names'.[26] Even finding a 'Thomas Estcourt' would not be conclusive (and a search of the digitised Fleet registers available on Ancestry revealed no such record). So while it is entirely possible that Lancelot found a reference to a Thomas marrying in the decade before 1742, it would have been a huge and unwarranted leap to connect it to Thomas Cresswell.[27]

So the evidential basis for this first alleged marriage is so flimsy as to be virtually worthless. But its fortuitous 'discovery' by Lancelot meant that he regarded Elizabeth as free to marry him – which they did in 1750.[28] In the absence of any proof that Elizabeth was validly married to Thomas, then Lancelot and Elizabeth's marriage must be presumed to have been valid. Sadly, it also proved very short-lived: Elizabeth was dead within the year.

Thomas never married again. In 1754, he was elected as the MP for Wootton Bassett, a post he held until 1774. He died in 1788 and is buried in the graveyard at Sherston in Wiltshire. His will set aside £200 to be used to erect a monument in the chancel of the church in memory of his uncle, his mother and himself – carefully stipulating that it should contain an inscription 'of the times of our respective births and burials only'.[29]

Had Elizabeth and Lancelot ever made good on their threats to prosecute Thomas for bigamy, he would have certainly been acquitted for lack of evidence. Elizabeth had no proof of any wedding: no record, no witnesses, no public cohabitation with Thomas, nor any acknowledgement by him that she was his wife. Similarly, if anyone had sought to annul Thomas' marriage to Ann, any such suit would similarly have failed for lack of evidence. So the simple answer as to why Thomas was never prosecuted is simply that the case against him was unprovable. But there is also a distinct possibility that he was not guilty of having committed bigamy even once, let alone twice, and that the alleged first and second marriages were a pure invention.

The Invented: A 'Gentleman of Great Property'

In June 1766, various newspapers reported that a 'Gentleman of great Property' in Surrey had been taken into custody for bigamy. He had, it was claimed, married 'a Lady

[26] ibid 217.

[27] Even if the lady in question had a particularly distinctive forename, there is nothing to suggest that Lancelot knew of her existence before undertaking his search of the registers. A search of the digitised registers reveals 16,694 matches to the name Thomas in the period.

[28] Boyd's 1st miscellaneous marriage index, 1415–1808.

[29] TNA, *Records of the Prerogative Court of Canterbury*, PROB11/1172.

of Fortune, his first Wife being living' and had entered into recognizances in the huge sum of £5,000 to appear at the next Guildford assizes.[30] But the Surrey assizes came and went without anyone being indicted for bigamy.[31]

The cynical reader might suspect that this was a case of a wealthy man being able to get away with bigamy. But in September that same year a virtually identical story appeared, though the sum stated was £3,000, the arrest happened in Southwark, and the trial was to take place at the Kingston assizes.[32] February 1767 saw a bumper crop of similar stories appearing – with the arrest again being reported as if it had just happened.[33] By June 1767 the story had changed again: it was still a gentleman from Surrey who had just been arrested, but this time he had married three wives, all of whom possessed considerable wealth.[34] And again, there was never any corresponding prosecution at the assizes.[35]

It would seem, then, that this story was a pure invention – mere journalistic 'filler' designed to pad column inches on a slow news day that was then picked up and recycled by other newspapers. As Jeremy Black has noted, most eighteenth-century newspapers were produced by cutting and pasting news items from other papers, with the result that 'many items were inaccurate, unchecked and conjectural'.[36]

Nor was this the only instance. Every so often there would be an account of an unnamed individual who had been arrested for bigamy, with the titillating hint that large sums of money were involved. There was, for example, the young sea officer who had married three women in two years, 'each with a genteel fortune',[37] the tradesman whose second wife had brought him a fortune of £6,000,[38] and the 'military candidate' who had married 'a young Lady of Fortune'.[39] Again, none of these can be matched to actual cases. Such stories may have created an impression that bigamy was more common than was actually the case.

So we should be equally cautious of claims about other unnamed bigamists. In 1763, the *Newcastle Courant* ran a story about wives remarrying while their husbands were at sea:

> A few days ago the following incident happened at Shields: A carpenter of that place having been impressed into his Majesty's service, his wife not hearing anything of him for some

[30] *Newcastle Chronicle*, 7 June 1766; *Coventry Standard*, 9 June 1766; *Salisbury and Winchester Journal*, 9 June 1766; *Sherbourne Mercury*, 9 June 1766.

[31] TNA, ASSI 94/1016 (30 July 1766).

[32] This was reported by the *Salisbury and Winchester Journal*, 8 September 1766 and the *Newcastle Courant*, 13 September 1766, with both claiming the arrest to have happened 'yesterday'.

[33] *London Evening Post*, 14–17 February 1767; *Oxford Journal*, 21 February 1767; *Kentish Weekly Post or Canterbury Journal*, 21 February 1767; *Newcastle Courant*, 21 February 1767; *Coventry Standard*, 23 February 1767; *Aris's Birmingham Gazette*, 23 February 1767; *Chester Courant*, 24 February 1767. Two months later, an identical report appeared in the *London Chronicle*, similarly claiming it had happened a few days earlier: *London Chronicle*, 28–30 April 1767.

[34] *Gloucester Journal*, 15 June 1767; *Aris's Birmingham Gazette*, 15 June 1767; *Kentish Weekly Post or Canterbury Journal*, 17 June 1767; *Newcastle Chronicle*, 20 June 1767; *Ipswich Journal*, 20 June 1767.

[35] TNA, ASSI 94/1022 (25 March 1767); ASSI 94/1028 (19 August 1767).

[36] J Black, *The English Press, 1621-1861* (Stroud, Sutton Publishing, 2001) 11.

[37] *London Evening Post*, 7–9 August 1759, 31 May–3 June 1766; *Chester Courant*, 3 February 1767.

[38] *Bath Chronicle and Weekly Gazette*, 12 November 1767; *Aris's Birmingham Gazette*, 16 November 1767; *Sherbourne Mercury*, 16 November 1767.

[39] *St James' Chronicle*, 1–3 November 1768; *Manchester Mercury*, 2 January 1770.

> months, and enquiry being made after him, she was informed he was dead; on which a master of a ship made his addresses to her, and they were married. But the first husband arriving at Shields, and finding his wife in the possession of another, applied to a gentleman in that neighbourhood for his advice and assistance, who summoned the parties before him, and settled the matter to the satisfaction of all.[40]

It might appear to be a plausible enough story. But apart from the lack of names, one has to wonder how the writer learnt of the incident if matters were resolved as privately as the story implies. The piece went on to claim that there had been 'some other incidents' among sailors' wives, one or two of whom had gone on to have children by the second husband, but that these had been 'amicably settled', and the absent husbands made aware that the remarriage was due to 'their negligence in not writing'.[41] Again, it might be true, but equally it might not.

The fact that some stories were invented does not mean that newspapers should be dismissed as a source: stories that specifically named the parties proved highly unlikely to be made up. It does, however, underline the importance of looking at a lot of newspaper reports, to be able to spot the ones that were recycled and get a sense of the likelihood of others having been invented, and to cross-check with other sources wherever possible.

The Undetected: Henry Cecil, 1790

Often, when we find a bigamist who was never prosecuted, it can be difficult to be sure whether this was because they were never detected, or because no one wished to prosecute them. But in the case of Henry Cecil, it seems highly likely that no one – apart from perhaps his second wife Sarah – ever knew that he had committed bigamy, at least during his lifetime.[42]

Henry was born into an aristocratic family, and many of the details of his life are well documented. Following the death of his grandfather, the eighth Earl of Exeter, he was brought up at the magnificent Burghley House by his uncle Brownlow, the ninth Earl. In May 1776, at the age of 22, he married heiress Emma Vernon at the fashionable church of St George, Hanover Square, and moved to her family home, Hanbury Hall in Worcestershire. Relatively little is known of their married life over the next decade or so, except that their only child, born in 1777, died at the age of just two months, and that they managed to run up a considerable amount of debt. Much more, however, is known about their separation.

In 1789, Emma confessed to Henry that for the last five years she had been in love with the local curate, William Sneyd. Henry (at least by his own account) tried to save his marriage, proposing first that they should live separately under the same roof and then

[40] *Newcastle Courant*, 29 January 1763. The story was sufficiently newsworthy to be repeated in several other newspapers: *Oxford Journal*, 5 February 1763; *Coventry Standard*, 7 February 1763; *Chester Courant*, 8 February 1763.

[41] ibid.

[42] This summary is based on R Probert, J Bailey and J Shaffer, *A Noble Affair: The Remarkable True Story of the Runaway Wife, the Bigamous Earl, and the Farmer's Daughter* (Kenilworth, Takeaway, 2013).

that he would take the blame for their separation. But Emma refused to give William up, and took advantage of what was intended to be their farewell meeting to run away with him. Cuckolded and deceived, Henry also left Hanbury Hall, although he promised to keep in touch with the local rector, the Reverend William Burslem.

We next find Henry in the Shropshire village of Great Bolas, passing under the name of John Jones. From there he wrote lengthy letters to the Reverend Burslem, rhapsodising about the peace and tranquillity of country life. And on 13 April 1790, he went through a ceremony of marriage with a young girl named Sarah Hoggins, the daughter of a local farmer – a detail he failed to mention in his correspondence with the rector.

Since Henry was still married to Emma, the marriage to Sarah was both void and bigamous. But Henry had at least made the first tentative steps towards ending his first marriage, having written to Burslem at the end of March 1790 to authorise him to employ 'some professional Man to initiate the proper steps for the obtaining a divorce betwixt myself and my now wife Emma Cecil'.[43] The first step, in June 1790, was to sue the Reverend William Sneyd for adultery with Emma in a lawsuit for what was euphemistically called 'criminal conversation'.[44] These proceedings having been successfully concluded, and damages of £1,000 awarded, Henry then sought a divorce *a mensa et thoro* on the basis of Emma's adultery. Once that had been granted, he could then petition Parliament to pass a private Act dissolving his marriage to Emma and allowing him to remarry legally. On 10 June 1791, King George III gave the Bill his Royal Assent, and the marriage of Henry and Emma was finally at an end.

Less than four months later, on 3 October, Henry and Sarah went through a second ceremony of marriage – this time in the small and unfashionable church of St Mildred, Bread Street, in the City of London, and with Henry using his true name. After a brief visit to Burghley House to introduce Sarah to his uncle Brownlow – and their future home – Henry and Sarah returned to Great Bolas. This was a strategic move, as by this time Sarah was pregnant. The birth of their first child, in February 1792, would have raised no eyebrows among the villagers, who thought that Henry (or rather 'John Jones') and Sarah had married in 1790. But Henry took care not to reveal it to those who were only aware of the 1791 wedding, only announcing the birth of their daughter Sophia a tactful nine months later. Inconveniently, Sarah became pregnant again almost immediately after giving birth – rather than after when she was supposed to have given birth – necessitating some further finessing of dates in Henry's subsequent correspondence.

Towards the end of 1793, Brownlow fell sick and died. Henry became the tenth Earl of Exeter, and he and Sarah, together with young Sophia, moved from Great Bolas to Burghley House. At least by this time, the fact that Sophia was five months older than she was meant to be would have been less obvious to all but the most suspicious observers. Tragically, Sarah's time as mistress of Burghley House was to be all too short: in 1797, after giving birth for the fourth time in five years, she died, aged just 24.

Given how much was written about Henry's divorce from Emma, and his marriage to Sarah, it seems safe to say that his bigamy was not public knowledge. Instead, nineteenth-century writers revelled in the romantic story of the young, modest girl who

[43] Burghley House, letter to Burslem, 30 March 1790.

[44] *The Remarkable Trial of the Rev. William Sneyd, for Seducing, Debauching, and Carrying Off, the wife of Henry Cecil, Esq.* (London, 1790).

was elevated to wealth and rank.[45] Only in the 1890s did investigation of the registers of Great Bolas reveal that the first wedding of 'John Jones' and Sarah Hoggins had preceded his divorce from Emma.[46] It also seems unlikely that Henry's bigamy was known even to his friends and acquaintances. His letters, as we have seen, show him carefully concealing the details that would expose his crime. Nor is there any reason to think that it would have been known in Great Bolas. Even if a newspaper reporting Henry's divorce from Emma had found its way to the village, no one would have had any reason to connect the story to their 'John Jones'. The only person who might possibly have known was Sarah. Henry would, after all, have had to come up with some reason as to why they had to go through a second wedding ceremony. Then again, it is perfectly possible to think of other reasons he might have given short of revealing that he was already married.

So Henry's case shows that it was possible for bigamists to escape detection. But we need to bear in mind the particular circumstances of his case. Emma's elopement meant that no one was looking for him, and he had the financial and intellectual resources to move across the country and spin different stories to different people. The main take-home message from his case is that bigamy just made one's life a lot more complicated.

The Left-behind Spouse: Ann Stimson, 1803

In 1795, a young woman named Ann Place married Mat Stimson.[47] Their daughter Annie was baptised the following year, alongside her cousin, the daughter of Ann's brother Francis.[48] A son, Matthew, followed in 1798. But in 1799, 24-year-old Mat was convicted of highway robbery. At his trial at the Old Bailey, the man he had robbed, John Field, told the court that Mat had stopped him while he was travelling down the Edgware Road and threatened him with a pistol: 'he said he had a wife and two children in much distress, and he swore by G-d he would shoot me if I did not immediately deliver my money'.[49] John handed over all the change he had – a gold half-guinea and four shillings – and, on being pressed further by Mat, his pocket-book, containing a banknote for £2. Mat then rode off. But within half an hour he had been arrested, and he immediately returned the money to John – with the exception of the shillings, which John said he could keep.

That was all the proof that was needed to convict Mat. But two witnesses spoke of his good character and of how his acts were borne out of desperation, one noting that he was out of employment and another that he had been ill for two months. The jury

[45] Among the works inspired by their story were Thomas Moore's 1822 poem 'You Remember Ellen' in his *Irish Melodies*, Tennyson's *The Lord of Burleigh*, first published in 1842, John Everett Millais' 1857 picture of the same name, and a 'pastoral cantata' composed by Francesco Schira in 1873.

[46] WO Woodall, 'The Lord of Burghley and Sarah Hoggins', *Notes and Queries*, 8th Series, Vol 1, 14 May 1892.

[47] Ancestry, *London Church of England Parish Registers*, P77/All/018 (marriage at All Saints, Fulham, 27 April 1795).

[48] Ancestry, *London Church of England Parish Registers*, MS07221/002 (baptism at St Sepulchre, Holborn, 5 September 1796).

[49] *OBP*, 8 May 1799 (Matthew *Stinson*).

recommended him to mercy, which was endorsed by the prosecutor.[50] His sentence of death was subsequently commuted to transportation for life,[51] and he was sent out to New South Wales on the *Earl Cornwallis*.

If Ann and her two young children had been in much distress before, Mat's departure must have made their situation even worse. And after Mat had been gone some months, a former suitor of Ann's, one Thomas Roydhouse, came back on the scene and began to court Ann again.[52] It would have been entirely understandable if Ann had jumped at the chance of marrying him there and then. As it was, she waited several years, during which time there was no news of Mat. She eventually married Thomas at St Martin in the Fields on 27 April 1803.[53]

Ann's brother Francis noted her remarriage in his diary. Neither of them could have imagined that this document would subsequently come to be regarded as an important historical source, with poor Ann's actions being used to illustrate the supposed ease and prevalence of bigamy.[54] Historian Lawrence Stone gave the impression that she was somewhat insouciant about the risk of committing bigamy, claiming that she 'soon remarried an old suitor, apparently without any qualms or objections on the grounds that she already had a husband who was presumably still alive'.[55]

On the other side of the world, Mat was indeed still alive, but Ann had no means of knowing this. In the absence of any news, it would not have been unreasonable for her to conclude that he might well be dead. And this is what the law would have presumed, had the validity of her remarriage to Thomas been called into question in any civil legal proceedings.[56] The presumption would have been in favour of its validity, and the onus would have been on those claiming otherwise to show that Mat was still alive. Similarly, for Ann to be prosecuted for bigamy, the prosecution would have had to provide evidence that Mat was alive when she married Thomas in 1803.

Stone also used Ann's case to argue that 'more or less permanent desertion' was 'regarded as morally dissolving the marriage'.[57] Again, this is difficult to square with the fact that she waited four years to remarry. More significantly, in all of the cases that I have reviewed, I have found no example of anyone expressing a belief that their first spouse's desertion meant that they had a *right* to remarry. Desertion might well provide a *reason* for a remarriage, particularly for a wife who had no other means of support, but that was a different matter. Husbands who had been deserted were more likely to advert to the fact that their wife had formed a new relationship (or, alternatively, that they believed she had died) when explaining their decision to remarry.

This is significant in terms of how we interpret the excuses and justifications that individuals *did* provide. Adultery was, after all, a ground for a divorce *a mensa et*

[50] ibid.

[51] TNA, *Home Office and Prison Commission: Prisons Records, Series 1*, PCOM 2, 1770-1951 (May 1799).

[52] M Thale (ed), *The Autobiography of Francis Place (1771-1854)* (Cambridge, Cambridge University Press, 1972) 135.

[53] Ancestry, *Westminster Church of England Parish Registers*, STM/PR/6/19.

[54] Stone, *The Family, Sex and Marriage* (n 1) 40; R Phillips, *Putting Asunder: A history of divorce in Western society* (Cambridge, Cambridge University Press, 1988) 298.

[55] ibid.

[56] *R v The Inhabitants of Twyning, in Gloucestershire* (1819) 2 Barn & Ald 386; 106 ER 407.

[57] Stone, *The Family, Sex and Marriage* (n 1) 40.

thoro, and – for those wealthy enough to obtain one – a full Parliamentary divorce. Desertion was not. As the ecclesiastical judge Sir William Scott had noted in *Evans v Evans*, granting a separation on that ground would simply 'confirm the desertion, and gratify the deserter'.[58] The fact that men did frequently advert to the idea that their wife's adultery justified them in remarrying, but that no equivalent argument was made in relation to desertion, is yet another illustration of the importance of the law in shaping beliefs.[59]

Sadly, Ann's story does not have a happy ending. As Francis recorded, they had all hoped that she would 'do well' after her marriage to Thomas:

> but she was not now the same sort of person she was when she married Stimson … her sedateness had now become a settled melancholy she was no longer neat, had no care for anything, made home uncomfortable to her husband who fell into despair lost his sober habits and took to drinking. In a short time his health became impaired, his business was neglected and he dropped gradually into a state of miserable poverty. My sister lingered on from melancholy to a state of perfect apathy and died miserably.[60]

The Strategically Absent Spouse: Sir Harcourt James Lees, 1887

Harriett Lees could hardly have done more to try to bring her husband to justice. The couple had married in Kensington register office in December 1872, their choice of venue being determined by the fact that both had previously been married and divorced by their former spouses.[61] After their wedding, they had lived together at various places in France and Germany as well as in England. Harcourt then deserted Harriett in September 1878, shortly before she was due to give birth to their fifth child.[62]

Some years later, Harriett discovered that Harcourt had gone through a bigamous ceremony of marriage with a woman named Flora Nelson at the Lewisham register office in July 1881. She traced him to Devon and informed him of her intention to obtain a divorce. He promised to provide for her and their children, but then promptly vanished. She informed the authorities and a warrant was issued for his arrest, but he evaded it by leaving the country. Even then she did not give up, pursuing him first to Antwerp and then to Hamburg, where – by pure chance – she put up at the hotel where he and his second wife were staying. Upon her telling him that a warrant was out for his arrest, he confidently replied 'I am safe here' – but he made doubly sure by leaving for America the following day.[63]

[58] *Evans v Evans* (1790) 1 Hag Con 35, 120; 161 ER 466.

[59] See further chapter 8.

[60] Thale (n 52) 135.

[61] Harriett had married Charles Moore in 1865 and had been divorced by him in 1868 on account of her adultery with Harcourt: TNA, *Divorce and Matrimonial Causes Files, Moore v Moore and Lees*, J77/88/970. Harcourt's wife Charlotte subsequently divorced him on the basis of his adultery with Harriett combined with his desertion: *Lees v Lees*, J77/113/1952.

[62] TNA, *Lees v Lees*, J77/368/1128.

[63] *Lees v Lees*, *The Times*, 28 March 1887.

Harcourt's confidence that he was safe from being prosecuted was well founded. Nor was he alone in escaping prosecution by leaving the country. Within my sample of 220 divorce petitions citing bigamy with adultery, a total of 54 husbands (25 per cent of the sample) had also gone overseas. In a few cases, the bigamous marriage had taken place in England or Wales but the bigamist had left the country shortly afterwards.[64] Donald Campbell Mackey Gordon, for example, had sailed for New Zealand with his new wife Louisa within a few weeks of their wedding.[65] John Glasiere had left the country and headed for South America, although in doing so he had also deserted his second wife.[66] More often the second marriage had taken place overseas, and the parties had stayed overseas.[67] Charlotte and Isaiah Deck entered into a deed of separation in 1848 and he headed for the US, where he remarried in 1853.[68] The marriage of Clara and John Thomas Walker ran into trouble almost immediately, with Clara's subsequent petition for divorce giving details of his cruelty and consorting with prostitutes; he left for Australia a little over a year after their first anniversary and went through a further ceremony in Sydney in 1859.[69] And William John Robson, who had been transported to Australia for committing forgery, committed bigamy there after being given his ticket of leave.[70]

Harcourt's absence did not preclude the court from granting Harriett a decree *nisi* based on his bigamy and adultery. In the event, however, Harriett did not obtain her divorce. After the decree *nisi* had been granted, the Queen's Proctor intervened, asking for more detail about Harcourt's adultery and the dates that their children had been born. He then provided evidence that Harriett had herself committed adultery. This was fatal to her petition, and the decree was rescinded.[71]

The Potentially Polygamous First Marriage: Roggee Goodfellow Sammy-Joe, 1966

In 1964, the matrimonial entanglements of a Nigerian law student named Roggee Goodfellow Sammy-Joe came before the Divorce Court.[72] The question for the judge was whether he was married to his third wife Catherine or to his fourth wife Frances – or indeed to neither of them. The reason why Sammy-Joe was keen to have the issue resolved was that two maintenance orders had been made against him by different magistrates, one in favour of Frances and one in favour of Catherine, for a combined total of £8 10 shillings per week.[73] He was advised that the way to decide the issue would

[64] TNA, *Horn v Horn*, J77/23/H4; *Rowbotham v Rowbotham*, J77/44/R3; *Gunning v Gunning*, J77/21/G75.
[65] TNA, *Gordon v Gordon*, J77/170/4224; *The Times*, 29 January 1877.
[66] TNA, *Glasiere v Glasiere*, J77/184/4734; *The Times*, 6 June 1877.
[67] See also TNA, *Dixon v Dixon*, J77/13/D8; *Standard*, 4 June 1860.
[68] TNA, *Deck v Deck*, J77/13/D3; *Bury & Norwich Post*, 29 May 1860, 3 July 1860.
[69] TNA, *Walker v Walker*, J77/58/W48; *The Times*, 2 June 1862.
[70] TNA, *Robson v Robson, The Times*, 23 November 1864; J77/46/R99.
[71] *Lees v Lees (the Queen's Proctor Showing Cause), The Times*, 26 October 1887.
[72] Since the spellings of his first name differ between different sources, I have referred to him by his surname.
[73] 'The two-wife tangle of Mr Sammy-Joe', *Western Daily Press*, 22 October 1964; '"Two-Wife" Poser Sets Judge a Problem', *Daily Mirror*, 23 October 1964.

be for him to seek two separate declarations in relation to each of these marriages and have the two cases heard together.[74]

Each of Sammy-Joe's four marriages had taken a different form. The first two had taken place while he was in Nigeria, and the last two while he was in England, but he had remained domiciled in Nigeria throughout. His case is probably the most complex of all those we have looked at in terms of the legal issues that it raised about the relationship between different sets of rules governing marriage, both within and across national borders.

Sammy-Joe's first marriage, to Victoria, had taken place in Nigeria in 1951. It had been conducted by native law and custom and as such was potentially polygamous. His second marriage, to Felicia, had also taken place in Nigeria, this time in 1954. Had this marriage also been conducted by native law and custom, it would have been a valid polygamous marriage under Nigerian law. However, the ceremony had taken place in a register office. As Mr Justice Rees explained, this type of marriage was intended to be monogamous, and it was not open to a man to have both a valid potentially polygamous marriage and a valid monogamous marriage at the same time. So this second marriage was void.

Sammy-Joe then came to England in 1954, shortly followed by Felicia. Their relationship broke down in 1961, and later that year he went through his third marriage ceremony. This, however, took place by proxy, while he was in England and Catherine was in Nigeria, and as such was incapable of creating a valid marriage under Nigerian law. Before this ceremony, he had attempted to divorce Victoria by returning her dowry, but the evidence indicated that his actions were insufficient to effect a divorce under Nigerian law. This meant that he was still married to Victoria and that his fourth marriage, to Frances – which took place at Willesden register office in 1962 – was also void. Mr Justice Rees accordingly granted Sammy-Joe decrees of nullity in relation to his third and fourth marriages, and set aside the orders of the magistrates requiring him to pay maintenance to Catherine and Frances.[75] He also warned Sammy-Joe that he might be facing criminal charges, and sent the text of his judgment to the Director of Public Prosecutions (DPP).

The DPP's files in the National Archives include a document setting out whether any of Sammy-Joe's multiple marriages constituted a criminal offence.[76] The conclusion was that he could probably not be prosecuted for bigamy. Only a few years earlier, it had been held in *R v Sarwan Singh* that a prosecution for bigamy could not be based on a potentially polygamous first marriage.[77] The only previous case to have touched on the issue was *R v Naguib*, back in 1917, which had expressly refrained from deciding the point. As the writer of the opinion noted, while it would be *possible* to charge Sammy-Joe with bigamy 'in the hope that a red judge would reverse *Sarwan Singh*', he was doubtful whether any judge would do so.[78]

[74] 'Nigerian asks: Which is my wife?', *Birmingham Daily Post*, 26 November 1964.

[75] Sammy-Joe subsequently tried to recover the £449 he had paid Catherine. Since the money had been deducted from his earnings, he issued a writ against the North London Magistrates' Court for making an attachment of earnings order and his employers for complying with it. It was struck out as showing no cause of action: *Sammy-Joe v GPO Mount Pleasant Office and Others* [1967] 1 WLR 370.

[76] TNA, DPP 2/4162, memo dated 4 April 1966.

[77] *R v Sarwan Singh* [1962] 3 All ER 612, 615. See further *Double Trouble*, ch 10.

[78] The reference to a 'red' judge overruling *Sarwan Singh* was a reference to the colour of the robes worn by assize judges (who would not be bound by a decision that, like *Sarwan Singh*, had been made at quarter sessions).

The writer also noted that there would also be challenges in prosecuting Sammy-Joe for any other offences. In order to prosecute him under the Perjury Act 1911 for making a false declaration in relation to his fourth marriage, it would have to be shown that he had made such a declaration 'knowingly and wilfully'.[79] There was the possibility of a prosecution under the Sexual Offences Act 1956 for procuring a woman to have sex with him by false pretences, but that would only succeed if it could be proved that he knew his marriage was void.[80] The only offence they were left with was that of falsely procuring a passport for Felicia,[81] and here any prosecution would be 'extremely stale'.[82]

The upshot was that it was decided that no action should be taken against Sammy-Joe. As the writer concluded, it was yet another example of the 'inadequacy' of the current law to deal with those who had married under a very different system of laws. It is a final reminder of just how complex the law of bigamy is.

[79] Perjury Act 1911, s 3(1)(a).

[80] Sexual Offences Act 1956, s 3.

[81] Under Criminal Justice Act 1925, s 36, knowingly making a false statement for the purpose of procuring a passport was (and remains) an offence punishable with imprisonment for up to two years or a fine of up to £100 or both.

[82] TNA, DPP 2/4162.

BIBLIOGRAPHY

Books and pamphlets

The Arraignment, Trial, and Examination of Mary Moders (London, 1663).

The Lawyers Clark trappanned by the crafty Whore of Canterbury (London, 1663).

The great tryall and arraignment of the late distressed lady otherwise called the late Germain princess (London, 1663).

An Exact and True Relation of the Examination, Tryal and Condemnation of the German Princess, alias Mary Carleton, at Justice-Hall in the Old Baily, January 17, 1672 (London, 1672).

The Memoires of Mary Carleton, commonly stiled the German Princess being a narrative of her life and death interwoven with many strange and pleasant passages, from the time of her birth to her execution at Tyburn, being the 22th of January 1672/3: with her behaviour in prison, her last speech, burial & epitaph (London, 1673).

The Deportment and Carriage of the German Princess, Immediately before her Execution; And her last Speech at Tyburn (London, 1673).

The Life and character of Mrs. Mary Moders, alias Mary Stedman, alias Mary Carleton, alias Mary -------, the famous German princess being an historical relation of her birth and fortunes, with the havock and spoil she committed upon the publick in the reign of King Charles the Second: together with her tragical fall at Tyburn, on the 22d of January 1678, added by way of appendix (London, 1673).

The miserable effects of grasping at riches By any Unlawful or Unseemly Methods; exemplified In the melancholy and remarkable Instance of Anxiety and Distress, at this Time laboured under by some Persons who once seemed by Nature formed for, and might have otherwise enjoyed, every Delight this Earth affords. With A Word of Advice to the interesting Parties, in Relation to their future Conduct (London, 1748).

The Remarkable Trial of the Rev. William Sneyd, for Seducing, Debauching, and Carrying Off, the wife of Henry Cecil, Esq. (London, 1790).

The Remarkable Trial of the Honourable James Stamp Sutton Cooke, accused of bigamy at the Old Bailey, on the 14th April 1812: wherein is proved the complete innocence of this much injured gentleman (London, 1823).

Archbold: Criminal Pleading, Evidence and Practice (Westlaw online edition, 2025).

JF Archbold, *A summary of the law relative to pleading and evidence in criminal cases*, 3rd ed (London, Pheney, Sweet, 1828).

——, *The new system of criminal procedure* (London, Shaw & Sons, 1852).

——, *The justice of the peace and parish officer: Vol IV*, 5th edn (London, Shaw & Sons, 1855).

——, *The justice of the peace and parish officer: Vol IV*, 6th edn (London, Shaw and Sons, 1859).

J Aston and O Anderson, *Deserted Wives and Economic Divorce in mid-Nineteenth Century England and Wales: For Wives Alone* (Oxford, Hart, 2024).

R Auchmuty, E Rackley and M Takayanagi (eds), *Women's Legal Landmarks in the Interwar Years: Not For Want of Trying* (Oxford, Hart, 2024).

J Ayliffe, *Parergon juris canonici anglicani* (London, 1726).

J Bailey, *Unquiet Lives: marriage and marriage breakdown in England, 1660-1800* (Cambridge, Cambridge University Press, 2003).

JH Baker, *An Introduction to English Legal History*, 5th edn (Oxford, Oxford University Press, 2019).

GL Banks, *The Manchester Man* (Manchester, Printwise Publications, 1991, first published 1876).

F Barret-Ducrocq, *Love in the Time of Victoria: Sexuality, Class and Gender in Nineteenth-Century London* (London, Verso, 1991, trans John Howe; original edn 1989).

F Beauman, *Shapely Ankle Preferr'd: A History of the Lonely Hearts Ad, 1695-2010* (London, Chatto & Windus, 2011).
E Bernbaum, *The Mary Carleton Narratives, 1663-1673: A Missing Chapter in the History of the English Novel* (Cambridge, Massachusetts, Harvard University Press, 1914).
H Berry, *The Castrato and His Wife* (Oxford, Oxford University Press, 2011).
W Blackstone, *Commentaries on the Laws of England: Vol 1* (Oxford, Clarendon Press, 1765).
B Boothby and L Temple, *A synopsis of the law relating to indictable offences*, 2nd edn (London, Wm Maxwell, 1854).
G Bray (ed), *The Anglican Canons, 1529-1947* (Woodbridge, Boydell & Brewer, 1998).
——, *Tudor Church Reform: The Henrician Canons of 1535 and the Reformatio Legum Ecclesiasticarum* (Woodbridge, Boydell & Brewer, 2000).
RL Brown, *A History of the Fleet Prison: The Anatomy of the Fleet* (London, The Edwin Ellen Press Ltd, 1996).
W Bruce, *Archbold's Pleading and Evidence in Criminal Cases* (London, Sweet, Stevens & Sons, 1871).
JC Bucknill and DH Tuke, *A manual of psychological medicine: The history, nosology, description, statistics, diagnosis, pathology, and treatment of insanity* (Philadelphia, Blanchard & Lea, 1858).
R Burn, *Ecclesiastical Law: Vol 2* (London, 1763).
M Carleton, *The case of Madam Mary Carleton, lately stiled the German Princess, truely stated with an historical relation of her birth, education, and fortunes; in an appeal to his illustrious Highness Prince Rupert* (London, 1663).
J Carleton, *The Replication; or Certain Vindicatory Depositions* (London, 1663) and *The Ultimum Vale of John Carleton, of the Middle Temple* (London, 1663).
JS Cockburn, *A History of the English Assizes, 1558-1714* (Cambridge, Cambridge University Press, 1972).
E Coke, *The third part of the Institutes of the laws of England concerning high treason, and other pleas of the crown, and criminall causes* (London, 1644).
H and P Coombs (eds), *Journal of a Somerset Rector 1803-34: John Skinner* (Oxford, Oxford University Press, 1971).
P Cox, R Shoemaker and H Shore, *Victims and Criminal Justice: A History* (Oxford, Oxford University Press, 2023).
TE Cresswell, *A Narrative of the Affair Between Mr Cresswell and Miss Scrope … By which may be discovered the Falsities, Misrepresentations etc in a Letter in the General Evening Post, October 31, signed Lancelot Lee* (London, 1748).
S Cretney, *Family Law in the Twentieth Century: A History* (Oxford, Oxford University Press, 2003).
E Crittall (ed), *A History of the County of Wiltshire: Volume 6* (London, 1962).
C Derry, *Lesbianism and the Criminal Law: Three Centuries of Legal Regulation in England and Wales* (Cham, Palgrave Macmillan, 2020).
Sir L Dibdin and Sir C Chadwyck Healey, *English Church Law and Divorce* (London, John Murray, 1912).
J-A Dubourdieu, *An appeal to the English nation; or the body of the French Protestants, and the honest proselytes, vindicated from the calumnies cast on them by one Malard and his associates* (London, 1718).
EH East, *A Treatise of the Pleas of the Crown: Vol 1* (London, 1803).
DR Fisher (ed), *The History of Parliament: the House of Commons 1820-1832* (Cambridge, Cambridge University Press, 2009).
R Fletcher, *The Shaking of the Foundations* (London, Routledge, 1988).
E Foyster, *The Trials of the King of Hampshire: Madness, Secrecy and Betrayal in Georgian England* (London, Oneworld Publications, 2016).
G Frost, *Living in Sin: Cohabiting as Husband and Wife in Nineteenth-Century England* (Manchester, Manchester University Press, 2008).
H Gally, *Some Considerations upon Clandestine Marriages* (London, J Hughes, 1750).
WNM Geary, *The law of marriage and family relations: a manual of practical law* (London, Adam and Charles Black, 1892).
FB Gent, *Vercingetorixa; or the German Princess Reduc'd to an English Habit* (1663).
C Gervat, *Elizabeth: The Scandalous Life of the Duchess of Kingston* (London, Century, 2003).
P Giblett, *A Refutation of the Calumnies of George Harrower, Lately Convicted at The Old Bailey Sessions, on a Charge of Bigamy* (London, 1816).
J Gillis, *For Better, For Worse: British Marriages 1600 to the Present* (Oxford, Oxford University Press, 1985).

L Gowing, *Domestic Dangers: Women, Words and Sex in Early Modern England* (Oxford, Clarendon Press, 1996).
E Griffin, *Liberty's Dawn: A People's History of the Industrial Revolution* (New Haven, Yale University Press, 2014).
R Gwynn, *Huguenot Heritage: The history and contribution of the Huguenots in Britain* (London, Routledge & Kegan Paul, 1985).
Sir M Hale, *Pleas of the Crown* (London, 1677).
JT Hammick, *The marriage law of England: a practical treatise on the legal incidents connected with the law of constitution of the matrimonial contract* (London, Shaw & Sons, 1887).
C Harding, B Hines, R Ireland and P Rawlings, *Imprisonment in England and Wales: A Concise History* (London, Croom Helm, 1985).
G Harrower, *The Refuter Refuted* (London, 1816).
BD Henning (ed), *The History of Parliament: the House of Commons 1660-1690* (Woodbridge, Boydell and Brewer, 1983).
E Higgs, *Making sense of the census: the manuscript returns for England and Wales, 1801-1901* (London, HMSO, 1989).
KT Hoppen, *The Mid-Victorian Generation, 1846-1886* (Oxford, Oxford University Press, 1998).
J Hoppit, *A Land of Liberty? England 1689-1727* (Oxford, Oxford University Press, 2002).
TB Howell, *A Complete Collection of State Trials and Proceedings for High Crimes and Other Misdemeanors: Vol XVI* (London, 1812).
J Hudson, *Crime and Consequence in Early Modern Literature and Law* (Edinburgh, Edinburgh University Press, 2022).
TB Hug, *Impostures in Early Modern England: Representations and Perceptions of Fraudulent Identities* (Manchester, Manchester University Press, 2010).
D Hume, *Commentaries on the Law of Scotland, respecting the description and punishment of crimes: Vol 2* (Edinburgh, 1797).
M Ingram, *Church Courts, Sex and Marriage in England, 1570-1640* (Cambridge, Cambridge University Press, 1987).
R Ireland, *Land of White Gloves? A history of crime and punishment in Wales* (London, Routledge, 2015).
J Jervis and WN Welsby, *Archbold's Pleading and evidence in criminal cases*, 14th edn (London, H Sweet, V&R Stevens and GS Norton, 1859).
J Jervis, *Archbold's Pleading and Evidence in Criminal Cases* 17th edn (London, H Sweet, 1871).
KJ Kesselring and T Stretton, *Marriage, Separation and Divorce in England, 1500-1700* (Oxford, Oxford University Press, 2022).
MJ Kietzman, *The Self-Fashioning of an Early Modern Englishwoman* (Aldershot, Ashgate, 2004).
F Kirkman, *The Counterfeit Lady Unveiled* (London, 1673).
M Kishlansky, *A Monarchy Transformed: Britain 1603-1714* (London, Penguin, 1997).
A Knapp and W Baldwin, *Criminal Chronology; or, The New Newgate Calendar; Being Interesting Memoirs of Notorious Characters, Who Have Been Convicted of Outrages on The Laws of England, During The Seventeenth Century; and Brought Down to The Present Time: Vol 2* (London, 1809).
N Lacey, *In Search of Criminal Responsibility: Ideas, Interests and Institutions* (Oxford, Oxford University Press, 2016).
JH Langbein, *The Origins of Adversary Criminal Trial* (Oxford, Oxford University Press, 2003, ppbk 2005).
R Latham and W Matthews (eds), *The Diary of Samuel Pepys, Vol 4: 1663* (Harper Collins, 1971).
S Lettmaier, *Spouses, Church, and State* (Tübingen, Mohr Siebeck, 2025).
M Malard, *The case, and humble petition of Michael Malard, never a monk, but pastor of the church of Belleville, in Beaujolois in France, To the Honourable Committee, newly Established for the Relief of the Proselytes* (London, 1717).
J Mannion, *Female Husbands: A Trans History* (Cambridge, Cambridge University Press, 2020).
M Matchinske (ed), *The Carleton Bigamy Trial* (New York/Toronto, Iter Press, 2023).
JB Maule (ed), *Burn's Justice of the Peace and Parish Officer*, 30th edn (London, H Sweet, 1869).
E Mavor, *The Virgin Mistress: A Study in Survival: The Life of the Duchess of Kingston* (London, Chatto & Windus, 1964).
M Mulholland, *The Murderer of Warren Street: The True Story of a Nineteenth-Century Revolutionary* (London, Hutchinson, 2018).

GC Oke, *The Magisterial Synopsis: a Practical Guide for Magistrates, their Clerks, Attorneys and Constables*, 7th edn (London, Butterworths, 1860).
RB Outhwaite, *Clandestine Marriage in England, 1500-1850* (London, Hambledon Press, 1995).
——, *The Rise and Fall of the English Ecclesiastical Courts, 1500-1860* (Cambridge, Cambridge University Press, 2006).
J Phegley, *Courtship and Marriage in Victorian England* (Santa Barbara, Praeger, 2012).
R Philips, *Putting Asunder: A history of divorce in Western society* (Cambridge, Cambridge University Press, 1988).
CG Pooley and J Turnbull, *Migration and Mobility in Britain Since the Eighteenth Century* (London, Routledge, 1998).
RA Pritchard and W Tarn Pritchard, *A digest of the law and practice of the Court for Divorce and Matrimonial Causes* (London, W Maxwell, 1864).
R Probert, *Marriage Law and Practice in the Long Eighteenth Century: A Reassessment* (Cambridge, Cambridge University Press, 2009).
——, *The Changing Legal Regulation of Cohabitation: From Fornicators to Family* (Cambridge, Cambridge University Press, 2012).
——, *Tying the Knot:* The Formation of Marriage, 1836–2020 (Cambridge, Cambridge University Press, 2021).
R Probert, J Bailey and J Shaffer, *A Noble Affair: The Remarkable True Story of the Runaway Wife, the Bigamous Earl, and the Farmer's Daughter* (Kenilworth, Takeaway, 2013).
R Probert, RC Akhtar and S Blake, *Belief in Marriage: The evidence for reforming weddings law* (Bristol, Bristol University Press, 2023).
E Rackley and R Auchmuty (eds), *Women's Legal Landmarks: Celebrating the History of Women and Law in the UK and Ireland* (Oxford, Hart, 2019).
M Richardson, 'The Maltreated and the Malcontents' (Bristol Radical History Group, 2016).
J Rickman, *Love, Lust and Licence in Early Modern England: Illicit Sex and the Nobility* (Aldershot, Ashgate, 2008).
H Roscoe, *A digest of the law of evidence in criminal cases* (London, Saunders & Benning, 1835).
D Rosman, *The Evolution of the English Churches, 1500-2000* (Cambridge, Cambridge University Press, 2003).
WO Russell, *A Treatise on Crimes and Misdemeanors* (London, 1819), 2nd edn (London, Butterworth and Son, 1826).
JFS Russell, *My Life and Adventures* (London, Cassell & Co, 1923).
J Scandura, *Down in the Dumps: Place, Modernity, American Depression* (Durham and London, Duke University Press, 2008).
E Scrope, *Miss Scrope's Answer to Mr Cresswell's Narrative* (London, 1749).
BJ Shapiro, *Beyond Reasonable Doubt and Probable Cause: Historical Perspectives on the Anglo-American Law of Evidence* (Berkeley and Los Angeles, University of California Press, 1991).
AWB Simpson, *Leading Cases in the Common Law* (Oxford, Oxford University Press, 1995).
KJM Smith, *Lawyers, Legislators and Theorists: Developments in English Criminal Jurisprudence, 1800–1957* (Oxford, Oxford University Press, 1998).
FM Sposini, *The Certification of Insanity: Local Origins and Imperial Consequences* (Palgrave Macmillan, 2023).
T Starkie, *A practical treatise of the law of evidence: Vol 3* (London, J & WT Clarke, 1824).
——, *A practical treatise of the law of evidence, and digest of proofs, in civil and criminal proceedings: Vol III*, 3rd edn (London, V &R Stevens and GS Norton, 1842).
S Staves, *Married Women's Separate Property in England, 1660-1833* (Cambridge, MA, Harvard University Press, 1990).
JF Stephen, *Roscoe's Digest of the Law of Evidence in Criminal Cases*, 7th edn (London, Stevens and Sons, 1868).
——, *A History of the Criminal Law of England: Vol 2* (London, Macmillan, 1883).
L Stone, *The Family, Sex and Marriage in England 1500-1800* (New York, Harper & Row, 1977).
——, *Road to Divorce: England 1530-1987* (Oxford, Oxford University Press, 1990).
——, *Uncertain Unions and Broken Lives: Intimate and Revealing Accounts of Marriage and Divorce in England* (Oxford, Oxford University Press, 1995).
M Sweet, *Inventing the Victorians: What We Think About Them and Why We're Wrong* (London, Faber and Faber, 2002).

M Thale (ed), *The Autobiography of Francis Place (1771-1854)* (Cambridge, Cambridge University Press, 1972).
EP Thompson, *The Making of the English Working Class* (London, Penguin, 1972, first published 1963).
FML Thompson, *The Rise of Respectable Society: A Social History of Victorian Britain, 1830-1900* (London, Fontana Press, 1988).
CH Timperley, *Annals of Manchester* (Manchester, Bancks & Co, 1839).
J Todd and E Spearing (eds), *Counterfeit Ladies: The Life and Death of Mal Cutpurse; The Case of Mary Carleton* (London, William Pickering, 1994).
S Varlow, *The Lady Penelope: The Lost Tale of Love and Politics in the Court of Elizabeth I* (London, Andre Deutsch, 2007).
J Warner, *Craze: Gin and Debauchery in an Age of Reason* (London, Profile Books Ltd, 2003).
J Witte Jr, *The Western Case for Monogamy Over Polygamy* (Cambridge, Cambridge University Press, 2015).
L Woodward, *The Age of Reform, 1815-1870* (Oxford, Oxford University Press, 1962).
K Wrightson, *English Society 1580-1680* (London, Routledge, 2002).

Articles

'Double Bigamy – Law and Second Marriage – The Seven-year Proviso' (1939) 103 *Justice of the Peace & Local Government Review* 1.
D Aikenhead Stroud, 'Fortune Telling and Mens Rea' (1921) 37 *Law Quarterly Review* 488.
WH Ainsworth, 'Enoch Arden' (1864) 132 *The New Monthly Magazine* 462.
O Anderson, 'State, Civil Society and Separation in Victorian Marriage' (1999) 163 *Past and Present* 161.
DT Andrew, 'The code of honour and its critics: the opposition to duelling in England, 1700-1850' (1980) 5 *Social History* 409.
J Aston, 'Petitions to the Court for Divorce and Matrimonial Causes: A New Methodological Approach to the History of Divorce, 1857-1923' (2022) 43 *Journal of Legal History* 161.
R Auchmuty, 'Whatever happened to Miss Bebb? *Bebb v The Law Society* and women's legal history' (2010) 31 *Legal Studies* 199.
J Bailey, '"I dye [sic] by Inches": locating wife beating in the concept of a privatization of marriage and violence in eighteenth-century England' (2006) 31 *Social History* 273.
WE Baxter, 'Tennyson's "Enoch Arden": Bigamy and Desertion' (1864) 143 *Notes and Queries* 256.
JM Beattie, 'Scales of Justice: Defense Counsel and the English Criminal Trial in the Eighteenth and Nineteenth Centuries' (1991) 9 *Law and History Review* 221.
G Black, 'The significance of sex in Scots Civil Law' (2024) 36 *Child and Family Law Quarterly* 321.
B Capp, 'Bigamous Marriage in Early Modern England' (2009) 52 *The Historical Journal* 537.
H Cocks, 'The cost of marriage and the matrimonial agency in late Victorian Britain' (2013) 38 *Social History* 66.
D Cox, '"Fitted both Morally and Physically to Fulfil his Proper Duties in the Battle of Life"? – The Effectiveness or Otherwise of Penal Servitude and Imprisonment 1853–2021' (2021) 60 *Howard Journal of Crime and Justice* 47.
P Crawford and S Mendelson, 'Sexual Identities in Early Modern England: The Marriage of Two Women in 1680' (1995) 7 *Gender & History* 361.
D Desert, 'The Strangers and the Established Church' (2003) 27 *Proceedings of the Huguenot Society of Great Britain and Ireland* 1.
C Durston, '"Unhallowed Wedlocks": The Regulation of Marriage During the English Revolution' (1988) 31 *Historical Journal* 45.
JF Field, 'Clandestine weddings at the Fleet Prison, c.1710-1750: who married there?' (2017) 32 *Continuity and Change* 349.
TP Gallanis, 'The Rise of Modern Evidence Law' (1999) 84 *Iowa Law Review* 499.
T Gilfoyle, 'The Hearts of Nineteenth-Century Men: Bigamy and Working-Class Marriage in New York City, 1800–1890' (1994) 19 *Prospects* 135.
S Gold, 'Xmas Bigamy' (1987) 137 *New Law Journal* 1199; (1988) 138 *New Law Journal* 157; 138 *New Law Journal* 359.
T Hitchcock and WJ Turkel, 'The Old Bailey Proceedings, 1674–1913: Text Mining for Evidence of Court Behaviour' (2016) 34 *Law and History Review* 929.

M Harding, 'The Curious Incident of the Marriage Act (no 2) 1537 and the Irish Statute Book' (2012) 32 *Legal Studies* 78.
J Horder, 'Provocation and loss of self-control' (1992) 108 *Law Quarterly Review* 191.
A Humphreys, '*Enoch Arden*, the Fatal Return, and the Silence of Annie' (1992) 30 *Victorian Poetry* 331.
L Leneman, 'English Marriages and Scottish Divorces in the Early Nineteenth Century' (1996) 17 *Journal of Legal History* 225.
K Lilley, '"These Novels of My Life": Mary Carleton's Crimes' (2010) 25 *Australian Feminist Studies* 265.
——, 'Mary Carleton's false additions: the case of the "German Princess"' (2010) 16(1) *Humanities Research* 79.
I Loudon, 'Puerperal insanity in the 19th century' (1988) 81 *Journal of the Royal Society of Medicine* 76.
K Lucenko, '"Meerly my own free Agent": Liberty and Civility in The Case of Madam Mary Carleton' (2019) 14 *Early Modern Women: An Interdisciplinary Journal* 50.
B McConnell, 'For bad or worse' (1992) 142 *New Law Journal* 1250.
RH Mnookin and L Kornhauser, 'Bargaining in the Shadow of the Law: The Case of Divorce' (1979) 88 *Yale Law Journal* 950.
G Newton, 'Clandestine marriage in early modern London: when, where and why?' (2014) 29 *Continuity and Change* 151.
M Parker, 'The draft Nuptial Agreements Bill and the abolition of the common law rule: "swept away" or swept under the carpet?' (2015) 27 *Child and Family Law Quarterly* 63.
R Probert 'The Double Standard of Morality in the Divorce and Matrimonial Causes Act 1857' (1999) 28 *Anglo-American Law Review* 73.
——, 'The Judicial Interpretation of Lord Hardwicke's Act of 1753' (2002) 23 *Journal of Legal History* 129.
——, 'Why do couples still believe in common law marriage?' [2007] *Family Law* 403.
——, '*R v Millis* reconsidered: binding contracts and bigamous marriages' (2008) 28 *Legal Studies* 337.
——, 'Common law marriage: myths and misunderstandings' (2008) 20 *Child and Family Law Quarterly* 1.
——, 'Control over Marriage in England and Wales, 1753–1823: The Clandestine Marriages Act of 1753 in Context' (2009) 27 *Law and History Review* 413.
——, '"A Banbury Story": cohabitation and marriage among the Victorian poor in 'notorious Neithrop' (2012) 19 *Cake and Cockhorse* 2.
——, 'The presumptions in favour of marriage' (2018) 77 *Cambridge Law Journal* 375.
——, '*R v Hall* and the changing perceptions of the crime of bigamy' (2019) 39 *Legal Studies* 1.
——, 'Escaping detection: illegal second marriages and the crime of bigamy' (2022) 6 *Journal of Genealogy and Family History* 27.
R Probert and L D'Arcy-Brown, 'The transportation of bigamists in early nineteenth century England and Wales' (2019) 40 *Journal of Legal History* 223.
R Probert, M Harding and B Dempsey, 'A Uniform Law of Marriage? The 1868 Royal Commission Reconsidered' (2018) 30 *Child and Family Law Quarterly* 217.
——, 'The presumptions in favour of marriage' (2018) 77 *Cambridge Law Journal* 375.
——, '*R v Hall* and the changing perceptions of the crime of bigamy' (2019) 39 *Legal Studies* 1.
——, 'Escaping detection: illegal second marriages and the crime of bigamy' (2022) 6 *Journal of Genealogy and Family History* 27.
G Quealy, 'Astrophil's Star: Locating Penelope Rich in the Sidney Constellation' (2023) 41 *Sidney Journal* 23.
P Sharpe, 'Bigamy among the Labouring Poor in Essex, 1754–1857' (1994) *Local Historian* 139.
M Sudai, 'Sex Ambiguity in Early Modern Common Law (1629–1787)' (2022) 47 *Law & Social Inquiry* 478.
AA Tait, 'The Beginning of the End of Coverture: A Reappraisal of the Married Woman's Separate Estate' (2014) 26 *Yale Journal of Law and Feminism* 165.
DM Turner, 'Popular Marriage and the Law: Tales of Bigamy at the Eighteenth-Century Old Bailey' (2005) 30 *London Journal* 6.
P Wallis, J Colson and D Chilosi, 'Structural Change and Economic Growth in the British Economy before the Industrial Revolution, 1500–1800' (2018) 78 *Journal of Economic History* 862.
D Watkins, 'Recovering the lost human stories of law: Finding Mrs Burns' (2013) 7 *Law and Humanities* 68.
G Williams, 'Bigamy and the Third Marriage' (1950) 13 *Modern Law Review* 417.
E Wilputte, 'Haywood's Tabloid Journalism: *Dalinda: or, The Double Marriage* and the Cresswell Bigamy Case' (2014) 4 *Journal for Early Modern Cultural Studies* 122.

WHD Winder, 'The Rule of Precedent in the Criminal Courts' (1941) 5 *Journal of Criminal Law* 242.
S Wolfram, 'Divorce in England 1700–1857' (1985) 5 *Oxford Journal of Legal Studies* 155.
WO Woodall, 'The Lord of Burghley and Sarah Hoggins', *Notes and Queries*, 8th Series, Vol 1, 14 May 1892.
GN Woolnough, 'A Victorian fraudster and bigamist: Gentleman or criminal?' (2019) 19 *Criminology & Criminal Justice* 439.
D Wright, '"Well-Behaved Women Don't Make History": Rethinking Family, Law, and History Through an Analysis of the First Nine Years of the English Divorce and Matrimonial Causes Court (1858–1866)' (2005) *Wisconsin Women's Law Journal* 211.
X You, 'Women's labour force participation in nineteenth-century England and Wales: evidence from the 1881 census enumerators' books' (2020) 73 *Economic History Review* 106.

Chapters

JH Baker, 'Criminal Courts and Procedure at Common Law 1550–1800' in JS Cockburn (ed), *Crime in England 1550–1800* (London, Methuen, 1977).
A Barlow, 'Modern Marriage Myths – the dichotomy between expectations of legal rationality and lived law' in R Akhtar, P Nash and R Probert (eds), *Cohabitation and Religious Marriage: Status, Similarities and Solutions* (Bristol, Bristol University Press, 2020).
D Bentley, 'Acquitting the Innocent. Convicting the Guilty. Delivering Justice?' in J Rowbotham and K Stevenson (eds), *Behaving Badly: Social Panic and Moral Outrage – Victorian and Modern Parallels* (Aldershot, Ashgate, 2003).
J Ellis, 'Regional and County Centres, 1700–1840' in P Clark (ed), *The Cambridge urban history of Britain: volume II, 1540–1840* (Cambridge, Cambridge University Press, 2000).
P Handler, 'Judges and the criminal law in England 1808–61' in P Brand and J Getzler, *Judges and Judging in the History of the Common Law and Civil Law: From Antiquity to Modern Times* (Cambridge, Cambridge University Press, 2012).
——, 'Legal development in Victorian criminal trials' in M Dyson and D Ibbetson (eds), *Law and Legal Process: Substantive Law and Procedure in English Legal History* (Cambridge, Cambridge University Press, 2013).
M Ingram, 'Breaking Vows: Adultery, Marital Ill-Treatment, and Divorce in England, 1450–1650' in JM Ferraro (ed), *A Cultural History of Marriage in the Renaissance and Early Modern Age* (London, Bloomsbury Academic, 2020).
RW Ireland, 'Sanctity, superstition and the death of Sarah Jacob' in A Musson and C Stebbings (eds), *Making Legal History: Approaches and Methodologies* (Cambridge, Cambridge University Press, 2012).
L Lammasniemi and K Sharma, 'Age of Marriage Act 1929' in R Auchmuty, E Rackley and M Takayanagi (eds), *Women's Legal Landmarks in the Interwar Years: Not For Want of Trying* (Oxford, Hart, 2024).
R Lamont, 'The Crown against …: The Victim and the State in the Pursuit of Criminal Prosecution, 1840–1985' in S Walklate and P Cox, *Victims Access to Justice: Historical and Comparative Perspectives* (London, Routledge, 2022).
S Lettmaier, 'Marriage Formation in Europe from the Late Middle Ages until the Late Eighteenth Century' in R Probert and S Thompson (eds), *Research Handbook on Marriage and Cohabitation* (Edward Elgar 2024).
H Marland, 'At home with puerperal mania: the domestic treatment of the insanity of childbirth in the nineteenth century' in P Bartlett and D Wright (eds), *Outside the Walls of the Asylum: The History of Care in the Community, 1750–2000* (London, Bloomsbury, 1999).
D McClean and M Hayes, 'But I Didn't Really Want to Get Married' in S Gilmore, J Herring and R Probert (eds), *Landmark Cases in Family Law* (Oxford, Hart, 2011).
R Probert, 'Parental Responsibility and Children's Partnership Choices', in R Probert, J Herring and S Gilmore (eds), *Responsible Parents and Parental Responsibility* (Oxford, Hart Publishing, 2009).
——, 'The Roos Case and Modern Family Law' in S Gilmore, J Herring and R Probert (eds), *Landmark Cases in Family Law* (Oxford, Hart, 2011).
——, 'Approaching sources critically: Challenging myths in the standard narratives' in R Auchmuty, C Derry and D Wright (eds), *Research Handbook on Gender, History and Law* (forthcoming).

AL Rowse, 'Bishop Thornborough: A Clerical Careerist' in R Ollard and P Tudor-Craig (eds), *For Veronica Wedgwood These: Studies in Seventeenth-Century* (London, Collins, 1986).
T Stretton, 'Marriage, separation and the common law in England, 1540–1660' in H Berry and E Foyster (eds), *The Family in Early Modern England* (Cambridge, Cambridge University Press, 2007).
A Sumner Holmes, '"Don't Frighten the Horses": The Russell Divorce Case' in G Robb and N Erber (eds), *Disorder in the Court: Trials and Sexual Conflict at the Turn of the Century* (Basingstoke, Palgrave Macmillan, 1999).

INDEX

www.ingramcontent.com/pod-product-compliance
Ingram Content Group UK Ltd.
Pitfield, Milton Keynes, MK11 3LW, UK
UKHW020241290926
15470UKWH00002B/677

9 781509 97948